Last Book Fund.

DURHAM CA
MUSIC MANU

# A Catalogue of
# DURHAM CATHEDRAL MUSIC MANUSCRIPTS

Compiled by
BRIAN CROSBY

PUBLISHED BY OXFORD UNIVERSITY PRESS
FOR THE
DEAN AND CHAPTER OF DURHAM
1986

Oxford University Press, Walton Street, Oxford OX2 6DP

Oxford New York Toronto
Delhi Bombay Calcutta Madras Karachi
Kuala Lumpur Singapore Hong Kong Tokyo
Nairobi Dar es Salaam Cape Town
Melbourne Auckland

and associated companies in
Beirut Berlin Ibadan Nicosia

Oxford is a trade mark of Oxford University Press

British Library Cataloguing in Publication Data
Durham Cathedral
A Catalogue of Durham Cathedral music
manuscripts.
1. Music—Manuscripts—Catalogs
I. Title   II. Crosby, Brian   III. Dean
and Chapter of Durham
016.78   ML135
ISBN 0–19–920155–2

Printed in Great Britain
at the University Printing House, Oxford
by David Stanford
Printer to the University

# PREFACE

In 1967 Canon A. H. Couratin, the Dean and Chapter Librarian, suggested that it would be useful to compile a catalogue of the cathedral's music manuscripts. This project was seen as complementing the work done by R. Alec Harman in *A Catalogue of the Printed Music and Books on Music in Durham Cathedral Library* (1968), which work was already at the printers.

Inventories of many of the sacred music manuscripts (see MS E36) and a slip catalogue listing the incidence of compositions under their composers had been assembled in the 1920s by Ernest H. Knight, an alto lay-clerk and assistant to the Librarian. He did not tackle the instrumental manuscripts, and even among the sacred items little headway was made with those which afforded no obvious clue as to their identity. Moreover, although Knight compiled lists of the many dated authorizations of payment found in the manuscripts, the background of those manuscripts was not explored.

Since Knight's time additions have been made to the cathedral's collection, and the fragments of monastic music have increasingly attracted attention. Again, of the Bamburgh Castle music collection deposited on indefinite loan in 1958 over forty of the finding numbers apply to manuscripts. All of these aspects are covered by the present catalogue, work at which has proceeded at times not conflicting with teaching commitments. It proved relatively straightforward to compile new inventories of the manuscripts, and to build up anew an index of cross-references. Tracking down the anonymous items, particularly those of an instrumental nature, has been more exacting, and has no real hope of completion. What has required the time has been the acquisition of background information from the cathedral's own considerable archives, and from elsewhere, for a goodly number of the manuscripts have proved to be 'foreign'. The production has been further delayed by the decision to re-cast the inventories as numerated summary lists under composers.

In a work as diverse as this, much is owed to many people. I must express my thanks to the Dean and Chapter of Durham for their support and for granting me almost unlimited access to the manuscripts; to two successive Headmasters of The Chorister School for tolerating my divided loyalties; to the staffs of the Dean and Chapter Library and of the Departments of Music and of Palaeography and Diplomatic in the University of Durham; to the librarians and staff of the many libraries elsewhere who have assisted me in my searches for related material; and to the many scholars who have been willing to pass on to me the fruits of their own research. In particular I should like to thank Donald Burrows for acquainting me with the Oxford connections; Alan Piper for his assistance with the monastic fragments, and especially for corroborating their dates on palaeographical grounds; and Roger Norris, the Deputy Librarian who has continually advised and encouraged me.

G. B. C.

# CONTENTS

# INTRODUCTION

Durham cathedral's music manuscripts, like its printed music, fall into two categories. Most belong to its own collection, the others to the Bamburgh collection deposited on indefinite loan in 1958.

Much of the cathedral's collection is domestic, being used by the organist or by some member of the choir during the daily services. Such manuscripts continued to be used until c.1884 when they were withdrawn and placed in the organ loft.[1] There they remained until 1908 when they were transferred to the Refectory, where space had become available through the removal of the monastic books to the Spendement. Transferred at that time to what has become known as the music closet were MSS A1–A9, B1, C1–C25 (surprising, unless some of what are now MSS C26–C28, C31–C34, were then C20, C22–C25), and E4–E11, together with about eighty unspecified part-books of the eighteenth and nineteenth centuries. Hughes speaks of the earlier books being 'lately repaired', and mentions that a catalogue [MS E36] and shelf list had been made of them but not of the later manuscripts.

Thus those which have survived as well as many of those which have disappeared have done so through being used, and through being known as stores of useful music. Not so the music of monastic times. That little of it has come down to the present day is hardly surprising, for the Dissolution of the monastery in 1539 marked the end of an era. Gone were the monastic offices; gone too was the use of Latin as the language of the liturgy. It was simply a question of time before most of its music was either lost or destroyed. The few extant fragments owe their preservation to the fact that, their

---

[1] H. D. Hughes, *A History of Durham Cathedral Library* (1925), pp. 29 *et seq.*

musical life over, they proved suitable in size and material to serve as end-papers and bindings for other books. But though they are only fragments, their very antiquity causes them highly to be esteemed. Portions there are of Missals and Breviaries noted; and two folios from a Processional [Incunable 15A] dated c.1400 represent a very early use of void notation (white notes). Notable among the instances of three-part polyphony are a Kyrie Trope in honour of St Cuthbert [MS A.III.11][1] and a troped Gloria [Communar's Cartulary], both dated c.1400. Added at about the same date to a manuscript now in the British Library is a 'Salve regina' set as a three-part canon.[2]

It was no doubt music such as the last three items which was being referred to in one of the complaints made during a Visitation of the monastery conducted c.1390 (I translate):

there were wont to be 'clerks' singing 'organum' and assisting the monks in the song which is called 'trebill' [i.e. three-part], and they are no longer there, to the great inconvenience and frustration of the brothers singing in the Quire.[3]

Speculation on what music was used or composed at Durham in monastic times is increased by the contracts with the lay cantors. These professional musicians had been introduced to ensure that the monastery's music was of the highest order. They were required to instruct certain monks and also the small band of eight choristers who sang the Lady Mass daily in the Galilee Chapel and the Jesus Mass every Friday evening at the Nave altar. The first such contract, with John Stele, is dated 1430, but *ad hoc* payments usually naming the recipient occur from 1414–15 onwards.[4] From c.1490 onwards it was stipulated that yearly they were to compose a

[1] See MS C.I.8 for two other Kyrie Tropes.
[2] Royal MS 7.A.VI; see N. Sandon, 'Mary, meditations, monks and music', *Early Music* (Jan. 1982, pp. 43–55).
[3] *Chapters of the English Black Monks*, ed. W. A. Pantin, iii (1937), 84.
[4] For details of the lay-cantors see B. Crosby, *Choristers and their Masters* (1980), pp. 8–12, 45.

four- or five-part Mass in honour either of St Cuthbert or
of Blessed Mary the Virgin or else some equivalent offering.
A single part of movements of the Mass [End Paper 25]
dating from the time of Stele is found among the muniments
at Durham; and a single part of 'Stella caeli' of possibly
earlier date was added to the British Library manuscript
mentioned above.[1] Both these parts employ stroke notation,
a short-lived device designed to assist non-professional
singers with the lengths of notes. The only example of music
known to have been composed by one of the cantors is a
fragment of the Mass 'Sancte Cuthberte' by Thomas Ashe-
well (at Durham c.1513–c.1527), and it too is in the British
Library.[2]

Before leaving the monastic period mention should be
made of some fourteenth century French, English, and Latin
motets [MS C.I.20]; and of an eleventh century antiphoner
[MS B.III.11] emanating from northern France. This antiphoner is noted with neumes, that is with a system of
notation not using lines, and where the signs—it would be
wrong to call them notes—indicate the direction the voice
has to move—they do not denote the pitch or duration of
the sounds. Four pre-Norman manuscripts [MSS A.II.17,
A.IV.19, B.III.32, B.IV.9], the first two in the possession of
the community of St Cuthbert before it came to Durham in
AD 995, also have minute sections noted with neumes.

Though for the period from 1540 to 1600 there is some
evidence of the acquisition of music, as far as can be ascer-
tained not even one contemporary note remains. As early as
1544 the newly constituted cathedral authorities acquired
music copies of Cranmer's Litany. John Brymley, the last of
Durham's monastic lay cantors, who survived the Dissolution of the monastery to become the new regime's first
Master of the Choristers and Organist, must have been active
at this time too. Copied into one of the early seventeenth
century manuscripts [MS C13] is part of the tenor part of

[1] See p. xii n. 2.    [2] Add. MS 30520.

his Te Deum and Benedictus. This must have been composed
in the 1540s, for the text of the Te Deum is older than that of
the Prayer Book of 1549, agreeing with that of the King's
Primer of 1535. Complete in the later manuscripts [MSS
E4–E11] are his 'Kerries', i.e. Responses to the Commandments in the Communion Service.

The financial year 1568–9 marked the purchase of 'paper
to make bookes for the singing men'. This was presumably at
the instigation of Dean Whittingham, who, jealous about the
cathedral's musical standing, was:

very carefull to provide the best songs and anthems that could be
got out of the Queen's chapell to furnish the quire with all . . .[1]

These books may well have been the set of books of 'Services
and Anthemes for men' in use in the 1660s,[2] of which set
no survivor remains. This hypothesis is supported by a few
Restoration manuscripts [MSS A3, C11, C17, C19] having
a corpus of music for men's voices, the composers of which—
Mundy, Sheppard, and Tallis—were all active in the mid-
sixteenth century.

Towards the end of the century, in 1597, William Smythe,
Minor Canon and Master of the Choristers and Organist,
was paid £2 'for a sett of singing bookes gylded'. It seems
likely that some of the covers of this set were used again
during the seventeenth century [on MSS C4, C5, C9, C10,
C17] and have come down to the present day.

What the cathedral's collection is best known for is its early
seventeenth century manuscripts.[3] No fewer than twenty-
nine books belonging to the period 1625 to 1640 still survive
at Durham, to which should be added the 'Dunnington–
Jefferson MS' [MS M29S], now in York Minster Library.
Five of the Durham books are organ books, the rest are part-

[1] 'The Life and Death of Mr. William Whittingham, Dean of Durham', p. 23;
in *Miscellany VI*, ed. M. A. E. Green (Camden Soc. for 1871).

[2] See Misc. Ch. 7116 for this and other descriptions of 17th cent. MSS.

[3] B. Crosby, 'Durham Cathedral's Liturgical Music Manuscripts, c.1620–
c.1640', *Durham University Journal* (Dec. 1973).

books. An examination of their contents divides the part-books into five sets, together with four composite books [MSS C11, C13, C16, E11a] designed for private use. Of two of the sets only singletons remain, but the others have four, six, and eight left of original complements of ten members each. That such was the size of each set is confirmed both by references to their production in the contemporary Chapter Act Books and Treasurer's Account Books, and also by a manuscript Inventory of Moveable Church Goods [Misc. Chs 7116, 7117] which has been dated at 1665.[1] For each of the sides Decani and Cantoris (and Durham is very much the exception in having Decani, the senior side, on the north) there were five books—one treble, two counter-tenor, and one bass. The expression 'part-book' is most apt, for each contained not even the whole of one voice part but only what its user had to sing. For instance, in the case of the counter-tenors, the Decani books did not include those antiphonal sections sung just by Cantoris; and in the case of solos, each was allotted to one particular individual and is found in only one of the four books.

The five early seventeenth century sets answered the needs of every conceivable occasion. Six books [MSS C4–C6, C7 (2nd fascicle), C9, C10] remain of a set of anthem books for general use. Their contents are arranged in two sections, full anthems and verse (i.e. having solo sections) anthems. The contemporary Tables of Contents disclose that this set was originally neither paginated nor foliated—it is the anthems themselves which are numbered within their different sections. One member [MS C8] remains of the set containing 'short services', i.e. full settings of the canticles in which there is no repetition of the text; and one member too [MS C18] of the set containing 'verse Services'. The other two sets are much more spectacular. Four books [MSS C2, C3, C7 (1st fascicle), C14] hold verse anthems 'for ffestivall daies' and general use. Their former section starts with 'This is the

---

[1] B. Crosby, 'A 17th-century Durham Inventory', *Musical Times* (Feb. 1978).

record of John' by Orlando Gibbons, set for the Fourth Sunday in Advent, and proceeds to work through the church's year. Many of the anthems are settings of the Collect for the particular day. After each feast day space was left so that other suitable anthems could be added as they became available—that several compositions by the contemporary Durham composers William Smith (a minor canon, not related to the earlier William Smythe), Henry Palmer, and John Geeres (both lay-clerks) were so added is evident from a slightly more hurried hand. The last set [MSS E4–E11] is immediately noteworthy on account of its physical size—the books measure 500 mm high by 300 mm wide. From the completeness of the corners of their pages it is likely that they were scarcely used—a situation rendered the more likely by the fact that the two books now missing had gone astray by 1665. They were intended for use on the six major feast days—Christmas, Epiphany, Easter, Ascension, Whitsunday, and All Saints' Day. Their music is divided up into liturgical groupings with spaces left between the groups. First come the preces and festal settings of the appropriate psalms; and then the various services divided up into groups for Matins, Communion, and Evensong without any service being assigned to any specific day.

Between 1625 and 1635 the principal copyists were John Todd (precentor; d. 1631) and Toby Brookinge (lay-clerk). They were paid at the rate of sometimes 3*d.*, sometimes 4*d.* per page, and Brookinge earned at least £14. 16*s.* 8*d.* from this activity between 1632 and 1634. This represents somewhere between 900 and 1200 pages, and is a sizeable amount when compared with his annual salary of £20. One is tempted to read between the lines in relation to his wife Magdalen collecting ? a further £6. 6*s.* 8*d.* 'for prickinge Antheames &c.'. Could it be she wished to prevent it from being spent in hostelries such as the one where in 1628 he had suffered grievous bodily harm when Richard Hucheson the organist had attacked him with a candlestick!

The motive force behind at least the two festal sets [see MSS C2, E4] was Prebendary John Cosin. A high-churchman of the Laudian school, he was keen to introduce at Durham all the latest London trends including those developments of the baroque period, the verse anthem and the verse service. The personal animosity this created in the mind of his colleague, the Calvinist Peter Smart, the latter's infamous sermon in July 1628 and the consequent litigation are all well known.[1] In 1635 Cosin added the Mastership of Peterhouse, Cambridge, to his preferments, and it is not inappropriate to observe that the work of no fewer than seven different Durham copyists has been identified in the Peterhouse Caroline manuscripts.

The organ books of the 1630s are distinctive too. They are all written on staves of six lines. William Smith copied some forty-one pages of his own compositions, including his Preces (but not his Responses) into the beginning of a new organ book [MS A1]. This book was completed in 1638 by Henry Palmer. The selfsame year and in 1639 Palmer transcribed two further organ books [MSS A6, A5], ending his labours with a holograph anthem entitled 'The end of all things is at hand' [MS A5, pp. 280–1]. It is not known whether he was referring to his work as a copyist, to the current political scene, or to his own unhappy domestic situation in which his first wife and one of his children had but recently died. As to the final two books, one [MS A3] has only a section from this period, and it is unlikely that the other [MS A2] had become a book at this stage. William Smith was responsible for some of its sections, but nearly all the rest is in the hand of John Todd with nearly twenty items bound into it still in their individual paper covers.

The early seventeenth century then was a period of great musical activity, with much fine music in the repertoire. The standard of performance in the 1630s is, however, somewhat

[1] *The Correspondence of John Cosin, D.D.*, vol. 1, ed. G. Ornsby (Surtees Soc. vol. 52; 1868), pp. 155 *et seq.*

open to question, especially when it is borne in mind that Nicholas Hobson, one of the lay-clerks, was attributed the age of eighty-two years when he married in 1637.[1]

After the Restoration, John Foster, a Durham chorister of the 1630s, was appointed Master of the Choristers and Organist. The manuscripts he had known as a boy continued to be used by him and by his successors until the early eighteenth century. Included in the replacement and additional copies are Durham MSS C1, C12, C15, C17, and C19; whilst British Library Add. MSS 30478 and 30479 were produced not for the choir but for George Davenport, chaplain to Bishop Cosin, and Prebendary Isaac Basire respectively. Thereafter, with the exception of a set of anthem and service books begun c.1710, it is harder to arrange the books in sets, for from 1724 onwards the need for copying was reduced. That year saw the publication of thirty of Croft's anthems in full vocal score. The Dean and Chapter is listed among the subscribers, though the number of copies is not stated. But the process had begun. It was no longer necessary to copy Croft's anthems into every part-book. Greene's anthems (pub. 1743) and Boyce's monumental three-volume collection of worthy cathedral music of the previous two hundred years (pub. 1760, 1768, 1773) and other such volumes continued to reduce the need for copying.

Among the copyists, Alexander Shaw (fl. 1664–82) who emulated the splendid hands of the 1630s, Matthew Owen (1688–95) who returned to round notation, Cuthbert Brass (1730–69), and John Mathews (1765–76) deserve mention for their clear work. Thomas Ebdon (organist, 1763–1811) made several transcripts of mainly his own anthems during the last ten years of his life; whilst Matthew Brown (1832–77) had his salary increased by £25 per annum in 1866 to compensate him following a decision to use the many single printed copies then being published by Novello and others.

Included in the cathedral's collection are manuscripts right

---

[1] St Giles' Register, p. 132.

up to the beginning of the twentieth century. This has been done partly for the sake of completeness, partly through the desire to put on record the contribution of Philip Armes (organist, 1862–1907). In 1874 he finally introduced a set of chants for the psalms—he had made an abortive attempt in 1863—adding in 1886 a second set to be used in alternate months [MS D12]. He also played a significant part in the fostering of interest in English Church music of the sixteenth and seventeenth centuries, himself editing anthems and services from the old Durham manuscripts [MSS D23, D26–D28].

The background information about the cathedral's own manuscripts has been extracted from a wealth of muniments. For the monastic period recourse has been made to the Priory Registers and to the Account Rolls of certain of the monastic officials. The copying projects of the 1620s and 1630s are described in the Act Books of the Dean and Chapter, and payments to named copyists are recorded in them and also in the three surviving Treasurer's Account Books of that period. These, like all the Treasurer's Books and Rolls, name the minor canons, lay-clerks, and choristers. From the late sixteenth century until the early twentieth the Account Books are further useful in that in them the recipients signed for their quarterly stipends. From 1678–9 onwards the details of all non-stipendiary payments are kept in a series of Audit Books, with those for music usually under the heading 'In Billis'. Some thirteen of the actual bills submitted by the copyists between 1677 and 1700, two for 1709, and three for 1728 to 1730 have been preserved,[1] their details both interesting and infuriating in that the books they refer to cannot always positively be identified. From c.1690 the manuscripts themselves abound with signed statements that the year's payment covered to the point in question. The evidence of the Audit Books makes it clear that the signature in each case is not that of the acknowledging copyist but of the

---

[1] Post-Dissolution Loose Papers; and Audit Bills.

authorizing Precentor. This situation became mandatory on 20 November 1702,[1] its object being to counteract unnecessary copying. By the middle of the nineteenth century the delegation of authority had changed. The payments for copying were made to William Henshaw, the Organist. His signature is in the manuscripts, but the indications are that others did the actual copying. As well as dating the manuscripts accurately the date-points make it clear what styles were practised by the various copyists. When the dates of composition of anthems and services are known, they also serve to show how quickly such music reached Durham.

But the cathedral's collection has its wider aspects too. A further liturgical manuscript [MS B1] is not of Durham origin.[2] With instrumental overtures and ritornellos, it was compiled in London c.1670, for whilst there are anthems by Henry Cooke, Humfrey, Blow, and Tucker, Purcell is conspicuous by his absence. To Prebendary Philip Falle (1656–1742), who was responsible for so many of the rare music books in the printed music collection, can be assigned three sets of part-books [MSS D2, D4, D5] and one book in score [MS D10] of music for viols. These date from the second half of the seventeenth century, and contain sonatas by Jenkins, Butler, and others. One set [MS D2] was used by John St Barbe, Bart., a pupil of Christopher Simpson, and a former owner of Broadlands near Romsey in Hampshire. A further book [MS A27] is of music for the viola da gamba, Falle's own instrument, and it is in his own hand. As nearly every item it contains is taken from the printed music books in his possession, it was evidently produced for his own convenience, to obviate carrying numerous books around with him. The extent of Falle's collection may be determined from his holograph catalogue [Add. MS 154], which ends with a statement bequeathing his books to the cathedral library.

[1] Act Book 4, p. 75.
[2] B. Crosby, 'An Early Restoration Liturgical Music Manuscript', *Music & Letters* (Oct. 1974).

That, however, was only a declaration of intent, for it was made in 1722, and the actual transfer did not take place until 1739.

Thomas Drake (minor canon, 1714–20) bequeathed in 1747 two of his own works: 'Messiah. A Christ-Mass Song' [MS D1] and a 'Te Deum' [MS E1]. The text of the latter was arranged in sapphic verses by Anthony Alsop who was contemporary with Drake at Oxford. Thomas Ebdon (1738–1811), who as chorister, lay-clerk, and organist, served the cathedral for no fewer than sixty-four years, left behind harpsichord sonatas and three-part glees [MSS D6, D11], whilst among incidental pieces in his hand [MS D3] are three by his daughter Mary and an Allegretto by Count Joseph Boruwlaski, the Polish dwarf. Ebdon was probably more at ease on the non-liturgical scene, and Manchester Public Library holds a book of Music Lessons which he devised in 1799 for a Miss Hubback of Stockton.[1]

John Mathews, a lay-clerk and copyist with a very fine hand, when he left for a similar position in Ireland, did not take with him the scores and single-parts of 'Joshua' [MSS A24, D8], and 'The king shall rejoice' and the 'Dettingen Te Deum' [MSS A32, D7], works which he had had bound in Salisbury before he came to Durham. In 1777 he sent back from Dublin two organ books [MSS A18, A19] in the hope that some of the music they contained might be deemed suitable for inclusion in the Durham repertoire. His covering letter mentions the popularity of the Jubilate at Durham; whilst the comment in Shenton's Communion Service that the Sursum Corda, Sanctus, and Gloria had been composed at Mathews's request sheds further light on contemporary Durham usage.

The widest range of manuscripts, probably most of MSS E12–E35, was collected and used by Richard Fawcett who was a Prebendary from 1778 until his death in 1782. Born in 1714, the second son of a Recorder of Durham, Fawcett was

---

[1] MS 740. Eb.31.

associated with Corpus Christi College, Oxford, from 1730 to 1754. In 1757 he was appointed to the living of Church Eaton, Staffordshire, returning to the north, to Gateshead and Newcastle, in 1766. Whilst at Oxford he was active musically, as can be gathered from his comments and annotations in the Durham manuscripts and in others in the Christ Church and Bodleian libraries.[1] The Durham collection embraces many non-liturgical aspects. There are sonatas and concertos by Handel and Geminiani, and organ music by J. S. Bach,[2] most of it lacking any ascription [MSS E13, E24–E26, E33, E34]. Never published are two holograph works for the violoncello by Giorgio Antoniotto d'Adorni [MSS E24(v), E27].[3] Handel is the most popular composer, for there are full scores of some of the Chandos anthems [MSS E14, E19, E21, E28], and scores and parts annotated by Fawcett of some of his oratorios and operas [MSS E12, E17, E20, E23, E35]. There are solo cantatas in Italian by Agostini, Melani, and Pacieri [MS E29]; and as at Oxford there are cantatas for two voices in Latin and Italian, possibly by Steffani [MS E22], and sections of two of Borri's Latin Masses [MS E31]. Loose in a coarse paper folder bearing Fawcett's initials and also its title is the hitherto missing holograph score of Galliard's opera 'Merlin, or the Devil of Stonehenge', together with portions of his ['Apollo and Daphne'] and [? 'The Triumphs of Love'] [MS E30]. Possibly belonging to Fawcett is a music book [MS E15] used in 1726 by the London-based Academy of Ancient Vocal Music. In c.1970 a name something like 'Estwicke'[4] was still visible on its covers, but no trace of this can now be found.

A set of eight part-books [MSS D13 and D14] containing the choruses only of eighteen anthems by Croft may be

[1] D. Burrows, 'Sources for Oxford Handel Performances in the First Half of the Eighteenth Century', *Music & Letters* (April 1980).

[2] B. Cooper, 'An unknown Bach source', *Musical Times* (Dec. 1972).

[3] Cf. Bod. Lib. MS Eng. Letters, D.45, pp. 399–424.

[4] i.e. Sampson Estwick (c.1657–1739), minor canon of St Paul's. He was at the meeting held in January 1725/6 (Brit. Lib. Add. MS 11732).

associated with Finedon, Northamptonshire. Finedon was
the family seat of Sir John Dolben (1684–1756), formerly
sub-Dean of the Chapel Royal, and later a Prebendary of
Durham. Sir John appointed James Kent, a pupil of Croft, as
his first private organist. More, however, needs to be known
about the books and about the 'J. Hands' of Birmingham
whose name is inside the front covers.[1] Equally obscure is the
history of a set of instrumental and vocal parts used for a late
(1757–62) performance of 'Esther' [MS D15]. At some stage
they were owned by a C. W. Wheeler, for a combination of
his initials, signature, and coat-of-arms of an angola goat and
the motto 'Aveto jure', is on every copy. Also by Handel is an
early version (c.1725) of 'Ottone' [MS D16], presented in
1928 by Algernon Armes, the eldest son of Philip Armes, the
former organist. Bound in red leather ornately tooled in gilt,
it is said to be in the hand of J. C. Smith the elder, Handel's
principal amanuensis. Lastly in the cathedral's collection is a
book [MS E37] which helped to pass away the time. It is
a book of hymns, both tunes and text, and was compiled in
1808 and 1809 by John Scurr of Whitby whilst he was held
prisoner at Givet in France. The purpose of the book otherwise is not clear, especially if the printed sources he refers to
were at hand.

The Bamburgh collection takes its name from Bamburgh
Castle, which had been purchased by Bishop Lord Crewe in
1704.[2] When he died in 1721 he left the revenue from three
estates in Northumberland and Durham to be administered
as a charity. In 1736 Thomas Sharp I (1693–1758), who
numbered Archdeacon of Northumberland and Prebendary
of Durham among his titles, became one of the trustees. He
was succeeded as trustee in 1758 by his eldest son, John III,
who subsequently emulated his father by being advanced to
the other two positions. It was John III who was instrumental

[1] 'Birm꙽ is found in Royal College of Music MSS 1101, 2230.
[2] C. J. Stranks, *The Charities of Nathaniel, Lord Crewe and Dr. John Sharp 1721–1976* (1976).

in having the keep of Bamburgh Castle restored, initially
to provide accommodation for its manorial courts, though
because there was no parsonage the incumbent of Bamburgh,
Thomas Sharp II (John's younger brother) lived there. When
Thomas II died in 1772, John succeeded to the living. He duly
sold his brother's library to the trustees for the use of the
public. His brother, it should be pointed out, had inherited
his father's half-share of the library begun by their grand-
father John I (1645–1714), sometime Archbishop of York.
John III himself had somewhat fortuitously[1] inherited via his
father his uncle John II's half-share, and when he died in 1792
his bequest brought together again the two parts of the
family library. Further bequests were made by other members of the Sharp family during the early part of the nineteenth century. Even though the castle was sold to Lord
Armstrong in 1894, the library remained there until 1958
when, with the exception of the music books which came to
the cathedral, it was transferred on indefinite loan to Durham
University Library.

Some forty of the Bamburgh finding numbers—about a
fifth of the music section—refer to manuscripts. They may
be conveniently divided into two major groups.

The first of these is of interest rather than moment, being
written by or for the members of the Sharp family and used
by them. Eleven of Thomas I's children survived infancy and
learned to play at least one instrument each. Used by the
young Sharps and in John III's possession from his college
days is a set of seven part-books [MSS M183–M189] containing printed and manuscript sections. Overtures to Handel's
operas predominate, and there are concertos by other early
eighteenth century composers. In one of the books [MS
M185, p. 81] is written 'Charles Sharp', 'James Sharp',
'Thomas Sharp 1741', and also 'John' and 'William'; and elsewhere in the same manuscript are 'John Wharton' [p. 3] and
'Francis Myddleton' and 'James Mason' [p. 84]. Also inscribed

[1] Gloucester Record Office, D3549, Box 15a.

'John Sharp. Trin. Coll.' are ten part-books of 'Alexander's Feast' by Handel [MS M172]. One can only speculate whether they were used at the Deanery performance of 1749.[1] That they were used at some later date may be gathered from Thomas Ebdon's[2] transcription into the violoncello book of part of the 1st Flute part. Similarly inscribed are two books [MSS M159, M204] of music for the violoncello, John III's own instrument. Acquired in 1762 at the earliest—to judge from the Archdeacon's bookplate—is a complete version of 'Dialogue in Amphitrion' by William Boyce [MS M205].

Two collections of hymns (some by Thomas Sharp II) with other sacred items [MSS M89, M174] are in an unidentified formal hand responsible for similar and larger collections at Cambridge (Ely MSS), Gloucester Record Office, Oxford (Tenbury MSS), Westminster Abbey, and York Minster. Their copyist may well have been active in London where James, William, and Granville Sharp had set up house, and where Thomas II held a further living as Rector of St Bartholomew the Less, Smithfield, from 1765 until his death. The London Sharps held concerts there and on their barges on the Thames. It was with one of them as a setting that Zoffany painted a family portrait (many with their instruments) in c.1780. They had an extensive music collection, which was sold in 1814.[3] Hardly any of it found its way to the Bamburgh collection; and the identity of the books given by Catherine Sharp (John III's niece) up to 1835 has not been established.

Very much to be associated with the Sharp family is a part-book for the 1st Violin of movements from concertos and overtures [MS M157]. These were transcribed by Cuthbert Brass, as were an Evening Service by [Edward Gregory] [MS M207], a Durham minor canon, and the verse anthem, 'O let my mouth be filled' [MS M206] by James Hesletine, Organist

[1] *Letters of Spencer Cowper*, ed. E. Hughes (Surtees Soc. vol. 165), p. 118.

[2] Organist, Durham, 1763–1811.

[3] J. B. Holland and J. LaRue, 'The Sharp Manuscript, London 1759–c1793', *Bulletin of the New York Public Library* (March 1969).

of Durham (1711–63) and brother-in-law to Thomas Sharp I. This last is a bonus, for the anthem is very imperfect in Durham's own manuscripts, a situation which tradition accounts for by asserting that Hesletine, supposing he had been slighted by the Dean and Chapter, destroyed as many of his compositions as he could lay his hands on. Fortunately, this destruction was restricted to the cathedral's own manuscripts, for Tenbury MSS 700 and 822, in the formal hand mentioned above, represent further anthems by him.

The full extent of John III's books, including music books, is afforded by the valuation lists compiled after his death.[1] For his music a certain amount of holograph evidence exists in the form of a loose sheet and a somewhat mutilated catalogue [MSS M174(ii), M194]. This last indicates that some items had come 'from Charles' (a brother) and some 'from Hon. Mr. Finch's Collect$^n$'.

The Finch connection and collection is itself a major topic, for John Sharp I, sometime Archbishop of York, had been chaplain to Sir Heneage Finch, the 1st Earl of Nottingham. The Hon. Edward Finch, his fifth son (1664–1738) was ordained in 1700, achieving the dignity of a Prebendary of York. He was a keen amateur musician and minor composer, two of his compositions being included in the six-volume collection of services and anthems made by Thomas Tudway for Lord Harley in the early eighteenth century.[2]

Bamburgh MS M70 was personal to Edward Finch. Many of its anonymous sonatas and catches are presumably by him, for on a number of pages there is a monogram incorporating under reflection the letters 'EF'. Moreover, 'The Cuckoo Sonata' [Rev pp. 41–4] appeared under his name in 1693 in *The Division Violin*. Among favourite items and arrangements are compositions by Thomas Benson, Master of the Choristers, York, Edward Salisbury and Carlo Quarlesi (i.e. Charles Quarles), Organists of York, and Abbot Steffani,

---

[1] Gloucester Record Office, D3549, Box 52.
[2] Brit. Lib. Harley MSS 7337–42.

sometime President of the Academy of Ancient Music [see MS E15]. MS M70 includes one of Steffani's motets, and three others were transcribed by Finch into eighty-seven pages of MS M192.

Finch was particularly impressed with Greene's 'Lord let me know mine end'—'the Best Anthym that ever was made' is how he described it.[1] It is therefore interesting that he had copied into MS M70 [Greene's] anthem, 'O Lord who shall dwell in thy tabernacle', which is unknown apart from the companion instrumental and vocal single parts in the same hand in Bodleian Library MS Mus. d.46. Their copyist was active not later than 1738, for Finch himself added the final 'Amen' to the same scribe's transcription on an anonymous Service in G. Amongst other items in MS M70 in this hand is Farinelli's 'Ossequioso Ringraziamento', together with an additional copy of the text (for which someone else has supplied an interlinear translation) on an envelope addressed to Finch. It must remain a matter of conjecture whether Finch met the famous Italian castrato during the latter's sojourn in London, 1734–7.

Reference must also be made of the way Finch indicated the different parts of six-part harmony when closely scored, for it and his method of blocking off sections, never mind his distinctive hand, help to determine what other manuscripts were his. Into this category fit two late seventeenth century part-books of music for viols [MSS M179–M180] which include eighteen sonatas by Jenkins not complete elsewhere; and of the same date a badly mutilated York bass part-book of anthems (all lost) and services [MS M170]. Slightly later are sonatas purporting to be by Ziani [MS M193/1],[2] the otherwise unknown Francesco Navarra of Mantua [MSS M175, M193/2–7], Finger [MSS M195–M197], and Pez [MS M200].

[1] Tenbury MS 1027; see Tenbury MSS 1024–7 for other music in common with MS M70.
[2] Dr Michael Talbot is confident that they are by Albinoni, who may also be responsible for some of the unidentified items of MSS M175 and M193/2–7.

How this music came into the possession of the Sharps is no mystery. The families had known each other since the previous generation, and following the death of Edward Finch in 1738, the current Earl of Nottingham wrote thus to Thomas Sharp I:

I received the favour of yours from Durham & shall be mighty glad if there are any scores or musical Compositions amongst my uncles books y$^t$ may be agreable to you ... I shall think them very well placed in your hands.[1]

Thomas clearly liked what he saw. That the Finch music did not become part of the Sharp family library is apparent from its dispersal. Apart from the four manuscripts at Tenbury already referred to, a further holograph manuscript is in Glasgow University Library.[2] Bearing the bookplate of the London Sharps, it is, like MS M70, a personal manuscript and includes a number of his own compositions.

There remains in the Bamburgh collection a handful of manuscripts devoid of Sharp signatures and Finch calligraphics. Simply because of their dates, an imperfect copy of Purcell's 'Hail bright Cecilia' [MS M102] must have belonged to Finch, whilst a violoncello concerto by Cervetto [MS M202] and a badly mutilated score of [Jommelli's] 'Oratorio Della Passione' [MSS M176–M177] knew no such connection.

[1] Gloucester Record Office, D3549, Box 77a.
[2] Euing MS R.d.39.

# THE FORMAT OF THE CATALOGUE

THE compilation of this catalogue called for two major issues to be resolved. With Durham's own manuscripts having prefixes A to E, just like the printed music, not to mention peculiarities like C2★, C19A, and E11a, it had to be decided whether the opportunity should be taken to allocate new and orderly finding numbers. Equally, it had to be determined whether there should be any foliation or further re-pagination of the later manuscripts, many of which had been paginated in the 1920s.

Though ideally such undertakings have much to recommend them, yet it was felt that they would raise as many problems as they would solve.

Scholars have worked at many of the manuscripts, and new systems of finding numbers and pagination would greatly reduce the value of their work. Not only that, but it would add to the work of the library staff. Nor would that be alleviated by providing correlating lists. As has transpired with the Caroline part-books at Peterhouse, such lists would not be a temporary or transitional measure, for the finding numbers have been used in many published books and articles. Moreover, to answer the needs of scholars, many of the manuscripts have been microfilmed, and whilst it would be relatively easy to alter their finding numbers, it would not be possible to impose a further system of pagination. Furthermore, foliation would simply go from front to back, and many of the Durham manuscripts are double-ended, each end having its own individuality. Consequently, both areas have been left as they were.

It was originally intended that the catalogue should include a full inventory of every manuscript, and a detailed index listing under composers the occurrences of each of their compositions. But the considerable repetition in the many books of anthems and services, the relative insignificance of some of the other items, together with economic considerations, have resulted in further thoughts, especially in relation to the inventories. The decisions that have been made are the result of consultations with the Department of Music in the University of Durham combined with an appraisal of the requests which have been made about the manuscripts. Enquirers have been more interested in individual composers, in particular works of those composers, in music for certain instruments, than in all the contents of any manuscript. What they have wanted to know about the manuscripts themselves has tended to be background information—date, provenance, copyists, related manuscripts, etc. The inventories, therefore, have been greatly reduced (though for the convenience of researchers full ones are available at the library). The detailed index, on the other hand, has become the most substantial part of the catalogue.

### The scope of the catalogue

The catalogue covers all the music manuscripts now in the possession of the Dean and Chapter of Durham, whether in the libraries of the cathedral or among the muniments in the care of the Department of Palaeography and Diplomatic in the University of Durham. Music used by the choir, sacred, secular, and instrumental donations, fragments of mediaeval music now serving as end papers of later manuscripts and incunables, inventories, and catalogues, all are included.

The date range is from the tenth century through to, for the sake of completeness of what is now an out-moded method of reproduction, the early years of the twentieth century.

*Editorial procedure*

Editorial assertions regarding the identity of a work or of its composer are indicated by [. . .]. The keys of chants and instrumental items, and the number of instrumental parts, though often not stated explicitly in the manuscripts, can hardly be regarded as discoveries, and accordingly are not normally so treated.

*The description of the manuscripts*

The monastic music is presented first, then the cathedral's later manuscripts, and finally the Bamburgh collection. For the first two groups shelf-order (starting with the 'A's) is adhered to, followed by certain sundry items and those among the muniments in the care of the Palaeography Department. The Bamburgh music is a numbered sequence having the prefix, 'M'.

In each case (apart from monastic and other fragments, where the physical details are advanced) the information is given in this order:

(1) Nature of the manuscript.

(2) Its relationship to other manuscripts as regards contents.

(3) Summary lists of contents. In the case of the organ books (most of the 'A' series), their individual nature has been appreciated. For each of them any anonymous items are followed by the known composers listed in alphabetical order, the relevant numbers allocated in the Index of Composers to each's composition following immediately in brackets, e.g. for MS A1:

Anon (71.72), Amner (2.), T. Boyce, Byrd (2.8.11.15– 17 . . .), etc. This system has also been applied to other highly individual manuscripts.

With the part-books, an attempt has been made to divide them into sets. For each set, its range of contents, excluding singletons, is listed under its most suitable member in fashion similar to that of the organ books.

Any additional items are listed under the manuscripts in which they occur. But even this system breaks down, for from *c.*1770 onwards some manuscripts serve to some extent to compensate for an insufficiency of the various printed volumes which had been purchased for the choir. Such situations too are commented upon.

In the case of the instrumental music, it has been deemed sufficient merely to mention the number of occasions a composer is featured, e.g. for MS A27:

Marais (40 items), Schenck (39), . . ., C. Simpson (12), etc.

The Index of Composers sheds further light on the scene.

With certain manuscripts, e.g. MS E24–E26, each of which could have been given a wide range of finding numbers had not their diverse contents already been explored, it has been felt desirable to subdivide them thus: E24(i), E24(ii), etc. In contrast, the descriptions, e.g. MS M193/1, M193/2, etc., are used where several part-books having similar contents, or single parts of the same work, are grouped under the same finding number.

(4) Background information:
  (*a*)  date: a substantiation in the form of a page reference indicates that it is a precentorial or other authorization.
  (*b*)  provenance (when not Durham), history, copyists, and other related matter.
  (*c*)  noteworthy covers and tables (of contents).

(5) Physical description:
  (*a*)  size in mm, height given first.
  (*b*)  most of the manuscripts are of paper, so only stated if to the contrary.
  (*c*)  number of folios, and details of current pagination, e.g. (invention):

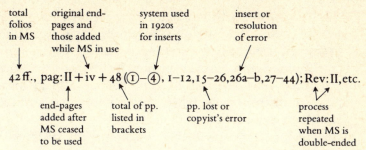

(*d*)  indication of number of unused manuscript pages.

(*e*)  most of the manuscripts have 5-lined staves, so only stated if otherwise.

(6)  Bibliography.

## Index of Composers and their Compositions

Preceded by the anonymous items, the composers are listed in alphabetical order. The information given about each composer is:

(1)  (*a*)  accepted form of surname, followed in brackets by significant variations of spelling found in the manuscripts.

(*b*)  style (where relevant), and Christian name(s).

(*c*)  year of birth and of death, or indication either when active or of date of manuscript. Further biographical details are provided for composers with Durham or York connections.

(2)  Where relevant, a restricted bibliography giving any eighteenth or early nineteenth century printed volumes of the composer's works used by the choir, together with certain modern thematic studies.

(3)  When more than one, the compositions under each composer are numbered. Apart from the anonymous items, the order of these compositions is liturgical, secular vocal, instrumental, theoretical works, and catalogues. Within the liturgical section the order is anthems and hymn tunes, services, and chants. The anthems and

songs are arranged alphabetically, the services and chants by keys, and the instrumental works by genre. Where a liturgical work is featured in one of the eighteenth or early nineteenth century printed collections this too is recorded. The question of authorship is also discussed, and comment is made when a work is not ascribed in any Durham manuscript.

(4) the manuscripts in which a work appears are given in finding order, no attention being paid to date, voice, or instrument.

(5) the designation, 'v', e.g. C11v, is used in conjunction with the finding numbers to denote the reverse end of a double-ended manuscript.

(6) the precise details of pagination are supplied to compensate for the lack of full inventories. The loss of just a few notes receives no mention; 'imp' is used where more than a stave has been torn away; 'inc', where a whole leaf has gone; and 'frag', where the item never was complete.

(7) the handling of services, with their many components, calls for further explanation. Consider part of the entry for one of *BLOW*'s services:

> 30. in e: Td, Be, J, K, C, Cd, Dm (*Boyce 3*)
>     A33: 191–219   B22: 116–25   B28: 185–202
>     C8: 424–32, 434 (—Td, Be; Dm inc)   etc.
>     Td, J, Cd, Dm
>     A15: 131–43   A22: 153–64   etc.

The description of the service by key is followed by the sum total of its components found in the manuscripts, and it is noted that an early published version occurs in the third volume of Boyce's *Cathedral Music*. The manuscripts which follow immediately without a separate heading contain all the components listed with the exception of MS C8, which lacks the Te Deum and Benedicite, and in which the Deus Misereatur is incomplete through page(s) being torn away. In this particular service it is felt desirable to give a sub-set of the components. It likewise is followed by the manuscripts in which the combination is to be found. Some of the services, like that by *TALLIS*, where certain manuscripts have a spurious Jubilate (hence, 'J'), have many sub-sets.

*Other Indexes*

To facilitate research a number of other Indexes are added:

(1) of century, or half century, when manuscript begun;
(2) of signatures in the manuscripts relating to payments;
(3) of copyists of Durham's own liturgical manuscripts;
(4) of musical genre;
(5) of titles and first lines.

# ABBREVIATIONS

PERSONAL experience of many of the liturgical items and an abundance of well-authenticated modern editions have greatly reduced the task of corroborating assertions. The only editions listed here are those early general collections purchased by the Dean and Chapter and used in conjunction with the manuscripts, and certain other collections on which the copyists had clearly drawn. Early editions of the works of individual composers and certain modern studies are recorded under those composers, whereas articles on individual manuscripts are mentioned under those manuscripts, as are related and useful manuscripts in other libraries.

*Bibliographical:*

| | |
|---|---|
| *Arnold* | *Cathedral Music: Being a Collection in Score*, ed. Samuel Arnold (4 vols; 1790) |
| *Boyce* | *Cathedral Music: Being a Collection in Score . . . By the Several English Masters of the last Two Hundred Years*, ed. William Boyce (3 vols; 1760, 1768, 1773) |
| *Boyce's Own, Croft, Crotch*, etc. | See Index of Composers |
| *Div Comp* | *The Divine Companion: Being a Collection of New And Easie Hymns and Anthems . . . for Henry Playford* (1701) |
| *Div Harm 1, 1731* | *Divine Harmony Six Select Anthems . . . by Mr Jnº Weldon* [1731] |
| *Div Harm 2, 1731* | *Divine Harmony The 2ᵈ Collection being Select Anthems . . . Compos'd by Several Eminent Authors* [1731] |
| *Div Harm 1798* | *Divine Harmony, being a collection of psalm and hymn tunes; . . . by the late . . . Phocion Henley . . .* |

*to which are added four psalm tunes . . . by the late . . . Thomas Sharp [II]* (1798)

| | |
|---|---|
| Gardiner | *Judah*, William Gardiner (1821; includes arrangements from Haydn, Mozart, and Beethoven) |
| Grove | *The New Grove Dictionary of Music and Musicians*, ed. S. Sadie (1980) |
| Ker, Anglo-Saxon | *Catalogue of Manuscripts containing Anglo-Saxon*, N. R. Ker (1957) |
| Ker, Medieval | *Medieval Manuscripts in British Libraries*, N. R. Ker (vol. 2; 1977) |
| Latrobe | *A Selection of Sacred Music*, ed. C. I. Latrobe (6 vols; 1806–26) |
| Mynors | *Durham Cathedral Manuscripts to the end of the Twelfth Century*, R. A. B. Mynors (1939) |
| Ouseley 2 | *Special Anthems for Certain Seasons*, ed. F. A. G. Ouseley (vol. 2; 1886) |
| Page | *Harmonia Sacra, A Collection of Anthems in Score*, ed. John Page (3 vols; 1800) |
| Pratt | *A Collection of Anthems in Score Selected from the Works of Handel, Haydn, Mozart, Clari, Leo and Carissimi*, ed. John Pratt (vol. 1; ?1828) |
| RISM | *Répertoire International Des Sources Musicales* (1971 +) |

*Liturgical*:

| | | | | |
|---|---|---|---|---|
| Be | Benedicite | | L | Litany |
| Bs | Benedictus | | M | Magnificat |
| C | Creed | | N | Nunc dimittis |
| Cd | Cantate domino | | Ps. | Psalm |
| Dm | Deus misereatur | | R | Responses |
| G | Glory be to God on high | | S | Sanctus |
| Go | Sentence before Gospel | | Sc | Sursum corda |
| J | Jubilate | | Td | Te deum |
| K | Responses to Commandments, Kyrie | | V | Venite |

# ABBREVIATIONS

*Miscellaneous (selected):*

| | | | |
|---|---|---|---|
| A | key of A major (other major keys represented similarly) | instr | instruments |
| | | l-c | lay-clerk |
| | | m-c | minor canon |
| | | Misc. Ch. | Miscellaneous Charter |
| a | key of A minor | | |
| add | additional (matter) | m of chor | Master of the Choristers |
| arr | arranged by, arrangement | | |
| | | org | Organist |
| ascrib | named in Durham MSS | pag | paginated |
| | | parchm | parchment |
| attrib to | now thought to be by | Pr. | printed book in Dean and Chapter Library, Durham |
| b. | born | | |
| bapt | baptised | preb | Prebendary |
| chor | chorister | prec | precentor |
| d. | died | pt | part |
| ed. | edited by | Rev | reverse end of double-ended MS |
| *fl.* | flourished | | |
| Forw | front end of double-ended MS | Table | Table of Contents |
| | | t. | tune |
| frag | transcription never finished | v | used with finding numbers (e.g. MS C11v) to denote reverse end of double-ended MS |
| hol | holograph | | |
| imp | more than one stave torn away | | |
| Inc. | Incunable | | |
| inc | leaf missing from MS | | |

# ADDENDUM, CORRIGENDUM, ET EXPLICANDUM

THE following came to light after the page-proof stage had been reached:

(1) p. 3. Dr Alma Browne's searches for further examples of early notation met with one small success:

**MS B.II.11** *Hieronymi et Aliorum Opuscula*, the last fascicle (ff. 107 *et seq.*) being *Epistole Fulberti Carnotensis Episcopi*. 11th cent. From France, and given by Bishop William St Calais (d. 1096). 325 × 238 mm. i + 138 ff.

Music: 11th cent. On f. 136 the incipits of two Fulbertian hymns headed 'In die Pentecostes' (Organum mentis tibi quęso nostrę temporans) and 'In die Natalis Domini' (Nuncium vobis fero de supernis) are noted with letter notation (a–p system). The melody each time is that of the hymn, 'Iste confessor'.

*Mynors*, no. 39; cf. A. C. Browne, 'The *a-p* system of Letter Notation', *Musica Disciplina* (1981).

(2) p. 205. Dr Robert Manning pointed out an error in the H. Purcell references, hence the division of no. 6.

(3) pp. 11–93 (*passim*), 249–71 (*passim*). Failure to set down in writing the policy on composers' initials has resulted in a number of inconsistencies. For example, with composers having the same surname initials have usually been given; but whilst the lesser T. Boyce and M. Ebdon are so indicated, W. Boyce and T. Ebdon almost invariably lack theirs.

# DESCRIPTION OF THE MANUSCRIPTS

## THE MONASTIC ITEMS

**MS A.II.17** The Durham Gospels (inc). 7th/8th cent. ? copied on Lindisfarne, and in the possession of the community of St Cuthbert (d. 687) from its earliest days on the island. 340 × 260 mm for ff. 2–102; 300 × 225 mm for ff. 103–11.

Music: late 10th cent. On f. 74ᵛ the Baptism of Jesus and the beginning of his genealogy (*see* Luke 3: 21–4) are pointed with inter-linear adiastematic neumes. In view of the provenance of the MS their form is unusual, having both German and French influences.

*The Durham Gospels*, ed. T. J. Brown (Early English Manuscripts in Facsimile, vol. 20; 1980), especially D. Hiley (p. 35); *Ker, Anglo-Saxon*, no. 105; *Mynors*, nos. 3 and 4.


**MS A.III.11** Main contents: Miscellanea theologica, including Prepositinus of Cremona, *Super Psalmos*; Peter Comestor, *Super Iohannem*; Gregory, *Dialogi* i–iv; Peter Chrysologus of Ravenna, *Sermones* extr.; Augustine, *Enchiridion*; Alcuin, *De virtutibus et viciis*. Mid 13th–mid 14th cent. f. 1 has early 15th cent. inscription, 'De libraria infra Capellam Prioris Dunelm'.

Music: *c*.1400. One parchment flyleaf (fol. ii) at front. 345 × 228 mm.

A fragment of three-part polyphony.

f. ii holds several textless movements of the Mass. On the first two systems is a [Kyrie] based on the Kyrie 'Lux et origo' (Graduale Romanum No. 1 = Vatican Kyrie No. 1); and on the remaining systems are a [Sanctus and Agnus Dei], the Cantus being on the middle stave, taken from Vatican Mass XV. The Kyrie Trope on f. iiᵛ is of Durham origin. In honour of St Cuthbert, it begins, 'Kyrie Cuthberti prece culpa ceno plebicete. Eleyson'. In all there are eight 'verses', for each of the four systems has two sets of words to its 'Eleyson'.

On staves of 5 brown lines, there being 15 staves on f. ii and 12 on f. ii^v. Notation is Ars Nova (minims, division dots, accidentals); the script textura. The 'K' of 'Kyrie' is large, decorated with pen-work in green and red, and extended along the top and down the side. f. ii^v bears the finding number, 'A. II. 11.' [*sic*].

*RISM*, BIV², pp. 216–18; *The Relics of St. Cuthbert*, ed. C. F. Battiscombe (1956), pp. 194–200; G. Reaney, in *Musica Disciplina* (1961), p. 23; *Grove*, vol. 13, p. 368.

**MS A.III.32**   An illuminated Sarum Missal, with a little notation.

The notation is substantial only at the more important feast days, including the Purification. The 'Blessing of the Wax' (ff. 124^v–28) is noted, as are the Prefaces (ff. 144–9), a Pater Noster (ff. 152–3^v), and the hymn 'O Redemptor summe' (ff. 112–12^v).

15th cent. Southern England. Plainchant notation on staves of 4 red lines. Textura script, two columns, rubricated. Large initials are blue, flourished in red, smaller initials red or blue.

333 × 228 mm. 340 ff.

**MS A.IV.6**   Main contents: *Daniel et Esdras glossata*. Late 12th cent. Given to St Alban's cell at Tynemouth, *c.*1200.

Music: *c.*1200. One folded parchment fragment (f. 1). 210 × 161 mm (unfolded).

On two staves on the largely blank inside are '[R.] Ave Maria gracia plena dominus tecum', and 'V. Benedicta [tu inter] mulieres et benedictus fructus ventris tui. Gloria patri et filio et spiritu . . .'

In black non-mensural notation on dry-point lines with rough vertical lines (?indicating where to breathe). Stuck on the lower part is an unidentified fragment in the same hand.

*Mynors*, no. 96.

**MS A.IV.19**   A Collectar (collects and short chapters read at the day-hours during the year), to which are added benedictions and other matter. 10th cent. With its text in Latin, probably from southern England, and inter-linear Northumbrian Saxon, it is thought that this MS came into the possession of the community of St Cuthbert during its stay at Chester-le-Street (AD 883–995). 251 × 172 mm. 89 ff., pag. 1–178.

Music: mid 11th cent. Two liturgical directives added in the left-hand margin of p. 94 have inter-linear adiastematic neumes. The higher, in Anglo-Saxon, has two such lines; the lower, in Latin, eight. They relate to the body of the text which has the heading, 'Benedictio Domus'.

*Rituale Ecclesiae Dunelmense*, ed. U. Lindelöf (Surtees Soc. vol. 140; 1927); *The Durham Ritual*, ed. T. J. Brown (Early English Manuscripts in Facsimile, vol. 16; 1969); *Ker, Anglo-Saxon*, no. 106; *Mynors*, no. 14.

**MS A.IV.23**  Main contents: Commentary on the Bible. 14th cent. A 14th cent. inscription (f. 222) refers to Robt. de Basefird, OP. In Durham by *c.*1500.

Music: *c.*1500. Part of one parchment leaf, 164 × 100 mm, inserted upside down at front of MS.

On the side facing the front cover are four staves of a single part of the latter part of a polyphonic setting of 'Gloria in excelsis Deo' (from 'unigenite Jesu Christe' to the end). The second and third staves on the other side have the text: '. . . laude dignissima quia . . . us noster Alle[luia]'; the other staves are blank.

The 5 staves on each side are of 5 red lines each. The notation of the Gloria is mensural, and 'void' with semi-minims in black, and with rests clearly indicated. On the other side black long-breve notation is employed. The script is cursive.

*RISM*, BIV⁴, pp. 606–7; G. Reaney, 'Some Little-Known Sources of Medieval Polyphony in England', *Musica Disciplina* (1961).

**MS B.II.11**  *See* p. xxxix.

**MS B.III.11**  Other contents: the first three fascicles are a collection of *Homilies* by Gregory the Great and others.

Music: 11th cent. Parchment. ff. 136–59 (the fourth and last fascicle). 317 × 245 mm.

An Antiphoner, noted with adiastemic neumes.

ff. 136–57ᵛ contain the Temporale, beginning with 'Tu exurgens' (Advent Sunday) and continuing through to Trinity Sunday (with added matter on f. 155ᵛ), the Histories of Job and Ezekiel, together with passages relating to the Song of the Three Holy Children (Book of Daniel). ff. 157ᵛ–9ᵛ give part of the Sanctorale

(Sts Sebastian, Agnes, and Vincent, the Purification of Blessed Mary the Virgin, St Agatha, and the Annunciation).

Written in northern France. The notation is substantial on ff. 136–47, 152–3, 155, and 158, but spasmodic elsewhere. Caroline script. ff. 136–43 are rubricated. On ff. 140ᵛ–2ᵛ the nine lections for the Feast of St Stephen are given in full.

*Pars Antiphonarii*, ed. W. H. Frere (facsimile by Plainsong and Mediaeval Music Soc., 1923); *Corpus Antiphonalium Officii*, vol. 1, ed. R. J. Hesbert (Rerum Ecclesiasticarum Documenta, Series Maior, Fontes, VII, 1963); *Mynors*, no. 42; *Grove*, vol. 1, p. 484.

**MS B.III.12**   Main contents: Gregory the Great, *Commentary on the Gospels*. 14th cent. At Durham by 1456.

Music: 14th cent. Two parchment folios (ff. 84–5) inserted at back. 307 × 208 mm.

From an Antiphoner.

The items on the first folio are for Palm Sunday and the next three days of Holy Week; those on the second are for the Second Sunday in Lent and the Monday following. Several of the psalms are not those of Sarum use.

f. 84 lacks staves and notation. Its text is spaced the same as on f. 85, each side of which has 16 staves each of 4 brown lines, the notation being plainchant. f. 85ᵛ is spoiled by glue, and the notation stops after seven lines. Textura script.

**MS B.III.32**   A Latin Hymnary with inter-linear Anglo-Saxon gloss together with Aelfric's *Grammar*. Mid 11th cent. ff. 2–55 contain the Hymns and Canticles for Matins throughout the year. Its glosses have Kentish forms. ff. 56–127 are associable with Christ Church, Canterbury. Given to the Cathedral by Thomas Wharton (d. 1714). 235 × 155 mm. 127 ff.

Music: mid 11th cent. On f. 14ᵛ the first verse of the Anglo-Saxon gloss of 'Ymnus in Epiphania Domini ad vesperam' ('Iesus refulsit omnium. Pius redemptor gentium') is noted with adiastematic neumes.

*The Anglo-Saxon Hymnarium*, ed. J. Stevenson (Surtees Soc. vol. 23; 1851); *Ker, Anglo-Saxon*, no. 107; *Mynors*, no. 22.

**MS B.IV.9**   Prudentius, *Poemata*. 10th cent. Belonged to the Cathedral Priory by c.1200. 250 × 165 mm. i + 171 ff.

Music: 10th cent. Parts of *Cathemerinon* (ff. 1–26) are noted with adiastematic neumes. There are a few above the text of 'Ymnus ante cibum' (ff. 5–5ᵛ), and 'Ymnus post cibum' (f. 8); some eleven lines above 'Hymnus ante somnum' (ff. 11ᵛ–12); some eighteen lines above 'Ymnus ieiuantium' (ff. 14–15); and two lines above 'Ymnus post ieiunium' (f. 17).

*Ker, Anglo-Saxon*, no. 108; *Mynors*, no. 18.


**MS C.I.8** Main contents: Gratian, *Decretum*, with gloss added later. Late 12th/early 13th cent. Belonged to the Cathedral Priory by 1395.

Music: early 14th cent. One parchment flyleaf (f. 1). 388 × 240 mm.

Two Kyrie Tropes (both inc), in three-part polyphony.

On f. 1 are the last three sentences of a Trope whose second last sentence begins 'Clemens creator eloy te tremunt omnes angeli'. The last system of this side and all of f. 1ᵛ are occupied by the first six sentences of 'O pater excelse'.

15 staves per side, each side having 5 systems. The staves are ruled in red, the top part always having 5 lines, the second part 4 on f. 1 and 5 on f. 1ᵛ, the lowest part usually 4 lines. The music is black long-breve on f. 1, to which are added semibreves, accidentals, division dots, and 'bar lines' on f. 1ᵛ. Textura script. On f. 1ᵛ the various initials indicated in the left hand margin have not been drawn in.

*RISM*, BIV¹, pp. 489–90.


**MS C.I.20** Main contents: Huguito, *Summa super derivationibus*; Isidore, *Etymologiae*. Mid 14th cent. Procured by Prior Wessington for Durham (f. 5) in early 15th cent.

Music: 14th cent. 8 parchment flyleaves, 340 × 222 mm; four (ff. 1–4) inserted at front, and four (ff. 336*, 337–9) at back.

On ff. 1–4 are seven polyphonic motets of English origin: (1) Herodis in pretorio (f. 1); (2) Fusa cum silentio (f. 1ᵛ); (3) Jesu fili dei patris (f. 2); (4) Princeps apostolice turme (f. 2ᵛ); (5) Dei preco fit baptista (f. 3); (6) Barrabas dimittitur dignus (f. 3); (7) Orto solo serene novitatis (ff. 3ᵛ–4); followed by (8) Virgo dei genetrix (to Gradual: Benedicta) (f. 4ᵛ); and (9) Deo gratias (f. 4ᵛ).

The various parts of the motets are given separately in Petronian notation on staves of 5 brown lines, 12 staves per page. The last two items are in Ars Nova, there being 4 systems of 3 staves each on f. 4$^v$. The text of the lowest part is rubricated. Textura script, with blue initials having red pen-work.

On ff. 336*, 337–9 are ten polyphonic motets, some in Latin, some in French, including two by [Philippe de Vitry (1291–1361)]: (1) Virginalis concio virginis (f. 336*); (2) [Amer amours est l'achoison] (f. 336*); (3) Ad lacrimas flentis dolorem (ff. 336*$^v$–7); (4) Vos quid admiramini [P. de Vitry] (ff. 336*$^v$–7); (5) O vos omnes quibus est aditus (f. 337$^v$); (6) [O canendo vulgo per compita] [P. de Vitry] (f. 337$^v$); (7) L'amoureuse flour d'este (f. 338); (8) Musicorum collegio in curia (ff. 338$^v$–9); (9) Apta caro plumis ingenio (ff. 338$^v$–9); (10) Mon chant en pliant (f. 339$^v$).

The motets, in varying degrees of completeness, are given part by part on staves of 6 brown lines, 13 staves per side. Notation is Ars Nova, with indication of rests, some direct signs, and several 'bars' of 5 longs in duration. Certain notes are rubricated (f. 336*, ll. 5–6). Textura script. The initials are alternately red and blue, and flourished in the other colour.

*RISM*, BIV$^2$, pp. 218–22; F. L. Harrison, 'Ars Nova in England: A New Source', *Musica Disciplina* (1967); *Grove*, vol. 17, pp. 657, 660, 661; 'Vos quid admiramini' is no. 58 in *Medieval Music*, W. T. Marrocco and N. Sandon (1977).

**MS C.III.12**  Main contents: Roffredo Epifanio of Benevento, *Libellus de ordine iudicorum*, *Libelli de iure canonico*; Bartholomew of Breschia, *Ordo iudicaris*, *Brocardica*; Hugelinus, *Distinctiones*. Later 13th cent. Belonged to the Cathedral Priory by the later 15th cent., perhaps given by William Doncaster (d. 1439).

Music: early 13th cent. Two parchment flyleaves (ff. 283–4), the larger 220 × 172 mm.

From a Gradual.

The items on f. 283 are for [Missa pro Fidelibus Defunctis]; and those on f. 284 for the [13th to 15th Sundays after Trinity].

A different rite from Sarum is indicated by the setting of 'Domine refugium factus es' for the 14th (and not the 11th) Sunday after Trinity. Plainchant notation, on 4 red lines. f. 283 (damaged) has 10 staves per side, f. 284, 13. Textura script, with alternate red and blue initials.

**MS C.III.29**  (Removed in 1982 from Incunables 32–4; Bartolus, *Super . . . digesti*, *Super . . . infortiati* (Venice, 1493 and 1494). Each vol. has original sides of binding. Given to the Cathedral in 1519 by Thomas Farne, Vicar of St Oswald's, Durham. Two bifolia were lightly attached inside each cover, having presumably previously served as padding inside the paste-downs. ff. 1–8 were in Inc. 34, ff. 9–16 in Inc. 33, and ff. 17–24 in Inc. 32.)

Music: early 14th cent. 12 parchment bifolia. 193 × 258 mm (open).

From a Breviary (Sanctorale).

The fully noted psalms, antiphons, and responsories are appointed for the Circumcision, the Octave of St Stephen, the Epiphany and its Octave, Septuagesima, and Sexagesima. Not Sarum use— additional matter embraces further passages on the Wedding at Cana, and the Creation of Woman, Adam after the Expulsion, and the descendants of Adam—possibly Franciscan.

Plainchant notation on staves of 4 red lines. Textura script, two columns per page; rubricated, with blue or red initials.

**Incunable 3** Printed contents: Bartholomeus de Glanville, *De proprietatibus rerum* (Strasbourg, 1491). With original blind-stamped sides of binding. Given in 1537 to Stephen Marley by Thomas Swalwell, both monks of Durham. Owned in 17th cent. by 'Sᵣ Thomas Temp[est], Baronet'.

Music: *c.*1200. Two parchment flyleaves, one inside each cover. 278 × 190 mm.

From a Breviary (Sanctorale).

On the front flyleaf are antiphons, responsories, and lections relating to Stephen P. (Aug. 2), and Invention of St Stephen M. (Aug. 3); and on that at the back, the conclusion of the last-named day (after a gap), St Affra (Aug. 5), and St Oswald (Aug. 5). Not Sarum use.

Some of the antiphons and responsories are noted in plainchant on staves of 4 red lines. Two columns per page, rubricated, and with alternate green and red initials.

**Incunable 4** Printed contents: Robertus Caracciolus de Licio, *Sermones Quadragesimales* (Strasbourg, 1497). Owned in 16th cent. by Henry Brandlying, and in 17th cent. by Sir Thomas Tempest, Baronet.

Music: *c.*1200. One inverted reversed parchment folio sewn

asymmetrically round the last gathering, originally pasted to back board. Now 186 × 150 mm, but part of side and top lost.

From a Breviary (Sanctorale).

The antiphons, verses, and psalms relate to Sts Peter and Paul (June 29), starting in the [Second Nocturn].

Music is in early non-mensural black notation on staves of 4 red lines, there being 7 staves on the side with the initial, and 9 on the other, the latter being greatly obscured by glue. Textura script, part of the red initial [P] being down the side of the page.

**Incunable 15A**   Printed contents: Nicolaus de Lyra, *Repertorium in postillam Bibliae* (Nuremberg, 1494). Binding: Oxford, *c*.1500. Inscribed in 1536 by William Wylom, monk of Durham; owned in 17th cent. by Sir Thomas Tempest.

Music: *c*.1400. Two parchment pastedowns, now lifted. 240 × 165 mm.

From a Processional.

The pastedown at the front (inverted and reversed) gives the instructions for Vespers on the Wednesday before Easter and for Maundy Thursday. Though gaps have been left for the notation of e.g. 'Quomodo sedet sola' (Lamentation of Jeremiah), it has not been supplied. That at the back deals with Easter Day, explaining that each verse of the Vespers' psalms 'Laudate pueri Dominum' and 'In exitu Israel' (Pss. 112 and 113) is followed by 'Alleluia'. Ps. 112 is set out on the recto, Ps. 113 on the verso. Both psalms are fully noted.

The plainsong chant is in single-part void notation (longs, breves, and semibreves, though these lack mensural significance) on staves of varying numbers of black lines. In script anglicana, and not well written. The informal nature of the fragment probably accounts for this very early example of void notation.

**Hunter MS 99**   A Manual.

Consists of (1) Office of the Dead (ff. 1–31); (2) Commendation of Souls (ff. 31–40); (3) Mass for the Dead (ff. 40–5); (4) Committal (ff. 45ᵛ–57ᵛ); and (5) other matter including lections commemorating St Cuthbert, pentitential psalms, and a Litany.

Early 15th cent. Written in England [? for use in the Durham region]. The text and musical notation of (1), (2; little notation here), and (4), the only noted sections, are also in Hunter MS 103.

Plainchant notation on staves of 4 red lines; its initials black with black pen-work. Textura script, rubricated. Large initials are blue with red flourishing, smaller initials blue or red. Owned in 16th cent. by 'Antho. Ovington' (f. 78ᵛ).

167 × 109 mm. ii + 80 + ii ff.

*Ker, Medieval*, pp. 503–4.

## Hunter MS 103   A Manual.

Consists of (1) Office of the Dead (ff. 1–51); (2) Commendation of Souls (ff. 51–64); and (3) Committal (inc; ff. 65–75ᵛ).

Mid 15th cent. Written in England. Text and musical notation as for Hunter MS 99, nos. (1), (2), and (4).

138 × 95 mm. ii + 75 + ii ff.

*Ker, Medieval*, pp. 505–6.

## Hunter MS 104   A Common-place Book, little used. Inscribed, 'Hannah Browne 1672' (p. iii).

Music: 15th cent. A fragment of one parchment folio wrapped round the back flyleaves. 32–46 × 174 mm.

From a [? Sarum] Breviary.

With 'Syon noli timere ecce deus', 'Egredietur dominus', and 'Rex noster' noted, the fragment pertains to the Saturday of the 1st Week of Advent, the Commemoration of the Blessed Virgin Mary, and the 2nd Sunday in Advent.

Notation is plainchant on staves of 4 red lines, the black initials decorated in black. Textura script, two columns, rubricated, with blue initials.

## Communar's Cartulary   (among Dean and Chapter muniments in the care of the Palaeography Department of the University of Durham)

Music: last quarter 14th cent. One parchment folio, 396 × 264 mm (open), folded and fastened sideways inside the front cover.

A troped three-part 'Gloria in excelsis Deo', the troped text being 'Spiritus et alme'.

On staves of 5 brown lines, 4 systems of 3 staves on each side of the folio. The notation is black, longs, breves, semibreves, and a few minims, with accidentals and division dots, direct signs, and 'bar' lines dividing it up into sections in 6/8 (𝄴) and 9/8 (⊙) time. These rhythmic alterations are also indicated by 'swallow-tailed' notes. Textura script. The initial 'E' is blue, flourished in red.

W. Summers, 'A New Source of Medieval English Polyphonic Music', *Music & Letters* (Oct. 1977); *Ker, Medieval*, p. 507.

**End Papers and Bindings, nos. 23–5** (among Dean and Chapter muniments in the care of the Palaeography Department of the University of Durham)

**No. 23**

14th cent. Small fragment of one parchment bifolium. 32 × 320 mm (open).

From a Breviary.

Remaining are some of the later verses of Ps. 111 ('Beatus vir qui timet'), portions of Ps. 113 ('In exitu Israel'), notice of the antiphon 'Nos qui vivimus' and of the chapter 'Dominus autem [dirigat]', and the opening of Ps. 114 ('Dilexi: quoniam exaudiet'). Ps. 111 through to Ps. 113 were prescribed for Vespers on Sundays, and Ps. 114 for Vespers on 'feria secunda', i.e. Mondays.

Plainchant notation on staves of 4 red lines. Textura script, two columns per page. Blue initials, decorated in red.

**No. 24**

15th cent. Two fragments from a parchment folio. 290 × 96 mm when put together.

Part of the Office of the Dead.

Though parts of Ps. 137 ('Confitebor tibi Domine') and Ps. 145 ('Lauda anima'), together with the various sentences are extant, there are only two systems of music, set to the antiphon, 'Opera manum tuarum Domine non despicias'.

Plainchant notation, on staves of 4 red lines. Textura script; initials blue or red. Only traces of 2nd column survive.

**No. 25** (formerly Misc. Ch. 7175)

Mid 15th cent. One damaged bifolium. [290] × 450 mm (open).

Barely legible is the end of an 'Agnus Dei' (f. 1). Then follows the Kyrie Trope, 'Kyrie fons bonitatis' (ff. 1ᵛ–2). Of its nine sections, nos. 3, 6, and 8 have not been transcribed. A 'Gloria in excelsis' (ff. 2–2ᵛ) and the opening of a ? 'Credo' (f. 2ᵛ) occupy the remainder. Scarcely any of f. 2ᵛ is legible.

Probably from a part-book, this bifolium being central in a gathering. The lengths of sections 3 and 6 of the Kyrie are indicated by rests, that of section 8 possibly so. Plainchant notation, on staves of 5 red lines, 9 staves per page. The music is grouped in units of one beat, the symbols used having no significance. The repeated elongated horizontal notes (stroke notation) may well be the method devised by John Stele (lay cantor, Durham, 1430–87) to help his inexperienced singers with notes of more than one beat in duration.

R. Bowers and A. Wathey, compilers, 'New Sources of English Fourteenth- and Fifteenth-Century Polyphony', *Early Music History*, vol. 3 (1983), 123–73, especially pp. 128–36.

# THE CATHEDRAL'S LATER MANUSCRIPTS

**MS A1**   Organ Book. Anthems, Services, and Fantasias.

Anon (71.72.), Amner (2.), T. Boyce, Byrd (2.8.11.15–17.21. 27.28.30.31.), Derrick, Geeres (1.2; 2. hol), O. Gibbons (1.6.13. 14.28.), Giles (4.5.14.), Hilton (1.), Hooper (3.), R. Hucheson (1.2.), M. Jeffries (2.), Morley (3.), J. Mundy (2.3.), W. Mundy (2.10.), Palmer 4.6; hol), R. Parsons [I] (1.2.), Patrick, Read (1.2.), W. Smith (1.4.6.7.9.10.13–20; ?22.?23; hol), Edw. Smythe (9.), Tallis (9.12.), T. Tomkins (3.4.9.), Tye (2.), Ward, Weelkes (1.), R. White (1.2.), W. White (1.2.), and Wilkinson (3.).

*c.*1633–8. Pp. 1–41 are a systematic holograph collection of most of the works of William Smith—and two fantasias in his hand at the back (pp. 328–33) may be further holograph material. Pp. 42–6, 50–67 were added by Brookinge, pp. 48–9 by Geeres (hol). The rest (Table and pp. 69–327) was copied out by Palmer, who in 1638 and 1639 also transcribed MSS A5 and A6. These three MSS embrace most of the repertoire of the 1630s (*see* MSS C4, C18, E4, C8, and C2), and this MS draws heavily on MS C4. Evidence of payments (undated) is found at the bottom of pp. 148, 188, 228, and 308. 'James Smart' (l-c, 1660–97) is written on the first flyleaf; whilst 'Mr. Will: Greggs, Alixander Shaw, January the 5th 1681[/2]' may indicate that Greggs was at first only Master of the Choristers. Tooled in gilt on leather covers (restored) is the early 17th cent. coat-of-arms of Durham Cathedral (cf. MSS C2, E4, and A.IV.32).

285 × 192 mm. 171 ff., pag: II + ii + 1–224 + II + 86 (227–312) + II + 22 (315–23, 323a–b, 324–34) + II. 6-lined staves.

J. Buttrey, 'William Smith of Durham', *Music & Letters* (July 1962).


**MS A2**   Organ Book. Anthems and Services.

Anon (42.), Alison, Batten (16.), Bull (1.), Byrd (4.21.27.31.), Carlton, Cobbold, East (2.), Fido, O. Gibbons (4.10.11.20.24. 27.29.), Giles (14.15.), Hooper (5.10–12.), R. Hucheson (2.), M. Jeffries (4.), Loosemore (1–3.), Morley (2.5.6.), J. Mundy (5.), Peerson (2.), Randall, W. Smith (9.; hol), Edw. Smythe (5.7.9.), D. Taylor, T. Tomkins (1.6.12.13.19.), Ward, Weelkes (2.4.6.), Wilkinson (9.14.), and Woodson.

Mainly 1620s and 1630s. This book is unique among Durham's MSS in that it incorporates nearly 20 items still in their individual paper covers. Many of the organ parts correspond to the services of MS C18, others to the anthems of MS C4. They are chiefly in the same hand—that of Todd—as those MSS. Todd copied pp. vi–30, 33–128, 206–43, 255–71, 290–308, 316–23, 363–72, 386–405; and W. Smith pp. 30–2, 130–61, 192–200, 244–54, 312–14, 324–33, 373–85). Dated 1639, pp. 162–88 are the work of Geeres. Though the Table is dated 1681, the book had been assembled some years before then—Foster, besides copying pp. 201–3, 309, 333–55, paginated the MS.

296 × 195 mm. 198 ff., pag: II + viii + 380 (1–6, 9–32, 35–48, 51–68, 70–189, 192–203, 206–23, 226–35, 238–83, 290–2, 292a–b, 293–319, 324–37, 337a, 338–70, 373–4, 377–8, 378a, 379–405) + iv + II. 6-lined staves.


**MS A3**   Organ Book. Anthems and Services.

Bevin, Blancks, Bryne (1.), Bull (3.), Byrd (12.30.), Cranford (1.), Derrick, J. Farrant, A. Ferrabosco, Foster (2.3.6.10.13; hol), Giles (3.4*.7.), Heardson, Hooper (1.4.8.), J. Hutchinson (2.4.), Loosemore (6.8.), Mudd (1.3.), Mundy (1*.2*.4–8.), W. Mundy (3.4.8.9.11.), Nicholls (2.), Palmer (12.), R. Parsons [II] (2.4.), Ravenscroft (1.), Rutter, Sheppard (2*.), El. Smyth, Stevenson (1.2.), Strogers (1.), Tallis (2.4.7*.10*.12*.), T. Tomkins (6.7.9. 13.14.), Weelkes (3.), and Wilson.

Partly 1630s, but mainly 1660s and 1670s. W. Smith copied pp. 17–28, 33–82; Foster the remainder. Well represented are the additions made in the 1660s to MS C11, including some of the possible contents (marked ★) of the now wholly lost set of 'Tenn Bookes of Services and Anthemes for men' (see Misc. Ch. 7116). The Table was written by White in c.1682.

284 × 183 mm. 219 ff., pag: II + 432 (1–10, 10a–b, 11–206, 209–73, 273a, 274–423, 428–35) + ii (436–7) + II. 6-lined staves.

**MS A4**   Organ, sometimes figured bass only. Anthems and Services.

Child (3.6.13–15.17–20.22.23.), Cranford (2.), C. Gibbons (4.), O. Gibbons (2.7.11.), Giles (1.12.), Greggs (4.6; hol), John Hawkins (1.2.), Hilton (4.), J. Hutchinson (5.), J. Jackson, [W.] King (3.), Mudd (2.4.5.), Portman (3.), H. Purcell (24.), Shaw (1–4; hol), T. Tomkins (2.11.), Tucker (1.2.4–6.8.10.), Tudway (2.), Turner (10.), and Wise (2.4–6.).

1679–c.1690. Pp. 1–130 and Rev pp. 1–131 were copied by Shaw who is so named in payments dated 30 Oct. 1679 (p. 104; Rev p. 92). The rest, apart from pp. 131–5, is in the hand of Greggs who succeeded Shaw as Organist in 1682.

298 × 196 mm. 175 ff., pag: II + 176 (1–73, 73a, 74–175); Rev: II + ii (parchm) + 168 (1–68, 73–119, 119a, 120–71). 6-lined staves.

**MS A5**   Organ Book. Anthems and Services.

Amner (1.), Byrd (3.6.), Cranford (3.), Dering, East (1.3.), R. Farrant (3.), Fido, Foster (1.5.8.9.11.12; hol), Geeres (3.), O. Gibbons (20.23.), Gibbs, Giles (4.9.11.), Hinde, Hooper (6.12.), Horseley, R. Hucheson (3.), Juxon, Morley (2.4.), J. Mundy (1.5.6.), Palmer (2.5.7.8; hol), Sheppard (3.), W. Smith (11.), Edw. Smythe (2.4.5.7.), Tallis (11.), J. Tomkins, T. Tomkins (12.15–19.), Tozar, Weelkes (2.5.), and R. White (2.).

Pp. 1–281 were copied in 1638 and 1639 by Palmer, who thereby brought to a conclusion his transcribing of the repertoire of the 1630s (see MSS A1, A6). His final anthem, one of his own entitled 'The end of all things', could be a reflection on the musical or political scene or on his own life—his first wife and one of his children had just died. Details of payment at the rate of 3d. per page are recorded on pp. 4, 67, 115, and 224 (imp). P. 224 also states that the preceding service had been composed by 'John Foster:- Chorister of the Church of Durham:- 1638:-'. The rest of the MS

14    DESCRIPTION OF THE MANUSCRIPTS

(pp. 282–99) dates from after 1660, and is mainly holograph, being in the hand of the same Foster. The Table dates from *c.*1682. On p. 301 there is the specification (in Foster's hand) of an organ (? that built by Dallam in 1661) having five stops on the Choir and eight on the Great.

283 × 190 mm. 153 ff., pag: II + iv + 296 (1–165, 167–240, 242–57, 259–99) + ii (300–1) + II. 6-lined staves.

**MS A6**   Organ Book. Anthems and Services.

Alison, Batten (1.2.5–8.11–13.15.16.20–3.), J. Bennet, Byrd (19.20.), Child (24.), East (2.), Farrant, O. Gibbons (15.), Giles (6.), Hilton (5.), Hooper (9.10.), Marson, Morley (5.6.), Palmer (3; hol), Parsley, Peerson (1.), Ravenscroft (2.3.), W. Smith (21.), Stonard (1–3.), Strogers (2.), Tallis (14.), Tye (6.), Warwick, Weelkes (6.7.), Wilkinson (1.2.4–12.14.), and Yarrow.

1638. The second of three books (*see* MSS A1, A5) into which Palmer transcribed the repertoire of the 1630s. Details of payment, on pp. 28 (imp), 83, 180, and 208, show that the copying was done in 1638, the rate being 3*d.* per page. Pp. 1a–2, 374, copied by Foster, and pp. 9–12a, 347–52, are later.

289 × 192 mm. 193 ff., pag: II + 382 (1, 1a–d, 2–12, 12a–b, 13–38, 38a–b, 39–374) + II. 6-lined staves.

**MS A7**   Organ Book. Anthems. Includes figured organ bass and open vocal scores.

Croft (3.19.43.52.53.64.67.71.), Foster (4.), Greene (4.7. 21–3.34.),Handel (1.), Wanless (1.), and Wise (10.). Of these only Croft (19.67.71.) and Greene (7.21–3.) are ascribed.

1720s and 1730s. Seven items also lack their titles. Present are a number of the hands of MS C21.

318 × 198 mm. 90 ff., pag: II + vi + 1–130; Rev: II + ii + 1–38.

**MS A8**   Organ Book. Services, Anthems, and Chants. Includes open vocal scores and single parts.

Aldrich (18.), Bembow, Blow (4.24.), Church (6.), Clarke (4.5 × 2.8.), Croft (6.29.32.54.57.58.), Galliard (1.), Goldwin (5.), Hine (1.), Morgan (dated Christmas 1731), Pepusch, Sir John Pryce (chants dated 1736 and 1738), H. Purcell (8 × 2.14.17 × 2.29. 32.), Tallis (11.13.15.), Turner (11.), and Weldon (7.8.10.12.).

1730s. Not of Durham origin; and compositions by Greene are noticeably absent. Bembow is unknown, and Morgan only tentatively identified, but Sir John Pryce, Bart., of Newton Hall, Montgomery (d. 1761), was an eccentric of some repute. Originally the MS extended to p. 140; groupings pp. 141–54 and pp. 155–79 each had their own system of pagination; whilst pp. 181–98 consist of treble, alto, and tenor single parts. The Table (p. iii) and the related further system of pagination indicate that pp. 141–98 enjoyed an existence distinct from the earlier pages.

317 × 200 mm. 106 ff., pag: IV + iv + 1–200 + IV.

**MS A9**   Organ Book. Anthems and Services.

Blow (3.17.28.), O. Gibbons (13.), Humfrey (6.7.11.), H. Purcell (8.17.36.), Tallis (9.), and Wise (1.). Of these only Blow (28.), Purcell (17.36.), and Wise (1.) are ascribed.

Early 18th cent. A comparison with his holograph anthem ('Unto thee have I cried') in Brit. Lib. Add. MS 30860 confirms Hesletine as the copyist. Names inside back cover include 'William Gwatkin' and 'Edmund Baker'.

297 × 198 mm. 54 ff., pag: II + 1–70 (with pp. 34–70 blank); Rev: II + 34 (1–5, 5a–b, 6–32). 6-lined staves.

**MS A10**   Organ. Anthems and Services; much in full score.

Beethoven (5.), Cherubini, Handel (19.32.), Hasse (1.), Haydn (7.11.17.), Mozart (4.), H. Purcell (22.25.), Rolle, Salvatore, Spohr (2.), and Winter. *Rev*: three services: Bishop (2.), Pilbrow, and Rogers (8.).

Dated 1826 (p. 24; Rev p. 23) to 1846 (p. 247; Rev p. 64). P. 168a is later.

282 × 226 mm. 150 ff., pag: II + vi + 220 (1–27, 29–69, 100–4, 104a, 105–68, 168a–b, 169–248); Rev: II + vi + 1–64.

**MS A11**   Organ Loft. Anthems and Services; the voice parts are given in open score, often with no organ reduction.

Edwards, Ferretti, Fussel, Graun (2.), Handel (10.25.), Luther, Moreira (2.), Tye (5.), and Young.

Dated 1826 (p. 85) to 1849 (p. 167).

281 × 228 mm. 89 ff., pag: IV + iv + 166 (1–32, 35–168) + IV. The slightly older pagination indicates that in pp. 1–82 are two

corpuses which enjoyed separate existences before the MS was assembled.

**MS A12**   Organ Book.

(*a*) 'Messiah' (pp. 1–123; starts 'Comfort ye') and 'Zadok the priest' (pp. 126–7; inc in middle), both by Handel; (*b*) 'Morning Service in D' (pp. 129–47; in C here; J inc) by H. Purcell; (*c*) 'Acquaint thyself with God' (pp. 149–59) by Greene and 'My song shall be alway' (pp. 159–68; inc) by H. Purcell.

Mid 18th cent. The MS may represent the binding together of several formerly independent groupings. In 'Messiah', 'For unto us' (p. 55), 'Behold the Lamb of God' (p. 59) and 'He was despised' (p. 67) were all paginated '1', though only in the last case does the pagination then continue. (*b*) and (*c*) were paginated 1–12, 15–21, and 1–20 respectively. All copied by Brass, with 'Messiah' probably dating from about 1751 when £6. 2s. 0d. was expended on 'Dr. Handell's Oratorio' (Audit Book A. VI).

291 × 237 mm for pp. 1–124, and 291 × 225 mm for pp. 125–68. 86 ff., pag: 172 (1–47, 47a–b, 48–54, 54a–b, 55–168). Later pp. torn away.

**MS A13**   Organ Loft, no. 4. Anthems and Services.

Anthems: Bacon (1.), Blake, Blow (9.), Boyce (3.), Croft (6.9.15.16.33.34.37.44.51.52.65.), Goldwin (5.), Greene (26.), Hall (3.5.), Handel (11.), Kent (8.10.), Marcello (2.), Pepusch, H. Purcell (32.), Tallis (11.), and Wise (3.11.). *Rev*: 14 services: Alcock, Aldrich (16.), Bevin, Bishop (2.), Blow (29.), Croft (70.71.), Gregory (1.), W. Hayes (16.), Kelway (3.), C. King (10.), Lamb (1.), Priest, and Raylton. With the exception of Blow (29.), these are all in MS B35.

Dated 1747 (p. 11) to 1771 (p. 132); Rev, 1750 (p. 78) to 1776 (p. 156). Copied by Brass (pp. 1–112; Rev pp. 5–124, 138–53), Ebdon (pp. 96a–b, 113–25; Rev pp. 1–4, 125–37, 154–6), and Mathews (pp. 126–32).

253 × 367 mm. 149 ff., pag: iv + 132 (1–54, 57–96, 96a–b, 97–132); Rev: iv + 1–158.

**MS A14**   Organ Book, no. 3. Anthems.

Aldrich (1.), Bassani (2.), Bishop (1.), Blow (7.), Byrd (4.), Clarke (16.), Croft (5.13.18.20.22.38.43.45.47.48 × 2.53.55.65.67.

68.71.), O. Gibbons (1.13.15.), Goldwin (6.), Greene (20.27.34.), Handel (5.), Humfrey (5.), H. Purcell (34.), and Weldon (8.).

Transcribed by Ebdon between 1764 (p. 130) and 1768 (p. 190), the last piece being added in 1783 (p. 199). On the first flyleaf at the back, in the same hand as the Table, on paper dated (from watermark) 1813, is the specification of a three-manual organ having twelve stops on the Great, five on the Echoes, and six on the Choir. This organ is probably that built by 'Father Smith' in 1683, but modified in 1748 and 1815.

237 × 290 mm. 105 ff., pag: vi + 198 (1–70, 73–200) + vi.

**MS A15**  Organ Book, no. 7. Services.

Aldrich (17.), Bacon (2.), Bishop (2.), Blow (28.30.31.), Bryne (2.), Byrd (30.), Child (20.22–4.), R. Farrant (3.), O. Gibbons (28.), [Greville], Hall and Hine, Kent (15.), C. King (8.), Patrick, Rogers (6.), Shenton (2.), Tallis (14.), and Travers (4.). These represent about half the contents of MS B7. Additional is Boyce (23.).

Dated 1767 (p. 80) to 1793 (p. 226). Copyists include Ebdon (pp. 1–103, 121–59) and Mathews (pp. 104–20).

268 × 373 mm. 119 ff., pag: ii + 1–234 (+ stubs of later pp.) + ii.

**MS A16**  Organ Loft, no. 6. Anthems.

Anon (39.), Baildon, Banks (1.), Boyce (11.), Creighton (1.), Friend (1.2.), Garth (3.), Goldwin (3.), Greene (8.), Handel (39.), Haydn (5.), W. Hayes (1.3.5–12.14; all but one in *Hayes*), Henley (2.), Hilton (3.), [C.] King (4.), Mozart (1.), Pleyel, H. Purcell (8.), Reynolds, Webbe (2–4; in *Webbe*), and Wise (10.).

Copied between 1796 (p. 129) and 1808 (p. 241) by Chrishop (pp. 1–129, 132–89) and Ebdon (pp. 130–1, 191–241). The remaining pp. were added in 1826 (p. 261).

259 × 367 mm. 134 ff., pag: iv + 1–262 + ii.

**MS A17**  Organ Loft, no. 11. 'Messiah' by Handel, and Anthems.

The anthems are: anon (44.), Bacon (1.), Boyce (4.), Greene (19.30.35.41.42.), Hesletine (2.3.), [Pergolesi] (3.), H. Purcell (14.), and Weldon (2.8.12.). Banks (2.) and Mason (2.3.) are later.

*c.*1770. The barely visible original pagination confirms that this volume represents the binding together in the 1810s of two earlier books. The second (pp. 83–216; formerly pp. 1–134) with

pp. 83–198 copied by Mathews (*see* 'Paid Sepr. 1768' on p. 198) is
the older. Of the 15 anthems in his hand no fewer than 12 are verse
anthems either for or transposed for the counter-tenor voice.
Mathews also began the transcription of 'Messiah' (pp. 1–7), but
gave way to Ebdon (pp. 8–81) on the verso of a folio.

243 × 342 mm, with pp. 199 *et seq.* 243 × 303 mm. 107 ff., pag:
iv + 208 (1–166, 175–216) + ii.

**MSS A18 and A19**   *A18*: Organ Loft, no. 14. Voice parts and
organ bass of Services, Anthems, and Chants.

Bevin, Broderip, Byrd (30.), Carter, Croft (72.), R. Farrant (3.),
O. Gibbons (28.), W. Hayes (17.), Higgins (1.2.), C. King (9.), Earl
of Mornington, Nares (16.18.19.), R. Roseingrave (1–4.), Shenton
(3.), Stephens (2.), Tallis (14.), Taylor, Walsh (1.2.), Wise (14.15.),
and Woodward.

*A19*: Organ Loft, no. 15. Description as for A18.

Boyce (9.22.), W. Hayes (8.11.), Murphy, H. Purcell (5.),
Shenton (1.2.), Travers (2.5.), [E. White], and Woodward.

1777. The contemporary Table for both books is at the front
of A18, and the pagination is continuous. A letter dated 'Dublin,
30th October, 1777' (A18: ii) reveals that the books were transcribed by John Mathews in the hope that the Durham choir might
thereby extend its repertoire. The Durham and Dublin repertoires
are compared, and the increased popularity of the Jubilate is
mentioned. Comments on A19: 422–3 disclose that Shenton had
composed the Sursum Corda, Sanctus, and Gloria at Mathews's
request to render his Service suitable for use at Durham. In ascrib-
ing 'Christ is risen' to H. Purcell, Mathews was following the
earlier 18th cent. Dublin MSS. Audit Book A.VII confirms that in
1777–8 Mr Wood, the intermediary named in the letter, duly
received Mathews's commission of £12. 15s. od. Before moving
to Dublin, Mathews had been in the Winchester, Salisbury, and
Durham choirs, and several other MSS (e.g. A17, A24, A32, D7,
and D8) are in his hand.

247 × 300 mm. *A18*: 193 ff., pag: IV + ii + 378 (1–160, 160a–b,
161–253, 253a–b, 254–74) + II; *A19*: 140 ff., pag: ii + 276 (375–
650) + ii.

**MS A20**   Organ Loft. Anthems.

Aldrich (5.12.13.15.), Allinson (1.), Banks (3.), Batten (3.5.12.),
Blow (5.7.14.), Boyce (22.), Child (8.13.), Clarke (9.12.), Corfe

(2.), Earle, R. Farrant (1.), Garth (2.), Goldwin (2.4.), Greene (22.),
Henley (2.), W. Jones, Kent (2.4.5.13.14.), Mason (5.), W. Mundy
(3.), Nares (10.), Pickering (1.), Porter, H. Purcell (9.19.20.32.),
Rogers (1.4.), Stroud, Tallis (9.), Tucker (6.), Turner (6.), Weldon
(3.4.12.), and Wise (2.).

Dated 1783 (p. 25) to 1795 (p. 184). Of the 50 items, some 19 are
represented in *Boyce 2* (1768). Though all the payments for copying during this period were made to Thomas Ebdon, only on
pp. 1–4, 16–32 are both notes and text in his hand. Chrishop transcribed pp. 85–91, 136–84.

235 × 334 mm. 95 ff., pag: iv + 1–184 + ii.

**MS A21**   Organ Loft. Anthems and Services.

All 11 anthems—Handel (8.), Haydn (1.6 × 2), Lotti, Mason
(1.), Pergolesi (1.2.), H. Purcell (16.27.), and Weldon (9. 10.)—are
in MS C22v. *Rev*: six services, by Boyce (24.), Clarke[-Whitfeld]
(4.), P. Hayes (4.), W. Hayes (15.), Kent (15.), Nares (16.), and
Walsh (1.) (cf. MS C20).

Dated 1830 (p. 38) to 1834 (p. 111); Rev, 1796 (p. 17) to 1814
(p. 109). Copyists include Radcliffe (Rev pp. 18–101).

269 × 370 mm. 132 ff., pag: iv + 1–46, with later pp. missing;
Rev: iv + 1–110.

**MS A22**   Organ. Services.

17 of the services of MS B7: Blow (28.30.31.), Bryne (2.),
Byrd (30.), Child (17.20.22–4.), Creighton (3.), R. Farrant (3.),
O. Gibbons (28.), Goodson, Patrick, H. Purcell (36.), and Tallis
(14.). A Cantate Domino by Fussel is later, as is a chant by 'M[ary].
E[bdon].' dated 1797.

Late 18th cent. Music transcribed mainly (pp. 25–9, 33–51,
54–192) by T. Ebdon, though text is in a variety of hands. The
Mary Ebdon chant (p. 29) was added by Chrishop.

245 × 300 mm. 85 ff., pag: II + ii + 162 (23–116, 129–30, 133–
98) + ii + II.

**MS A23**   Organ parts of 'Messiah' and of the Coronation
anthem, 'Zadok the priest', both by Handel. Included are two
versions of 'How beautiful upon the mountains', and the 'Original
Version of the Recit. "But who may abide" as performed in
Ireland'.

Copied *c.*1800 by Chrishop. There may be some connection between this MS and the payment in 1794 of £6. 17s. 4d. 'for prs of Handels works' (in Payments Book 2, but not in Audit Book A.VIII).

238 × 300 mm. 156 ff., pag: iv + 306 (1–10, 10a–b, 11–304) + ii.

**MS A24**  Full score of the Oratorio, 'Joshua', by G. F. Handel.

*c.* 1760. Copied by Mathews whilst he was still at Salisbury, and brought with him when he transferred his allegiance to Durham in 1764. All 30 single parts enumerated on p. iii survive, now forming MS D8.

238 × 295 mm. 167 ff., pag: x + 1–322 + ii.

**MS A25**  Organ Book. Anthems.

Allinson (2.), Blow (2.3.5.10.12.13.15.17.19.21.22.25–7.), [Carissimi] (1.), Clarke (12.), Croft (20.54.57.), Greggs (1–3.5; hol), Jas Hawkins (1–3.), G. Holmes (2.), Humfrey (1.10–12.), Isham (2.), W. Norris (1–2.), H. Purcell (1.6a.14.17.23.30.34.35.), Tudway (3–7.), and Turner (4.5.).

*c.*1695–*c.*1710. In the hand of Greggs (cf. MSS A4, A33). The 'Awake put on thy strength' attributed erroneously to Wise in the Table agrees with Tenbury MS 1227b, where the copyist ascribes it to 'Giacomo Carissimi'. The 'Dr. Pickering' mentioned as the arranger at the top of the Tenbury version was a Prebendary of Durham, 1692–1711.

236 × 353 mm. 124 ff., pag: II + iv + 1–240 + II. 6-lined staves, pp. 1–39 only.

**M A26**  Organ Book, no. 1. Anthems [and Service].

Battishill (1.), Boyce (1.4 × 2.5.15.21.), Croft (12.15.17.35.39. 64.65.), Fiocco, Garth (1.), Greene (40.), Handel (1.44.), [P.] Hayes (1.), Kent (9.), Locke (3.), Marcello (3.), Mason/[Ebdon] (6.), Nares (1.), and H. Purcell (2.37.).

Dated 1768 (p. 82) to 1787 (p. 193) and 1793 (p. 206). Copyists include Brass (pp. 1–17), Ebdon (pp. 18–96, 107–93), and Mathews (pp. 97–106).

234 × 332 mm. 106 ff., pag: ii + ii (parchm) + 1–206 + ii.

**MS A27**  Music for the viola da gamba.

Nearly half the collection is drawn from Marais (1–3; 40 items) and Schenck 1.2; 39 items). Other composers are: Blancourt, Du Buisson, Dufaut, Falle (2.3; hol), Finger, (3.), Fiore (2 items), Hacquart (16 items), Heudelinne (1.2; 9 items), Mace, A. Poole, Ste Colombe le fils (1–5; 10 items), C. Simpson (1.2; 12 items), Snep (16 items), and [F.] Steffkin. Eight items are anonymous (anon 89.).

Early 18th cent. Compiled, with items in the same key grouped together, by Philip Falle for his own convenience mainly from printed sources in his own collection. His references are detailed, and where two page numbers are given, the first refers to the solo part-book, the second to the continuo. The MS is not listed in Falle's own catalogue of his music (Durham Add. MS 154).

219 × 285 mm. 173 ff., pag: iv + 1–342, pp. 328 *et seq.* being blank.

M. Urquhart, 'Prebendary Philip Falle (1656–1742) and the Durham Bass Viol Manuscript A27', *Chelys* (1973–4).

**MSS A28 and A29**   *A28*: Organ Loft, no. 10. Anthems.

Aldrich (2.5.6.15.), Bassani (2.), Blow (1.5.10.17.20.27.), Byrd (4.), Church (5.), Clarke (5.9.), Croft (5.18.19.28.43.64.71.), Goldwin (1.4.), Greene (6.16.20.21.26.34.36.), [Howard], Humfrey (1.2.5.6.8.10.12.), H. Purcell (1.2.8.9.14.17.19.20.34.), Stroud, Turner (6.), Weldon (3.4.), and Wise (1.2.8.10.).

*A29*: Organ Loft, no. 8. Anthems and Services.

Aldrich (9.10.), Avison, Blow (11.14.), Bull (4.), Byrd (21.), Child (10.), Clarke (4.), Creighton (3.), Croft (3.6.13.29 × 2.35. 41.48 × 2.71.), O. Gibbons (13.15.), Greene (1.2.4.7.8.10.12.13. 18.19.22–4.27.28.33.37.38.41.42.), Locke (3.), Nares (4.8.14.15.), H. Purcell (31.36.), Rogers (4.), Tallis (11.), Walkley, Wanless (1.3.), Weldon (5.), and Wise (12.13.).

Mid 18th cent. The two MSS were part of the same project. Pp. 232–45 have been lost, for the partly visible original pagination of A29 begins at p. 246. A29 is dated 1741 (p. 89; Rev p. 25) and 1744 (p. 191; Rev p. 47), whereas A28 is devoid of payments. Transcribed by Brass, whose later cul-de-lampe first occurs on A29: 66.

268 × 370 mm. *A28*: 118 ff., pag: iv + 230 (1–21, 21a, 22–33, 38–75, 75a–b, 76–98, 100–18, 120–43, 143a–b, 144–231) + ii. *A29*: 142 ff., pag: ii + 1–215; Rev: iv + 1–63.

**MS A30**  Organ. Anthems.

A holograph collection of 44 different anthems by Thomas Ebdon.

*c*.1800–11 (p. 128). The anthems, many of which express personal distress, were added as they were composed. All bear his name, and nearly all have the date of composition as well. They are all included, without dates, in MS A31, and many feature in the second printed volume of his sacred works (pub. 1811). From the alignment of the staves it is probable that the missing pp. 1–44 now form the opening 44 pp. of MS A31.

270 × 370 mm. 43 ff., pag: 86 (45–130).

**MS A31**  Organ Book. Service, Anthems, and Chants.

The complete liturgical works (holograph) of Thomas Ebdon. *Rev*: five anthems, by Boyce (8.), Handel (4.15.35.), and Isaac.

Pp. 1–44 and 45–89 are respectively early 19th cent. transcripts of volumes of his music published *c*.1790 and in 1811. Of the remaining compositions (pp. 90–148), the last (the only item to bear his name) was composed in June 1811, some three months before his death. From the alignment of the staves it is probable that in order to expedite the completion of this orderly collection Ebdon merely transferred pp. 1–44 from MS A30 to the present volume. *Rev*: introduced after Ebdon's time, Radcliffe copying pp. 1–23. The date 1713 (p. 23) is an error for 1813.

267 × 372 mm. 90 ff., pag: II + ii + 1–148; Rev: II + 1–26.

**MS A32**  Full score of 'The king shall rejoice' and the 'Dettingen Grand Te Deum Laudamus', both by G. F. Handel.

*c*.1760. Transcribed by Mathews. All but two of the single parts enumerated on p. iii survive, now forming MS D7. The value of the score and all parts, £3. 16s. 4¼d., is given on p. iii; and that of the value of this book, £2. 2s. 0d., inside the back cover. A reference there to Edward Easton, a Salisbury bookbinder, dates the MS not later than 1764 when Mathews transferred to Durham.

240 × 299 mm. 81 ff., pag: iv + 1–154 + iv.

**MS A33**  Organ Book. Anthems and Services.

Anon (25.), Aldrich (4.7.), Allinson (1.4.), Blow (1.16.20.24. 28.30.31.), Child (14.21.), Club Anthem, Hall (1.), Jas Hawkins (3.), Humfrey (2.3.5–8.13.), Locke (4.), M. Wundy (3.), Preston,

H. Purcell (2.8.9.18–20.33.36.), Tucker (3.), Tudway (1.), Turner (1.6.9.), and Wise (1.).

*c*.1690–1700. Originally foliated, this MS was copied by Greggs (cf. MSS A4 and A25), but contains no composition by him. A payment on p. 254 is dated 'Jan. 11. 1699[/1700]'.

241 × 348 mm. 131 ff., pag: II + ii + 1–256 + II. 6-lined staves.

**MS A34** Organ Loft, no. 2. Services and Anthems, in open vocal score.

Services by Bishop (2.), Chard (1.), Child (23. 24.), Croft (70.), R. Farrant (3.), O. Gibbons (28.), Kelway (1.2.), Penson (1.), Raylton, Rogers (5.7.), and Tallis (14.), are with the exception of Child (23.) and Croft (70.) listed under MS C20. *Rev*: the anthems are Boyce (9.), Hall (4.), Handel (18.24.), P. Hayes (2.3.), Mozart (5.), Sarti, and Tye (4.).

Dated 1819 (p. 120; Rev p. 16) and 1820 (p. 264; Rev p. 82).

231 × 330 mm. 192 ff., pag: vi + 1–301 (p. 301 = Rev p. 82); Rev: 78 (5–82).

**MS A35** Services, in open vocal score, with some organ bass.

Barrow, B. Cooke (2.), R. Cooke, Croft (70.), Rogers (8.), and Wise (13.).

Early 19th cent. (paper 1809). Not of Durham origin, the pencil comment 'from Dean Goodenough's Library. James Higgs' (p. i) indicating a connection with Wells. Given by Dr C. W. Eden to Mr A. J. Thurlow in 1974, and donated to the Library in September 1980.

224 × 291 mm. 90 ff., pag: ii + 1–176 + ii.

**MS B1** Organ Book. Anthems and Services; the representation ranging from organ bass of verse sections only through to vocal score and full score with symphonies and ritornellos.

Anon (31.36.40.45†.53†.55★.61★.67★.68.), Blett, Blow (18†.), Child (9.16.), H. Cooke (1★. 2★.), J. Ferrabosco (1–3.), [? T. Ford] (1†.), C. Gibbons (2.3.), O. Gibbons (10.), Hinde, Hitchecocke, T. Holmes, Hosier (1–6.), Humfrey (1†.2.5†.6.9★.10★.), [? Isaak], [G. Jeffreys], [H. Lawes] (1.), W. Lawes (1.2.), Locke (1.3.), Loggins, [Portman] (3.), Rogers (2.8.), Tallis (14.), Silas Taylor,

★ = full score of symphonies; † = bass part of symphonies.

T. Tomkins (7.10.), Tucker (1.2.9.), [Turner] (11.), [Wilkinson] (3.), and Wise (2.5.7.).

*c*.1665–75. Not of Durham origin. Many of the composers had strong London connections in the 1660s and 1670s. Humfrey is well represented, a holograph anthem by Hitchecocke is dated '[16]69', whilst Purcell is conspicuous by his absence. Unique are six anthems by Richard Hosier (? at King's College, Cambridge in 1637; ? at Bristol in 1661), and it is felt that the MS is in his hand, not least because of 'Hallelujah' sections similar in style to those of his own anthems added to other anthems. Humfrey (9.) and anon (53.) are present in the 18th cent. MSS of the Dublin cathedrals and at Trinity College, Dublin—the latter is ascribed to 'Isaac' in the somewhat later Tables to Trinity College MSS 4777 and 4778. 'Thomas Blunderfild' and 'John Blunderfild' (? = Blundevile) are written inside the front cover.

345 × 224 mm. 133 ff., pag: II + 174 (1–85, 85a, 86, 86a, 87–173; p. 173 = Rev p. 86); Rev: II + 88 (1–54, 54a–b, 55–86).

B. Crosby, 'An Early Restoration Liturgical Music Manuscript', *Music & Letters* (Oct. 1974).

**MS B3**   Tenor [Cantoris]. Services and Anthems.

Three-quarters of the services of MS B18, followed by the nine services of *Boyce 1* (in volume order). Added later were G. Elvey (3.), C. King (8.), Nares (18.), and S. S. Wesley (9.). *Rev*: the anthems—Barnby, Chawner, Greatheed, Macfarren, Monk, Ottley, Ouseley (1.4.6.9.11.), Stainer (1–3.), and S. S. Wesley (5.)—are with the exception of that by Wesley all drawn from *Ouseley 2*.

Dated 1816 (p. 4) to 1846 (p. 263), with additions in 1886 (p. 300), the date of the Rev end (Rev pp. 53, 61). Pp. 263–300 and all of Rev were copied by Walker.

364 × 225 mm. 189 ff., pag: II + viii + 1–300; Rev: II + iv + 1–62.

**MS B4**   Tenor Cantoris, iii. Anthems.

Considerable agreement with the corpuses listed under MSS B18v, C22v, and D21. Additional are Beethoven (7.), Croft (65.), Goss (1.), and Handel (19.), together with a transcript of *Crotch*.

Dated 1817 (p. 23) to 1848 (p. 217), with additions until 1872 (p. 228). Brown was responsible for pp. 145–6, 167–8, 217–28. 'The Last of MS.' is added in pencil after the date on p. 228, a comment no doubt bewailing Chapter's decision to purchase printed folio and octavo editions rather than employ a copyist.

360 × 225 mm. 142 ff., pag: xiv + 1–256 (with further pp. cut away) + xiv. Pp. 229 *et seq.* are blank.

**MS B5**   Tenor Decani, no. 1. Services.

Of the same set as MS B7, having about two-thirds of its services.

Dated 1750 (p. 233) to 1766 (p. 295). Copyists include Brass (pp. 3–80, 88–106, 114–257, 259–73), Ebdon (pp. 273–86), and Mathews (pp. 289–301) who also restored the bottom of many of the earlier pages. A further restoration took place during the first half of the 19th century.

369 × 240 mm. 151 ff., pag: iv + 296 (1–88, 103–240, 243–312) + ii.

**MS B6**   Tenor Decani, no. 4. [Anthems and a few Services].

May be considered with MS B12, still having in spite of missing pages about three-fifths of that corpus. Additional is 'In the midst of life' by H. P. Simpson, and these services: Blow (29.), Croft (71.), and Priest.

Dated 1746 (p. 11) to 1799 (p. 205); Rev, 1748 (p. 13) to 1761 (p. 68). Copyists include Brass (pp. 1–168; Rev pp. 1–18, 21–64, 67, 68), and Mathews (pp. 170–92; Rev pp. 19–20, 69–70).

363 × 232 mm. 133 ff., pag: viii + 182 (1–58, 69–114, 123–58, 163–205; p. 205 = Rev p. 70); Rev: vi + 1–70.

**MS B7**   Tenor Cantoris, no. 6. Services.

MSS B5, B7, B19, B22, B23, B28, and C30 (cf. MS C31) may be regarded as a set. Drawing on this repertoire, though much shorter in length, are MSS A15, A22, B8v, B13v, and B16v. Lacking most of the 17th cent. compositions are MSS A13v, B17v, B29v, B31v, B32v, B33v, B35 (q.v.), and B36v. Apart from settings found in only one MS, the comprehensive list of services is: Alcock, Aldrich (16.18.), Bacon (2.), Bevin, Bishop (2.), Blow (28–31.), Bryne (2.), Byrd (30.), Child (17.20.22–4.), Creighton (3.), Croft (70.71.), Ebdon (62.), R. Farrant (3.), O. Gibbons (28.), Goodson, Greene (43.), Gregory (1.), [Greville], Hall and Hine, W. Hayes (16.), Kelway (3.), Kent (15.), C. King (7.8.10.), Lamb (1.), Mason (7.), Nares (15.), Ogle, Patrick, Pleyel (hymn), Priest, H. Purcell

(36.37.), Raylton, Rogers (6.), Shenton (2.), Stephens (1.), Tallis (11.14.), Travers (4.), Walkley, Wanless (1.), and Wise (12.13.). Some eight of these are not in B7.

Dated 1748 (p. 235) to 1799 (p. 351). Copied by Brass (pp. 1–307), Ebdon (pp. 308–14, 335–49), Mathews (pp. 315–34), Chrishop (pp. 350–2) and others. Pp. 1–133 draw heavily upon the repertoire of the late 17th cent. (cf. MS C32).

371 × 233 mm. 182 ff., pag: vi + 354 (1–70, 72–81, 81a, 82–100, 102–46, 146a, 147–354) + iv.

**MS B8**    Tenor Cantoris. Anthems and Services.

About half of the anthems of MS B35v, together with anon (43.), Croft (28.), Earle, Ebdon (4.), Greene (8.), H. Purcell (2.), and Weldon (12.). *Rev*: about three-fifths of the services of MS B7.

Dated 1752 (p. 27) to 1796 (p. 110); Rev, 1752 (p. 47) to 1791 (p. 220). Copied by Brass (pp. 1–39, 46–81; Rev pp. 1–189), Ebdon (pp. 40–5; Rev pp. 190–6), Mathews (pp. 82–3; Rev pp. 197–202), Chrishop (pp. 98–109; Rev p. 221), and others.

371 × 235 mm. 172 ff., pag: II + iv + 1–110; Rev: II + iv + 1–222.

**MS B9**    Tenor Cantoris. Anthems.

Two-thirds of the anthems of MS B12, together with Banks (3.), Blow (3.), Croft (71.), W. Hayes (5.), Isaac, Pilbrow, Pleyel, Weldon (8.), and a transcript of *Kent 1*, in volume order.

Dated 1749 (p. 115) to 1799 (p. 209); Rev, 1749 (p. 41) to 1794 (p. 99). Copyists include Brass (pp. 1–172; Rev pp. 1–57), Mathews (pp. 172–91; Rev pp. 58–69), Friend (Rev pp. 76–7), and Chrishop (pp. 196–207, 209; Rev pp. 100–5).

364 × 230 mm. 168 ff., pag: II + viii + 1–214; Rev: II + ii + 1–108.

**MS B10**    Counter-tenor Cantoris, no. 3. Anthems.

Three-fifths of the anthems of MS B12, together with Batten (3.4.9.12.), Byrd (12.), Club Anthem, Falle (1.), Foster (4.), Hilton (1.), Hooper (3.), Humfrey (7.), W. Lawes (2.), Morley (3.), W. Mundy (2.), and Read (1.).

The MS antedates the group it has been compared with, a situation evident from the additional items all of which belong to the repertoire of the 1690s. The first hand, ? active in the 1720s, was responsible for pp. 1–154; Brass copied pp. 154–221, 224–349 between 1741 (p. 161) and 1756 (p. 348); the remainder being added by Mathews in 1771 (p. 370).

352 × 237 mm. 189 ff., pag: II + vi + 368 (1–265, 268–370) + II.

## MS B11    Tenor. Anthems.

Apart from now lacking the last 16 anthems of the Ebdon corpus, the contents, which include (pp. 11–37) a transcript of *Kent 1* in volume order, are substantially the same as those of MS B16. Additional is Aldrich (15.).

Dated 1791 (p. 5) to 1808 (p. 108). Pp. 38–57, 61–82 were copied by Chrishop; and pp. 85–104, 108–14, in the hand of Ebdon, are holograph.

373 × 235 mm. 60 ff., pag: II + ii + 1–114 + II.

## MS B12    Alto Cantoris. Anthems.

MSS B6, B9, B10, B12, B17, B24, B26, B29, B32, and B36 may be considered together. The difference in their lengths is accounted for by the extent of the inclusion of anthems by Croft and Greene, itself related to the cathedral's holding of the printed works of those composers. The following common corpus is a combination of most of the anthems of the earlier MS C21 and the contemporary MS B35v: Aldrich (1.5.6.9.10.13.15.), Allinson (1.), Avison, Bacon (1.), Banks (1.), Bassani (2.), Battishill (1.), Bishop (1.), Blake, Blow (5–7.9.10.14–17.20.23.27.), G. Bononcini (1.), Boyce (1.3–5.21.), Bull (4.), Byrd (4.21.), Child (1.5.8.10.11.13.), Church (5.), Clarke (4.5.9.12.16.), Corfe (2.), Croft (3.5.6.9.12. 13.15–18.20.22.28.29.32–5.37–9.41–5.47.48.51–6.58.59.64.65.67. 68.), Earle, Ebdon (4.7.58.), Fiocco, Garth (1.2.), O. Gibbons (1.13.15.), Goldwin (1.2.4.), Greene (6–8.16.19–22.26.30.34.35.), Hall (3.5.), Handel (1.9–11.17.20.21.29.34.39.44.), Henley (2.), Hesletine (2.3.), Hine (1.), [Howard], Humfrey (1–3.5.6.8.10.12.), Kent (1.8–10.), Locke (3.5.), Marcello (2.), Mason (5.6.), W. Mundy (3.), Nares (4.8.11.14.), Porter, H. Purcell (1.2.4.8.9.17. 19.20.31.32.34.), Rogers (4.), Shenton (1.), Stroud, Tallis (9.), Tucker (6.), Turner (6.), Weldon (3–5.12.) and Wise (1–3.8.10.11.). B12 has about four-fifths of these plus Croft (8.) and Greene (14.).

This is either an additional copy or a replacement, for pp. 1–272 were all transcribed by Mathews in 1768. He added pp. 273–345 (p. 339 is dated 1773); and a later hand completed the MS in 1791.

377 × 242 mm. 182 ff., pag: II + viii + 352 (1–74, 77–354) + II.

**MS B13**   Contratenor Cantoris. Anthems and Services.

Two-thirds of the anthems of MS B35v, together with Croft (38.58.), O. Gibbons (1.), Goldwin (5.), Humfrey (6.), and Pepusch. *Rev*: The surviving 23 services (pp. 1–36 are lost), and Pleyel's Hymn are all listed under MS B7.

Dated 1746 (p. 10) to 1796 (p. 167); Rev, 1750 (p. 53) to 1791 (p. 194). Copied by Brass (pp. 1–136; Rev pp. 37–141), Ebdon (Rev pp. 142–8), and Mathews (pp. 137–62; Rev pp. 148–70). The MS was brought briefly out of retirement in 1949—see the comment 'Cogan v. Gregory. 22.2.[19]49' (p. 139).

370 × 235 mm. 186 ff., pag: II + vi + 1–168; Rev: XXXVIII + 158 (37–194).

**MS B15**   Contratenor Decani. Anthems and Services.

The anthems are those of MSS C22v and D21 together with Corfe (2.), Durante, Handel (21.38.), Hesletine (3.), Sabadini, and Wolf. Loose in the MS are two copies of the decani alto part of Haydn's 'Lord we pray thee'. *Rev*: ten of the later services of MS B18—Arnold (2.), Child (24.), B. Cooke (2.), Havergal (2.), Kelway (2.), Penson (1.), Pilbrow, Rogers (5.7.), and J. S. Smith— and eight from MS D21v—S. Elvey, Mendelssohn (9.10.), Nares (17.), Rogers (8.), Shenton (2.), Walmisley (11.), and Young.

Dated 1819 (p. 13) to 1852 (p. 238), with a much later addition by Lisle in 1909 (p. 239); Rev, 1819 (p. 20) to 1852 (p. 119).

366 × 236 mm. 193 ff., pag: IV + iv + 242 (1–220, 220a–b, 221– 40); Rev: IV + iv + 1–128.

**MS B16**   Alto Decani. Anthems and Services.

*Forw*: MSS B11, B16, and B34 are later developments of MS B35v. Their common corpus is: the core of 49 anthems by Ebdon interspersed with Corfe (1.), Garth (3.), and Mozart (1.) (cf. MS B18v), together with Aldrich (1.8.12.), Banks (1.3.), Byrd (4.), Corfe (2.), Earle, Ebdon (4.), Friend (1.2.), Greene (8.), Handel (39.), Haydn (5.), Henley (2.), Kent (1–7.9.11–14: i.e. *Kent 1*), Mason (7.), Pleyel, Shenton (1.), H. P. Simpson, and Weldon (12.). Additional in B16 are Child (4.) and Croft (5.). *Rev*: 18 of the services listed under MS B7.

Dated 1793 (p. 42) to 1810 (p. 136); Rev, 1793 (p. 91) and 1794 (p. 151). Copyists include Friend (pp. 4–17; Rev pp. 1–78), Chrishop (pp. 44–68, 70–95; Rev pp. 138–52), and Ebdon (pp. 96– 112, 116–43; hol).

384 × 245 mm. 159 ff., pag: IV + iv + 1–149; Rev: IV + ii + 1–155.

## MS B17 Contratenor, no. 2. Anthems and Services.

*Forw and part of Rev*: About three-fifths of the anthems of MS B12. Additional are Batten (3.4.9.12.), Hilton (1.), [Pergolesi] (3.), and Tallis (11.14.). *Rest of Rev*: nearly all the services of MS B35v, together with Mason's 'O Lord how manifold'.

Dated 1735 (p. 29) to 1794 (p. 156); Rev, 1735 (p. 25) and 1772 (p. 180). Copyists include Brass (pp. 1–90, 95–117, 119–21; Rev pp. 1–160), Ebdon (pp. 90–5, 118–19; Rev pp. 161–6, 169–71) and Mathews (pp. 123–46; Rev pp. 167–8, 172–85).

361 × 235 mm. 183 ff., pag: IV + iv + 160 (1–27, 27a, 28–64, 64a, 65–145, 145a–b, 146–56); Rev: II + iv + 1–72 + IV + 116 (77–192).

## MS B18 Alto Cantoris. Services and Anthems.

*Forw*: MSS B3, B15v, B18, B30, C20, C22, C23, C24, C25, and D22 may be considered together. The range of services is: Arnold (2.), Boyce (24.), Chard (1.), Child (23.24.), Clarke[-Whitfeld] (4.), B. Cooke (2.), R. Cooke, Croft (72.), R. Farrant (3.), Fussel, O. Gibbons (28.), Handel (4.), Havergal (2.), Jommelli (2.), Kelway (1.2.), C. King (9.), Marsh, Mason (7.), Nares (16.), Ogle, Patrick, Penson (1.), Pilbrow, Rogers (5.7.), J. S. Smith, Tallis (14.), and Walsh (1.). B18 has two-thirds of these. *Rev*: MSS B4, B18v, C20v, C23v, and C24v have most of these anthems in common: Boyce (8.), Clarke[-Whitfeld] (3.), B. Cooke (1.), Croft (7.10.), Edwards, Ferretti, Graun (2.), Handel (15.25.31.35.41.), Isaac, Moreira (2.), Mozart (5.), Penson (1.), (*sic*), Pickering (1.), Tallis (5.), and Tye (5.); together with some 49 anthems by Ebdon interspersed with Corfe (1.), Garth (3.), and Mozart (1.). This 'Ebdon' corpus is found in MSS B11, B16, B33, B34, C23v, C24v, and D18. Additional in B18 are Blow (7.20), Croft (18.), Ebdon (4.), Fiocco, Friend (1.2.), Haydn (5.), Luther, and H. Purcell (8.9.).

Dated 1813 (p. 31) to 1819 (p. 110); Rev, 1804 (p. 37) to 1819 (p. 116). Copied by Chrishop (Rev pp. 25–7), Ebdon (Rev pp. 28–44, 47–77; hol) and Radcliffe (pp. 15–36; Rev pp. 82–90).

360 × 230 mm. 118 ff., pag: II + ii + 1–110; Rev: II + ii + 1–118.

## MS B19 Contratenor Cantoris. Services.

Of the same set as MS B7, having, though in a different order, almost two-thirds of those services.

Dated 1731 (p. 31) through 1755 (p. 364) to 1791 (p. 400; music is earlier). Copied by Brass (pp. 1–371), Mathews (pp. 372, 380–400), Ebdon (pp. 372b–9), and Chrishop (p. 401).

358 × 235 mm. 204 ff., pag: II + ii + 402 (1–372, 372a–b, 373–88, 391–402) + II.

## MS B20   Counter-tenor Cantoris. Anthems and Services.

Of the same set as MS C21, Blake, Croft (16.), Kent (8.10.), and Wise (10.) being additional here. About a third of the anthems have been misplaced. They are at the reverse end, followed by about half the corpus of services, Blow (29.), and Mason (7.).

Dated c.1714 (p. 10) to 1755 (p. 142); Rev, c.1734 (p. 80) to 1755 (p. 140). Copyists include Leeke (pp. 1–37), Laye (Rev pp. 1–5), and Brass (pp. 57–143; Rev pp. 55–140).

305 × 195 mm. 149 ff., pag: II + x + 1–142; Rev: II + iv + 138 (1–74, 77–140).

## MS B21   Counter-tenor Cantoris. Anthems and Services.

Of the same set as MS C21. 11 of the later anthems are missing. Additional are Boyce (5.), Croft (19.), O. Gibbons (15.), and Weldon (8.). *Rev*: Owing to wear and tear contains only about half the services; additional are Aldrich (9.), Blow (14.), Child (10.13.), Handel (8.), Hesletine (1.), Ogle, and Tallis (9.).

Dated c.1714 (p. 7) to 1739 (p. 204); Rev, c.1732 (p. 12) to 1737 (p. 71). Copyists include Leeke (pp. 3–5), Laye (pp. 7–40, 41–5, 52–3; Rev pp. 9–16), and Brass (pp. 88–206; Rev pp. 36–71). Mathews added pp. 206–7, Rev pp. 72–8 in 1772, Chrishop p. 208 in the 1790s.

310 × 190 mm. 200 ff., pag: II + viii + 1–208; Rev: II + ii + 1–78.

## MS B22   Alto. Services.

A later copy based on MS B7, now having about three-fifths of those services. Additional is Humfrey (13.).

Mathews transcribed pp. 1–53, 71–170 between 1768 (p. 47) and 1774 (p. 53), the remaining pages being copied in 1791 (p. 63). From Mathews's own pagination it is clear that B22 was formerly two MSS—pp. 9–47 were pp. 80–128, whilst pp. 71–170 remain unaltered. This latter corpus is presumably part of Mathews's own book into which 172 pp. were copied in 1768. The pagination also discloses that pp. 1–27 have been badly disturbed.

373 × 257 mm. 83 ff., pag: II + iii + 159 (1–63, 71–108, 111–50, 153–70) + II.

**MS B23**   Treble Primo, Decani. Services.

About three-quarters of the services of MS B7. Additional is 'O Lord grant the king' by Banks.

Pp. 3–165 were transcribed by Mathews by 1776, additions being made until 1791. Made from parchment purchased for that purpose in 1772–3 (Audit Book A.VII; cf. MS B24).

Parchment. 330 × 242 mm. 93 ff., pag: II + ii + 1–16 + II + 160 (19–54, 57–74, 79–154, 157–86) + II. At least eight pp. have been cut away after p. 186.

**MS B24**   Treble Secundo, Cantoris, no. 16. Anthems.

Seven-tenths of the anthems of MS B12. Additional are Greene (1.28.33.42.), and Mason (2.).

Mathews copied pp. 1–101 by 1776, additions being made until 1791 (p. 109). Made from parchment purchased for that purpose in 1772–3 (Audit Book A.VII; cf. MS B23).

Parchment. 311 × 235 mm. 62 ff., pag: VI (paper) + ii + 1–114 + II (paper). Pp. 1–30 have been restored to their original pagination.

**MS B26**   Bass Cantoris. Anthems.

Nearly half the anthems of MS B12, together with Friend (1.2.), Handel (5.), Kent (2.5.), and Marcello (3.).

Late 18th cent. Pp. 143 *et seq.* are later, with p. 174 dated 1795; pp. 157–74 were copied by Chrishop. Inscribed, in fashion similar to MS C30: 'I give this book containing 174 Pages of MS. Music to the Cathedral Church of Durham. Francis H. Egerton' (p. ii). Egerton was a Prebendary from 1780 to 1829, but it has not been established whether the MSS were transcribed especially for him.

373 × 236 mm. 91 ff., pag: II + iv + 1–174 + II.

**MS B27**   Bass Cantoris. Anthems and Services.

Pp. 1–142, 192–242 are drawn mainly from MS C27; the rest, apart from O. Gibbons (1.) and a Kyrie by Miss Ogle, are in the early part of MS C21. Among additions in pencil are the hymn tune 'German' by [Croft], and a chant by Henshaw (org, 1813–62)— the only evidence of any composing activity on his part to emerge. *Rev*: three services—Croft (71.), H. Purcell (37.), and Rogers (6.)—and 'O clap your hands' by Greene.

Dated *c*.1714 (Funeral of Queen Anne; p. 47) to 'Jan. 28th 1717/8' (p. 242). Copied by Laye (pp. 1–147, 180–242; Rev pp. 1–24) and the early copyists of MS C21. *Rev*: the initials 'J.W.' (p. 9) are those of John Waring (prec, 1721–33).

365 × 240 mm. 142 ff., pag: iv + 256 (1–34, 37–96, 99–102, 105–70, 173–6, 179–214, 217–68); Rev: 1–24.

**MS B28**  Precentor's Book, [Bass], no. 3. Services.

Though not in the same order the contents are substantially the same as those of MS B7. Additional are Child (18.), and Foster (13.).

Pp. 68–78, 88–156, 185–200, 205–16, 225–310 were copied by Brass between 1732 (p. 258) and 1741 (p. 310). Mathews replaced and added pp. 389–97, 3–67, 79–87, 157–84, 201–4, 217–24, 311–88 in 1771 (p. 397). Chrishop added p. 398 in 1799.

317 × 195 mm. 202 ff., pag: II + ii + 398 (389–400, 3–388) + II.

**MS B29**  Bass. Anthems and Services.

To be considered with MS B12, having about two-thirds of those anthems. Additional are Aldrich (2.), and H. Purcell (14.). *Rev*: 13 of the services of MS B35, together with Blow (31.).

Dated *c*.1745 (p. 206) to 1771 (p. 286); Rev, 1742 (p. 6) to 1768 (p. 87). Copied by Brass (pp. 1–269; Rev pp. 1–81), Mathews (pp. 209, 270–86; Rev pp. 82–4, 88–90), and Ebdon (Rev pp. 85–7).

368 × 235 mm. 195 ff., pag: II + vi + 284 (1–231, 234–86); Rev: II + iv + 92 (1–73, 73a–b, 74–90).

**MS B30**  Bass. Services.

Half the services of MS B18, most of those of MS D21v; and Aldrich (17.), Boyce (23.), C. King (5.8.10.), Nares (18.) (all from *Arnold*), H. Purcell (37.), more of Tallis (14.), and S. S. Wesley (10.); and Bach's, 'Behold us Lord before thee'.

Pp. 1–163 are dated 1839 (p. 26) to 1867 (p. 163). Walker copied the remaining pages.

365 × 233 mm. 99 ff., pag: IV + ii + 188 (1–140, 149–90, 209–14) + IV.

**MS B31**   Bass Cantoris, no. 4. Anthems and Services.

Three-quarters of the anthems of MS B35v, together with Aldrich (5.), Allinson (1.), Byrd (4.), Clarke (9.), Greene (20.30.), and Kent (2.6.). *Rev*: 17 of the services of MS B35.

Dated 1745 (p. 3) to 1791 (p. 131); Rev, 1745 (p. 11) to 1776 (p. 124). Copyists include Brass (pp. 1–89; Rev pp. 1–99), Mathews (pp. 90–122; Rev pp. 100–24), and Chrishop (Rev p. 9).

367 × 232 mm. 134 ff., pag: II + vi + 130 (3–70, 73–106, 111–38); Rev: II × iv + 1–124.

**MS B32**   Bass Cantoris, no. 5. Anthems and Services.

Of the same set as MS B12, having nearly half of its anthems. Additional are Croft (25.66.). *Rev*: 15 of the services of MS B35.

Dated 1736 (p. 52) to 1771 (p. 98); Rev, 1741 (p. 7) to 1771 (p. 80). Copied by Brass (pp. 7–66, 72–94; Rev pp. 1–73), Ebdon (pp. 67–71), Mathews (pp. 94–9; Rev pp. 74–80), and others.

366 × 236 mm. 91 ff., pag: iv + 92 (7–99; p. 99 = Rev p. 80); Rev: vi + 1–80.

**MS B33**   Bass Decani, no. 3. Anthems and Services.

May be considered with MS B35v, having nearly all of its anthems, together with Aldrich (6.), Blow (17.), Clarke (5.12.16.), Croft (18.), Goldwin (2.), Humfrey (12.), H. Purcell (1.17.), Turner (4.), and Wise (8.10.11.). 19 anthems of the Ebdon corpus and Garth (3.) (*see* MS B18v), Greene (32.), and Nares (3.4.7.13.) were added much later. *Rev*: 12 of the services of MS B35 remain, together with two anthems—Garth (2.), and Turner (6.).

Dated 1746 (p. 10) to 1796 (p. 173); Rev, 1750 (p. 33) to 1791 (p. 116). Copied by Brass (pp. 1–120, 125–34, 137–8a; Rev pp. 1–73), Ebdon (pp. 120–5, 135, 174–87; Rev pp. 74–80, 83–4), Mathews (pp. 139–66; Rev pp. 81–2, 87–110), Chrishop (pp. 169–72), and others. Pp. 187–95 and Rev pp. 121–6 were added in 1841.

365 × 240 mm. 145 ff., pag: 196 (1–34, 34a–b, 35–135, 137–8, 138a, 139–95; p. 195 = Rev p. 126); Rev: 94 (31–84, 87–126).

**MS B34**   Bass Decani. Anthems and Services.

The anthems are those of MS B16, together with Aldrich (5.), Allinson (1.), Battishill (1.), Blake, Boyce (8.), Clarke (9.), Croft (18.), Crotch (chant), Fiocco, Garth (2.), Goldwin (4.), Greene (20.), Handel (11.15.35.), Isaac, W. Jones, Mason (5.6.), Nares

(11.), Porter, and Stroud. *Rev*: six services Child (23.24.), Hall and Hine, C. King (8.), Ogle, and Shenton (2.).

Dated 1791 (p. 5) to 1810 (p. 168); Rev, 1791 (p. 22). Copyists include Friend (pp. 14–42), Chrishop (pp. 89–122), Ebdon (pp. 124–43, 145–76; hol), and Radcliffe (pp. 178–99).

376 × 240 mm. 121 ff., pag: II + vi + 1–199; Rev: II + ii + 31 (1–8, 19–41).

**MS B35**    Bass. Services and Anthems.

*Forw*: MSS A13v, B17v, B29v, B31v, B32v, B33v, B35, and B36v, form a sub-set related to MS B7, the significant difference being the omission of most of the 16th and 17th cent. compositions. Apart from settings found in only one MS the comprehensive list of contents is: Alcock, Aldrich (16.), Bacon (2.), Bevin, Bishop (2.), Creighton (3.), Croft (70.71.), Ebdon (62.), Goodson, Gregory (1.), W. Hayes (16.), Kelway (3.), Kent (15.), C. King (7.10.), Lamb (1.), Nares (15.), Priest, H. Purcell (36. 37.), Raylton, Shenton (2.), Tallis (11.), Travers (4.), Walkley, Wanless (1.), and Wise (12.13.). Additional in B35 are Greville, and C. King (8.).

*Rev*: MSS B8, B13, B31, B33, and B35v, are related to MS B12. The main difference is the considerable and sometimes complete reduction of the anthems of MS C21, and of those by the late 16th and early 17th cent. composers listed under MS B12. The revised common corpus is: Aldrich (1.), Bacon (1.), Banks (1.3.), Battishill (1.), Bishop (1.), Blake, Blow (5–7.9.23.), Boyce (1.3–5.21.), Corfe (2.), Croft (5.9.13.16.29.39.41.43.44.47.48.64.65.), Ebdon (7.58.), Fiocco, Garth (1.2.), Hall (3.5.), Handel (1.9–11.17.20.34.39.44.), Hesletine (3.), Hine (1.), Humfrey (1.5.10.), Kent (8.10.), Locke (3.), Marcello (2.), Mason (5.6.), Porter, H. Purcell (4.34.), Shenton (1.), and Wise (1.3.). B35v has five-sixths of these plus Avison, Clarke (4.), Nares (8.11.14.), Turner (6.), Weldon (5.), and Wise (2.).

Dated 1741 (p. 45) to 1791 (p. 192); Rev, 1741 (p. 6) to 1796 (p. 148). Copyists include Brass (pp. 1–147; Rev pp. 3–97), Ebdon (pp. 148–54; Rev pp. 97–103), Mathews (pp. 154–72; Rev pp. 1, 2, 103–33) and Chrishop (Rev pp. 144–7).

363 × 235 mm. 175 ff., pag: IV + iv + 186 (1–52, 59–192); Rev: II + viii + 146 (1–84, 87–148).

**MS B36**    Bass, no. 1. Anthems and Services.

About a third of the anthems of MS B12, together with Handel

(7.). *Rev*: 20 of the services of MS B35, plus Greene (43.), and Hall and Hine.

Dated 1737 (p. 26) to 1775 (p. 160) and 1796 (p. 161); Rev, 1737 (p. 22) to 1771 (p. 119). Copied by Brass (pp. 1–118; Rev pp. 1–113), and Mathews (pp. 119–60; Rev pp. 113–19).

377 × 235 mm. 146 ff., pag: II + iv + 1–161; Rev: II + ii + 121 (1–45, 45a, 46–91, 96–119, 131–5).

## MS C1  Medius. Anthems and Services.

On the smaller pages are the anthems of MS C4 (though nearly all the full section has been lost), W. Smith's responses, the special anthems of MS C2, and the service by Tallis. The larger pages hold many of the services, preces, and festal psalms of MSS C8, C18, and E4; many of the general anthems of MS C2 (these are in a block); and services by T. Boyce, Hilton, and Marson.

?1660s. The different sizes of leaves indicate that more than one original MS is represented here. That they were replacement copies, produced to allow the continued use of the repertoire of the 1630s, is apparent from the extension to the C4 series being in the basic hand here, and from the 'Puritan hat' watermark of the smaller pages. The MS is a mine for the names of early 18th cent. choristers: 'Cuthbert Brass not his Book 1724/5' (inside front cover); 'John Cowen his Boke' (p. 39); 'Humphrey Norton, Francis Blackett, Richard Willson, James Richardson, Durham, John Stout, Stephen Colling, Durham, Cuth Brass, Stephen Colling his Booke 1721' (p. 100). 'Joseph Stevenson 1736' (p. 185, cf. p. 208), 'Robert Paxton' (p. 207, also p. 224), 'Christopher Mitcalf' (p. 224), and 'Thomas Leigh, 1727' (inside back cover). In addition, 'A. W.' is scratched on the front cover.

285 × 190 mm, and after p. 141, 291 × 190 mm. 158 ff., pag: II + 312 (1–3, 3a–b, 4–310) + II. Pp. 1–130 draw on early pp. 49–190, and pp. 141–310 on early pp. 226–368, 373–96.

## MS C2  I Contratenor Decani. Anthems.

MSS C2, C3, and C7 (1st fascicle), and C14 are the survivors of a set of ten anthem books 'for Festivall daies' (*see* Misc. Ch. 7116). Containing mainly verse anthems, each book has two sections—anthems for the feast days of the church's year, with pages left blank after each day to allow for additions; and those for general use.

Allocated to feast days: Batten (8.17.), Bull (1.), Byrd (6.23.),

Cranford (3.), Dering, East (1.2.), Geeres (1.), O. Gibbons (2.4.10.11.14.17.23.24.), R. Gibbs, Giles (1.2.), Hooper (2.5.10.), Juxon, J. Mundy (5.), Palmer (1–4.), W. Smith (1.4.6.10.11.), Edw. Smythe (2.), J. Tomkins, T. Tomkins (2.4.5.9.16.), and Weelkes (1.2.5.); with 'How is the gold become dim', by Elias Smyth, added some time after 1649.

For general use: Alison, Amner (1.), Batten (2.5–7.11.13.15.), Byrd (9.), Child (3.8.), Cranford (1.2.), Gale, C. Gibbons (1.), O. Gibbons (15.), Giles (3.5.7.12.), Hilton (2.4.), Hinde, Hooper (4.), R. Hucheson (3.), M. Jeffries (1–3.), Loosemore (2.), Mudd (1.), W. Mundy (3.4.), R. Parsons [II] (1.), Peerson (1.), Portman (2.), Ravenscroft (2.), Stevenson (1.), Strogers (1.), Tallis (2.), T. Tomkins (1.11.13–15.), Tozar, Weelkes (3.), and Wilkinson (1–11.).

Added to this MS after 1660 were: Aldrich (13.), Child (1.2.5.7.10–12.16; in 1675), Croft (68.), Goldwin (2.), Isham, [W.] King (2.), Nicholls (1.), and Wise (9.).

1630s. As with the other members of the set, the initials have not been drawn in, whilst a slightly different ink and more hurried style indicate several very early additions in the spaces left for that purpose. Transcribed by Brookinge. Elias Smyth (p. 198) and White (pp. 1–4, 9, 12–13, 17–18, 129, 152) extended it in the 1670s; with Laye's work (pp. 21–4, 28–30, 66–7) attested 'A. Y[app].' (p. 67; prec, 1711–16). The same basic contents, together with the preces and psalms of MS E4, are found in the same hand in the 'Dunnington-Jefferson MS', now in York Minster Library (MS M 29 S). That MS was probably used by Prebendary John Cosin, for its Table is arranged differently, having headings such as 'Prayer', 'Penitence', and 'Praise', just like the Caroline part-books at Peterhouse. C2 still has its original Table, and its leather covers (restored) bear tooled in gilt the cathedral's early 17th cent. coat-of-arms (cf. MSS A1 and E4; and A.IV.32).

307 × 205 mm. 106 ff., pag: II + iv + 200 (1–54, 56–76, 78–165, 167–200, 202–4) + iv + II.

W. K. Ford, 'An English Liturgical Partbook of the 17th Century', *Journal of the American Musicological Society*, xii, nos. 2–3 (1959).

**MS C2★**  Counter-tenor. Anthems.

Two-thirds of the full anthems of MS C4; with Allinson (1.), Humfrey (8.), [W.] King (3.), Pickering (1.), and Tudway (3.) added later.

*c.*1700, as indicated by the king being named as 'William' in Byrd's anthem (p. 3). Pp. 1–42 were copied by Softley. The additions include an anthem by Pickering (preb, Durham, 1692–1711; cf. MS A25). How extensive this MS may have been is uncertain; what remains demonstrates the stability of the repertoire.

309 × 192 mm. 26 ff., pag: II + 1–48 + II.

## MS C3  II Contratenor Decani. Anthems.

Of the same set as MS C2. Added later were the 'Club Anthem', and 'Thou O God art praised' by [?Jn Hawkins].

1630s. Like MS C2 this volume has its original Table. Copied by Brookinge; with p. 27 added by Shaw, and p. 162 by Owen. Tooled in gilt on its covers (restored) is the cathedral's early 17th cent. coat-of-arms. 'Tho. Laye' (l-c, 1710–29) is scratched on the front cover.

305 × 201 mm. 83 ff., pag: IV + 48 (3–50) + II + 14 (53–66) + II + 32(69–100) + IV + 20(105–24) + IV + 18(129–46) + IV + 4(159–62) + II + 2 (175–6) + iv + II.

## MS C4  II Contratenor Decani. Anthems.

MSS C4, C5, C6, C7 (2nd fascicle), C9, and C10, are the survivors of the set of 'Tenn Bookes in folio of full and Verse Anthemes' (*see* Misc. Ch. 7116). These anthems are in two distinct groups.

Full are: Batten (1.), Byrd (2.11.12.15–17.19–21.), Geeres (2.3; hol), O. Gibbons (1.13.), Giles (6.), Hilton (1.), Hooper (1.3.8.), M. Jeffries (2.), Morley (3.), J. Mundy (2.3.), W. Mundy (2.), Palmer (7.), R. Parsons [I] (1.2.), Read (1.), Rutter, Tallis (4.9.), D. Taylor, T. Tomkins (3.), Tye (2.), Warwick, Weelkes (4.), R. White (1.2.), and W. White (1.2.).

Verse are: Batten (16.), Bull (2.3.), Byrd (1.3.6.), East (3.), Fido, O. Gibbons (6.7.10.11.20.23.24.), Giles (1.4.5.8.10.), Hinde, Hooper (5–7.), R. Hucheson (1.2.), Morley (2.4.), J. Mundy (1.4.6.), W. Mundy (1.6.), R. Parsons [II] (3.), Peerson (2.), Portman (1.4.), W. Smith (7.9.), Edw. Smythe (2.4.7.), T. Tomkins (4.6.7.12.17.), Ward, and Weelkes (2.).

Depending on their state of preservation the MSS include varying numbers of the following 15 early post-Restoration additions: Byrd (8.), Foster (3–6.10.11.13.), Giles (11.), Hooper (9.), Mudd (3.), Nicholls (2.), Tallis (7.), Wilson, and Yarrow. Of these C4 has but two.

1620s and 1630s. Todd started copying all the members of this set, transcribing full anthems 1–27 (1–28 in MS C7)—at which point there is a holograph anthem by Geeres—and verse anthems 1–20. Then either to expedite completion or to extend the scheme the work was shared out, Brookinge copying up the Cantoris books as far as full anthem 37 and verse anthem 42. A further full anthem and verse anthems 43–9 were added a little later to all the books by Brookinge, whilst Geeres brought the full section to a close with another holograph composition.

MSS C4 and C10 still have their original Tables, which in this set refer to neither pagination nor foliation—it is the anthems themselves which are numbered. MSS C4, C5, C9, and C10 also have their original leather covers (restored) with gilt tooling, covers which possibly date from 1597. Further covers are on MS C17 which was re-written c.1675. MS C4 pp. 17–26 are replacement copies dating from c.1670.

293 × 183 mm. 51 ff., pag: II + vi + 1–92 + II.

## MS C5   II Contratenor Cantoris. Anthems.

Of the same set as MS C4. Full anthems 1–4 are now missing, nos. 5–6 are only fragments. Loosemore (4.) and H. Purcell (32.) are later.

1620s and 1630s. Original leather covers (restored), tooled in gilt. 'Thomas Parkinson' (chor 1667–72, l-c 1675–1720) is inscribed on pp. 54, 55.

293 × 188 mm. 52 ff., pag: II + 100 (①–②, 1–45, 45a–b, 46–96) + II.

## MS C6   I Contratenor Decani. Anthems.

Of the same set as MS C4. Now lacks full anthems 1–2 and verse anthems 1, 45–50. Humfrey (5.) is later.

1620s and 1630s. The Table, dated 1682 and the work of White, gives little indication of the possible extent of the MS. Owen added pp. 1–2 in 1693. 'Niccolis'—there were several singers named Nicholls in the 17th cent.—survives on a fragment pasted inside the back cover.

290 × 187 mm. 52 ff., pag: II + iv (parchm) + 1–96 + II.

## MS C7   [I Contratenor Cantoris]. Anthems.

Bound together to form this volume are two early 17th cent.

part-books. The first belongs to the same set as MS C2, the second to the MS C4 series together with its extension. The other anthems added after 1660 have much in common with the new items in the main corpus of MS C34. Jn Hawkins (1.), [G.] Holmes (1.), and Turner (5.) are additional here.

1620s and 1630s; with considerable additions by White (Table, pp. 131–7, 328–39, 343–50), Owen (pp. 138–82, 351–84, 386–406), Greggs (pp. 12–13, 182–91), Thoresby (pp. 196–201), Softley (pp. 205–8, 406–14), and Leeke (pp. 1–2, 213–14) until the beginning of the 18th cent. Duplications in the additions indicate that the two fascicles enjoyed distinct existences throughout this period. William Smith has crossed out the text of 'The secret sins' by [W. Mundy] replacing it with 'The Lord is only my support'.

298 × 191 mm for 109 ff., pag: II + vi + 1–208 + II; and 286 × 185 mm for the remaining 105 ff., pag: iv (parchm) + 202 (213–414) + ii (parchm) + II. In all, 214 ff. The pagination was revised in the 1920s.

## MS C8  Counter-tenor. Services.

In the oldest parts are: Byrd (30.), Coste, Derrick, R. Farrant (3.), O. Gibbons (28.), Hooper (11.), Hughes, W. Mundy (9.10.), Parsley, Parsons of Wells, Patrick, Read (2.), Stevenson (2.), Strogers (2.), Tallis (14.), T. Tomkins (18.), and Tye (6.). Added before 1640 were: Foster (12.), Palmer (12.), and W. Smith (19.20.). Added from 1660 onwards were: Blow (28.30.31.), Child (17.18.), Foster (13.), Goldwin (2; anthem), Humfrey (13.), C. King (7.), Loosemore (8.), Mundy (8.), Parsons [R II] of Exeter (4.), Tallis (11; Litany), Travers (4.), and Wanless (1; Litany).

c.1630, with additions until 1739. The sole survivor of a set of ten books 'for short services' (see Misc. Ch. 7116), a set intended for regular use. The original services are numbered 1–14, and are arranged in three sections for use at Matins, Communion, and Evensong respectively. Most of the items lack initials. Todd was the original copyist, Brookinge adding a number of local compositions (p. 158-f. (7ᵛ); pp. 188–97, 229–36) by 1640. The line inserted by Palmer on p. 181 is his only contribution in the Durham part-books. In the later part are three indications of payment: 'E. K[irkby].' (p. 446; prec 1682–8), 'J. M[ilner]. May 21. [16]93' (p. 458; prec 1688–1705), and 'Pd. 1739' (p. 547). Its copyists include Owen (pp. 424–459), Softley (pp. 460–506), and Brass (pp. 517–50). An inscription on the old calf cover mounted inside the front cover shows that the MS was owned by 'Chr. Mickleton, Dep: Regr̄ar', '1716'. Inscribed elsewhere are 'Cuth: Wilson' (p. 69; chor 1740–50, l-c 1751–80) and 'John Banks' (p. ii; chor 1770–83).

292 × 182 mm. 218 ff., pag: ii + II + 428 (1–2, 5–102, 107–20, 139–60, ff. ①–⑧, pp. 161–2, 165–70, 173–202, 207–36, 241–314, 316–29, 400–5, 407–8, 424–32, 434–510, 515–50) + ii + II.

**MS C9**   Tenor Decani. Anthems.

Of the same set as MS C4. Now lacks full anthems 1–18 and verse anthems 20–6. Additional is [W.] King (3.).

1620s and 1630s. White added p. 25 in the 1670s. Original leather covers (restored), tooled in gilt.

293 × 188 mm. 45 ff., pag: II + 4 (1–4) + II + 40 (5–44) + VI + 28 (45–72) + II + 4 (73–6) + II.

**MS C10**   Tenor Cantoris. Anthems.

Of the same set as MS C4. Full anthems 1–4.7.8.15.16.28.29 are now lacking; nos. 5.6.13.14. only fragments. Later are all the set's early post-Restoration additions, also Blow (29.), Fiocco, Jn Hawkins (1.), Hesletine (3.), Nicholls (1.), H. Purcell (32.), and Turner (10.).

1620s and 1630s. With the exception of pp. 87–8, where Geeres has copied out the words of 'The first psa. appointed for the fast of the 8th July instead of Venite exultemus', pp. 86 *et seq.* date from after 1660. Later copyists include White (pp. 106–10), Leeke (pp. 112–13), and Laye (pp. 114–15), showing that the set was still used in the 1710s. On p. iv is written 'James Smart' (tenor l-c 1660–97). The MS has its original Table and leather covers (restored) tooled in gilt.

295 × 188 mm. 66 ff., pag: II + viii + 1–118 + ii + II.

**MS C11**   Tenor Decani. Anthems.

A comprehensive book containing in its first hand the anthems of MSS C2 and C4, together with Hooper (9.), Mudd (3.), W. Mundy (3.4.), Parsons of Exeter (2.), Stevenson (1.), Tallis (2.), and Yarrow. Added after 1660 were: Amner (1.), Batten (11.12.14.), Blow (14.24.), Bryne (1.), Byrd (12.), Child (1.2.5–8. 10–12.), East (3.), Foster (1–5.7–11.), C. Gibbons (4.), Giles (4★.), Greggs (6.), Jn Hawkins (1.2.), Heardson, Hilton (2.), Hooper (9.), R. Hucheson (3.), Humfrey (5.), J. Hutchinson (1–4.), W. King (1.3.), H. Lawes (2.), Loosemore (1.2.4.6.), Mudd (1–5.), Mundy

(1–3; all ★), Nicholls (1.2.), H. Purcell (9.24.), Sheppard (2★.), El. Smyth, Edw. Smythe (7.), Stonard (2.), Strogers (1.), Tallis (7.10.12; all ★), T. Tomkins (3.13.), Tucker (1.3–9.), Weelkes (1.3.), Wilson, and Wise (4–6.).

Late 1630s, with additions to c.1680. This is the companion volume to MS C13, for like that MS it is for the tenor voice, and the edges of its pages are gilded and gauffered and decorated in green and red. Brookinge, the copyist of the original part (pp. 1–83; Rev pp. 1–83, 87–155, with a calculation relating to payment on p. 156), was responsible at about the same time for MSS C13, C16, and E11a, and for over 200 pp. in the Peterhouse MSS. Pp. 85–146 and Rev pp. 83–6, 156–64, added probably by Shaw c.1664 (see 'A' on Rev p. 161), include possible contents of the missing set of part-books for men's voices (marked ★). Shaw was active later (pp. 147–51; Rev pp. 156–65), as was White (pp. 151–2; Rev pp. 166–233, with p. 171 dated 1675). 'John Sudbery his book' and 'Denis Grenvell', written on a back flyleaf, indicate that the MS was used by two successive Deans of Durham (1661–84 and 1684–91, respectively). Besides having 'Tenor. De . . .' tooled in gilt the covers are also stamped, 'Bassus Decan . . .'.

298 × 197 mm. 283 ff., pag: II + 1–282; Rev: II + xiv + 266 (1–97, 99–156, 156a, 157–8, 158a, 159, 159a, 160, 160a, 161, 161a–b, 162–3, 165–73, 173a, 174–90, 192–262). Pp. 153–282 and Rev pp. 234–62 are blank.

## MS C12   Tenor Cantoris. Anthems and Services.

Pp. ①–30 draw extensively on the full anthems of MS C4. The remainder embraces 32 of the post-Restoration additions to MS C11, Alison and Carr (anthems), and Child in A minor. Rev: the services are very much those of the slightly later MS C32. Lacking are Blow (28.31.), H. Purcell (36.), and Weelkes (7.); additional are Batten (21.22.), O. Gibbons (29.), Morley (5.), Shaw (4.), and the tenor part of 20 chants dating from c.1683 (see MS C28) and of two early 18th cent. chants by 'J. H[esletine].'

Late 17th cent. The presence in the basic hand of five anthems by Tucker (acquired c.1679) and of services by Shaw and Nicholls (who shared the reins of office after the death of Foster in 1677) points to a date c.1680. Later copyists include Shaw (pp. 70a–b; Rev pp. 265–72), White (pp. 71–88; Rev pp. 15–44, 237–44), Owen (Rev pp. 4–12, 45–66), and Greggs (pp. 1–3, 13–14, 66–8,

244–8; p. 248 is dated 1693). Among boyish scribblings are 'George Chrishop' (p. 41), 'Old grunting Acton' (Rev p. 15), and 'Acton we see in human shape. Mutch like a munkey or an ape 1796' (Rev p. 161). Chrishop was deputy organist and teacher of the choristers, 1796–1803; Acton was a lay-clerk, 1782–1817.

308 × 196 mm. 188 ff., pag: II + 94 (①–⑥, 1–88); Rev: II + 1–44 + II + 228 (45–272) + II + 3 (273–5; p. 275 = Forw p. 88). Pp. ①–⑥, 1–69 were originally pp. 1–75; and Rev pp. 69–237 were formerly pp. 1–58, 61–90, 93–175, with pp. 248–63 once being pp. 186–201.

## MS C13    Tenor Decani. Services.

A comprehensive book embracing the original contents of and early additions to MS C8; most of MS C18 (omitting, like MS E11a, Farrant, Frost, R. Gibbs, M. Jeffries (4.), Randall, and Weelkes (8.)); and all of MS E4. Also in the original hand are T. Boyce, Brymley (1.), Child (24.), [J.] Farrant, Hilton (5.), Marson, Palmer (11.), R. Parsons [II] (4.), Thorne, Weelkes (7.), and Wilkinson (12.13). Added in the 1660s were Batten (18–20.), Bevin, Byrd (30.), [J.] Farrant (again), [J.] Holmes, Loosemore (8.), and Shaw (4.); and in 1671 Bryne (2.), and Foster (13.).

Late 1630s. In the same hand, and with its pages also gilded and gauffered and decorated in green and red, this is the companion volume to MS C11. Unlike the MSS on which it draws, the services here are not arranged in liturgical groupings. Brookinge's calculations relating to what he should be paid at the rate of 3d. per page are on p. 304 and Rev p. 107. Shaw was probably responsible for Rev pp. 107–74 in c.1664; and added pp. ⑬–⑱, and Rev pp. ⑤–⑫ in 1671 (so Rev p. ⑫). White copied Rev pp. 29–30. 'Christopher Wardall', 'Ralph Thurkeld', and 'William Pye', who wrote their names on p. ① during the 18th cent., were never members of the cathedral foundation. The covers (like those of MS C11) indicate they once held a bass part.

297 × 193 mm. 252 ff., pag: II + xii (①–⑫) + 300 (⑬–⑱, 1–189, 200–304); Rev: II + iv (①–④) + 184 (⑤–⑭, 1–174).

## MS C14    Tenor Cantoris. Anthems and Service.

Of the same set as MS C2, the copyist including W. Smith (15.) by error. Added after 1660 were most of the new items of MS C34, and, at the reverse end, Blow in G.

1630s, with additions until c.1715. White inserted the corpus of anthems by Child at the front c.1675 (pp. 1–2, 4, 8–9, 12, 14–16;

cf. MS C2), added pp. 77, 161–72, and in 1682 re-wrote the Table.
Other later copyists include Owen (pp. 173–204, 205–13, 228–35;
Rev pp. 1–9), Thoresby (pp. 85–8, 130, 236), Softley (pp. 111–12),
Leeke (pp. 40–2), and Laye (p. 110). Lay-clerks James Smart
(1660–97), Robert Softley (1697–1704), Richard Elford (1695–9;
afterwards in London where he achieved fame as a counter-tenor),
and Robert Hutchinson (1699–1700), who wrote their names
in a column inside the front cover, were presumably some of the
users of the book. Inscribed on the same page is 'J. Wilkinson'.
His position is less clear, for no lay-clerk of that name is known,
and he who was a chorister (1661–3) transferred immediately to
sackbutter.

293 × 197 mm. 131 ff., pag: II + ii (parchm) + 1–247; Rev:
II + 1–9.

## MS C15   Tenor. Anthems.

Opens (pp. 1–64) with nearly all the full anthems of MS C4
together with nine of the post-Restoration additions to that set.
Then follow most of the new items found under the slightly later
MS C34; and Child (2.), Croft (42.), Hooper (4.), R. Hucheson
(3.), M. Jeffries (3.), Mudd (1.3.), and W. Mundy (3.4.), many of
which are drawn from MS C2.

A post-Restoration replacement copy facilitating the continued
use of the repertoire of the 1630s. Pp. 78–9, in the hand of Elias
Smyth, cannot be later than 1676; the later pages were copied
by White (Table; pp. 79–98, 145–54), Owen (pp. 99–103,
122–35, 154–200, 205–20), Greggs (pp. 103–21, 201–4), Thoresby
(p. 136) and Softley (pp. 137–44). As well as scathing comments
on performance (e.g. pp. 86, 89), and lists of the choristers of
1798 (pp. 203, 221), there is the assertion 'George Chrishop
Organist of the Cathedral Church of Durham' (p. 213). This is
not some boyish self-glorification, for during the period 1796–
1803 Chrishop was paid for teaching and for copying music
(*see* Index of Copyists).

293 × 192 mm. 118 ff., pag: II + vi (parchm) + 1–148 + II + 72
(149–220) + iv (parchm) + II.

## MS C16   Bass. Anthems.

A compendium containing most of the anthems of MSS C2 and
C4 together with Palmer (5.). Added after 1660 were: Amner
(1.), Bryne (1.), Foster (5.10.11.), Giles (11.), R. Hucheson (3.),

J. Hutchinson (2.4.), Loosemore (2.6.), Mudd (1.), W. Mundy (3.), Nicholls (2.), R. Parsons [II] (2.), Strogers (1.), and Wilson.

Late 1630s. Copied by Brookinge and of the same date as MS C11, this MS too has its pages gilded and gauffered. Pp. 81–100, 239–44, 359–61 were added after 1660. The gilt tooling on the covers agrees with that on MS E11a.

299 × 192 mm. 219 ff., pag: IV + x + 418 (1–54, 56–84, 84a, 85–131, 133–290, 293–301, 303–422) + iv + II; with pp. 101–33, 245–93, and 362–402 blank.

## MS C17    Bass Cantoris. Anthems.

Nearly all the full anthems of MS C4, together with about two-fifths of MS C2. Its other anthems are very much the same as those added to MS C11 after the Restoration, including those for men's voices.

This MS re-uses the covers of the member of the C4 series it was replacing. Each of the three pages of its contemporary Table is dated 1675; and inside the back cover is 'Writt. by John White 1679', a statement corroborated by the known acquisition of anthems by Tucker (*see* pp. 183–9) in 1679. Stuck inside the front cover is the Service Sheet (ms, and imp) for June 1680.

311 × 201 mm. 103 ff., pag: II + viii + 1–192 + ii + II.

B. Crosby, 'A Service Sheet from June 1680', *Musical Times* (June 1980).

## MS C18    Bassus Decani. Services and Festal Psalms.

Batten (21.), Blancks, Byrd (31.), Farrant, Frost, O. Gibbons (27.29.), J. Gibbs, Giles (14.15.), Hooper (11.12.), M. Jeffries (4.), Morley (5.6.), W. Mundy (8.11.), Parsons of Wells, R. Parsons [I] (4.), Randall, Edw. Smythe (9.), T. Tomkins (19.), and Weelkes (6.8.).

1620s and 1630s. The sole survivor of a set of ten books 'with black Covers for verse Services' (*see* Misc. Ch. 7116). Its principal (pp. 3–73) and second hands (pp. 75–9), Todd and Brookinge, worked on the other sets dating from this period (*see* MSS C2, C4, C8, and E4); the third hand (pp. 80–94) has not been identified. Many of the corresponding organ parts—also copied by Todd— enjoyed individual existences before they were bound into MS A2. The embossed covers have gilt tooling.

341 × 226 mm. 47 ff., pag: II + 90 (3–84, 87–94) + II.

**MS C19**   Bass Decani, no. 4. Anthems and Services.

The earliest part (pp. 1–80, 145–292, 329–30, 341–403) repeats most of the anthems of MSS C4 and C2, the early post-Restoration additions to those series, and the anthems for men's voices (*see* MS C11). More of the later part of MS C11 is represented, and other additions make its contents compatible with those of MSS C34, C21, and B12. Not in any of those MSS are anon (52.), Church (1.), Hesletine (1.), and G. Holmes (1.). *Rev*: With the exception of the later Kyrie by Mason, the 12 services are from those listed under MS C21v.

1660s through to *c*.1771. Like Brit. Lib. Add. MS 30479, the basic part is in the hand of Shaw, pp. 80–1 being added by him in 1671. Other copyists include White (pp. 294–307), Softley (pp. 83–97), Leeke (pp. 308–17), Laye (pp. 99–117, 318–27, 331–3, 404–8; Rev pp. 3–12), Brass (pp. 334–40, 409–82; Rev pp. 21–76), and Mathews (pp. 483–90).

300 × 190 mm. 289 ff., pag: II + vi + 1–490; Rev: II + ii + 1–76. Pp. 1–14, 15–80, 145–293 were originally pp. 37–50, 59–125, 126–273 (with several numeration errors).

**MS C19A**   Tenor. Anthems and Services.

Of the same set as MS C21. *Forw*: now lacks the last 16 anthems; additional are H. Purcell (17.32.34), and Wise (2.). *Rev*: adds Blow (17.28.29.), Byrd (24.), and O. Gibbons (28.).

Dated 1730 (p. 87) to 1738 (p. 168); Rev, 1718 (p. 9) to 1737 (p. 101). Copyists include Laye (pp. 26, 29–34, 35–46; Rev pp. 9–39) and Brass (pp. 66–171; Rev pp. 54–101). Mathews re-copied pp. 1–24 in 1772 (p. 24), repairing Rev (e.g. p. 8) at the same time.

308 × 200 mm. 144 ff., pag: IV + iv + 1–171; Rev: IV + ii + 103 (105–6, 1–101).

**MS C20**   Alto Cantoris. Services and Anthems.

To be considered with MS B18. *Forw*: has most of the services; additional are Luther's Hymn (printed) and Raylton. *Rev*: lacks the 'Ebdon' corpus, but includes most of the other anthems. Adds about half of the anthems of MS C22v.

Dated 1813 (p. 19) to 1826 (p. 144); Rev, 1817 (p. 30) to 1826 (p. 89). Radcliffe copied pp. 1–25, Rev. pp. 1–10.

283 × 235 mm. 123 ff., pag: ii + II + 148 (1–58, 58a–b, 59–84, 84a–b, 85–144); Rev: ii + II + 1–90.

**MS C21**   Tenor. Anthems and Services.

Double-ended, the anthems being at one end and the services at the other, MSS B20, B21, C19A, C21, C29, and C35 are all members of the same set.

Apart from items appearing in only one MS, the anthems are: Aldrich (2.3.5.10.13.15.), Avison, Bassani (2.), G. Bononcini (1.), Bull (4.), Byrd (4.21.), Church (5.), Clarke (4.9.), Croft (5.6.8.12. 15.18.28.32–9.41–3.48.51.53.56.58.59.64.65.67.68.), Falle (1.), Goldwin (1.2.4.6.), Greene (1.4–7.10–12.14–16.20–3.25.26.34. 36.39.41.), Handel (1.21.29.44.), Jas Hawkins (2.), [Howard], Humfrey (2.), Locke (3.), Marcello (2.), W. Mundy (3.), Nares (4.8.11.14.), H. Purcell (3.19.31.32.), Stroud, Turner (8.), and Weldon (3–5.).

Similarly, the services are: Aldrich (16.18.), Bacon (2; added later), Croft (71.), Dean, Goodson, Greene (43.), Hall and Hine, C. King (7.), Lamb (1.), Patrick, H. Purcell (36.37.), Rogers (6.), Tallis (11.14.), Travers (4.), Tudway (8.), Walkley, Wanless (1.), and Wise (12.13.).

Additional in C21 are Battishill (1.), Fiocco, Mason (5.6.) (all anthems); Creighton (3.), and Nares (15.) (services); and a chant (tenor only) by T. Davis.

Dated: c.1710 (pp. 3–8) to 1744 (p. 195) and c.1775 (p. 201); Rev, 1718 (p. 13) to 1742 (p. 143). The copyists include Leeke (pp. 3–8), Laye (pp. 9–35, 41–57; Rev pp. 1–48), Brass (pp. 78–198; Rev pp. 49–159), and Mathews (pp. 198–201). A copyist with a hand resembling that of James Kent's in Brit. Lib. Add. MS 31461 transcribed pp. 57–77; but those responsible for pp. 36–41 and Handel (1.), and for Bononcini and Croft (32.) have not been identified. In most cases each copied the same items into all members of the set.

301 × 188 mm. 183 ff., pag: IV + 200 (3–130, 130a, 131–201); Rev: IV + 158 (1–75, 78–108, 108a–b, 109–59; p. 159 = Forw p. 201).

**MS C22**   Precentor's Book, Bass. Services and Anthems.

About half the services of MS B18. *Rev*: MSS B4, B15, C20v, C22v, D20v, and D22v have the following corpus of anthems in common: Beethoven (5.), Boyce (6.9.13.), Clarke[-Whitfeld] (2.), Croft (49.), O. Gibbons (20.), Hall (2.4.), Handel (8.10.18.24.32.),

Hasse (1.), Haydn (1.3–7.10.11.17.), P. Hayes (2.3.), Lotti,
Luther, Mason (1.), Mozart (5.), Pergolesi (1.2.), H. Purcell
(4.16.22.25.27.), Rolle, Salvatore, Sarti, Spohr (2.), Tye (4.),
Webbe (3.), Weldon (9.10.). Additional in C22 are Allinson (1.),
Garth (2.), Handel (39.), and Mendelssohn (2.).

Dated 1817 (p. 16) to 1843 (p. 91); Rev, 1819 (p. 28) to 1843
(p. 150).

278 × 228 mm. 127 ff., pag: vi + 1–91; Rev: vi + 1–151.

## MS C23   Bass. Services and Anthems.

To be considered with MS B18. *Forw*: the services are: Blow
(29.), Boyce (16.), Chard (1.), Clarke[-Whitfeld] (4.), R. Cooke,
Fussel, Handel (4.), C. King (9.), Nares (16.), and Walsh (1.). *Rev*:
most of the anthems, together with Handel (44.).

Dated 1813 (p. 20) to 1826 (p. 70); Rev, 1807 (p. 20) to 1826
(p. 116). Ebdon copied Rev pp. 1–60 (mostly hol), and Radcliffe
pp. 1–26 and Rev pp. 62–88.

278 × 228 mm. 101 ff., pag: vi + 1–70; Rev: viii + 1–118.

## MS C24   Bass. Services and Anthems.

Services as for MS C23, with Croft (72.) instead of Blow (29.).
*Rev*: most of the anthems of MS B18.

Dated 1813 (p. 21) to 1817 (p. 78); Rev, 1804 (p. 12) to 1817
(p. 107). Copyists include Ebdon (Rev pp. 1–23, 25–60; hol), and
Radcliffe (pp. 1–26, Rev pp. 62–88).

280 × 227 mm. 100 ff., pag: VI + 1–78; Rev: VIII + 1–108.

## MS C25   Bass. Services.

Most of the services of MS B18, together with Bishop (2.).

Dated 1813 (p. 20) to 1826 (p. 138), pp. 1–26 being copied by
Radcliffe (cf. MS C23). MSS C20, C23, C24, and C25 were begun
at the same time.

277 + 235 mm. 71 ff., pag: IV + 1–138.

## MS C26   Bass. Services and Anthems.

Compared with the services of MS C32, the oldest part lacks
only J. Farrant and T. Tomkins (18.). Added later were Aldrich
(18.), Croft (71.), H. Purcell (32.36.), Rogers (6.), and Tudway
(8.). *Rev*: nine chants (bass part only; cf. MSS C12 and C28)

followed by anthems by Croft (8.32.39.42.), Goldwin (6.), Greene (14.20.), Stroud, and Weldon (3.4.).

The earliest part (pp. 1–140, 181–294) was copied by Owen early in the 1690s. Additions through to 1718 (p. 347) were made by Softley (pp. 305–15), Leeke (pp. 317–27), Laye (pp. 146–73, 327–47; Rev pp. 4–14), and others.

335 × 225 mm. 198 ff., pag: IV + 1–348; Rev: IV + 40 (3–42).

## MS C27    Bass. Anthems.

The oldest sections are very much as MS C34. Additional are Aldrich (5.6.), Byrd (2.), Child (3.17.), Clarke (2.5.12.14.16.), Croft (5.11.18.44.45.57.58.64.68.), Fiocco, O. Gibbons (10.), Hesletine (1.4.), Humfrey (1.11.), J. Mundy (2.), H. Purcell (1.), Tudway (3.7.), Turner (4.), and Wise (10.11.). Some 22 of these are in MS B12.

Begun in the 1690s, the earliest parts (pp. 1–58, 67–91, 116–62, 182–292) were copied by Owen. The remainder was added early in the 18th cent.—see 'P[exall]. F[orster]. June 21, 1711' (p. 377)— chiefly by Softley (pp. 328–36), Leeke (pp. 60, 94–6, 163–74, 340–3, 346–82), Parkinson (pp. 92, 336–8), and Laye (pp. 61–6, 97–115, 175–81, 383–411).

342 × 234 mm. 211 ff., pag: IV + 414 (1–3, 3a, 4–388, 388a–b, 389–411) + IV.

## MS C28    Bass. Anthems and Chants.

Originally very much as MS C34. The bass part of 25 early chants (pp. 507f–h; cf. MSS C12 and C26) includes ['Canterbury' and 'Imperial' (see anon 32.), Blow (32.), Child (25.), Humfrey (14.), Purcell, H. Purcell (39.), T. Purcell, and Turner (11.)]. Other additions made the MS usable with MSS C21 and B12. Anthems by Aldrich (8.12.), W. Jones, and Kent (2.3.5.7.9.13.14; all in *Kent 1*) are not in any of those MSS (cf. MS B16).

The earliest parts (pp. 1–60, 65–109, 129–42, 161–323) were transcribed by Owen in the 1690s. Softley added pp. 61–3, 323–8, 400–22 and Brass pp. 110–28, 143–60, 426–507, 508–45; and the MS continued to be added to until 1794 (p. 605). With Brass active in this MS until 1772 (p. 545) as opposed to 1761 in other MSS, the possibility arises of it being the MS he himself used. Some of the chants have been identified from Brit. Lib. Add. MS 17784, which gives nos. 1–21 in the same order; others from an unnumbered MS at Chichester.

340 × 245 mm. 283 ff., pag: IV + xiv + 542 (1–329, 400–507, 507a–h, 508–91, 593–605) + ii + II.

## MS C29    Bass Cantoris, no. 7. Services and Anthems.

Of the same set as MS C21, plus Croft (45.) and Hesletine (3.).

Payments range from 'A. Y[app].' (p. 8; prec, 1711–16) to 1741 (p. 139); Rev, 'A.Y.' (p. 7) to 1744 (p. 192). Copyists include Leeke (pp. 1–8), Laye (pp. 8–24, 44–6; Rev pp. 1–29, 32, 37–9), and Brass (pp. 61–147; Rev pp. 39, 62–194). Four early anthems missing from Rev are found preceding the services at the front of the MS.

308 × 188 mm. 173 ff., pag: ii + 148 (1–120, 120a, 121–2, 122a, 123–47; p. 147 = Rev p. 194); Rev: vi + 190 (1–14, 21–103, 105–36, 136a, 137–85, 185a–b, 186–94).

## MS C30    Bass, no. 9. Services.

About three-fifths of the services of MS B7.

Late 18th cent. Inscribed: 'I give this book containing 222 Pages of MS Music to the Cathedral Church of Durham. Fras. H. Egerton' (p. iii). Egerton (preb, 1780–1829) also donated MS B26. Chrishop copied pp. 223–5.

294 × 226 mm. 112 ff., pag: iv + 220 (1–201, 212–30), with later pages torn away.

## MS C31    Bass. Services.

The oldest part is similar in content to MS C32, lacking only services by J. Farrant, Hilton (5.), W. Mundy (9.), and T. Tomkins (18.). Though the services added later are very like those of MS B35, it is more accurate to say that they were all that were necessary to make the contents comparable to those of MS B7.

The oldest parts (pp. 1–150, 185–311) were transcribed by Owen in the early 1690s; the rest dates from before 1750, Brass being the copyist.

345 × 244 mm. 223 ff., pag: IV + 438 (1–160, 162–81, 185–442) + IV.

## MS C32    Bass. Services.

The oldest parts of MSS C26, C31, C32, and C33 are the work of one copyist (cf. MS C34). With minor differences their common corpus is: Batten (18.), Bevin, Blow (28.30.31.), T. Boyce, Bryne (2.), Byrd (30.), Child (17–24.), Derrick,

J. Farrant, R. Farrant (3.), Foster (13.), O. Gibbons (28.), Hilton (5.), Humfrey (13.), Loosemore (8.), W. Mundy (10.), Nicholls (3.), R. Parsons [II] (4.), Patrick, H. Purcell (36.), Read (2.), Tallis (14.), T. Tomkins (18.), Tucker (10.), Weelkes (7.), and Wilkinson (12.).

1690s. Copied entirely by Owen. Pp. 1–149 draw heavily on the repertoire of the 1630s as represented by MS C8. Like MS C34, its companion volume, it is bound in black leather and belonged (so pp. 104, 176) to John Montague, Dean of Durham, 1700–28.

340 × 250 mm. 160 ff., pag: IV + viii + 1–304 + IV, with pp. 150–60, 284–304 blank.

**MS C33**  Bass. Services [and Anthems].

All the services of MS C32, together with services and anthems by Bacon (1.2.), Blow (29.), Boyce (4.), Child (more of 20.), Foster (more of 13.), Gregory (1.), H. Purcell (37.), and Stephens (1.).

1690s. The oldest parts (pp. 118–73, 189–226, 231–317) were copied by Owen. As for pp. 1–117, 317–28, Mathews in 1771 (p. 328) simply re-copied the older pages, adding the extra items.

295 × 191 mm. 170 ff., pag: IV + iv (parchm) + 1–328 + IV.

**MS C34**  Bass. Anthems.

The oldest parts of MSS C27, C28, and C34 stem from the same copyist (*see* MS C32). They include some 35 of the anthems of the 1630s and 1660s together with those added by their copyist to MSS C7, C14, and C15. Including a number of slightly later additions the common corpus is: anon (37.), Aldrich (4.7.9.13.), Alison, Allinson (1–4.), Batten (3.4.7.9.10.12.), Blow (1.3.5.10.12–17. 20–2.24.26.27.29.), Byrd (12.15.16.20), Child (1.5.6.8.10.11. 13.14.), Clarke (15.), Club Anthem, Croft (20.34.), Forcer, Foster (4.5.8.11.), Geeres (3.), O. Gibbons (6.13.15.20.23.), Goldwin (2.), Greggs (1.3–6.), Hall (1.), Jas Hawkins (3.), Jn Hawkins (2.), Hesletine (3.), Hilton (1.), Hooper (3.4.9.), Humfrey (2.3.5–8. 10.12.), J. Hutchinson (1–4.), W. King (1.), H. Lawes (2.), W. Lawes (2.), Locke (3.4.), Loosemore (6.), Morley (3.), Mudd (2.4.5.), W. Mundy (2.), Nicholls (1.2.), W. Norris (1.2.), R. Parsons [I] (1.2.), R. Parsons [II] (2.), Peerson (1.), Pickering (1.), Preston, H. Purcell (2.6a.8.9.11.14.17–20.23.24.30.33–5.), Read, Rogers (4.), Rutter, Tallis (4.7.9.), T. Tomkins (14.17.), Tucker (1–6.8.9.), Tudway (1.5.), Turner (6.10.), Warwick, Weelkes (4.), R. White (1.), Wilson, and Wise (1.2.4.6.8.9.).

Additional in C34 are Byrd (17.), Croft (33.), Hodge (1.2.), and Wanless (2.).

Early 1690s. Bound distinctively in black leather like MS C32, its companion volume, this was not an ordinary choir book. On the recto of the back flyleaf is written, 'this book belongeth to John Montague Dean of Durham' (1700–28). The books, however, were probably written for his predecessor, for the Audit Book for 1692–3 records the binding of 'Mr Deanes Songe Bookes', the copyist (apart from pp. 90–5, 121–8, 305–19) being Owen.

339 × 247 mm. 172 ff., pag: IV + x + 324 (1–307, 312–28) + ii + IV.

**MS C35**  Tenor. Services and Anthems.

Of the same set as MS C21. Bacon (2.) and Handel (7.) are additional.

Dated 1735 (p. 55) to 1741 (p. 98); Rev, 1718 (p. 13) to 1741 (p. 177). Copyists include Leeke (Rev pp. 1–5), Laye (pp. 15–22, 25–35; Rev pp. 5–15, 21–7), and Brass (pp. 41–98; Rev pp. 17, 47–182). Mathews added and re-copied pp. 99–14 [*sic*], 23–4, Rev p. 27a in 1772. Compared with MS C21, this MS lacks anthems from both the beginning and the end.

309 × 190 mm. 149 ff., pag: II + ii + 104 (99–104, 1–98); Rev: II + iv + 184 (1–18, 18a, 19–27, 27a, 28–68, 68a, 69–178, 180–2).

**MS D1**  Full score of 'Messiah. A Christ-Mass Song for Voices and Instruments', a romantic work by [Thomas Drake].

1st quarter 18th cent. Holograph. Corelli's VIIIth Concerto [Op. 6], entitled 'Fatto per la notte di Natale', was used as its Overture (so p. xviii), and the work begins 'The night was dark and silent'. Though the MS itself merely records that it was donated in 1747 by Thomas Drake, Vicar of Norham, Minor Canon of Durham Cathedral 1714–20, the Book of Acquisitions (MS A.IV.32, f. 87) makes it clear that Drake had composed both this work and 'Hymnus Ambrosianus' (MS E1).

296 × 233 mm. 61 ff., pag: xviii + 1–100 + iv.

**MS D2**  Three part-books of Sonatas, etc., some for two violins and a bass, others for viols.

Music by [Jenkins] (1–3; 15 items) predominates. Other composers are: Abel, Becker, Butler (1–4.), Farinel, Mat[t]eis, Nicolai

(1.), Norcombe (1.), Schmelzer (1.2.), Schnittelbach, Young (1–3.6.), Zamponi, and anon (74–82.).

c.1680. Original numbers 32–44, by [Jenkins], are in virtually the same order in Brit. Lib. Add. MS 29369. Somewhat unusual is the use of numbers instead of vowels in certain names, viz. 'B5tl2[r]', 'M1t23s', and 'N3C4L13'. On a flyleaf of D2/2 there is 'for the honorabl. Sir John St. Barbe Bart neare Rumsey in Hampsheere'. St Barbe (1655–1723), a previous owner of Broadlands, was a pupil of Christopher Simpson who dedicated *The Principles of Practical Music* (1665) to him. Similarly, in D2/3, there is 'John Freyd 1678', and, in pencil, 'in the old Jorry belo the Church att a barber. M$^s$. Steffken'. These MSS, and MSS A27, D4, D5, and D10, formed part of Philip Falle's donation (*see* Durham Add. MS 154).

312 × 204 mm. *D2/1*, Viol: 1$^o$: 39 ff., pag: iv + 1–70 + iv; *D2/2*, Viol:2$^o$: 40 ff., pag: iv + 1–72 + iv; *D2/3*, Bass: 32 ff., pag: iv + 1–56 + iv.

**MS D3** 'Pieces for the Forte Piano, Violin or Flute', by Thomas Ebdon [and others].

Some 58 incidental pieces entitled Andante, Allegro, Minuetto, Rondo, Vivace, March, etc. Nos. 15, 33, and 34 bear the initials 'M. E.' (no doubt Mary Ebdon, his daughter), whilst no. 56 is ascribed to the Polish dwarf, Count Joseph Boruwlaski.

c.1800. Transcribed by T. Ebdon, two of the Marches being dated 1788 (p. 27) and 1797 (p. 28).

295 × 240 mm. 22 ff., pag: ii + 1–40 + ii.

**MS D4** 'Fantasies for three Viols', in separate part-books.

Jenkins (4–6; 6 items), P. Poul (1–3; composer? unique to D4), Schutz, Young (4.5.), and anon (83.84.). Young (4.5.) and Poul (1.) are attributed elsewhere to Jenkins.

Late 17th cent. Given to the Library by Philip Falle (*see* MS D2 and Durham Add. MS 154), but at some time owned by 'A Koon' whose name is written on the front flyleaf of each book.

312 × 204 mm. *D4/1*, [Viol 1$^o$]: 14 ff., pag: ii + 1–24 + ii; *D4/2*, [Viol 2$^o$]: 14 ff., pag: ii + 1–25 + i; *D4/3*, [Bass]: 6 ff., pag: ii + 1–8 + ii.

**MS D5** Three part-books of Sonatas, etc., some for violin, viola [da gamba], and bass, others for two viola da gamba and bass.

Composers are Butler (1.3.4.), Claussen, Jenkins (5–7; 5 items), Young (4.), Zamponi, and anon (85–7.).

Late 17th cent. Given to the Library by Philip Falle (*see* MS D2 and Durham Add. MS 154).

310 × 202 mm. 12 ff. each, pag: 1–24. *D5/1*, Violin; *D5/2*, Viola; *D5/3*, Bass.

**MS D6**   A mainly holograph collection of varying numbers of the single parts of some 13 harpsichord sonatas and concertos by Thomas Ebdon.

Seven are dated, and belong to the period 1769 to June 1781. None of them features in Ebdon's *Six Sonatas for the Harpsichord . . . two Violins and a Violoncello (c.*1765).

247 × 345 mm (harpsichord parts, in coarse paper covers), and 303 × 246 mm (instrumental parts). In all some 212 pp., of which 31 are blank.

**MS D7**   25 single parts of 'Dettingen Grand Te Deum Laudamus' and 'The King shall rejoice', both by G. F. Handel.

*c.*1760. In the hand of Mathews. A comparison with the list in MS A32, the companion full score, shows that all 10 vocal parts are still extant, whilst of the 17 instrumental parts only one Violino Primo and one Violoncello part are now missing.

251 × 305 mm (vocal parts), and 303 × 243 mm (instrumental parts). In all 302 pp., 3 being blank.

**MS D8**   30 single parts of the Oratorio 'Joshua', by G. F. Handel.

*c.*1760. In the hand of Mathews. A comparison with the list in MS A24, the companion full score, shows that the original complement of 13 vocal and 17 instrumental parts is still intact.

Mainly 243 × 305 mm, though 10 instrumental parts are 305 × 245 mm. In all 612 pp., 13 being blank.

**MS D9**   Songs and Catches.

Anon (26.28.33.69.), Blow (34.35.), Courteville (1–3.), Ellis, R. King (2.), Locke (6.), Logg, H. Purcell (40–3.47–50.), and Turner (12.); with the text only of songs by Godfrey and Marvell. Apart from the textual items, only Courteville (3.) and Purcell (41.43.49.) are ascribed.

Early 18th cent. Inside the front cover are the names 'Falle' (not autograph, nor is this MS referred to in Durham Add. MS 154) and 'Roland Bainbridge his Book'; and at the back 'S$^r$ Thomas Michaell George Shotton Esquir'.

100 × 207 mm. 29 ff., pag: 1–50; Rev: 1–8.

**MS D10**   Full score of music for viols.

Butler (1–12; 18 items), Jenkins (9.10.), Nicolai (2–4.), Norcombe (2.), T. Steffkin, Webster, Young (1.3.7–10.), [Zamponi], and anon (90.). Elsewhere Nicolai (2.) is attributed to Jenkins, and Zamponi to Butler.

Late 17th cent. The MS falls into three sections: pp. 1–33 contain Sonatas for two and three viola da gamba with bass continuo; pp. 90–175 mainly Divisions for solo viola da gamba, together with three Suites; and pp. 212–30 trios for two violins and a viola da gamba. Given to the Library by Philip Falle (*see* MS D2 and Durham Add. MS 154).

115 × 230 mm. 161 ff., pag: ii + 1–318 + ii; with pp. 34–89, 176–211, and 231–318 blank.

**MS D11**   11 Catches and Glees, for three voices, by Thomas Ebdon (nos. 65–75).

Late 18th or early 19th cent. Holograph. A solo version of 'The Lapland Song' (no. 75) was published in his *Six Favorite Songs* (Op. 4, no. 4 [*c*.1797]).

160 × 230 mm. 25 ff., pag: 1–50.

**MS D12**   Ten late 19th and early 20th cent. chant books used in the cathedral until *c*.1947 when they were replaced by a printed collection (pub. 1939) which drew extensively on them.

Because of the enormous number—over 400, though there are duplications—and because of their minor importance, especially bearing in mind the lateness of the MSS, no description of the chants is given here, nor are they included in the major index. This list of composers (* denotes Durham connection) must suffice:

J. Alcock, H. Aldrich, *P. Armes, S. Arnold, R. A. Atkins, T. Attwood, T. Ayleward, E. Ayrton, J. Barnby, [J.] Barrett, J. Barrow, J. Battishill, arr from Beethoven, A. Bennett, W. S. Bennett, W. R. Bexfield, J. Blow, W. Boyce, J. F. Bridge, J. L. Brownsmith, Z. Buck, E. Bunnett, J. Camidge, M. Camidge, G. S. Carter, F. Champneys, E. T. Chipp, B. Cooke, R. Cooke,

*V. K. Cooper, Corfe, H. A. Coward, W. Crotch, E. J. Crow, *A. D. Culley, [E.] Cutler, de Lacy, T. S. Dupuis, Dutton, *J. B. Dykes, *T. Ebdon, G. J. Elvey, S. Elvey, R. Farrant, W. Felton, L. Flintoft, J. Foster, *Rev. C. Fowler, E. J. Frost, P. Fussell, G. M. Garrett, H. J. Gauntlett, C. Gibbons, W. B. Gilbert, R. P. Good-enough, R. Goodson, J. Goss, *E. Greatorex, M. Greene, W. H. Havergal, P. Hayes, W. Hayes, G. Heathcote, P. Henley, F. A. J(?G). Hervey, H. Hiles, J. Hindle, W. Hine, Hodges, E. J. Hopkins, J. L. Hopkins, P. Humfrey, W. Jacobs, J. Jones, T. Kel-way, Kenningham, C. King, *Rev. Canon Kynaston, R. Langdon, arr from H. Lawes, W. Lee, *A. G. Leigh, J. Lemon, *F. Lingard, G. A. Macfarren, J. Marsh, S. Matthews, E. G. Monk, W. Morley, Earl of Mornington, J. Nares, J. Naylor, J. Nicholson, T. Norris, V. Novello, H. S. Oakeley, F. A. G. Ouseley, H. H. Pierson, [J.] Pring, Purcell, K. J. Pye, [T.] Pymar, J. Randall, S. Reay, E. F. Rimbault, Jn Robinson, Joseph Robinson, H. Rogers, J. L. Rogers, *T. Rogers, R. Roseingrave, G. C. Rowden, W. Russell, St. Audries, W. Savage, H. Skeats jun, H. Smart, M. Smith, J. Soaper, [?F.] Southgate, W. Speare, S. Spofforth, from Spohr, J. Stainer, [C. V.] Stanford, C. Steggall, C. E. Stephens, S. J. Stephens, T. Tallis, ?Tenterton, J. Travers, J. Turle, W. Turner, Bp. [T.] Turton, Walker, T. A. Walmisley, T. Wanless, J. Weldon, S. Wesley, S. S. Wesley, H. West, C. J. Whittington, C. A. Wickes, Winn, Woods, R. Woodward, and [J.] Worgan.

Until 1967, D12 embraced only D12/1. Since then D12/2–5 have been transferred from the choir library, D12/10 donated by G. H. Christie in 1967, and D12/6–9 given in 1974 by Dr C. W. Eden (Organist, 1936–74), the compiler of the printed collection. Though in most of the MSS Philip Armes (Organist, 1862–1907; copied all except D12/10) states that he selected Set A in 1874 and enlarged it in 1886 when he introduced Set B, in D12/9 he claims that Set A dated back to 1863. This latter claim is supported by the Chapter Minutes for 31 October 1863, where it is stated that the new chants may be used for a further week when the old ones are to be resumed—it looks as if Armes had introduced them without seeking permission. Several books contain chants for Feast Days and for the Canticles, whilst D12/10 includes a selection for men's voices.

**D12/1**: Alto, Set A and chants for Feast Days, etc. Described as 'The Chants used in Durham Cathedral. (Oct$^r$. 1874)'. Signed 'P.A. 25.9.74' (p. 32). 240 × 154 mm. 24 ff., pag: 1–48.

**D12/2**: Alto Cantoris. Double-ended. *Forw*: has Set A which was

'Selected & arranged by P.A. in 1874. Enlarged in 1886' (p. 63). Followed by chants for Feast Days, etc. *Rev*: has Set B, which was 'Selected & arranged by P.A. July 1886' (p. 63). Once both sets were in use, Set A was used in odd months, Set B in the even. 164 × 231 mm. 82 ff., pag: ii + 97 (Forw) + 63 (Rev) + ii.

**D12/3**: Tenor Decani. Details as D12/2.

**D12/4**: Tenor Cantoris. Details as D12/2, apart from: 83 ff., pag: ii + 99 (Forw) + 63 (Rev) + ii, with comment about Set A on p. 65.

**D12/5**: Bass Cantoris, no. 2. Details as D12/2, apart from: 85 ff., pag: iv + 97 (Forw) + 63 (Rev) + vi.

**D12/6**: Full, Set A. 'The Chants used in Durham Cathedral. Selected and arranged by Philip Armes' (p. 1), the 1874 and 1886 dates being recorded on p. 63. 300 × 241 mm. 33 ff., pag: ii + 1–64.

**D12/7**: Full, Set B. 'Selected July 1886. P.A.' (p. 63). At the bottom of p. 2 there is '. . . Friday Oct. 1. 1886', presumably the date when Set B was brought into use. 300 × 241 mm. 32 ff., pag: 1–64.

**D12/8**: Full, chants for Feast Days, etc. 300 × 241 mm. 21 ff., pag: ii + 1–40.

**D12/9**: Bass, Set A, Set B, and chants for Feast Days, etc. The original owner was 'J. T. Fowler, Apr. 26. 1902, Most kindly copied for me by Dr. Armes. J.T.F.' (p. v). 'The "A" Coll$^n$ was selected & arranged by P.A. in 1863, Enlarged in 1874, and again in 1886' (p. 18); and Set B in 1886 (p. 36). 305 × 242 mm. 29 ff., pag: vi + 1–48 + iv, with pp. 43 *et seq.* blank.

**D12/10**: Full, Set A, Set B, and 'Evening Chants for Men's Voices'. Set B is dated 1886 (p. 127), and the chants for men's voices were 'Arranged by Dr. Armes Oct: 1901' (p. 129). 'Copied by Joseph S. Lisle, June 1st 1913' (p. 144). In 1933 it was owned by G. H. Christie. 312 × 233 mm. 86 ff., pag: vi + 1–160 + vi, pp. 145 *et seq.* being blank.

**MSS D13** and **D14**  A set of eight part-books containing, in the same order, only the choruses of 18 of Croft's verse anthems (nos. 1.3.4.12.15.19.25.28.35.38.39.43.55.57.60.64.66.67.).

Early 18th cent. Different clefs and a different style of writing, especially in the Tables, point to the last two or three anthems—it varies from MS to MS—being transcribed at a later date, possibly by a different hand. Gates, Hughes, and Freemantle are named as soloists in 'O praise God in his sanctuary', and Hughes in 'O give

thanks . . . and call'. 'O praise God in his sanctuary' was composed
for the opening of the organ at Finedon, Northants., in 1717, and
these Gentlemen of the Chapel Royal were present on that
occasion. Although Kent was the first organist there, it has not
been established whether the MSS were connected with Finedon.
Written inside the front cover of each book is 'J. Hands'. This name
also appears in similar fashion in Royal College of Music MSS 1101
and 2230, 'Birmingham' being added in both in contracted form.
Hands must have been either connected with or interested in Croft
who had earlier owned both those MSS.

155 × 203 mm. Three fifths of each book is blank. *D13/1*,
T[reble] C[antoris]; *D13/2*, C[ounter-tenor] C[antoris]; *D13/3*,
T[enor] C[antoris]; *D13/4*, C[antoris] B[ass]: each 52 ff., pag:
iv + 1–96 + iv; *D14/1*, T[reble] D[ecani]: 56 ff., pag: iv + 1–104
+ iv; *D14/2*, C[ounter-tenor] D[ecani]: 53 ff., pag: iv + 1–98 + iv;
*D14/3*, T[enor] D[ecani]: 58 ff., pag: iv + 1–108 + iv; *D14/4*, B[ass]
D[ecani]: details as for *D14/1*.

**MS D15**  11 vocal and 20 instrumental single parts of the
Cannons' (1720) version of 'The Oratorio of Esther', by [Handel].

? Early 18th cent. The singers named on the covers are: Sig^ra
Frasi (Esther), Richard Steel (Boy's part), Mrs Scott (Priestess),
Mr Tho. Baildon (Alto), Mr Beard (Assuerus and Mordecai), Mr
Joseph Baildon (2nd Tenor), and Mr Wass (Haman). This indicates
a late performance of the work, for Mrs Scott did not marry until
1757, and Thomas Baildon died in 1762. The initials 'CWW' and
a crest consisting of an Angola goat and the motto 'Avito jure'
have been stamped on all the coarse paper covers. In addition, the
name 'C. W. Wheeler' is written in ink on the covers of all the
non-vocal parts. One of that name lived from 1792 to 1863—but
Arne and Mrs Cibber feature in the same family tree (*Fowke alias
Wheeler*, by J. M. Wheeler, p. '67'). Further single part fragments
of ? a different performance of 'Esther' are grouped under MS
E35(iii). Some verse and some dance instructions are loose at the
back of D15/13.

240 × 300 mm for the voice and organ bass parts, the instrumental parts being 296 × 237 mm. In all 752 pp., of which one is
printed and 48 either blank or other matter.

**MS D16**  Full score of 'Opera Ottone' by [Handel], the text being
in Italian. Added in a later hand is a two-stave realization of
[Handel's] 'Overture to Radamistus'.

*c.*1725. The early date is proposed because of the absence of four arias added to the work on 26 March 1723, and the MS is said to be in the hand of J. C. Smith the elder. Presented to the Library in 1928 by Algernon Armes, eldest son of Philip Armes (org, 1862–1907).

224 × 282 mm. 105 ff., pag: ii + 1–206 + ii. Red leather cover, ornately tooled in gilt, the edges of the pages gilded also.

## MS D17    Bass Decani, no. 8. Anthems and Services.

With nine anthems from *Walmisley*, seven from *Wesley*, thirteen from *Greene*, and five from *Gibbons* (two now attrib to Loosemore), this late MS served to compensate for an insufficiency of those printed volumes. Remaining anthems are: Armes (1.), Beckwith (1.), Callcott, Dykes (2.), G. J. Elvey (2.), Goss (2.), Handel (37.), Kent (9.), Mendelssohn (6.), Mozart (2.), and Tallis (10.). *Rev*: five services from *Walmisley* are followed by Aldrich (18.), Armes (3.), Attwood, Bryne (2.), Goss (3.), Hopkins, Skelton, Turle (2.), and S. S. Wesley (10.), only those by Aldrich and Bryne being in any other Durham MS.

Dated 1867 (p. 73) to 1872 (p. 125); Rev, 1864 (p. 54) to 1869 (p. 119). Brown began both ends (to p. 125 and Rev p. 119); Walker completed them.

326 × 233 mm. 158 ff., pag: II + ii + 160 (1–38, 67–188); Rev: II + ii + 1–148.

## MS D18    Bass. Anthems and Services.

Of the same set as MS D21. *Forw*: most of the anthems together with half the Ebdon corpus plus Corfe (1.) and Garth (3.) (cf. MS B18v); and Beckwith (1.), Blow (3.5.7.), Byrd (5.18.), Child (14.), O. Gibbons (15.16.), Handel (20.32.34.), H. Purcell (19–21.35.), Tallis (9.), and Tye (3.). *Rev*: most of the services. Additional are Blow (28.), Boyce (2.), Chard (1.), Croft (71.), Clarke[-Whitfeld] (4.), O. Gibbons (28.), Goldwin (7.), C. King (5.6.), and Patrick, most of these being from the *Boyce* and *Arnold* volumes.

Dated 1848 (p. 224; Rev p. 151) to 1851 (p. 294; Rev p. 179). Copied by Brown.

355 × 252 mm. 234 ff., pag: II + ii + 1–294; Rev: II + 168 (11–179; p. 179 = Forw p. 294).

## MS D19    Alto. Anthems and Services.

Of the same set as MS D21. *Forw*: most of the anthems, together with Banks (1.), Blow (20.), Boyce (3.), Goldwin (3.), Greene (7.20.37.), Handel (1.8.), Haydn (3.), Hilton (3.), C. King (2.), Marenzio (3.), Nares (2–6.8–10.12.13; nine are in *Nares*), Richardson, Rogers (3.), Stroud, Tucker (6.), and all of *Pratt* (in order). *Rev*: 10 of the 12 services of *Arnold 2 and 3* and Handel's 'Dettingen Te Deum' are interrupted by Hudson and followed by the services of MS D21v.

Dated 1844 (p. 66; Rev p. 145) to 1850 (p. 229; Rev p. 202). Copied by Brown.

339 × 250 mm. 216 ff., pag: II + iv + 228 (1–216, 219–30); Rev: II + ii + 194 (1–156, 165–202).

**MS D20**  Alto. Services and Anthems.

All six services from *Arnold 1*, five from *Boyce 1*, and Arnold (2.), B. Cooke (2.), and Havergal (2.). *Rev*: two-thirds of the corpus of anthems of MS C22v, together with Blake, Clarke (9.), Handel (1.20.), Nares (2.), and S. Wesley; and, in blocks, eight anthems from *Arnold 1*, six from *Hayes*, and all (in order) of *Pratt*.

Dated 1839 (p. 7) to 1843 (p. 189); Rev, 1829 (p. 3) to 1844 (p. 184).

370 × 240 mm. 191 ff., pag: II + ii + 1–188 (p. 189 = Rev p. 184); Rev: II + iv + 1–184.

**MS D21**  Bass. Anthems and Services.

MSS B4 (anthems), B15, B30 (services), D18, D19, and D21, may be considered together.

*Forw*: the common corpus of anthems is: Arnold (1.), Battye, Beckwith (2.), Beethoven (1.2.4.8.), Camidge, Cherubini, Clarke-Whitfeld (1.), Crotch (7.), G. J. Elvey (1.2.), Graun (1.4.), Handel (26.30.), Havergal (1.), Haydn (9.12–14.16.), Himmel, E. J. Hopkins, Ions, W. Jackson, Marcello (1.), Mendelssohn (1.2.5.7.8.), Moreira (1.), Mozart (2–4.6.), T. Norris, Novello (1.2.), Paisiello, Pickering (1.), Reynolds, Spohr (1.), Tallis (5.), Walmisley (9.), and Winter. Additional in D21 are Allinson (1.), Beethoven (5.), Boyce (9.), Garth (2.), Graun (3.), Greene (1.16.23.28.34.42.), Handel (37.), Haydn (2.), Mendelssohn (6.), and a transcript in no particular order of *Crotch*. *Rev*: the common corpus of services is: Bryne (2.), Child (20.), Dykes (4.), S. Elvey, Mendelssohn (9.10.), Nares (17.), H. Purcell (36.), Rogers (8.), Shenton (2.), Walmisley (11.), and Young (2.). Additional in D21v are Croft (72.), Marsh, and S. S. Wesley (9.).

Dated 185[?] (p. 215; Rev p. 101) to 1865 (p. 217; Rev p. 120). Copied by Brown.

353 × 254 mm. 177 ff., pag: IV + iv + 218 (1–120, 120a–b, 121–217; p. 217 = Rev p. 120); Rev: IV + iv + 1–120.

**MS D22** Bass Cantoris, no. 3. Services and Anthems.

About half the services listed under MS B18 together with Aldrich (17.), Child (20.), King (5.8.), and Nares (18.), from the printed volumes; and Tallis (5; hymn). *Rev*: most of the anthems of MS C22v, together with Boyce (2.), Ferretti, Graun (2.), Greene (29.), Moreira (2.), H. Purcell (32.), Tallis (7.), and Travers (1.), and seven anthems from *Kent 1*.

Dated 1819 (p. 7) to 1848 (p. 103); Rev, 1817 (p. 4) to 1839 (p. 134).

279 × 229 mm. 126 ff., pag: IV + iv + 1–104; Rev: IV + ii + 1–134.

**MS D23** Tenor Cantoris. Anthems and Services.

Bound into this MS which reflects the re-awakening of interest in English church music of the 16th and 17th cents. are further copies of the sets listed under MSS D25–D28. Other revived works are: anon (57.), Clarke (7.13.)*, Croft (21.23.26.27.31.46.)*, R. King (1.)*, H. Purcell (6b.7.24.26.28.), Tallis (3.6.), Turner (3.7.)*, and Tye (1.). Later works are: Armes (3.), Bach (1.3.), Beethoven (2.6.), Mendelssohn (3.), Mozart (9.), Paisiello, H. H. Pierson (1–3.), and Süssmayr.

Dated 1856 (p. 84) to 1899 (p. 221). Pp. 51–84 were copied by Brown. Pp. 86–144, 157–232 were transcribed and in many cases reconstructed by Armes, who dates his work accurately and names his sources. Some eleven anthems (marked *) are taken from Playford's *Divine Companion* (1701). The printed contents are tenor parts of *Cathedral Music, Services & Anthems*, by F. A. G. Ouseley, and Creighton in E♭ and W. Hayes in E♭.

Various sizes from 292 × 205 mm to 353 × 245 mm. 123 ff., pag: x + 232 (1–232) + iv, with pp. 1–50, 145–56 printed.

**MS D24** Six single parts of three anthems, by Callcott, [Hilton] (3.), and Novello (2.).

Paper dated 1855. Copied by Brown. Never bound into any volume, but ?used on tower on 29 May until at least 1907.

All 341 × 250 mm; 4 pp. each. *D24/1–3*, Alto; *D24/4, 5*, Tenor; and *D24/6*, Bass.

**MS D25**  Five treble parts of 'Service in C for Double Choir' by Sir F. G. Ouseley.

An authorization of payment (at end of D25/3) is witnessed 'Paid Sept$^r$. 29th. 1856. W. Henshaw'. Copied by Brown. Only D25/3 is complete, the others lacking the last three bars of the Gloria to the Nunc Dimittis. Decani and Cantoris merely refer to the side using the copies, for each supplies both treble parts. The old pagination indicates that these parts were formerly in volumes. *See* MS E2 for a holograph full score.

*D25/1*, Treble Decani: 333 × 236 mm. 14 ff., pag: 1–28 (formerly 49–76); *D25/2*, Treble Decani: 341 × 245 mm. 14 ff., pag: 1–28 (formerly 49–76); *D25/3*, Treble Cantoris: 341 × 245 mm. 16 ff., pag: 1–32 (formerly 49–66, 66a–b, 67–78); *D25/4, 5*, Treble Cantoris: details as D25/2.

**MS D26**  Nine part-books containing 'Services and Anthems found in Old MSS.'.

The only service is Rogers (8.); the anthems are: Blow (24*.), Child (8.16.), Clarke (6*.10.17*.), O. Gibbons (17.27.), Humfrey (6.7.9.10.), H. Purcell (18.33.), Tallis (12.), Weldon (1.11.13.)*, and Wise (5.).

Transcribed between September 1884 and 1892 and in many cases edited by Armes, who indicates clearly what he has reconstructed and states his manuscript and printed sources. He had recourse to an Ouseley MS. (? the Batten Organ Book), as well as to the cathedral's own MSS; and six anthems (marked *) were taken from Walsh's *Divine Harmony* (1731). A further tenor part is bound into MS D23.

340 × 243 mm. Card covers. Each 20 ff., pag: 1–40. *D26/1*, Alto Decani; *D26/2, 3*, Alto Cantoris; *D26/4*, Tenor Decani; *D26/5*, Tenor Cantoris; *D26/6, 7*, Bass Decani; *D26/8, 9*, Bass Cantoris.

**MS D27**  Ten single parts of 'Shepherd in G' (2nd Service; originally in F).

1888. Transcribed by Armes who also edited it, arranging a Kyrie from the composer's Benedictus. The original pagination shows that the parts were formerly in volumes similar to MS D23. *See* MSS D23 and D28/11 for further parts.

303 × 230 mm. Each 8 ff., pag: 1–16, with p. 16 blank. *D27/1*, Alto Decani; *D27/2, 3*, Alto Cantoris; *D27/4*, Tenor Decani; *D27/5, 6*, Tenor Cantoris; *D27/7, 8*, Bass Decani; *D27/9, 10*, Bass Cantoris.

## MS D28   11 single parts of 'Pelham Humphreys in E minor'; with D28/11 adding Sheppard's Second Service.

1888 for D28/1–10; 1 March 1891 for D28/11. Re-scored and transcribed by Armes. Formerly incorporated in volumes. *See* MS D23 for a further part of the Humfrey, and MS D27 for other parts of the Sheppard.

310 × 231 mm for D28/1; 307 × 247 mm for the others. D28/1–10: 12 pp. each; D28/11: 22 pp. *D28/1–3*, Alto; *D28/4, 5*, Tenor; *D28/6–11*, Bass, D28/10 being the Precentor's copy.

## MS D29   Full vocal score of 'The Burial Service' by Dykes.

1893 at the latest, being used (so p. 8) at the funerals of F. A. Ker, MA, 7 March 1893, and Wm. Hy. Grice (lay-clerk) 29 [April] [18]96. The setting was first used at the funeral of Dean Waddington in 1869 (so J. T. Fowler in *Life and Letters of John Bacchus Dykes* (1897), p. 124). *See* MS D37 for 21 single parts.

312 × 245 mm. 8 pp.

## MSS D30–D35   Six treble books. Anthems and Services.

Selections from the choruses of 12 anthems from *Boyce's Own*, 7 from *Hayes*, and 15 from *Croft*, show the continued popularity of those volumes. Other anthems are: anon (57.), Alderson, Armes (2.), G. B. Arnold, Arnott, Bach (2.), Battishill (2–4.), Beethoven (3.), [J. L.] Bennett (1.), Calkin, Child (8.16.), Church (2–4.), Clarke (7.13.)★, Creighton (2.), Croft (2.21★.23★.26★.27★.31★. 46★.), Crotch (4.), Dykes (3.), O. Gibbons (4.14.17.), E. Greatorex, Greene (8.37.), Handel (10.), Haydn (16.), R. King (1★.), Kynaston (1.), Mendelssohn (3.4.), Nicholson, Ouseley (2.3.5.7.8.10.), Powley (1.2.), H. Purcell (12.), Tallis (3.6.), Turle (1.), Turner (3.7.)★, and Tye (1.). *Rev*: the services are: [J. L.] Bennett (2.), Bryne (2.), Kynaston (2.), Powley (3.), Russell, Smart, and Walmisley (11.15.).

Dated 1892 to 1902. Transcribed chiefly by Armes (org) and C. H. Nutton and G. W. Shaw (former chors). Some 11 items (marked ★) are from Playford's *Divine Companion* (1701).

*D30*: 293 × 235 mm. 119 ff., pag: iv + 166 (1–118, 121–68); Rev: iv + 64 (4–67), with more pp. gone; *D31*: 295 × 235 mm. 120 ff., pag: iv + 164 (1–120, 123–66); Rev: vi + 66 (1, 1a, 2–59, 62–7); *D32*: 299 × 235 mm. 123 ff., pag: iv + 168 (1–159, 159a–b, 160–6); Rev: iv + 70 (1, 1a, 2–56, 59–60, 57–8, 61–9), with more pp. gone; *D33*: 291 × 233 mm. 123 ff., pag: vi + 172 (3–174); Rev: 68 (1, 1a, 2–17, 20–69); *D34*: 293 × 232 mm. 119 ff., pag: iv + 168 (3–124, 127–47, 147a–b, 148–70); Rev: ii + 64 (1, 1a, 2–23, 24–37, 38–53, 54–63), with more pp. gone; *D35*: 295 × 240 mm. 119 ff., pag: iv + 162 (1–116, 121–66); Rev: iv + 68 (1, 1a, 2–67).

**MS D36**  Open vocal score with organ bass of 'Service in D for Matins and Communion', by J. Marsh.

Paper dated 1817. The service was included in the repertoire by 1819. Removed from a volume.

348 × 257 mm. 20 pp. (formerly pp. 57–76).

**MS D37**  21 part-books containing 'Burial Service' by Revd J. B. Dykes. This includes the 'Burial Chant' by Revd W. Felton, and has added to it 'Thou knowest Lord' by [H.] Purcell.

Paper dated 1852, with D37/21 somewhat later. Copied by Brown, apart from D37/9, a later transcript by Armes. Various 20th cent. lay-clerks have inscribed their names in copies used by them. *See* MS D29 for a full score.

Each: 208 × 170 mm; 12 pp.; except D37/9: 200 × 170 mm; 8 pp. *D37/1–10*, Treble; *D37/11–13*, Alto; *D37/14–16*, Tenor; *D37/17–21*, Bass.

**MS E1**  Full score of 'Hymnus Ambrosianus' (i.e. Te Deum) by [Thomas Drake].

1st quarter 18th cent. Holograph. The Latin text, which starts 'Te Deum laeto celebramus hymno', is arranged in sapphic verses by Anthony Alsop (d. 1726), who was contemporary with Drake at Oxford. Bequeathed to the Library in 1747 together with MS D1.

419 × 264 mm. 53 ff., pag: xiv + 1–88 + iv.

**MS E2**  Full score of 'Service in C for Double Choir' by F. A. G. Ouseley.

Dated 1856, and dedicated to Revd J. B. Dykes. Holograph, apart from Sc. *See* MS D25 for five Treble copies.

356 × 267 mm. 42 ff., pag: vi + 76 (1–48, 48a–b, 49–74) + ii.

**MS E3**   Full score of 'Israel in Egypt', by [Handel].

Mid 18th cent. Transcribed by Brass.

382 × 245 mm. 173 ff., pag: IV + iv + 1–218 + IV + 112 (223–334) + IV. Pp. 219–22 have been lost.

**MSS E4–E11**   Eight part-books (Medius, Contratenor, Tenor, Bassus), containing Preces, Festal Psalms, and Services.

Brymley (2.), Byrd (28.29.31.), O. Gibbons (26.27.), Giles (14.), Morley (5.), [J. Mundy] (5.), W. Mundy (8.), R. Parsons [I] (3.), Sheppard (3.), W. Smith (14–18.), and Edw. Smythe (8.9.); with Batten (22.23.) added only slightly later.

*c.*1630. Only the Primus Contratenor Decani and Bassus Decani Books are missing from this fine set of Service Books 'in Folio Maiori') (*see* Misc. Ch. 7116). The books, which are impressive for their size and for their diamond-shaped notation—both of which aspects are reminiscent of Brit. Lib. Add. MS 30520—were intended for use on major feast days only. Each book falls into four sections—preces and festal psalms, and music for Matins, Communion, and Evensong—with space left between the sections to allow for additions to be made. The initials are mainly lacking; and the partly trimmed away naming of the parts in their gatherings is a clear pointer to the method of production. Todd was responsible for the original part of the Decani books, but the Cantoris books were worked upon by two other scribes. Brookinge, the more important of these, also added the two services by Batten, the Tables, and the system of pagination to all the MSS. The original leather covers (restored) bear the cathedral's coat-of-arms of the early 17th cent. (cf. MSS A1, C2, and A.IV.32).

*E4*, Medius Decani: 498 × 295 mm. 90 ff., pag: II + iv + 172 (1–141, 141a–b, 142–70) + II; 31 pp. blank. *E5*, Medius Cantoris: 501 × 297 mm. 91 ff., pag: II + vi + 1–172 + II; 23 pp. blank. *E6*, Secundus Contratenor Decani: 499 × 291 mm. 86 ff., pag: II + iv + 1–164 + II; 33 pp. blank. *E7*, Primus Contratenor Cantoris: 495 × 296 mm. 91 ff., pag: II + iv + 1–174 + II; 23 pp. blank. *E8*, Secundus Contratenor Cantoris: 499 × 298 mm. 89 ff., pag: II + iv + 1–170 + II; 30 pp. blank. *E9*, Tenor Decani: 499 × 293 mm. 85 ff., pag: II + iv + 162 (1–8, 11–164) + II; 35 pp. blank. *E10*, Tenor Cantoris: 500 × 298 mm. 84 ff., pag: II + iv + 160 (1–75, 78–90, 93–164) + II; 26 pp. blank. *E11*, Bassus Cantoris: 500 × 296 mm. 83 ff., pag: II + iv + 158 (1–79, 90–100, 103–66, 169–72) + II; 37 pp. blank.

**MS E11a**    Alto. Services, with hymn tunes and secular items added later.

Embraces all the original contents and early additions to MS C8; most of MS C18 (*see* MS C13 for omissions); and all of MS E4 except R. Parsons [I] (3.). Also in the original hand are Batten (20.), T. Boyce, Child (24.), J. Farrant, Hilton (5.), Marson, Palmer (11.), W. Smith (21.), Weelkes (6.7.), and Wilkinson (12.13.).

Added in the 18th cent. were these 'Psalm Tunes Common M$^{rs}$' (i.e. hymn tunes): Old 100th, St Ann (or Leeds), St David, St James, St Mary, St Peter, Southwell, Wakefield, Westminster (all melody only); Beverley, Cambridge, Canterbury (or Low Dutch), Windsor, York (all melody + bass). Also a mixture of sacred and secular music by anon (58.), J. O. [y'] Astorga (1.2.), [Dezède], F. D[ixon]. (1.2.), Green, R. Martin, and [H. Purcell] (45.); a 'Solo Pasticcio' drawn from Corelli, Tartini, and Geminiani; and articles on Yorkshire priories together with a translation of a French inscription.

Late 1630s. Like the MSS on which it draws this MS arranges its services in liturgical groupings for Communion, Evensong, and Matins. It does not claim to be comprehensive—in the Table (partly in the hand of Geeres) 'see my little book' occurs on more than one occasion. Transcribed by Brookinge at about the same time as MSS C11, C13, C16, and many folios at Peterhouse. The gilt tooling on the covers agrees with that on MS C16.

Of the later contributors F. Dixon was active in the 1780s. He included an item by Robert Martin of Launceston, in which area the Duke of Newcastle had one of his estates. On p. i is 'Edward Forster e libris J. F. Forster'.

E11a is sometimes called the 'Clumber MS' on account of its being discovered in the Duke of Newcastle's Library at Clumber when that collection was put for sale at Sotheby's in 1938. It was purchased by a Mr Edison Dick of Chicago, but he was prevailed upon by Edmund H. Fellowes to restore the MS to its place of origin.

355 × 216 mm, with part of the Table 301 × 195 mm. 267 ff., pag: II + x + 518 (253–314, 325–458, 461–532, 537–40, 1–36, 36a–l, 37–234) + ii + II. This pagination, left in its original state, shows a major misplacing on rebinding. Some 88 pp. are blank.

**MS E12**    Full score of the 'Oratorio of Deborah' by [Handel].

*c.*1740. Owned by Richard Fawcett who transcribed pp. 69–70, 152–63, 188–200, inserting them into a copy said to be in the hand of S4. Fawcett ended his days as a Prebendary of Durham (1778–82), but much of his collection of music (probably most of MSS E12 to E35) dates from 1730 to 1754 when he was associated with Corpus Christi College, Oxford, and active on the Oxford musical scene.

431 × 279 mm. 102 ff., pag: ii + 1–200 + ii.

D. Burrows, 'Sources for Oxford Handel Performances in the First Half of the Eighteenth Century', *Music & Letters* (April 1980); B. Cooper, 'An unknown Bach source', *Musical Times* (Dec. 1972).

**MS E13**   Full scores of 12 concertos by Geminiani.

Mid 18th cent. The concertos, which lack references and are in no particular order, are those of [Op. 2 and Op. 3]. In the hand of Fawcett (*see* MS E12), who described the first as 'Concerto del S$^r$. Geminiani'. The Table (p. i) gives an arrangement (inc) into two sets.

283 × 237 mm. 72 ff., pag: vi + 1–136 + ii.

**MS E14**   Full score of the Chandos anthem, 'O praise the Lord with one consent', by Handel.

Mid 18th cent. 'Ri: Fawcett' is written on the first flyleaf, and the MS is in his hand (*see* MS E12).

228 × 292 mm. 40 ff., pag: ii + 1–76 + ii.

**MS E15**   Vocal score of motets and solo items, with keyboard accompaniment.

Anon (39.), Handel (2.12.43.), Marenzio (1.2.), Morley (1.), Steffani (3.), and Stradella (1.2.), together with a discourse in Italian on Consonance and Dissonance (anon 125.).

1726. The MS emanates from London, and two comments connect it with the Academy of Ancient Music. The first of these is explicit: 'A Musick Meeting being held at y$^e$ Crown Tavern near S$^t$ Clements M$^r$ Galliard at y$^e$ head of it, & cheifly for Grave ancient vocell Musick. Wee began it w$^{th}$ y$^s$ following Song [Dolorosi martir] of Lucas de Marenzio Jan 7 – 1725/6'. This date is the same as the first date in the surviving Minute Book of the Society (Brit. Lib. Add. MS 11732). A name, something like 'Estwicke', who headed the list of those present at that first meeting, was in 1968 still visible on the vellum cover.

208 × 279 mm. 32 ff., pag: 1–64.

**MS E16**   Full score of 'Sign$^r$ [G.] Bononcini's Funeral Anthem' (When Saul was king).

Mid 18th cent. Owned by Richard Fawcett (*see* MS E12) whose name is written in pencil inside the front cover.

220 × 288 mm. 17 ff., pag: ii + 1–30 + ii.

**MS E17**   Full score of 'Acis and Galatea' by [Handel].

Mid 18th cent. The ms portions are in the hand of Fawcett (*see* MS E12), as are the single parts found under MS E26.

243 × 298 mm. 123 ff., pag: 1–246. Of these, 167 pp. are ms, 25 printed, and the rest blank. Many of the blanks were originally sealed together with wax.

**MS E18**   Instrumental score and 11 single parts of the 'Overture to the Opera of Artaxerxes', by Gio. Adolfo Hasse.

Mid 18th cent. Mostly in the same hand as MSS E20(i) and E26(i) and (iv); Fawcett (*see* MS E12) was responsible for the 2nd Violin and both Corno parts (E18/5, 11, 12).

*E18/1*, full score: 233 × 291 mm. 32 pp., the last four being blank. *E18/2–12*, single parts: 303 × 239 mm. Some 31 pp. (out of 40) are ms.

**MS E19**   Full score of the Chandos anthem, 'O sing unto the Lord', by Handel.

Mid 18th cent. At one time owned by Richard Fawcett (*see* MS E12), whose name is written inside the front cover.

240 × 303 mm. 24 ff., pag: 1–48, pp. 47–8 being blank.

**MS E20**   Music by Handel, assembled by Richard Fawcett (*see* MS E12), and performed at Oxford, possibly in 1738. Unascrib apart from one part in each of (iii) and (iv).

(i) Eight vocal and eleven instrumental single parts of 'Alexander's Feast'.

Fawcett's hand is much in evidence. In seven books the Overture, which seems to have been copied separately, is in the same hand as MS E18. Named performers are: Eversman (*fl.* 1724–39) and Davenport (1st Violin principal) both crossed out and replaced by Eversman and Pickel (on p. 6 is the partially erased comment, 'For Mr. Festing'); Rowland (2nd Violin), replaced by Moseley and Phillips; Cha . . . (cello; p. 14 has a solo for Mr Brown); Hudson (cello); Lowe (Hautbois 2ndo); 'Rapin 75' (1st Canto); 'Rapin 74' and Powell (d. 1744) (Contratenor).

Mainly 300 × 240 mm, with some 240 × 300 mm; 382 pp., of which 31 blank.

(ii) ten single parts of portions of 'Alexander's Feast'.

Fawcett responsible for nearly all of it. 'Mr. Hays' is mentioned as a vocal soloist in the 2nd Flute part.

297 × 240 mm; 36 pp., of which 9 blank.

(iii) 15 single parts of 'Concerto Grosso in C major' [= Concertante], which served as the Interlude in 'Alexander's Feast'.

Much is in Fawcett's hand. The cello part mentions 'Mr. Brown'.

296 × 239 mm; 66 pp., of which 12 blank.

(iv) Six instrumental parts of [Cantata I: Cecilia volgi un sguardo]. The Basso part includes a section of [Cantata II: Carco sempre di Gloria].

Fawcett responsible for all except the Basso part.

297 × 240 mm; 16 pp., of which 7 blank.

**MS E21**   Full score of the Chandos anthem, 'My song shall be alway', by Handel.

Mid 18th cent.

240 × 302 mm. 32 ff., pag: 1–64.

**MS E22**   Six Cantatas in Latin and one in Italian, for two voices, together with figured bass, by [?Steffani] (nos. 7–13).

Late 17th or early 18th cent. Contents are in same order as in Bod. Lib. MS Mus. d. 100, where ascription to Steffani is possibly in a later hand.

271 × 224 mm. 63 ff., pag: ii + 1–122 + ii.

**MS E23**   Full score, six vocal single parts, and two (out of eleven, so details on cover of Full score) instrumental single parts of 'Ode to St. Cecilia's Day' (From harmony, from heavenly harmony), by Handel.

Mid 18th cent. The score is said to be in the hand of S4. Some 18 pp. of the part-books were transcribed by Fawcett (*see* MS E12). The 1st Violin part (E23/8) has as its cover a sheet of a 1741/2 newspaper. The bass singers are named as Messrs. Clements and Wheeler.

*E23/1*, Full score: 302 × 240 mm. 112 pp., the last 3 blank. *E23/2–7, 9*, single parts: 238 × 297 mm. *E23/8*: 297 × 238 mm. Single parts total 40 pp., of which 8 blank.

**MS E24** Mid 18th cent. A collection of loose sheets and unsewn gatherings. The coarse paper folder has, in the hand of Richard Fawcett, 'MSS. Lessons for yᵉ Harpsichord'.

(i) Translation in Fawcett's hand of the 9th chapter of *L'Armonico Practico al Cimbalo di Francesco Gasparini Lucchesi* (1745).

Much is on the back of 'envelopes' sent by 'Wm. Ord', 'Jo. Duresme' (The Lord Bishop of Durham), and 'Jo. Eing'ton' to 'The Revd. Dr. Fawcett, Fellow of C. C. College, Oxford', and therefore to be dated 1748–54. *See* (iv) below.

190–210 × 154–165 mm. 18 pp.

(ii)  1. two staves in b on the inside; theory in Fawcett's hand on the outside.

332 × 212 mm. 4 pp.

2. frag of envelope addressed to '. . . Bertie/ . . . Hall near/ [A]therston/Warwickshire'.

190 × 229 mm. 2 pp.

(iii) Modulations, &c, some from [Antoniotto's *L'Arte Armonica* (1760)]. Some in hand of Fawcett.

Various sizes. 18 pp.

(iv)  1. the Italian article of (i).

305 × 187 mm. 12 pp.

2. examples relating to the above article.
3. modulation according to Antoniotto, but not in his *L'Arte Armonica*. Holograph.

305 × 238 mm.   2. 4 pp.;   3. 2 pp.

(v) 'Sonata [in e] a Violoncello E Basso (N.6)' by Giorgio Antoniotto.

There are two versions of the Sarabande. Holograph, as is a concerto by him found under MS E27. Neither work forms part of his Op. 1.

335 × 212 mm. 10 pp.

(vi) Full score (6 staves) of an anonymous Concerto in G (anon 114.).

In hand of Fawcett. More complete because some removed from MS E26.

298 × 244 mm. 20 pp.

(vii) Transposed version of [*A Treatise of Good Taste* (1749), Ex. I, by Geminiani].

In Fawcett's hand.

305 × 245 mm. 4 pp., but 3 are blank.

(viii) Three anonymous pieces keyboard items, in E♭, d, and g (anon 124.).

In the hand of Fawcett.

304 × 243 mm. 4 pp.

(ix) 2nd violin ripieno part of end of [Op. 6, Concerto 6, by Handel].

290 × 224 mm. 2 pp.

(x) Fantasia and Fugue in b (BWV 951a) by [J. S. Bach].

295 × 234 mm. 12 pp., 6 being blank.

(xi) Pp.  1–13  Toccata in c (BWV 911) by [J. S. Bach]
       14–27  'Preludium Manualiter' [Toccata in d (BWV 913) by J. S. Bach]
       27–28  15 bars of Fantasia in d (BWV 905) by [J. S. Bach]
       33–37  Fugue in e—last movement (BWV 914) by [J. S. Bach]
       41     Toccata in c [1st movement of the same]
       45     18½ bars of Fugue in F, by [Handel]
? in the hand of Fawcett.

244 × 304 mm. 48 pp.

(xii)  1. The Hertfordshire Militia March in C.
       2. Harpsichord Sonata in F (frag).

240 × 298 mm. 4 pp.

B. Cooper, 'An unknown Bach source', *Musical Times* (Dec. 1972).

**MS E25** Mid 18th cent. A collection of loose sheets and unsewn gatherings, which as they have been identified have been arranged in a more logical order. On the coarse paper cover Richard Fawcett has written 'Organ Concerto Mr. Handel in B♭'—possibly referring to (v) below.

Nos. (i)–(vii) are full scores of some of the [Concertos of Op. 6, by Handel].
(i) [No. 1] (end only). 237 × 303 mm. 2 pp.
(ii) [No. 2] (inc). 237 × 303 mm. 4 pp.
(iii) Pp.  1–14 [No. 3] (inc).
        15–46 [No. 4] (inc). 237 × 303 mm. 48 pp.
(iv) [No. 6]. 240 × 305 mm. 32 pp.
(v) [No. 7] (inc). 240 × 305 mm. 10 pp.
(vi) [No. 11] (inc in middle). In hand of S2. 240 × 300 mm. 16 pp.
(vii) [No. 12]. 240 × 304 mm. 36 pp.

Nos. (viii)–(xiii) are full scores of the [Concertos of Op. 4, by Geminiani].

(viii) [No. 1] (inc). Removed from MS E26. 243 × 315 mm. 8 pp.
(ix) [No. 2]. Transcribed by Fawcett. 243 × 318 mm. 28 pp.
(x) 'Concerto 3'. 243 × 320 mm. 20 pp.
(xi) [No. 4]. Transcribed by Fawcett. 243 × 320 mm. 26 pp.
(xii) [No. 5]. Pp. 1–4 are a replacement by Fawcett.

243 × 318 mm. 32 pp.

(xiii) 'Concerto 6'. 243 × 315 mm. 16 pp.

Nos. (xiv), (xv), and (xvii)–(xx) were transcribed by Fawcett.

(xiv) (a) pp. 1–31 [*Pièces de Clavecin* (1st Collection; 1743), Suites 1–4, by Geminiani]
(b) pp. 32–4 [*A Treatise of Good Taste* (1749), Exs. I & II, by Geminiani]

242 × 306 mm. 34 pp.

(xv) An adaptation of the 1st Suite of (xiv). 240 × 303 mm. 4 pp.
(xvi) Two copies, the second incomplete, of 28 variations on the [Sarabande theme from Corelli, Op. 5, No. 7; possibly by Geminiani].

Geminiani has been suggested by Layton Ring on stylistic and technical grounds.

238 × 303 mm. 10 pp. + 4 pp.

(xvii) Full score of an anonymous 'Concerto' in E♭ (anon 113.).

242 × 300 mm. 28 pp.

(xviii) 1st 11 bars of [Overture in 'Amadigi', by Handel).

242 × 300 mm. 4 pp., 3 of them blank.

(xix) 2nd Tromba part of ['Zadok the priest', by Handel].

236 × 297 mm. 2 pp.

(xx) One line in B♭.

239 × 291 mm. 2 pp.


**MS E26**  Mid 18th cent. A collection of loose sheets and unsewn gatherings. All in a coarse paper folder inscribed 'Organ Concerto in G. Mr. Handel'. Some pages have been transferred to MSS E24 and E25 in the interest of completeness.

(i)  Nine single parts of [Op. 4, Concerto 1, by Handel].

Five of the parts were transcribed by Fawcett, and three by the hand responsible for MS E18.

Organ part, 242 × 302 mm, 16 pp.; others, 304 × 240 mm, 34 pp.

(ii)  Portions of ['Aci, Galatea e Polifemo (2)' by Handel]:

1.  Part of a score in Italian. In hand of S2. 242 × 304 mm. 54 pp.
2.  Italian version (inc) of Aci's part (contralto). In the hand of S1, with addenda by Fawcett. 242 × 307 mm. 40 pp., pag 9–48.
3.  Ascrib 1st Violin part of ['Mi palpita il cor']. 238 × 298 mm. 2 pp.

(iii)  Five instrumental parts of portions of 'Acis and Galatea' by [Handel].

Copied by Fawcett. Two of the parts mention songs for Mr Powell (d. 1744).

300 × 242 mm. 32 pp. in all, 6 blank.

(iv)  Seven single parts of [Op. 4, Concerto 1] by Hasse.

In the same hand as MS E18.

300 × 240 mm. In all, 24 pp.

(v)  Portions of 'As pants the hart' ('B' version) by [Handel]:
1.  The opening of the score (Overture + first five words);
2.  1st Violin Concertino part of the Overture;
3.  1st Violin Concertino part.

1. copied by S4; others by Fawcett.

300 × 242 mm. 6 pp. + 2 pp. + 6 pp.

(vi)  Full score of 'Verdi prati selve amene' ['Alcina'], by [Handel].

237 × 302 mm. 8 pp.

(vii) 13 instrumental parts of an unknown cantata in F. Included are recits. 'Va e la Natura', 'O come vaga appare Cosi adorno', and 'Si si mia dolce Irene' (anon 49.62.70.).

Instrumentalists named on the copies are: Banister, Scarpentini, and Dagron (1st Violins); ?Salrin and Seal (2nd Violins); Barton (Basso); and Potts (Bassoon).

Each 300 × 240 mm. 4 pp.; except Violoncello, 232 × 297 mm. 2 pp.

(viii) 1. Oboe part to part of [tenor solo 'One thing have I desired', from ['The Lord is my light', by Handel].
2. Unidentified item in C.

288 × 229 mm. 2 pp.

(ix) An anonymous six-part score in F (inc; anon 111.).

Copied by Fawcett. Found in full in MS E33.

305 × 242 mm. 8 pp.

(x) Score of 'Angelico splendor' (inc), an insert in ['Israel in Egypt', by Handel].

Transcribed by Fawcett.

292 × 238 mm. 4 pp.

(xi) Preces and Responses by [Tallis].

245 × 304 mm. 2 pp.

**MS E27** Nine-part score of 'Concerto Violoncello [in A] . . . di Giorg: Antoniotto de A[dorni]'.

Mid 18th cent. Holograph, as is a sonata by him found under MS E24(v). Neither work forms part of his Op. 1.

338 × 218 mm. 16 ff., pag: 1–32.

**MS E28** Full score and three single parts of the opening of the Chandos Anthem, 'O come let us sing', by Handel.

Mid 18th cent. E28/1 and E28/2 give the opening Sinfonia and part of the first verse; E28/3 gives all the Sinfonia, and E28/4 only its first movement. E28/2 is in the hand of Fawcett (*see* MS E12).

300 × 242 mm. *E28/1*, Full score: 16 pp.; *E28/2*, 1st Violin: 8 pp.; *E28/3*, Basso: 4 pp.; *E28/4*, Basso: 4 pp.

**MS E29**

(i): 'Piu' non puole il mio core', by Alessandro Melani; a solo cantata for the soprano voice, accompanied by two violins and bass continuo.

(ii): Five solo cantatas, three anonymous, for the bass voice with bass continuo.

The cantatas are 'Pe'r L'ampio mar d'Amore mentre scorre' (pp. 1–11); 'Stell' amica ver'me non selegnar' (pp. 12–15); 'L'ucello in Gabbia: In Palaggio Regal da' tetto d'oro' (inc), by Pacieri (pp. 17–48); '. . . Se di me' l'antica gloria' (inc; ends 'L'Aquila Imperatrice') (pp. 59–70); and 'Là dove all'herbe in seno d'un' pargoletto Rio', by P. Simone Agostini (pp. 71–86).

Late 17th or early 18th cent.

220 × 285 mm. *E29(i)*: 12 ff., pag: 1–24; *E29(ii)*: 38 ff., pag: 76 (1–48, 59–86).

**MS E30** (MS E30 originally referred to a box containing a miscellany. Its contents have been re-arranged as MSS E30–E36).

(i): Full score (hol; ?inc) of 'Merlin or the Devil of Stone Henge, the words by Theobald, set by Mr. Galliard' (so coarse paper folder).

Dated 1734. On folios arranged in three sewn gatherings, the score includes stage directions. The Overture is followed by the song, 'Lo! the companion of thy crime'. Singing characters are Devil, Ghost [of Faustus], the Mountebank's Zany, Time, Charon, and Chorus. Mrs Cantrell, Mrs Clive, and Mr Laguerre are named as extra soloists, and Mr Baker as the kettle-drummer. Owned by Richard Fawcett (initials in pencil on folder).

330 × 215 mm. 50 ff.

(ii): Full score (hol; ?inc) of ['Apollo and Daphne'] and [?'The Triumphs of Love'], both by [Galliard]; together with, (on p. 16), the textless treble, alto, and bass (twice) of an anonymous '2 Kyrie'.

*c.*1734. Within the same folder. The suggested identification is based on the fact that the opening song, 'Smiling graces, pleasures gay', and five other numbers are the same as in 'Songs in the New Entertainment Call'd Apollo & Daphne', a printed addendum to Brit. Lib. Add. MS 31588. The characters are Diana and Venus (sung respectively by Mrs Chambers and Mrs Barb[i]er; both as in the printed collection); Bacchus, Pan, and Silenus; and Silence, Mystery, and Morpheus. A song for Mr Hall (d. Oct. 1734) is missing—there is the comment 'Mr. Rich has it'. The description in the printed collection may not be entirely accurate, for *The London Stage* includes the last three characters in the cast of 'Apollo and Daphne', listing the others under 'The Triumphs of Love', which admittedly was usually part of the same entertainment.

330 × 215 mm. 29 ff.

## MS E31   (formerly part of MS E30).

Four single part-books containing sections of the four-part Mass (K, G) and of the five-part Mass (C) by Gio. Batt. Borri.

2nd quarter, 18th cent. Copied by Thomas Ford, who knew Fawcett (*see* MS E12) at Oxford and copied the same items in Bod. Lib. MS Mus. Sch. d. 232. In E31/4 the Soprano (not the Viola) part of the Creed is given.

160 × 208 mm. 6 ff. each, pag: 1–12. *E31/1*, Alto; *E31/2*, Tenore; *E31/3*, Viol: 2do; *E31/4*, Tenore viola di melia e soprano.

## MS E32   (formerly part of MS E30).

Music for the harpsichord.

A collection of trumpet tunes, dances, metrical psalm interludes and chants, and the condensed instrumental part of songs and Overtures. Corelli (3 × 3.), Handel (88.94.), Hayden, Lamb (2.), and Tudway (9.) are ascribed; and [Carey, Clarke (18.), Handel (85.86.), Mancini (five excerpts from 'Hydaspe') and H. Purcell (51.52.)] have been identified. Among music still to be attributed are dances entitled 'Scaramouch', 'Punch', 'Irish Man', 'Tall Man's Dance', and 'Peasants', the melody of [The Vicar of Bray], and the accompaniment (inc) to 'Appear all ye graces' (*see* anon 27.32 × 2. 39.46.51.66.124.).

The date, 'Monday April 19. 1717', is written inside the back cover.

160 × 204 mm. 44 ff., pag: 1–88.

## MS E33   (formerly part of MS E30).

Five instrumental part-books.

*Forw*: three concertos, in F, F, and b (anon 110–12.), followed by the 'Overture in Sosarmes' by [Handel]. The first concerto is [Op. 3, Concerto 4 in f dur—1st edit. of 1734, possibly by Handel], and the second is the same as MS E26(ix). *Rev*: accompaniment only of six arias by [Handel] taken from 'Atlanta', ['Ariodante' (4 items)], and ['L'Allegro'].

Mid 18th cent. Forw is in the same hand as MS E34(ii). Fawcett (*see* MS E12) responsible for Rev and its labels.

290 × 241 mm. *E33/1*, Hoboy Primo (Rev: 1st Violin Ripieno): 16 ff., pag: 1–24; Rev: 1–8; *E33/2*, Hoboy Secundo (Rev: 2nd Violin Ripieno): 14 ff., pag: 1–20; Rev: 1–8; *E33/3*, 2nd Violin: details as E33/1; *E33/4*, Viola: details as E33/2; *E33/5*, Violoncello and Bassoon: 20 ff., pag: 1–32; Rev: 1–8.

**MS E34**   (formerly part of MS E30).

Parts of Concertos by [Handel]. Used by Richard Fawcett (*see* MS E12) at Oxford during the 2nd quarter of the 18th cent.

(i) 'Concerto Grosso No. 6' [= Op. 6, No. 6]. Only three violin parts survive.

287 × 220 mm; 8 + 8 + 6 pp.

(ii) Seven 'Parts of y$^e$ Concerto in y$^e$ Opera of Otho' [= Op. 3, No. 6, 1st movement].

The coarse paper folder is labelled in the hand of Fawcett; the parts are in the same hand as MS E33 (Forw).

300 × 243 mm; 7 × 2 pp.

**MS E35**   (formerly part of MS E30).

Parts of anthems and oratorios by [Handel]. Used by Richard Fawcett at Oxford during the 2nd quarter of the 18th cent.

(i) Canto 2$^{do}$ and Viola parts of ['The ways of Zion'], the former adapted for use with 'Israel in Egypt'.

In the hand of S1, apart from the outer bifolio of the Canto 2$^{do}$ part. Canto 2$^{do}$, 240 × 305 mm; 16 pp. Viola, 307 × 243 mm; 16 pp.

(ii) Sections of the full score of 'Judas Maccabaeus'.

Transcribed by Fawcett.

245 × 305 mm; 40 pp., in unsewn gatherings.

(iii) Six vocal and six instrumental parts of sections of 'Esther'.

Four of the vocal parts were copied by Fawcett (*see* MS E12) and the coarse paper folder is in his hand. The second Canto primo part has on it, 'sent y$^e$ same to Mr. Hayes', whilst the first of the Alto parts includes an extract from 'Zadok the priest'. Cf. MS D15 for copies used at a later performance.

300 × 242 mm, and smaller; in all 34 pp., 12 of them being blank.

**MS E36** (formerly part of MS E30).

E. H. Knight's Catalogue of 'Durham Cathedral Library, Manuscript Music'.

Its four sections are: '(A) Alphabetical List of Composers; (B) Name Index; (C) List of Contents [in finding order for each MS]; (D) Subject Index [i.e. titles and first lines].'

Dated November 1928. Knight was an alto lay-clerk and an assistant to the Cathedral Librarian. His catalogue covers MSS A1–A34; B1, B5–B13, B16–B24, B26–B29, B31–B36; C1–C19A, C21, C26–C35; D1, D7, D8, D13–15; E1, E3–E11, E11a (later), E12, and E16; though no inventory of MS A27 was compiled. MSS B3, B4, B15, B30, C20, and C22–C25 were not covered, the reason being that they were 'modern'; and it was stated that MSS B2, B14, and B25 did not exist.

Knight inserted detailed lists of contents inside the MSS he covered; and made lists of the dated authorizations of payment. He also compiled a slip index of the occurrence of the compositions found in the MSS.

329 × 205 mm. 88 ff., pag: iv + 1–168 + iv.


**MS E37** 'A Collection of Psalms and Anthems and Hymns for use of The Church and Meetings', both words and music being given. Much use is made of the hymns of Wesley, Lady Huntingdon, G. Whitefield [sic], and Dr Watts.

The named tunes (spelling as in MS) are: Abingdon (twice), Aldrich, America (2), Angelsea, Antigua (2), Ashley, Athlone, Ayliff Street, Baltimore, Bampton (2), Bath Abbey, Bath Chapel (5), Bedford (2), Bennetts (4), Bermandsey, Bexley (3), Boston, Bowden, Braintree (2), Bramcoate, Breadby (4), Brighton (2), Bristol (3), Burford, Caermarthen, Cambridge New (5), Canterbury (2), Carlisle (3), Chard, Cheniton, Chimes, Colebrook (2), Condescention, Cookham, Coombs, Cornish, Crowle, Cumberland, Darwell's 46th, Denbigh, Deptford, Derby (4), Devizes (2), Devon (8), Devotion, Dorsitshire, [Easter Hymn], Ewel, Falkin Street (2), Farringdon, Feversham, Finsbury (3), Fletchers (2), Follett, Foster (2), Fotness (3), Foundery, Fulham (3), Funeral, Furman, Gainsborough, Geard (2), Gosport (2), Greenwich New (3), Grove House, Gr[o]ve, Halifax, Hamilton (2), Hammond (2), Hampton, Handon, Hanhover (4), Harts (2), Haughton, Haunt, Henley (2), Hemmings, Hephzibah, Hopkins (3), Hoxton, Huddersfield, Hull (2), Irish (9), Islington (3), Jewin Street (2),

Jordon, Judes, Judgment, Kentuckey, Kingsbridge, Langdon, Lebanon, Leeds, Leoni, Limehouse, Lisbon, Liverpool, London, London New, Lowell (2), Macclesfield, Magdalen, Malbarey/ Marlbrough (2), Mansfield, Marks, Martins Lane, Miall, Michaels, Middlesex, Milbrook = Morning Song (2), Milburnport, Miles Lane, Missionary (4), Mitcham, Monmouth, Moorfields (2), Morning Hymn, Musicians, Newbery (2), Newcastle, Newcourt, Newington/Nunsington (4), New Jerusalem (2), New Sabbath (4), Old 50th, Old 100th (5), Old Otford, Olivers (2), Oxford, Pearce, Peckham (2), Pithay, Pool, Portsmouth New, Portugal (5), Portugal New (4), Prescott Street, Redemption, Resurrection (2), Rothwell, Ryland, St George/Georges (4), St Luke (4), Salem, Salim New (2), Salisbury, Savannah, Simons, Southamton (2), Staffordshire, Staughton (2), Stocks, Stockton (3), Stratford (2), Stratham, Sussex, Sydenham, Tinemouth or Providence College, Truro (2), Uxbridge (2), Verulam (2), Walsal (6), Wareham (5), Wark, Wells, Weston Favel (4), West Street, Wiltshire (5), Winchester, Wirksworth (3), Yorkshire (2).

Unnamed tunes: pp. 38, 42 (2 tunes), 44, 46, 88, 103, 104, 105, 107, 108, 109, 114, 135(2), 141(2), 146, 148, 158, 159 = 166 = 207, 160, 167, 178, 186(2), 188, 231, 233, 253, 278.

Written out (so p. 284) by John Scurr whilst he was in Givet prison. A native of Whitby, he had been on the Henley when it was captured by the French on 8 December 1806. Givet was reached on 13 January 1807. Copying started (see p. 7) on 28 March 1808. Inside the front cover is 'W.W. 1949', the 'William Waples, Sunderland' whose bookplate is inside the back cover. Earlier it had belonged to Henry James Blake; and in August 1846 it was presented by a Mr Smith to James Devis of Birmingham. 'Barten Bath' is gilded on red leather stuck on the cover.

117 × 208 mm. 143 ff., newly pag: 1–286. The original has pp. 1–17 twice over, old pp. 76–150 are lost, and there is an insertion between old pp. 305 and 306.

**MS E38**  Eight songs for the solo voice and one duet, in German, with accompaniment.

Anon (35.), Banck, Curschmann (1.2.), C. Keller, Schubert (1.2.), and Thalberg (1.2.).

2nd half 19th cent. Tooled on cover is 'German Manuscript', 'George E. Schmettau'. Given by Dr C. W. Eden to Mr A. J. Thurlow in 1974, and donated to the Library in September 1980.

257 × 304 mm. 14 ff., pag: ii + 24 (1–12, 15–26) + ii.

**K.II.31** Printed contents: James Usher, *A Body of Divinity*, and *Immanuel, or the Mystery of the Incarnation of the Son of God* (1649).

Music: ?*c*.1660. On the verso of the 2nd last flyleaf (288 × 186 mm) is the melody of the 'Proper Tune' to Ps. 119.

Written in diamond-shaped notation on two staves of five lines each, with a third staff unused. The melody is roughly the same as the Tenor or Plainsong used by G. Farnaby in Ravenscroft, *The Whole Booke of Psalmes* (1621).

**Add. MS 154** Catalogue of Philip Falle's Music Books.

Arranged in four sections, viz., Theoretical, Sacred Vocal, Profane Vocal, and Instrumental Works, the last section being subdivided under Harpsichord, Lute, Viol, Flute, and Violin (solo and in concert).

1722. Holograph. Falle (1656–1742) was chaplain to William III in 1694, later becoming a Prebendary of Durham (1700–42). The catalogue gives over 170 groupings, of which about 150 survive at Durham. Many of these are rare items. The descriptions of the printed works include the place of publication and the date. Only four of the groupings are manuscript—but five candidates exist in MSS A27, D2, D4, D5, and D10. Of these Falle probably ignored MS A27, for it is merely his own transcript of mainly printed items which interested him. The Book of Acquisitions (MS A.IV.32, f. 87v) gives 1739 as the date of the bequest, but the catalogue itself shows that the decision had been made much earlier. It closes (p. 16) with the statement: 'All the Books in this Catalogue (w^ch at present are in my Study here at Shenley) I give and bequeath to be reposited in the Library at Durham . . . Witness my hand this 25th of June 1722. Ph. Falle.'

297 × 184 mm. 12 ff., pag: II + 1–18 + IV.

R. A. Harman, *A Catalogue of the Printed Music and Books on Music in Durham Cathedral Library* (1968); P. A. Evans, 'Seventeenth-Century Chamber Music Manuscripts at Durham', *Music & Letters* (July 1955); M. Urquhart, *Musical Research in Durham Cathedral Library: 'Mr John Jenkins in Particular'* (Durham Cathedral Lecture 1979).

**Hunter MS 33** Main contents: A Minor Canon's Commonplace Book. Early 17th cent. Possibly belonged to John Miller (not known) whose name is written inside the front cover. The last contributor was James Greene, Sacrist at Durham both before and after the Commonwealth period. His entries shed light on the period 1640–60. 297 × 205 mm. i + 69 + i ff.

Music: c.1640. On an inserted bifolium (ff. 6–7). 277 × 180 mm.

The bell part (f. 6ᵛ) and separate bass and treble parts (f. 7) of 'What strikes the clocke', by 'Mr. [Edward] Gibbons of Exceter'.

The bell part represents the striking of the hour from four to twelve inclusive, each hour being 'tolled' in the relevant number of repeated minim beats. Textless, apart from the first four words fitted to the treble part. Transcribed by Greene.

**Hunter MS 125**   Notebook of Elias Smyth, minor canon 1628–76 (*see* Index of Copyists). Pp. 221–3 include details of the choral establishment, 1660–2. 147 × 95 mm. 170 ff.

Music: ?c.1630. On a loosened back pastedown is a minute unidentified textless fragment.

**Miscellaneous Charters 7116 and 7117** (among Dean and Chapter muniments in the care of the Palaeography Department of the University of Durham)

**Misc. Ch. 7116**

A parchment roll (2074 × 216 mm) headed, 'An Inventorie of all the Vestments Ornaments Song Bookes and other moveable goods belonging to the Cathedrall Church of Durham delivered and committed to yᵉ charge and Custody of James Greene [d. 1667] Clerke and Sacrist of the said Church . . .'

At the time [c.1665] of the Inventory the Cathedral boasted 'Two paire of Organs'. A slightly later comment records: 'one pair of them is lately [1665] sold to Houghton[-le-Spring]'.

The section, 'In the Song Schoole', lists 'Two Sackbutts and Two Cornetts'. These had been in use as early as 1628, for Prebendary Smart had objected to them. They were played throughout the 1630s, and from 1660 until 1680, when the sackbutts ceased. The cornets continued until 1696 and March 1697/8 respectively. Also in the Song School were what might well be described as the textbooks used by John Foster, Master of the Choristers and Organist, 1661–77:

'Item Psalterium Carolinum composed by Dr. Wilson in three
    parts
Item Sʳ William Leightons divine Lamentation in ffower parts
Item Dowlands Songes in ffower parts

Item Jones Ultimum Vale to Musick in ffower parts

Item y^e Psalmes of David composed in fower parts for voices & Instrm^ts

Item Morleys Introduction to Musick

Item Consort Lessons for six Instrum^ts set by exquisite Authors . . .      . . .

Item Morleys ffower parts

Item Orianaes ffower parts'.

Only the first mentioned was a recent [1657] work, a not surprising situation as Foster had been a chorister in the 1630s (*see* MS A5, p. 224).

Then follows a section headed, 'In the Quire are these Bookes':

'Item Tenn Bookes in Folio Maiori whereof two wanting [MSS E4–E11, still only two "wanting"]

Item Tenn Bookes in folio with black Covers for verse Services [MS C18]

Item Tenn Books in fo: for short services [MS C8] and a base Booke of Services & Anthemes [not extant]

Item Tenn Bookes in fo: for ffestivall daies [MSS C2, C3, C7, C14; and York MS M29S]

Item Tenn Bookes in folio of full and Verse Anthemes [MSS C4, C5, C6, C7, C9, C10; and the cover of MS C17]

Item Tenn Bookes of Services and Anthemes for men [none extant; but cf. MSS A3, C11, C17, C19]

Item ffower Organ Bookes [four of MSS A1, A2, A3, A5, A6]

Item fower Parchm^t Bookes 2 Decani 2 Cantoris' [none extant].

This present catalogue shows that the first five sets and most of the Organ Books had been produced before 1640, and it is gratifying that so many of them are still in their place of origin. Also surviving are four private MSS (MSS C11, C13, C16, and E11a) which date from the 1630s; and a number of post-Restoration replacement copies (e.g. MSS C1, C12, C15, C17, C19).

## Misc. Ch. 7117

An imperfect revision of Misc. Ch. 7116. *c.*1665. Parchment roll. 2194 × 216 mm.

B. Crosby, 'A 17th-century Durham Inventory', *Musical Times* (Feb. 1978); P. le Huray, *Music and the Reformation in England, 1549–1660* (1967); J. M. Morehen, *Sources of English Cathedral Music, c.1600–1640* (Ph.D. thesis, Cambridge, 1969); R. T. Daniel and P. le Huray, compilers, *The Sources of English Church Music,*

*1549–1660*, 2 vols. (Early English Church Music, Supplementary Vol. 1; 1972); B. Crosby, 'Durham Cathedral's Liturgical Music Manuscripts, *c.*1620–*c.*1640', *Durham University Journal* (Dec. 1973); J. Bunker Clark, *Transposition in Seventeenth Century Organ Accompaniments and the Transposing Organ* (1974).

# THE BAMBURGH MANUSCRIPTS

**MS M69**  Music for the harpsichord.

A work-book with at least 16 pp. devoted to theory, with examples drawn from Corelli, Heck, Lampe, Rameau, 'T.S.' (p. 17), Tireman, and Vincent. Chelleri, Corelli (1 × 3.), Galuppi, Greene (44.), Jones, Nussen, Rameau (3.), Stanley[/Handel], and Vincent are the named composers; [Arne (2.), Felton (2.), Garth (4.), Lanzetti (1.), and Rameau (1.2.)] have so far been identified, as have variations on the [National Anthem] and 'Un Leçon Français' (*see* anon 122–4).

*c.*1770. Elsewhere instead of his initials the compiler states 'of my own adding' (p. 32). The use (pp. 28, 29) of Heck's *A complete System of Harmony* (1768) narrows the field to Thomas Sharp II (1725–72); and the naming of 'Wm.' in the instructions (pp. 21, 29) indicates the function of the book. It has not been established whether this William was his brother (1729–1810) or some other relative. The principal copyist was also responsible for some of the same pieces in MSS M108 and M216, and for MS M201(i).

286 × 233 mm. 47 ff., pag: 1–94, with little more than stubs of pp. 3–12.

**MS M70**  Sonatas and other instrumental items, anthem, canticles, chants, motets, songs, and catches.

Anon (34.38.47.60.63.65.102–9.), Benson, Bocchi (1.2.), Borri (1.), Byrd (14.), Lord Chesterfield, Corelli (2.3.5.), Farinel, Farinelli, [Finch] (4.6–9.), Geminiani (3.), Greene (17.23.31.), Handel (67.79.), Loeillet, Quarles, Salisbury (1.), Steffani (1.4.), and [Worrel].

Early 18th cent. A comparison with Euing MS R.d.39 (Glasgow Univ. Library) confirms the impression that the main part of this MS is in the hand of the Hon. Revd Edward Finch, Prebendary of York Minster. Many of the anonymous items are probably holograph, for the 'Cuckoo Sonata' (Rev pp. 41–4) is attributed to him in *The Division Violin* (1693), and a symmetrical monogram incorporating the letters 'EF' occurs on p. i and Rev pp. 12, 41, 51, and 56. Finch was the original owner of several of the Bamburgh MSS, his hand being evident in MSS M170, M179–80, M200, and particularly in MS M192. Others of his MSS are at York, whilst Tenbury MSS 1024–7, besides having much in his hand, duplicate parts of the present MS (e.g. pp. 70–83, 90–1; Rev pp. 116–21, 128). Tenbury MS 1026 describes Worrel as a 'young Lawyer'. He and Finch were members of the 'Crown Club'. Not in Finch's hand are pp. 92–153 and Rev pp. 157–78. Their copyist was active not later than 1738, for Finch himself was responsible for the final 'Amen' of anon (60.). Accompanying the 'Ossequioso Ringraziamento' by Farinelli is a further copy of the Italian text in the same hand. It is on an envelope addressed to Finch and someone else has supplied an inter-linear translation. Some of the copyist's work is now found at Oxford, for bound into Bod. Lib. MS Mus. d. 46 are the companion single parts of 'O Lord who shall dwell' by [Greene].

289 × 223 mm. 201 ff., pag: VI + ii + 1–192; Rev: VI + viii + 188 (1–178, 178a–b, 179–86). Blanks include pp. 154–92.

**M71** Printed contents: *Crotch's Specimens*, vol. 1 (1807).

Manuscript: 6 single and 27 double chants.

Battishill (3 chants), Boyce, Brown, Chard, Cooke, Crotch (3), Dupuis (2), [Felton], Goodenough, Wm. Gregory, Henley, Millard, Parnel, Perkins, Randall (2), Robinson, Scott, Shears, Soaper, and Woodward, with seven anon.

Early 19th cent.

298 × 236 mm. 6 ff., pag: 12 (167–78), added at the back.

**MS M88** Nine solos for the soprano voice, with accompaniment, from Odes and Oratorios by [Handel] (48.50 × 2.55.60.62. 64 × 2.75.)

2nd half of 18th cent. In the same hand as MS M90.

295 × 231 mm. 49 ff., pag: ii + 1–94 + ii, with pp. 48 *et seq.* blank.

**MS M89** Vocal score of five hymn tunes by the Revd Thomas Sharp [II]; and, in a different hand, the melody of 'O deck thy hair with the heather bell' (anon 50.).

2nd half of 18th cent. One of the hymn tunes is arranged from a Sonata by Boyce, and the other four are featured in *Divine Harmony* (1798), where Sharp is described as 'formerly Rector of St. Bartholomew the Less, West Smithfield'. Durham MS M174, Ely MS 23 (now in Cambridge Univ. Library), and several St Paul's, Westminster Abbey, and Tenbury MSS are in a very similar hand.

290 × 239 mm. 25 ff., pag: 1–48 + ii, with pp. 29, 30, 32 *et seq.* blank.

**MS M90**  Two and three-part vocal score of 18 different Hymn Tunes, divided for a no longer apparent reason into two groups.

The tunes are 'Balmborough'*, Cambridge, [*Divine Companion*, Hymn V], Dutch Tune, Edmunton, Greenwich, Leyden*, [Old 100th], Rothbury†, St Ann, St Edward, St Mary, St Nicholas, Southwell, Whitton†, and Windsor, with two unidentified. Clarke, Paxton and Henry Purcell are the only named composers, though two tunes (marked *) are by Thomas Sharp [II] (MS M89), and two others (marked †), because of local topography, presumably are.

2nd half of 18th cent. Some of the text is in the same hand as MS M88.

258 × 160 mm. 24 ff., pag: 48 (7–54), with pp. lost from both ends.

**MS M102**  Full score (inc) of 'St. Cecilia's Song' (Hail bright Cecilia) by H. Purcell.

Early 18th cent.

322 × 202 mm. 55 ff., pag: iv + 104 (1–68, 77–112) + ii; pp. 89 *et seq.* being blank.

**MS M108**  Music for the harpsichord.

In this work-book only Felton (2.3.) bear either ascription or title. Identified are [Lanzetti] (1.2.), [Rameau] (1.2.), and ['Un Leçon Français'] (*see* anon 123.124.).

Mid 18th cent. The MS has music in common with MS M69. The hand, apart from p. 1, is that of MS M201(i) and the main part of MS M69.

236 × 290 mm. 30 ff., pag: 1–56; Rev: 1–4; with all but 13 pp. blank.

**MS M157** 1st Violin part-book.

Overtures, and movements from concertos and sonatas by Alberti (2 items), Corelli (4.5 × 3), Geminiani (1.2 × 3), Handel (66.68.71.72.76–8.81.90 × 6), Hasse (3.), [J. S.] Humphries, [D.] Scarlatti, Schickhardt, Tessarini, and Valentini.

Mid 18th cent. Entitled 'Praxis Musica', this MS was transcribed by Cuthbert Brass.

180 × 240 mm. 70 ff., pag: 140 (31–170), with pp. 117 *et seq.* blank, and evidence of pages torn away from each end.

**MS M159** Seven sonatas, in B♭, G, B♭, g, B♭, C, and E♭, for 'Solo Violino con basso obligato', both parts being given (cf. anon 121.). The composers have not been established, for though nos. 5–7 were originally ascribed to Tartini, that ascription was crossed out at an early date in nos. 6 and 7.

Mid 18th cent. The MS was acquired (?written) by John Sharp III whilst at Trinity College, Cambridge.

255 × 368 mm. 34 ff., pag: ii + 1–64 + ii, pp. 40 *et seq.* being blank.

**MS M170** Bass. Anthems and Services.

The surviving services are: Aldrich (18.), Blow (28.31.), Child (20.22.), Goldwin (7.), Goodson, Nalson (1.), H. Purcell (36.38.), Rogers (6.), Smewen, and Wise (13.).

Late 17th and early 18th cents. The MS, which was originally double-ended, has been so badly mutilated that no anthem remains. Tables written inside the covers enable what has been lost to be determined—they also indicate a high degree of agreement with Bod. Lib. MS Eng. Liturg. c. 4. Although 'J. Sharp, Durham' and 'J. Sharp, Hartburn' are written inside the front and back covers respectively, the MS is not of Durham origin but emanates from York. The first (pp. 76–9) and second copyists (pp. 96–130) are not known, the fourth (pp. 135–57) was John Cooper. The third copyist (pp. 131–4) may be the 'Mr. Bardon' who in 1712 was responsible for the transcription at York of Purcell in G minor. The version here does not include Roseingrave's Gloria to the Nunc Dimittis, repeating that to the Magnificat. The York connection is supported by the inclusion, before the mutilation of the MS, of compositions by Finch, J. Hutchinson, and Smewen; and a comment in Finch's hand (p. 96) indicates earlier ownership.

309 × 200 mm. 33 gilded ff., pag: 66 (76–9, 96–157); + loose sheet.

**MS M172**   Five vocal and five instrumental part-books of 'Alexander's Feast', by Handel.

Mid 18th cent. At the back of the cello book (M172/8) Thomas Ebdon has transcribed part of the 1st Flute part. 'P. Strada' and 'P. Beard' are tooled in gilt on red leather stuck on the covers of M172/1 and M172/3 respectively. Little more than the covers of 1st Oboe copy (M172/9) survive, and M172/2–4 have pp. torn away. All the books are inscribed 'John Sharp. Trin. Coll.', and bear his Archdeacon's bookplate. An inventory compiled at the time of his death in 1792 (Gloucester Record Office, D3549, Box 52) shows that three books have gone astray since then.

296 × 223 mm. *M172/1*, [Soprano]: 8 ff., pag: ii + 1–12 + ii; *M172/2*, Canto 1mo: 7 ff., pag: 1–14; *M172/3*, [Tenor]: 6 ff., pag: 1–12; *M172/4*, Tenor: 6 ff., pag: 1–12; *M172/5*, Basso: 10 ff., pag: ii + 1–16 + ii; *M172/6*, Violino 2do: 12 ff., pag: 1–22 + ii; *M172/7*, Viola: 7 ff., pag: 1–12 + ii; *M172/8*, Violoncello: 14 ff., pag: ii + 1–24 + ii; *M172/9*, Hautboy 1mo: 4 ff., pag: 1–6 + ii; *M172/10*, Hautboy 2do: 10 ff., pag: 1–18 + ii. In all, 45 pp. are blank.

**MS M173**   'Select Pieces of Sacred Music Adapted for Two Oboes, Ger$^n$. Flutes, or Violins—1797'.

21 items—mainly anthems and arias—[Arne] (1.), Byrd (14.), Handel (10.20.57.59.63.65.), Kent (3.6.), Mason (5.), Nares (10.), and three hymn tunes, viz., [Easter Hymn] (p. 28), [Surrey] (Ps. 23; p. 16), and to 'Sound his praise abroad' (p. 17).

230 × 292 mm. 28 ff., pag: iv + 1–48 + iv.

**MS M174**

(i) Vocal score of 16 mainly three-part Canons, Anthems, and Hymns.

Anon (54.), [Byrd] (14.), T. Clark★, Clarke (1★.11.13★.), Croft (23★.26★.31★.40.), Ford (2.), [Greene] (3.), Henley (1.3.), [R.] King (1★.), and W. Webb.

2nd half of 18th cent. Seven of the items (marked ★) appeared in *Divine Companion* (1701; dedicated to John Sharp [I], Archbishop of York), and those by Henley in *Divine Harmony* (1798). All except those by Henley are featured in virtually the same order in another manuscript belonging to the Sharps, now in Gloucester Record Office (D3549, Box 54) and it is from there that the attribution to Greene is taken. 'Bamborough Castle' is written inside the front cover of M174, which is in a hand similar to that of MS M89.

236 × 297 mm. 22 ff., pag: 1–44; with pp. 22 *et seq.* blank.

(ii) A holograph list, under two headings, of some of John Sharp III's music.

Composers mentioned are:
Of printed works: Avison, Alberti, Albinoni, Corelli, Corelli/Geminiani, Courteville, Finger, Andrea Fiore, Geminiani, Haym, Marini, Nicolai Matteis, H. Purcell, Scarlatti/Avison, Schickhardt, Sherard, Torelli, and Valentini. Also a number of printed Collections of Music.

Of works in manuscript: Corelli, Corelli/Geminiani, Courteville, Finch, Finger, Gasparini, Lully, [Mancini], Pez, Stradella, and Ziani.

2nd half of 18th cent. *See* MS M194 for a fuller catalogue.

207 × 167 mm. One folio loose inside M174(i).

**MS M175** Sinfonias and sonatas, some of them for brass ensemble, in full score.

Corelli (6.), Navarra (1–2.), [A. Veracini], and anon (92–9.).

*c.*1700. The two sinfonias by Navarra (the 2nd is headed 'Maes. di Cap^la di S. A. S. di Mant . . . 1697') and anon 97–9 are also in MS M193/2–7. Anon 97 and 99 may be by Albinoni.

221 × 292 mm. 47 ff., pag: 1–94. At least two gatherings have been lost from the beginning.

**MSS M176** and **M177** Full score of 'Oratorio Della Passione', by [Jommelli].

Mid 18th cent. In two parts, M176 being 'Parte Prima'. M176 has been badly mutilated, five gatherings at the front and over five at the back being torn away. M177 has lost just over a gathering from the beginning, but thereafter is complete apart from 4 pp. missing between pp. 118 and 119 (cf. Brit. Lib. Add. MS 14136).

214 × 282 mm. *M176*: 10 ff., pag: 1–20; *M177*: 60 ff., pag: 1–120.

**MSS M179 and M180**   Two part-books—each labelled 'A'—of trios for viols or flutes.

Jenkins (11.12.), [?G.] Keller, and anon (88.); with minute fragments of [Finch's] anthems, 'Grant we beseech thee merciful Lord' and 'Bow thine ear' added later.

*c*.1700. The labels are further inscribed 'Secundo' and 'Primo' respectively, but this is misleading, and applies only to the first grouping in each MS. Each book now contains various parts—two are in tablature—of four groups labelled A, B, C, D, though most of these have been mutilated and are incomplete. B has 'Mr Jenkins' written at the end of its last piece, whilst D includes 'The pleasing slumber' known to be by him. The first item of A has 'Signior Keller' written above it; but C affords no written clue whatsoever. Different qualities of paper and different number of staves postulate early individual existences for some of the groups. Inside each cover is written 'J. Sharp: Trin: Coll', but at least some of the MSS had previously belonged to Edward Finch (*see* e.g. M179, p. 28).

147 × 200 mm. *M179*: 100 ff., pag: ii + 198 (1–114, ff. 115–23, pp. 124–36, 136a, 137–88), with stubs of later pp.; *M180*: 94 ff., pag: 188 (1–92, 92a–b, 93–121, 121a, 122–85), with later pp. lost.

I. H. Stoltzfus, *The Lyra Viol in Consort with other instruments* (Ph.D. thesis, Louisiana, 1982).

**MSS M183–M189**   Seven instrumental part-books—each labelled 'C'—containing both manuscript and printed collections of Overtures and Concertos.

Manuscript are Overtures to Operas by [G. Bononcini, Keiser, A. M. Bononcini, Mancini, Handel (47.63.73.74.79.80.82–5.)] and [M.] Veracini; 'Minuet in F' by Geminiani; and parts of Lampe's 'Cuckoo' Concerto. The printed music consists of *Overtures* (3rd, 5th, and 6th Collections) by Handel; *Harmonia Mundi* (2nd Collection); *Two Concertos* (1742) by Avison; and further parts of *The Cuckoo Concerto*.

Mid 18th cent. All the MSS bear the name 'J. Sharp', with 'Trin. Coll.' added later; whilst M185 has (p. 81) 'Charles Sharp; James Sharp; Thomas Sharp 1741' and also 'John' and 'William'. It thus appears that these books were one of the sets used by the young Sharp family. Other names mentioned are 'John Wharton' (ibid., p. 3), 'Francis Myddleton' and 'James Mason' (ibid., p. 84).

The MS parts measure 380 × 245 mm; some pp. are partly torn away.

*M183*, Hautboy Primo: 36 ff., pag: ii + 1–27 (ms, with 1–20 imp), 28–70 (printed); *M184*, Hautboy Secundo: 31 ff., pag: ii + 1–24 (ms), 25–56 (pr), 57–8 (ms) + ii; *M185*, Violino Primo: 45 ff., pag: iv + 1–22 (ms), 23–54 (pr), 55–74 (ms), 75–84 (pr) + ii; *M186*, Violino Secundo: 36 ff., pag: iv + 1–22 (ms), 23–66 (pr) + ii; *M187*, Viola: 37 ff., pag: iv + 1–22 (ms), 23–68 (pr) + ii; *M188*, Violoncello: 39 ff., pag: iv + 1–22 (ms), 23–72 (pr) + ii; *M189*, Basso: 49 ff., pag: iv + 1–24 (ms), 25–86 (pr), 87–8 (ms), 89–92 (pr) + ii.

**MS M192**   Full scores of Bull (4.), Handel (40.), Steffani (2.5.6.), and the Adagio from [Op. 7], Concerto 3, by [G.] Valentini.

Early 18th cent. Pp. 1–104, 306–13 are in the hand of the Hon. Revd Edward Finch.

365 × 247 mm. 189 ff., pag: 1–378. Blanks include pp. 314–78.

**MS M193**

**M193/1**: Five-part score of six sonatas, in B♭, g, e, f, A, and F, ascrib to [P. A.] Ziani. Added later were the catch, 'Oil and vinegar are two pretty things' by [H. Hall], and 'Next winter comes slowly' by [H. Purcell]. On a large folded sheet stuck inside the front cover are five six-part pieces (anon 101.). The first, in C, has the words 'soe gracious'; then follow 'Gowers Allmain' in F, 'Gallyard' in F, 'Allens Gallyard' in F, and 'Jo^n. Lasses Allmaine' in d.

Early 18th cent. Christ Church MS 3 agrees as regards original contents, composer, size, and hand. Although the first three sonatas appear to be an arrangement in three groups of four of the first twelve of *Ziani's Aires or Sonatas in 3 Parts* (Op. 1, 1703), Michael Talbot suggests Albinoni as their composer. The catch, 'Oil and vinegar', in the hand of Edward Finch, connect the MS with York, as does the comment, 'for Mr. Wanlass' (org, York, 1689–1711), which is written on the second side of the inserted sheet.

455 × 287 mm. 24 ff., pag: ①–④ + ii + 1–40 + ii.

**M193/2–7**: At the outset these six part-books held twelve sonatas—an unascribed 'Sonata Gamutt' (anon 100.), the six by Ziani, an anonymous one in g (anon 97.), two by Navarra, in C and a, and two further unascribed sonatas, both in D (anon 98.99.).

A five-part piece in C by Keller, and movements from two Masses by Borri are later.

Early 18th cent. The full scores of anon 97–9 and of the two sonatas by Navarra are also in MS M175. The presence of music copied by Edward Finch (e.g. M193/2, p. 24) and by one of the hands of MS M170 (M193/3, p. 29) again connects the MSS with York. Anon 97 and 99 may be by Albinoni.

330 × 212 mm. *M193/2*, 1st Treble, Trumpett, Tromba: 18 ff., pag: 1–36; *M193/3*, 2nd Treble, 1st Violin: 19 ff., pag: 1–38; *M193/4*, Alto, 3rd Treble, 2nd Violin: 20 ff., pag: 1–40; *M193/5*, Tenor: 4 ff., pag: 1–8, with later pp. torn away; *M193/6*, Bass: 19 ff., pag: 1–38; *M193/7*, Bass: 20 ff., pag: 1–40.

**MS M194**   A holograph catalogue (inc) of some of the printed and manuscript music owned by 'John Sharp [III], Trin. Coll.'.

Listed in order are works by Avison, [G. B. Bononcini, Keiser, A. M. Bononcini, Mancini, Handel], Arne, Charke, Prelleur, John Frederick Lampe, Keller, Finger, Jenkins, Flackton, Salvatore Lanzetti, Galliard, Carey, Leveridge, Pepusch, Bennegar, Hasse, H[esletine], Heighington, Leonardo Pescatore, Tireman, Francesco Barbella, Antonio Vivaldi, Nicolo Fiorenza, Gravina, Pergolesi, Solnitz, Carlo Cailo, Pietro Marchitelli, Claudio Roreri, Porpora, Francisco Gizziello, Lewis Granom, Gregory Werner, and Purcell.

2nd half of 18th cent. Certain of the works are described as being 'from Charles' [a brother], and others 'from Hon. Mr. Finch's Collect$^n$' (*see* MS M70). See too a list of some of John Sharp III's music on a piece of paper loose inside MS M174.

96 × 189 mm. 22 ff., pag: 44 (12–13, 16–23, 28–38, 38a, 39–40, 43–62).

**M195**   Printed contents: the four single parts of *Sonatas for three Violins and a Bass* by Godfrey Finger (Op. 1; 1688).

Manuscript: performance modifications to, and the rectifying of incompleteness in, the above single parts.

Early 18th cent. The 3rd Violin part (M195/3) has sewn into it transcripts to the C clef of Sonatas 10–12. On paper (3 ff.; 274 × 288 mm), these are in the hand of Edward Finch. The Bass part (M195/4) is incomplete, and is made good to some extent by M195/5 (5 ff.; 263 × 307 mm) which contains Sonatas 8 (inc), 9–11, and 12 inc). cf. MS M196.

**MS M196** The 1st and 2nd Violin parts of '3 Sonatas for 3 Violins & a Base', being [Op. 1, Sonatas 8, 9, and 7] by Godfrey Finger.

Early 18th cent. Transcribed by Edward Finch. Cf. M195.

327 × 204 mm. *M196/1*, 1st Violin: 10 pp., 3 blank; *M196/2*, 2nd Violin: 12 pp., 5 blank.

**MS M197** (formerly in M214) Three parts of two pieces for three flutes, by Godfrey Finger: (i) Pastorelle in G; and (ii) a three-movement Sonata in F.

Early 18th cent. Each part of the Sonata is also transposed to D, the transposer being Edward Finch.

224 × 294 mm. Each part, 4 pp.; 24 pp. in all.

**MS M199** (formerly in M215) The four single parts of a 'Sonata à 4 [in F] del sig$^r$ Arcangelo Corelli'.

Early 18th cent.

268 × 195 mm. Each part, 4 pp.

**MS M200** (formerly in M214) The 1st Violin (M200/1) and 2nd Violin (M200/2) parts of six Sonatas from [*Duplex genius*] by 'Sign$^r$ Johanes Christophorus Pez'; together with (p. 16) [Edward Finch's] holograph arrangement of 'The Old 100th' (Hymn tune) in 5, 6, and 7 parts.

Early 18th cent. Although numbered 1 to 6 here, the Sonatas are nos. 1–3, 7, 5, and 8 in the published edition.

330 × 208 mm. Each part, 16 pp.

**MS M201** (formerly in M215)

(i) Score of Op. 2 Sonata 3 for two violoncellos by Lanzetti.

Mid 18th cent. In same hand as some of MS M69 and M108.

303 × 241 mm. 4 pp.

(ii) 3rd part of a Sonata in d for three flutes by G. Keller.

Early 18th cent. In the same hand as Bod. Lib. MS Mus. Sch. c.44, f. 72.

277 × 215 mm; 2 pp.

**MS M202** Seven single parts of 'Concerto Violoncello' in G by Cervetto.

2nd half of 18th cent. The harpsichord part has the cello part added in pencil, a situation which compensates for the disappearance of a separate solo part.

205 × 303 mm. Total of 20 pp., 4 being blank.

**MS M203**  Four of the single parts (2nd and 3rd Violins, Viola, Bass) of 'Concerto No. 14' in d (anon 115.).

?Early 18th cent. At the end of the Viola part (M203/3) is written 'Finis Gallipoli copiavit', whilst the initials 'V. M.' are on the outside of the Bass part (M203/4).

213 × 276 mm. Total of 12 pp.

**MS M204**  15 short pieces (pp. 3–11; anon 119.) for the violoncello and continuo, both parts being given. Followed by 'A Collection of Solos for the Hoboy D'Amour' (p. 13)—there are four complete short items (pp. 14–16; anon 120.).

Mid 18th cent. 'F, 4 parts, Basso . . .' is written on the front cover. Owned by John Sharp [III] whilst at 'Trin. Coll.' [Cambridge], in his hand, the Archdeacon of Northumberland bookplate being added later.

203 × 292 mm. 9 ff., pag: ii + 1–16, with further pages torn away.

**MS M205** (formerly in M214)  Full score of 'Dialogue in Amphitrion' by Dr Boyce.

2nd half 18th cent. There are three movements: Plutus, 'Away with Fables philosophers hold'; Wit, 'Plutus vain is all your vaunting'; and Plutus and Wit, 'In vain would your jargon'. The MS bears the bookplate of John Sharp [III], Prebendary of Durham and Archdeacon of Northumberland, who has also written his name and 'Durham' on the first page.

295 × 242 mm. 10 ff., pag: 1–20, pp. 18–20 being blank.

**MS M206** (formerly in M214)  Full score of 'O let my mouth be filled', a verse anthem for the bass voice, by James Hesletine.

Mid 18th cent. Transcribed by Cuthbert Brass, copyist of many of Durham's liturgical MSS. Following a disagreement with the Dean and Chapter of Durham, Hesletine, a pupil of Blow, is said to have destroyed many of his compositions.

290 × 238 mm. 10 ff., pag: 1–20.

**MS M207** (formerly in M216)   Full score of 'Evening Service in Eb' by [E. Gregory].

*c.*1748 (*see* e.g. MS B7, p. 235). Transcribed by Brass (*see* MS M206).

300 × 276 mm. 26 ff., pag: 1–52.

**MS M208** (formerly in M214)   A three-movement keyboard item in c (anon 73.), entitled 'Solo'; followed by the Rounds 'When Gammar Gurton first I knew' by [Edward Finch] (4 pts), and 'Observe with care and judgment' (7 pts; anon 47.); and the opening of another keyboard piece.

Early 18th cent. Transcribed by Finch. As the first of the Rounds is ascribed to Finch in Euing MS R.d.39 (Glasgow University Library), and as the second is in his hand at Durham in MS M70, both personal MSS, it too is possibly by him.

240 × 305 mm. 8 pp., in the form of two bifolia sewn together.

**M211–M216**   Together with the Bamburgh music books are six folders. These Harman seems not to have found, for none of their printed items is mentioned in his catalogue of the cathedral's printed music. To avoid a further system of references the folders have been re-numbered, their old numbers being preserved in the units figures.

**M211–13:** In these there remain five, four, and three printed works respectively. It is not known what may have been removed.

**M214:** Three printed works remain. MS M197, Pr. M198, MSS M200, M205, M206, and M208 were formerly in here.

**M215:** Only minor MS music remains. This includes a song entitled, 'The Complaint' (anon 30.), and several hymn tunes, some of them by [Thomas Sharp II]. MSS M199 and M201 were removed from here.

**M216:** Only MS music remains. This includes another copy of [Un Leçon Français] (anon 123.), and four single parts from three sonatas and concertos (anon 116–18.). Brass (*see* MS M206) copied anon 118. MS M207 was formerly in here.

# INDEX OF COMPOSERS
# AND THEIR COMPOSITIONS

## ANONYMOUS

A number of tentative identifications (indicated, e.g. [?FORD]) are entered both here and under their suggested composers.

### A. VOCAL

*Mediaeval polyphony* (14th cent. and motets, unless stated otherwise)
1. Ad lacrimas flentis dolorem
   C.I.20, ff. 336*v–7
2. [Amer amours est l'achoison]
   C.I.20, f. 336*
3. Apta caro plumis ingenio
   C.I.20, ff. 338v–9
4. Barrabas dimittitur dignus
   C.I.20, f. 3
5. . . . Clemens creator eloy te tremunt omnes angeli (3-pt Kyrie Trope; inc)
   C.I.8, f. 1
6. Dei preco fit baptista
   C.I.20, f. 3
7. Deo gratias
   C.I.20, f. 4v
8. Fusa cum silentio
   C.I.20, f.1v
9. Gloria in excelsis (*c*.1400; 3-pt, troped)
   Communar's Cartulary
10. Gloria in excelsis (*c*.1500; single pt, inc)
    A.IV.23
11. Herodis in pretorio
    C.I.20, f. 1
12. Jesu fili dei patris
    C.I.20, f. 2
13. Kyrie Cuthberti prece culpa (*c*.1400; 3-pt Kyrie Trope)
    A.III.11, f. 1v
14. Kyrie + Sanctus + Agnus Dei (*c*.1400; 3-pt, textless)
    A.III.11, f. 1

15. L'amoureuse flour d'esté
    C.I.20, f. 338
16. Mon chant en pliant
    C.I.20, f. 339$^v$
17. Musicorum collegio in curia
    C.I.20, ff. 338$^v$–9
18. O pater excelse (3-pt Kyrie Trope, inc)
    C.I.8, f. 1$^v$
19. Orto solo serene novitatis
    C.I.20, ff. 3$^v$–4
20. O vos omnes quibus est aditus
    C.I.20, f. 337$^v$
21. Princeps apostolice turme
    C.I.20, f. 2$^v$
22. Spiritus et alme (c.1400; single pt of Gloria Trope)
    Communar's Cartulary
23. Virginalis concio virginis
    C.I.20, f. 336★
24. Virgo dei genetrix
    C.I.20, f. 4$^v$

*Later items* (unsegregated):

25. Textless anthem (organ pt; beginning lost)
    A33:23–4
26. A dove a sparrow a parrot
    D9v:8
27. Appear all ye graces
    E32:48–50, 52
28. Arise O God into thy resting place (anthem; frag)
    D9:42–3
29. Begging we will go (*see* 'The craftsman makes . . .')
30. Behold the sweet flowers around (The Complaint)
    M215
31. By the waters of Babylon (verse anthem; full score)
    B1v:32–5
32. Chants:
    (a) late 17th/early 18th cent. collections
        ['Canterbury'], numbered 2
            C12v:273 (tenor)  C26v:3 (bass)  C28:507f (bass)
        ['Imperial'], numbered 1
            C12v:273 (tenor)  C26v:3 (bass)  C28:507f (bass)
        4 single chants, in g, g, F, e, numbered 22–5
            C28:507h (bass)

ANONYMOUS (*cont.*)

  single chant in A
   E32:76 (treble + bass)
  single chant in B♭
   E32:87
 (b) 19th cent. collections (not even ascrib chants are listed in Index of Composers)
   D12/1–10 M71:167–8 sundry pt-books have chants in pencil

33. Crown me with roses (duet)
  D9:16–17
34. Good morrow gossip Joan
  M70:60–1
35. Guten Abend lieber Mondenschein (Der Mondenschein)
  E38:18–19
36. Hallelujah (chorus of anthem)
  B1:173
37. Hear my prayer O Lord and hide not (anthem)
  C7:370–1 (alto) C14: 202–3 (tenor) C15:198 (tenor)
38. Ho che liquor ho che sapor (Canon à 6; same as 'Observe with care . . .') [?FINCH]
  M70:49
39. Hymn tunes (the description of the MSS includes a list of any unascrib tunes)
  A16:215 (Old 100th) E11a: 305–9 E15:63 (Old 100th)
  E32:75–6 (Windsor, with Interludes) E37 M90
  M173:16–17, 28
  *See* Metrical Psalm Interludes
40. I will magnify thee (frag of anthem)
  Biv:9
41. '2 Kyrie' in a (no text; treble, alto, and bass)
  E30(ii):16
42. [Kyrie] in d (no text)
  A2:162
43. Kyrie in G (in pencil)
  B8:93
44. Like as the hart (verse anthem; full score)
  A17:136–43
45. Look shepherds look (verse anthem; full score) [?FORD]
  B1:16–20
46. Metrical Psalm Interludes
  E32:37 (Ps. 113) E32:43 (Ps. 100) E32:44 (Ps. 25)
  E32:75–6 (Windsor)

47. Observe with care and judgment (Canon à 7; same as 'Ho che liquor')
     [?FINCH]
     M70:49   M70:53   M208:6–7
48. O come let us humble ourselves (text only; used as alternative to
     Venite, 8 July 1640)
     C10:87–8
49. O come vaga appare Cosi adorno (recit of ?cantata)
     E26(vii)
50. O deck thy hair with the heather bell (frag)
     M89:31
51. Of all the simple things we do [?CAREY]
     E32:32
52. O God wherefore art thou absent (verse anthem; bass only)
     C19:237–9
53. O how amiable (verse anthem; full score) [?ISAAK]
     B1:170–2
54. O praise the Lord all ye nations (imp)
     M174:2
55. O sing praises (verse anthem; full score)
     B1:161–4
56. Pe'r L'ampio mar d'Amore mentre scorre (solo cantata)
     E29(ii):1–11
57. Rejoice in the Lord alway (anthem; attrib to REDFORD in these
     19th cent. MSS)
     D23:219–20   D30–5:41–2
58. Sancta Dei Genetrix (18th cent. transcript)
     E11a:352
59. . . . Se di me' l'antica gloria (solo cantata; inc)
     E29(ii):59–70
60. Service in G: Td, J, C (full vocal score; copied by 1738)
     M70:92–108, 148–53
61. Sing O daughter of Sion (verse anthem; full score + violin pt of last
     chorus)
     B1v:26–31
62. Si si mia dolce Irene (recit of ?cantata)
     E26(vii)
63. Smile smile blest isle [?FINCH]
     M70:62–3
64. Stell' amica ver' me non selegnar (solo cantata)
     E29(ii):12–15
65. The craftsman makes a mighty pother
     M70v:128–55
66. [The Vicar of Bray] (melody only)
     E32:85

ANONYMOUS (*cont.*)

67. The voice of my beloved (verse anthem; full score)
   B1:156–60
68. [?They] that go down (part of organ bass)
   B1:172
69. Tobacco is an Indian weed
   D9:49
70. Va e la Natura (recit of ?cantata)
   E26(vii)

B. INSTRUMENTAL

*For ?organ:*
71. Fantasia [I] in d [?W. SMITH]
   A1:328–30
72. Fantasia [II] in d (imp) [?W. SMITH]
   A1:331–3
73. 'Solo' in c
   M208:1–5

*For 2 viols and bass continuo:*
74. Sonata 1, in g
   D2/1–3:1
75. Sonata 2, in A (only 2 pts)
   D2/1,2:2–3
76. Sonata 7, in B♭
   D2/1,2:7   D2/3:9
77. Sonata 9, in D
   D2/1,2:9   D2/3:11
78. Sonata 10, in e
   D2/1,2:10–11   D2/3:12
79. Sonata 13, in D
   D2/1,2:14–15   D2/3:15
80. Sonata 15, in C
   D2/1–3:18–19
81. Sonata 24, in D
   D2/1:35   D2/2:37   D2/3:31
82. Sonata 27, in g
   D2/1:39–41   D2/2:41–3   D2/3:36–7
83. Fantasia in G
   D4/1,2:10–12   D4/3:4
84. Sonata in B♭
   D4/1:23–4   D4/2:24–5
85. Sonata in d
   D5/1–3:6–7

86. Sonata in g
    D5/1–3:8–9
87. Suite in A
    D5/1–3: 16–17
88. 30 sonatas (all imp), forming 'Set C'
    M179:131–59 (2nd Treble)    M180:62–91 (1st Treble)

*For the viola da gamba:*

89. 8 short pieces
    A27:83–5, 101–2, 249–50, 311–12
90. Sonatino in D
    D10:90–3

*For 3 flutes:*

91. 12 sonatas (all imp), forming 'Set A' [?G. KELLER]
    M179:3–25 (Treble)    M180:2–? [*sic*] (1st flute)
    M180:169–85 (Treble)

*For string and/or brass ensemble:*

92. Sonata à 3 in F
    M175:1 (end only)
93. Sonata à 4 in D
    M175:91–22
94. Sonata à 4 in c
    M175:22–9
95. [Sonata] à 4 in F
    M175:29–36
96. Sonata à 4 in d
    M175:37–42
97. Sonata à 5 in g (score and pts) [?ALBINONI]
    M175:58–68    M193/2–4, 6, 7:14–15
98. [Sonata] à 5 and 6 in D (score and pts)
    M175:69–88    M193/2–4, 6, 7:20–1
99. Serenatto à 6 in D (score and pts) [? ALBINONI]
    M175:89–93    M193/2, 4, 6:22    M193/3, 7:22–3
100. 'Sonata Gamutt', à 5
    M193/2–7:1
101. In 6-pt score: 'Gowers Allmain', 'Gallyard', 'Allens Gallyard' [all
    in F], 'Joⁿ. Lasses Allmaine' [in d], 'soe gracious' [in C]
    M193/1:①–④
102. Minuet à 5 in D [some of nos. 102–9 may be by FINCH]
    M70:8–9
103. ? à 4 in C
    M70:24–5    M70:28–33

**Anonymous** (*cont.*)

104. Concerto 3za à 4 in C
     M70:26–7
105. ? à 4 in d
     M70:36–7
106. Fugue à 5 in d
     M70:37–41
107. Cantabile Fugue à 5 in d
     M70:41–5
108. ? à 4 in B♭
     M70:54–8
109. ? à 2 in A (slightly later hand)
     M70:57
110. Concerto 1, in F (pts) [?HANDEL]
     E33/1–5:1–3
111. Concerto 2 in F (score and pts)
     E26(ix)   E33/1–3:4–6   E33/4:3–5   E33/5:6–7
112. Concerto Grosso, in b (pts)
     E33/1, 2:9–10   E33/3:10–11   E33/4:8–9   E33/5: 11–12
113. Concerto in E♭ (score)
     E25(xvii)
114. Concerto in G (score)
     E24(vi)
115. Concerto no. 14, in d, by 'V. M.'
     M203 (inc)
116. 2nd violin concertino pt of [Sonata in g]
     M216
117. 1st violin concertino pt of [Concerto in e] (+bass pt of Adagio
     movement)
     M216
118. 1st violin and cello pts of 'Concerto Quartro' in F
     M216

*For violoncello and continuo*:

119. 15 short pieces
     M204:3–11

*For 'Hoboy D'Amour'*:

120. 4 solos
     M204:14–16

*For violin and continuo*:

121. 7 sonatas, in B♭, G, B♭, g, B♭, C, E♭. Nos. 5–7 are ascrib to
     TARTINI, but in nos. 6–7 this has been crossed out
     M159:1–39

*Miscellaneous keyboard reductions*:

122. [British National Anthem] + variations
     M69:18–19
123. 'Un leçon français [ = Baa baa black sheep] + variations
     M69:62–5   M69:90   M108v:2–4   M216
124. Trumpet tunes, marches, dance tunes, etc.
     E24(ii), (viii), and (xii)   E32:1–7, 8, 23, 28–32, 33–7, 42, 45–52, 56,
     63–4, 84, 86–7   M69:14, 17–23, 26–33, 40–5, 49–51, 56, 57–61,
     66–9, 76–7, 84–5, 90   M108:5, 8, 10   M108v:1–2   M215
     M216

C. THEORETICAL

125. Discourse on Consonance and Dissonance (in Italian)
     E15:63–4

ABEL (ABELL), Clamor Heinrich (1634–96)
'Cuccu' Sonata à 3 in G
   D2/1: 26–7   D2/2:28–9   D2/3:24–5

AGOSTINI (AUGUSTINI), Pietro Simone (*c*.1635–80)
Là dove all'herbe in seno d'un pargoletto Rio
   E29(ii):71–86

ALBERTI, [Giuseppe Matteo] (1685–1751)
[Op. 1]
Concerto 4
   M157:33 (Presto)
Concerto 5
   M157:50–1 (Allegro Assai)

ALBINONI, Tomaso Giovanni (1671–1751)
Sonatas possibly by him, but ascrib to ZIANI. *See also* ANON (97.99.)

ALCOCK, John (1715–1806)
In e: Td, J, K, C, M, N
   A13v:94–112   B5:244–54 (N inc)   B7:269–80   B8v:47–58
   B13v:63–74   B17v:124–34   B19:340–59   B22:154–61
   B31v:61–71   B32v:52–9   B33v:44–55   B35:120–31
   B36v:81–91 (N inc)   C31:425–32 (-K, C)

ALDERSON, M. F. (MSS late 19th cent.)
Rend your hearts
   D30:155   D31–3:153   D34:157   D35:153

ALDRICH, Henry (1648–1710)
  1. All people that on earth (ascrib to TALLIS in *Arnold 1* and in B11,
     B16, C28)

ALDRICH, HENRY (*cont.*)

A14:178–9   B6:177   B9:172   B10:370   B11:44–6   B12:6–7
B13:151   B16:50–1   B29:272   B31:94   B32:97   B33:141
B35v:105–6   C28:563–5

2. Comfort ye my people

A28:43–7   B21:145–8   B29:69–72   C19A:129–32   C21:124–7
C28:160   C29v:125–9   C35v:98–101

3. For Zion's sake (arr from CARISSIMI)

B21:148–50   C19A:132–5   C21:128–30   C28:444–5
C29v:129–32   C35v:102–4

4. Give the king thy judgments

A33:20–2   C7:353   C14:177   C15:156–7   C27:248–51
C28:161–4   C34:129–32

5. God is our hope and strength (*Page 1*)

A20:30–2   A28:33 (inc)   B6v:29–30   B9v:6–7   B10:37–9
B12:20–1   B17v:19–20   B20:27–8 (imp)   B21:25–6   B24:40–1
B26:50   B27:239–40   B29:65–6   B31:136   B32:34–5   B34:18
C19:116–17   C19A:18–20   C21:15–17   C27:61–2   C28:112–13
C29v:6–7   C35v:10–11

6. I am well pleased (arr from CARISSIMI—ascrib to him in B27)
(*Arnold 3*)

A28:39–43   B6:40–3   B9:93–6   B10:95–9   B12:46–9
B17:101–4   B24:77   B27:33–4, 37   B29:73–5   B33:29–32
C19:322–3 (imp)   C27:358–62   C28:437

7. I waited patiently

A33:104–11   C7:364–5   C14:191–3   C15:184–91   C27:242–7
C28:175–81   C34:164–70

8. Not unto us O Lord (*Arnold 1*)

B11:41–3   B16:47–8   C28:558–60   D20v:89–90

9. O give thanks unto the Lord for he is gracious (*Boyce 2*)

A29:6–7   B6v:34–5   B9v:11   B10:55–6   B12:28–9   B17v:18
B21v:9–10   B24:36–7   B26:53   B27:227–8   B29:69
C7:355–6   C14:178–9   C15:167–8   C27:78   C28:86–7   C34:72

10. O Lord I have heard

A29:82–7   B12:153–4   B17:32–3   B20:123–4   B36:63–4
C21:183–4   C29v:183–4   C35v:175–7

11. O Lord my God (arr from BULL's 'Almighty God who by the
leading')

12. O praise the Lord all ye heathen (*Arnold 1*)

A20:182–3   B11:43–4   B16:49–50   C28:561–3   D20v:90–2

13. Out of the deep (*Boyce 2*)

A20:8–9   B6v:32–4   B9v:9–11   B10:35–7   B12:19–20
B17v:18–19   B20:9–10   B21:7–9   B24:37   B26:50–1

ALLINSON, THOMAS (*cont.*)
4. Why do the heathen
   A33:30–3   C7:184–7   C14:215–19   C15:103–6   C27:90–1 (inc)
   C28:101–5   C34:81–5

AMNER, John (1579–1641)
1. I will sing unto the Lord
   A5:269–72   C1:247   C2:194   C11v:161–1b   C14:159–60
   C16:240   C17:176   C19:288
2. Cesar's Service: V, Td, J, K, C, M, N
   A1:250–69

ANTONIOTTO, Giorgio (1681–1766)
Nos. 1 and 2 (both hol) do not form part of Op. 1, his only known published instrumental work; no. 4 (hol) is not from his *L'Arte Armonica*
1. Violoncello concerto in A
   E27:1–29
2. Violoncello sonata in e
   E24(v)
3. Examples from *L'Arte Armonica* (1760)
   E24(iii)
4. The Art of Modulation
   E24(iv)

ARMES, Philip (1836–1908; org, Durham, 1862–1907) (*see* Index of Copyists)
Author unknown, 'Philip Armes', *Musical Times* (Feb. 1900).
1. I will sing a new song
   D17:1–11
2. The Lord is my light (Amen added 17 June 1896)
   D30–5:66–9
3. In A: Td, Bs, K, C, Sc, S, G, Cd, Dm
   Td, Bs, Cd, Dm
   D23:125–36 (hol; Oct 1888)
   K, C, Sc, S, G
   D17v:63–8
4. Arr BEETHOVEN (3.6.), BLOW (24.), CLARKE (6.7.13.17.), CROFT (21.23.26.27.31.46.), O. GIBBONS (17.27.), HUMFREY (9.13.), R. KING (1.), H. PURCELL (12.18.33.), SHEPPARD (3.), TURNER (3.7.), WELDON (1.11.13.)

ARNE, Thomas Augustine (1710–78)
1. How cheerful along the gay mead (Abel; ascrib to HANDEL)
   M173:11 (for 2 oboes)

BACH, JOHANN SEBASTIAN (*cont.*)

3. With all my heart I love thee (Chorale)
   D23:137

*Instrumental* (all unascrib):

4. Fantasia and Fugue in b (BWV 951a)
   E24(x)
5. Fantasia in d (BWV 905)
   E24(xi):27–8 (inc)
6. Toccata and Fugue in e (BWV 914)
   E24(xi):41, 33–7
7. Toccata in c (BWV 911)
   E24(xi):1–13
8. [Toccata] in d (BWV 913)
   E24(xi):14–27

BACON, [Robert] (d. 1759)

1. The Lord is king
   A13:96a–b   A13:126–32   A17:175–81 (inc)   B6:180–2
   B9:173–5   B10:363–6   B12:326–8   B13:152–3   B17:136–7
   B31:105–6   B33:156–8   B35v:117–19   B36:120–2   C19:486–7
   C33:110–12
2. In A re, a: Td, J
   A15:104–12   B5:290–5   B7:323–9   B13v:156–61   B17v:175–80
   B19:383–8 (J inc)   B21v:72–8   B28:176–82   B31v:113–19
   B33v:93–9   B35:162–7   B36v:113–19   C19Av:ii, 105–6 (Td inc)
   C33:88–95   C35:99–103

BAILDON, Joseph (*c.*1727–74)

Behold how good and joyful (*Page 2*)
    A16:208–14

BANCK (BANK), Charles (1809–89)

Gut' Nacht fahr' wohl (Gute Nacht aus der Ferne)
    E38:20–1

BANKS, Ralph (1767–1841; chor, Durham, 1774–88, acting as 'Teacher of the choristers', Nov. 1785 to Nov. 1788; org, Rochester, 1788–1840)

1. O Lord grant the king (*Page 3*)
   A16:66–70   B6:202–3   B8:110   B9:208   B11:60   B13:167
   B16:69   B23:186 (inc)   B33:173   B34:101   B35v:148   B36:161
   D19:16–17
2. O Lord how glorious
   A17:207–15

3. O sing unto the Lord a new song
A20:103–19  B8:94–7  B9:192–5  B11:7–10  B16:18–26
B34:7–13  B35v:137–43

BARNBY, Joseph (1838–96)
O Lord God to whom vengeance belongeth (*Ouseley 2*)
B3v:26–8

BARROW, Thomas (d. 1789)
In F: Td, J, M, N
A35:145–75

BASSANI, Giovanni Battista (*c.*1657–1716)
1. As for me I will call
B6v:67
2. I will magnify thee O God my king
A14:66–70  A28:207–11  B12:90  B20v:81  B21:160
B24:13–14  C19A:142  C21:136–7  C29v:140  C35v:111–12

[BATH, George] (*fl. c.*1625)
Hear my prayer O Lord and consider (authorship not established;
possibly by CRANFORD)

BATTEN, Adrian (1591–1637)
1. Almighty God which in thy wrath ('In the time of the Plague')
A6:260–4  C2*:35–6  C4:24  C5:17  C6:23  C7:233  C10:15
2. Blessed are those that are undefiled
A6:252–4  C2:115–16  C3:89  C11v:12–13  C14:74  C16:182
C19:222–3
3. Deliver us O Lord (*Boyce 2*)
A20:69  B10:5–6  B17v:13  C7:352 (inc)  C14:174–5
C15:100 (imp)  C19:88–9  C27:55  C28:69  C34:53
4. Haste thee O God [I]
B10:4–5  B17v:11–12  C7:353 (inc)  C14:176–7  C15:102–3
C19:85–6  C27:50–1  C28:66–7  C34:50–1
5. Hear my prayer O God and hide not
A6:265–9  A20:70–2  C1:260–1  C2:135–6  C3:108  C7:72
C11v:53–4  C14:92–3  C16:206–8  C17:157–8  C19:244–6
6. Hear my prayer O Lord and with thine ears
A6:275–8  C1:262–3  C2:137–8  C3:109–10  C7:73–4
C11v:55–6  C14:94–5  C16:208–10  C19:247–9
7. Holy holy holy Lord God Almighty
A6:96–9  C1:251  C2:117–18  C3:90  C7:59  C11v:15
C14:75  C16:197–8  C17:150–1  C19:224–5  C27:310–11
C28:137–8  C34:108–9

BATTEN, ADRIAN (*cont.*)

8. I heard a voice (St Michael and All Angels)
  A6:247–51  C1:127–8  C2:94–6  C3:72  C7:48  C11v:139–40
  C14:56  C16:346–8  C19:240–2

9. My soul truly waiteth
  B10:6–7  B17v:12  C14:175  C15:101  C19:87–8  C27:52
  C28:68  C34:52

10. O clap your hands
  C7:351–2  C14:173–4  C15:99 (imp)  C19:83–4
  C27:53–4 (imp)  C28:65–6  C34:49–50

11. O Lord thou hast searched
  A6:270–4  C1:258  C2:133  C3:106  C7:70  C11v:66–7
  C11v:176–7  C14:90  C16:204–6  C17:155–6  C19:210–12

12. O praise the Lord all ye heathen (*Boyce 2*)
  A6:374  A20:69–70  B10:3  B17v:13  C11:107–8  C12:46
  C15:79  C17:81  C19:24–5  C27:53  C28:70  C34:54

13. Out of the deep [II]
  A6:255–9  C1:268–9  C2:161–2  C3:131  C7:91  C11v:72–3
  C14:115  C16:225–6  C17:165–6  C19:271–2

14. Out of the deep [III]
  C11:106–7  C17:80

15. Ponder my words
  A6:239–42  C1:259  C2:134–5  C3:107  C7:71  C11v:78–9
  C14:91–2  C16:196–7  C17:156–7  C19:243–4

16. Praise the Lord O my soul and all
  A2:324–8  A6:90–5  C1:35–7  C4:71–2  C5:69–70  C6:72–3
  C7:286–7  C9:45–6  C10:59–60  C11v:7–9  C16:146–8
  C17:131–3  C19:181–4

17. Turn thou us O good Lord (Ash Wednesday)
  C1:98–9  C2:25–6  C3:19–20  C7:14–15  C11v:97, 99
  C14:17–18  C16:305–7  C19:350–2

18. For Meanes, in D sol re: Td, Bs, K, C, M, N
  C12v:173–82  C13v:115–27  C26:37–46  C31:42–52  C32:30–8
  C33:69–75

19. 1st Service in E fa: K, C, M, N
  C13v:107–14

20. First Verse Service: V, Td, J, K, C, M, N
  Td, J, M, N
  A6:183–204 (+V, K, C)  C1:193–5 (−Td, J)
  C13v:75–9, 90–2 (+K)  E11a:221–7, 493–6

21. Second Verse Service: V, Td, J, K, C, M, N
  A6:205–32  C1:195–8 (M, N only)  C12v:249–52 (M, N only)
  C13v:80–4, 92–5 (−V, C)  C18:91–4 (−V, C, N; M inc)
  E11a:227–32, 497–9 (−V, K, C)

22. Third Verse Service: M, N
   A6:104–12  C1:199–200  C12v:252–6  C13v:96–8  E4:163–6
   E5:163–6  E6:155–8  E7:165–9  E8:163–6  E9:157–9
   E10:154–7  E11:163–6  E11a:500–3
23. Fourth Verse Service: M, N
   A6:233–8  C1:202–4 (both imp)  C13v:99–100  E4, E5:167–9
   E6:159–61  E7:170–2  E8:167–9  E9:160–2  E10:158–60
   E11:169  E11a:503–6

BATTISHILL, Jonathan (1738–1801)
   1. Call to remembrance (*Page 1*)
      A26:70–2  A26:85–9  B6v:69–70  B9v:67–9  B12:333–5
      B13:157–9  B17:142–4  B24:33–4  B26:18–20
      B31:111–12 (inc)  B33:159–61  B34:43–5  B35v:126–8
      B36:122–4  C21:198–201
   2. Deliver us O Lord (*Page 3*)
      D30–4:142  D35:140
   3. I will sing unto the Lord
      D30–4:127  D35:125
   4. O Lord look down
      D30–4:135–6  D35:133–4

BATTYE, James (1803–58)
My soul truly waiteth (Gresham Prize Competition 1845)
   B15:164–8  D18:234–9  D19:187–92  D21:45–9

BECKER (BECKERN), Dietrich (1623–79)
Sonata à 3 in D (Pr. C72, No. 41)
   D2/1:36–7  D2/2:38–9  D2/3:32–3

BECKWITH, John Christmas (1750–1809)
   1. My soul is weary of life
      D17:142–51  D18:201–8
   2. The Lord is very great
      B4:167–73  B15:100–6  D19:71–9  D21:120–6

BEETHOVEN, Ludwig van (1770–1827)
   1. Blessed is he that cometh (Mass in C, arr LINGARD)
      B4:196–203  B15:123–9  D18:10–18  D19:99–107  D21:8–16
   2. Eternal God, Almighty Power (*Gardiner*, no. 6)
      B15:146–7  D18:214–15  D19:164–5  D21:29–30  D23:139–40
   3. Glory be to God on high (arr ARMES, Feb. 1902)
      D30:162–5  D31, D32:160–3  D33:166–9  D34:162–5
      D35:160–3

BEETHOVEN, LUDWIG VAN (*cont.*)
  4. Great God of all
       B15:152–3   D18:218–21   D19:171–3   D21:39–41
  5. Hallelujah to the Father (Mount of Olives)
       A10:169–98   B4:145–9   B15:79–82   C22v:145–9   D20v:100–4
       D21:91–4
  6. He is blessed (arr ARMES)
       D23:141–4
  7. O praise Jehovah's goodness
       B4:221–8
  8. Praise the Lord O my soul and all (from Kyrie in C)
       B15:180–1   D18:254–6   D19:199–201   D21:64–6

BEMBOW, E. (MS *c.*1730)
My heart is fixed
  A8:95–100 ( + cornet part)

BENNET, John (b. *c.*1575–80; *fl.* 1599–1614)
O God of Gods
  A6:159–64

BENNETT, [J. Lionel S. D.] (Durham; m–c, 1893–1901; assist org, 1895–1901)
  1. I will lay me down
       D31–4:145–7   D35:143–5
  2. In A: Td, Bs, M, N
       D30v:33–42   D31v–3v:31–40   D34v:31–7, 38–40   D35v:31–40

BENSON, Thomas (m of chor, York, 1698–1742)
Gigue, added to FINCH, Sonata 6
  M70v:33

BEVIN, Elway (*c.*1554–1638)
In Dorian Mode: Td, Bs, 'J', K, C, M, N (*Boyce 1*)
Td, Bs, K, C, M, N
  A3:306–25   A13v:138–51   B3:157–73   B5:263–72   B7:297–307
  B8v:178–89   B13v:132–42   B16v:46–59   B17v:152–60
  B31v:78–88   B32v:65–73   B33v:63–73   B35:138–47
  B36v:103–13   C12v:139–48   C13v:162–74   C26:18–27
  C31:31–41   C32:39–47   C33:80–8   D20:131–46
'J' (from Bs: arr SHENTON)
  A18:13–17

BISHOP, John (*c.*1665–1737)
  1. Withdraw not thou thy mercy
       A14:169–72   B6:169–70   B8:82–3   B9:176–7   B12:124–5

B13:137–8  B17:122–3  B24:71  B29:270–1  B31:101–2
B32:98  B33:139–40  B35v:119–21  C19:488
2. In D: Td, Bs, Cd, Dm
B5:258–62, 273–9  B7:283–7, 308–14  B8v:62–6, 190–6
B13v:77–80, 142–8  B17v:137–41, 161–6  B23:90–6  B28:320–9
B31v:74–8, 108–13  B33v:59–62, 74–80  B35:134–7, 148–54
Td, Bs
A15:93–103  A34:265–301  B22:164–7  C25:95–102
Cd, Dm
A10v:1–22  A13v:118–24  B16v:133–8  B19:364–71
B32v:62–5  B36v:96–8 (Cd inc)  C31:411–16

## BLAKE, [Edward] (1708–65)

I have set God always (*Page 2*)
A13:85–90  B6v:64–6  B8:35–7  B9v:50–2  B12:91–2
B13:95–7  B17:86–7  B20:140–2  B24:7–9  B26:34–5
B31:68–70 (inc)  B32:77–9  B33:115–17  B34:20–2
B35v:82–4 (inc)  B36:111–13  C28:480–4  D20v:178–80

## BLANCOURT (MS *c*.1700)

Gigue in d, 'ex MSS'
A27:66–7

## BLANCKS (BLANKS), [Edward] (*c*.1550–1633)

To PARSONS of Wells's Flatt Service: M, N
A3:275–84  C13:275–9  C18:71–3 (N imp)  E11a:437–42

## BLETT, John (MS *c*.1670)

Ad te Domine: Thou Lord art my strength
B1:77–80

## BLOW, John (1649–1708)

1. And I heard a great voice (earlier version of 'I was in the spirit')
   A28:121–2  A33:83–5  C7:390–2  C27:306–10  C28:308–11
   C34:287–90
2. Christ being raised
   A25:9–13
3. God is our hope and strength (*Boyce 2*)
   A9v:27–9  A25:38–9  B9:44–6  C7:366–7  C14:194–5
   C15:182–3  C27:82–3  C28:96–7  C34:74–6  D18:50–6
4. How art thou fallen (Lucifer's Fall)
   A8:122–5
5. I beheld and lo (*Boyce 3*)
   A20:130–5  A25:119–25  A28:103–8  B6:45–8  B8:75–7
   B9:38–40  B10:255–60  B12:115–18  B24:74  B26:103–10

BLOW, JOHN (*cont.*)

B27:100–2 (inc)   B29:83–5   B31:81–3   B33:65–7
C7:205–8 (inc)   C7:413–14   C14:237–41   C15:141–4
C27:293–6   C28:323–7   C34:305–7, 312   D18:84–95

6. I said in the cutting off
B6:3–6   B9:29–31   B10:233–6   B12:166–7   B13:8–10
B17:42–4   B29:212–15   B31:11–13   B33:3–5   B35v:24–6
B36:84–7

7. I was in the spirit (*Boyce 2*) (cf. 'And I heard a great voice')
A14:1–7   A20:120–5   B6:25–8   B8:72–4   B9:34–7   B10:252–5
B12:120–2   B18v:16   B24:73   B27:113–17   B29:92–5
B31:78–80   B33:48–50   B35v:89–92   D18:95–107

8. I will always give thanks (*see* CLUB ANTHEM)

9. Lift up your heads
A13:91–4   B6:163–4   B8:54–5   B9v:56–7   B12:128–30
B13:133–4   B17:116–17   B24:41–2   B29:268–9   B31:84–6
B32:89–90   B33:133–4   B35v:96–7   C28:526–8

10. Lord how are they increased
A25:40–4   A28:116–18, 120   B6:53–4   B9:49–50   B12:199–200
B27:110–11   C7:405–6   C27:290–1   C28:222–3   C34:184–5

11. My God my soul is vexed (*Boyce 2*)
A29:50–1

12. O be joyful in God
A25:98–104   B27:90–4   C14:236   C27:297–300   C28:414–17

13. O give thanks unto the Lord and call
A25:59–61   C28:315–19   C34:291–5

14. O God wherefore art thou absent (*Boyce 2*)
A20:26–8   A29:12–13   B6v:25–7   B9:46–7 (notes frag)
B9v:35–6   B10:45–6   B12:41–2   B17v:15–16   B21v:15–16
B24:38   B26:56   B27:206–7   B29:82–3   B32:33–4   C7:334–5
C11v:231–2   C14:165–6   C27:81–2   C28:98–9   C34:73–4

15. O Lord I have sinned (*Boyce 3*)
A25:1–5   B6:48–50   B9:42–4   B10:167–70   C7:201–3
C7:406–7   C14:186–7   C15:178–81   C27:223–5   C28:312–14
C34:282–4

16. O Lord thou hast searched (*Boyce 3*)
A33:78–82   B10:277–8   B12:157   B17:57   B27:140–2
C14:184–5   C15:176–7   C27:228–31   C28:205–8   C34:171–4

17. O sing unto God (*Boyce 3*)
A9:18–24   A25:90–7   A28:110–15   B6:51–3   B9:47–9
B10:260–4   B12:196–9   B24:73   B27:86–9   B29:90–2
B33:36–8   C14:241–4   C19A:34   C27:301–4   C28:410–13

18. O sing unto the Lord a new song
    B1v:84–6
19. Save me O God (*Boyce 2*)
    A25:6–8
20. Sing we merrily (*Page 2*)
    A28:123–6   A33:40–3   B6:35–6   B6:167–8   B9:41–2
    B12:55–7   B18v:14–15   B24:38–9   B27:111–13   B29:88–9
    C7:174–5   C14:213   C15:212   C27:226–7 (imp)   C28:306–7
    C34:285–6   D19:29–33
21. The Lord even the most mighty
    A25:88–9   C7:400–1   C14:230–1   C15:216 (inc)   C27:271–6
    C28:189–95   C34:149–54
22. The Lord is king
    A25:62–5   C28:320–3   C34:295–8
23. The Lord is my shepherd
    B6:8–11   B9:31–4   B10:225–8   B12:164–5   B13:3–5
    B17:38–40   B29:217–20   B31:6–8   B33:8–10   B35v:19–21
    B36:80–2
24. Turn thee unto me (*Div Harm 2, 1731*; D MSS arr ARMES)
    A8:194   A33:2–5   C7:182–3   C11v:221–2   C14:214–15
    C15:201–2   C27:291–2   C27:304–5   C28:209–10   C34:175–6
    D23:110–11   D26/1–5:26–7   D26/6–9:27–8
25. Turn us again O Lord
    A25:112–18
26. We will rejoice
    A25:105–11   C27:332   C28:422
27. When Israel came out
    A25:30–2   A28:108–10   B6:54–6   B9:50–2   B10:162–6
    B12:256–60   B29:86–8   C7:196–9   C14:244–7   C27:319–22
    C28:406–9   C34:312–15
28. In A, A re: Td, J, K, C, Cd, Dm (*Boyce 1*)
    A9v:9–26   A15:51–61   A22:88–102   A33:135–52   B3:211–28
    B5:128–39   B7:115–26   B8v:166–77   B19:168–84   B22:95–103
    B23:14–16, 19–20 (C, Cd inc)   B28:203–15   C8:459–71
    C19Av:76–86   C26:273–82   C30:138–44 (−K, C)   C31:276–86
    C32:264–74   C33:307–17   D18v:87–92 (just Cd, Dm)
    M170:96–103
29. In D: S, G
    A13v:152–3   B6v:67–8   B8v:177–8   B13v:128–30
    B20v:138–40   B22:168   B23:84–5   B28:182–4   C10:109–10
    C15:97–8   C19Av:6   C23:69–70   C27:161–2   C28:507c–e
    C30:226–7   C33:186–8

Blow, John (*cont.*)

30. In e: Td, Be, J, K, C, Cd, Dm (*Boyce 3*)
    A33:191–219   B22:116–25   B28:185–202
    C8:424–32, 434 (–Td, Be; Dm inc)   C12v:45–56   C26:283–94
    C31:287–301   C32:242–55   C33:274–87
    Td, J, Cd, Dm
    A15:131–43   A22:153–64   B5:120–8   B7:107–15   B8v: 159–66
    B19:184–96   B23:34–9   C30:160–6
31. In G, in Gamut: Td, J, K, C, M, N (*Boyce 1*)
    A15:70–80   A33:118–34   B3:240–53   B22:80–7   B28:311–19
    C8:447–58   C14v:1–9   C26:264–72   C31:267–75   C32:256–64
    C33:288–96
    Td, J, M, N
    A22:145–52   B5:115–20 (Td inc)   B7:100–2, 107   B8v:152–8
    B19:197–207   B23:24–9   B29v:15–20   C30:154–9
    M170:137–43
    K, C (different from above)
    B22:87–9
32. Unascrib single chant in e, numbered 4
    C12v:273 (tenor)   C26v:3 (bass)   C28:507f (bass)

*Secular items* (both unascrib):
33. Come here's a good health
    D9v:1
34. I knew brother Tarr
    D9v:5–7


BOCCHI, Lorenzo (*fl. c.*1720)
   1. Sonata in G
      M70v:62–5
   2. Arrangements of FINCH's sonatas
      M70v:66–75


[BONONCINI, Antonio Maria] (1677–1726)
Camilla, Overture
   M185–6:3   M189:4


BONONCINI, Giovanni (1670–1747)
   1. When Saul was king
      B12:193–6   B17:11–12   B20v:11–12   B21:50–2   B27:148–50
      B32:57–8   B36:17–18   C19A:158–9   C29v:159–60   C35:137–8
      E16:1–30
   2. Astartus, Overture (unascrib)
      M186–9:1

3. Thomyris, Overture (unascrib)
   M185–6:5   M189:5

BORRI, Giovanni Battista (*fl.* 1655–88)
  1. O praise the Lord all ye heathen (from Gloria of 4-pt Mass)
     M70v:100–15
  2. 4-pt Mass (cf. above): K, G
     E31/1, 2:1–6   E31/3, 4:1–7   M193/2:24–7   M193/2:29–33
     M193/3:25–9   M193/4:25–7   M193/6:25–9   M193/7:25–8
  3. 5-pt Mass: C
     E31/1, 2:7–9   E31/3, 4:8–11   M193/2:34 (inc)   M193/3:32–3
     M193/4:29–31   M193/6:30–2   M193/7:29–31

BORUWLASKI, Count Joseph (Polish dwarf, b. *c.*1739; came to England, 1782; d. Durham, 1837)
Allegretto in G
  D3:38–9

BOYCE, Thomas (early 17th cent.)
Short Service: Td, Bs, K, C, M, N
  A1:238–49   C1:287–91 (− Bs; Td inc)   C12v:117–24 (− N; M inc)
  C13:159–67   C26:28–36   C31:21–30   C32:21–9   C33:13–18
  E11a:87–90, 281–3, 407–9

BOYCE, William (1711–79)
★ = *Fifteen Anthems together with a Te Deum and Jubilate . . . by William Boyce*, ed. P. Hayes (1780)
† = *A Collection of Anthems And a Short Service . . . by the late William Boyce*, ed. P. Hayes (1790)
  1. ★Be thou my judge
     A26:1–5   B6:179   B9:173   B10:359–63   B12:321–3
     B13:142–5   B17:133–6   B24:93   B29:281–3   B31:103–4
     B32:99   B33:151–2   B35v:112–13   C19:484   D30–5:4
  2. Blessing and glory (*Arnold 3*)
     D22v:132–3
  3. ★By the waters of Babylon
     A13:42–7   B8:1–3   B9v:44–6   B10:286–90   B12:92–4
     B13:27–9 (inc)   B17:58–60   B24:18–19   B26:67–70
     B29:231, 234–6   B31:25–8   B32:72–4   B33:81–4   B35v:38–40
     C28:473–7   D19:62–6
  4. ★Give the king thy judgments
     A17:181–8   A26:5–9   A26:165–71   B6:182–3   B9v:63–4
     B10:366–9   B12:328–33   B13:154–6   B17:138–41   B24:93
     B29:283–6   B31:106 (inc)   B33:153–6   B35v:114–17   C19:485
     C33:112–17

BOYCE, WILLIAM (*cont.*)

5. *If we believe (Easter Day)
   A26:14–17   B6:173–6   B9v:59–61   B10:356–9   B12:100–3
   B13:148–51   B17:131–3   B21:206–7   B24:89–90   B29:276–7
   B31:92–3   B32:95   B33:145   B35v:107–8   B36:119
   C19:483–4

6. †I have surely built thee an house
   B4:150–5   B15:84–7   D20v:105–9

7. †Lord who shall dwell
   D30–5:20–3

8. O come hither and behold (from 'O be joyful in God all ye lands')
   A31v:13–17   B18v:86–7   B34:192–9   C20v:6–7   C23v:77–85
   C24v:77–85

9. †O give thanks unto the Lord and call
   A19:503–26   A34v:17–46   B4:25–30   B15:4–10   C20v:38–45
   C22v:10–16   D21:99–107   D22v:6–13   D30–5:5

10. *O praise the Lord ye that fear him
    D30, D32:1–2   D33:172–3   D34:168–9   D35:1–2

11. *O sing unto the Lord a new song
    A16:96–111   D30–5:9–11

12. Out of the deep of sad distress (from BOYCE's Sonata; Hymn arr
    T. SHARP)

13. †O where shall wisdom be found
    B4:36–40   B15:10–13   C20v:52–6   C22v:24–8   D22v:20–4

14. *Praise the Lord ye servants
    D30–5:3

15. *Sing O heavens
    A26:201–6   D30–5:12–13

16. *Sing praises to the Lord
    D30–5:6–7

17. †Sing unto the Lord and praise
    D30–5:18–19

18. *Teach me O Lord
    D30–5:8

19. †The heavens declare
    D30–5:16–17

20. †The Lord is king, and hath put on
    D30–5:14–15

21. †The Lord is my light
    A26:10–14   B6:176   B9v:62–3   B10:352–6   B12:324–6
    B13:145–8   B17:126–8   B24:2   B29:277–81   B31:98–101
    B32:98   B33:147–50   B35v:108–11   C19:487–8

22. ★Turn thee unto me
    A19:527–35    A20:18–21
23. ★In A: Td, J (*Arnold 3*)
    A15:182–90    B30:209–11 (Td inc)    D19v:24–9
24. †In C: Td, J
    A21v:102–9    B18:37–41    C20:26–31    C23:31–5    C24:27–31
    C25:27–32

*Secular item*:
25. Away with the Fables philosophers hold (Dialogue in Amphitrion)
    M205:1–17

BRIMLEY, John (*see* BRYMLEY, John)

BRODERIP, [William] (1683–1727)
In D: Cd, Dm
    A18:205–28

BROSCHI, Carlo (*see* FARINELLI)

BRYMLEY, John (*c.*1502–76; Durham; monastic lay cantor, 1536–9; m of chor and org 1540–76)
  1. Td, Bs (Td to words of 1535 King's Primer)
     C13:189, 200–2
  2. K (to SHEPPARD's [Second] Creed)
     C13:222–3    E4:112    E5:114    E6:107    E7:114–15    E8:115
     E9:105    E10:110–11    E11:118–19    E11a:286–7

BRYNE (BRYAN), Albertus (*c.*1621–71)
  1. I heard a voice
     A3:382–6    C11v:158–158a    C16:242–4    C17:149    C17:180–1
     C19:219–21
  2. In G, Short Service: Td, J, K, C, M, N (*Arnold 2*)
     A15:165–74    A22:129–30, 133–4 (−Td; C, M inc)    B5:71–9
     B7:72–81    B8v:137–45    B13v:171–5, 178–80 (−K, C)
     B22:25–7, 12–13, 10–11    B23:106–11    B28:147–58
     C12v:210–19 (imp except K)    C13v:⑤–⑫ (Td inc)    C26:47–54
     C30:107–12 (−K, C)    C31:53–62    C32:48–55    C33:22–9
     D17v:119–33    D18v:54–8 (just K, C)    D19v:96–111
     D30v:47–54    D31v–5v: 45–52

BULL, John (*c.*1562–1628)
  1. Almighty God who by the leading (Epiphany) (The 'Star' Anthem;
     cf. 'O Lord my God')
     A2:265–9    C1:96–8    C2:19–21    C3:15–16    C7:11–12
     C11v:95–6    C14:13–14    C16:303–4    C19:348–50

BULL, JOHN (cont.)
2. Deliver me O God
   C1:24   C4:62   C5:60   C6:61–2   C7:271–2   C9:42   C10:49
   C19:164
3. In thee O Lord
   A3:1–7   C1:47–9   C4:78   C5:76–7   C6:82–3   C7:295–6
   C9:53   C10:68   C11v:27–8   C16:164   C17:138   C19:194–5
4. O Lord my God (Boyce 3) (alternative words by ALDRICH to
   'Almighty God who by the leading')
   A29:1–4   B6:86–7   B9:101–3   B12:1–3   B17:9–10   B20v:93–5
   B21:184–6   B24:92–3   B29:55–6   B32:53–4   B36:18–19
   C19A:155–6   C21:152–3   C28:521–2   C29v:152–3
   C35v:130–1   M192:306–13


BUTLER (BOTLER), Henry (Heinrich, Henrich) (c.1590–1652)

E. V. V. Phillips, The Divisions and Sonatas of Henry Butler (Ph.D. thesis,
Saint Louis, Missouri, 1982)

Sonatas à 3 viols:
1. In G
   D2/1:28–9   D2/2:30–1   D2/3:34–5   D5/1–3:14–15   D10:215–17
2. In e
   D2/1:29   D2/2:31   D2/3:35   D10:218
3. In F
   D2/1:31   D2/2:33   D2/3:27   D5/1–3:1   D10:212–14
4. In g (authorship uncertain; 'B5tl2[r]' in D2/2, ZAMPONI in D5,
   unascrib in D10)
   D2/1:42–3   D2/2:44–5   D2/3:38–9   D5/1–3:4–5   D10:219–22
Divisions and Preludes for solo viola da gamba:
5. 1 set in a (twice)
   D10:94–7, 112–15
6. 5 sets, in a, C, C, D, d
   D10:108–11, 116–24, 124–8, 129–31, 132–8
7. 1 set in e (ascrib to YOUNG; possibly by BUTLER)
   D10:139–42
8. [Prelude] in F
   D10:143
9. 3 sets, all in F
   D10:143–8, 149, 150–1
10. 1 set in G
    D10:156–9
11. [Prelude] in e
    D10:160

12. [Sonata] in e
     D10:160–1

BYRD, William (1543–1623)
  1. Alack when I look back
     C4:49   C5:47   C7:253–4   C9:27   C10:35
  2. Arise O Lord why sleepest thou
     A1:317–19   C1:1–2   C4:40–1   C5:32–3   C6:38–9   C7:248
     C9:19–20   C10:28   C11:41–2   C12:26–7   C15:42–3   C16:36–7
     C17:43–4   C19:15 (inc)   C27:30–1
  3. Behold O God the sad
     A5:5–7   C1:21   C4:60   C5:58   C6:57–8   C7:267–8   C9:39
     C10:46   C19:161–2
  4. Be not wroth (2nd part of 'Let not thy wrath'; see 'Bow thine ear' and
     'Thy holy city')
     A2:309 (frag)   A14:9–11   A28:30–2   B6v:55–6   B9v:31–2
     B12:18–19   B16:143–9   B17v:22–3   B20:86–7   B21:138–40
     B24:46   B26:44   B29:52–3   B31:88–9   B32:46   B34:30–1
     B36:6–7   C19:336–7   C19A:122–3   C21:110–12   C28:156–8
     C29v:112–13   C35v:91–3
  5. Bow thine ear (later text of 'Be not wroth') (Boyce 2)
     D18:18–20
  6. Christ rising again (Easter)
     A5:55–9   C1:58–60   C2:47–8   C3:37–8   C4:86–7   C5:85–6
     C6:95–6 (imp)   C7:27–8   C7:305–6   C9:61–2   C10:78–80
     C11v:112–13   C14:29–30   C16:316–17   C19:363–5
  7. Deliver me from mine enemies (now attrib to R. PARSONS [I])
  8. Have mercy upon me O God (ascrib to O. GIBBONS)
     A1:78–80   C1:72   C9:76 (imp)   C10:102–3   C11v:85–6
     C19:217
  9. Hear my prayer O Lord and consider
     C2:141   C3:113   C7:76–7   C11v:57–8   C14:97–8   C16:212
     C19:252
 10. Hear my prayer O Lord and hide not (see Preces & Pss., Epiphany)
 11. How long shall mine enemies
     A1:216–18   C4:46   C5:21   C6:27   C7:237   C9:8   C10:19
     C11:54–5   C15:32–3   C16:64–5   C17:31–2   C19:8–9
 12. Let not thy wrath (Ne irascaris Domine) (same as 'O Lord turn thy
     wrath away'; 2nd part of this was later used separately under the
     titles, 'Be not wroth', and 'Bow thine ear')
     A3:95–100   B10:14–17   C4:37–8   C5:29–31   C6:35–6
     C7:245–6   C9:16–18   C10:25–6   C11:130–3   C15:40 (inc)
     C17:40–2   C27:20–2   C28:13–15

BYRD, WILLIAM (*cont.*)

13. Lift up your heads (*see* Preces & Pss., Ascension Evensong)
14. Non nobis Domine (Canon à 3)
    M70:46–9 (arr LOEILLET)   M173:28 (for 2 oboes)   M174:1
15. O God the proud
    A1:281–2  C2*:6–7  C4:8  C5:2  C6:8  C7:218  C11:49–50
    C12:6–7  C15:10–11  C16:62–3  C17:8  C27:4  C28:9–10
    C34:5–6
16. O Lord give ear
    A1:290–1  C2*:13  C4:16  C5:10  C6:16  C7:226 (imp)
    C11:52  C12:22–3  C15:122  C16:35  C17:18  C27:9  C28:12
    C34:7
17. O Lord make thy servant
    A1:320–1  C2*:3–4  C4:6  C5:② (imp)  C6:6  C7:216
    C10:2 (imp)  C11:38–9  C12:3–4  C15:7–8  C16:76–7  C17:6
    C34:48
18. O Lord turn thy wrath away (alternative text to 'Let not thy wrath')
    (*Boyce 2*)
    D18:28–30 (1st pt only)
19. Prevent us O Lord
    A6:181–2  C2*:39  C4:34  C5:26  C6:32  C7:242  C9:13
    C11:53–4  C12:29–30  C15:36–7  C16:40–1  C17:37–8
    C19:14 (inc)
20. Save me God
    A6:84–6  C2*:8–9  C4:12  C5:6  C6:12  C7:222  C10:6
    C11:57–8  C15:15–16  C16:37–8  C17:12–13  C27:7–9 (imp)
    C28:7–8  C34:3–5
21. Sing joyfully (*Boyce 2*)
    A1:167–9  A2:159–61  A29:20–1  B6v:57–8  B9v:32–3
    B12:86–8  B20:88–9  B21:140–1  B29:53–4  B32:59–60
    B36:51–2  C2*:26–7  C4:9  C5:3  C6:9  C7:219  C10:3
    C11:16–17  C12:8–9  C15:11–12  C16:4–5  C17:9–10
    C19A:124–5  C21:112–14  C28:158–9  C29v:113–15
    C35v:93–5
22. Teach me O Lord (*see* Preces & Pss., Epiphany)
23. Thou O God that guidest (King's Day) (ascrib to GILES)
    C2:105–6  C3:78–9  C7:54–5  C11v:152  C14:63  C16:358–9
    C19:394–5
24. Thy holy city (earlier text of 'Be not wroth')
    C19A:107–8
25. When Israel came out (*see* Preces & Pss., Epiphany)
26. Preces (*see* Preces & Pss. below)

27. Responses (no Preces)
   A1:129   A2:55
28. Preces & Pss., Epiphany (When Israel came out; Hear my prayer
   O Lord and hide not; Teach me O Lord)
   A1:132–4 (all imp)   C1:205–8   C13v:6–8   E4–8:9–12   E9:11
   E10–11:9–12   E11a:6–8
29. Preces & Ps., Ascension Evensong (Lift up your heads)
   C1:299–302 (Preces imp)   C13v:17–19   E4–11:25–8   E11a:17–19
30. Short Service, in d: Td, Bs, 'J', K, C, M, N (*Boyce 3*)
   Td, Bs, K, C, M, N
   A1:302–12, 315–16 (M inc)   A3:326 (K, C only)   B28:25–34
   C8:12–18, 167–70, 247–52   C12v:15–23 (all imp)   C13:10–18
   C13v:158–61 (K, C only)   C26:9–17, 168–70   C30:35–45
   C31:11–20   C32:12–20   C33:30–8, 178–80
   E11a:40–4, 255–7, 364–6
   Td, Bs, M, N
   A15:211–20   A22:54–63   B5:10–17   B7:10–16   B8v:75–83
   B13v:91–8   B22:17–24   B23:128–32
   'J' (from Bs; arr SHENTON)
   A18:18–22
31. Great Service: Preces, V, Td, Bs, K, C, M, N
   V, Td, Bs, K, C, M, N
   A1:134–66 (−V; Td imp)   A2:130–58 (−V)   C13:244–60 (−V)
   C18:43–54 (+Preces)   E4:81–9, 120–3, 147–52
   E5:81–91, 121–4, 145–51   E6:78–86, 114–17, 141–6
   E7:81–91, 122–5, 147–53   E8:80–9, 123–5, 147–53
   E9:75–84, 111–14, 141–6   E10:79–89, 117–19, 140–4
   E11:90–8, 125–8, 149–54   E11a:170–9, 300–3, 432–7

CALKIN, [John Baptiste] (1827–1905)

Behold now praise the Lord
   D30:156–7   D31, D32:154–5   D33:154–6   D34:153–4
   D35:154–5

CALLCOTT, [John Wall] (1766–1821)

Give peace in our time
   D17:106–7   D24/1–6:3–4

CAMIDGE, John (jun; 1790–1859)

Holy holy holy Lord God of Hosts
   B15:153–6   D18:221–4   D19:173–6   D21:42–4

[CAREY, Henry] (*c.*1687–1743)

I'll range around
   E32:24

**CARISSIMI, Giacomo** (1605–74)
1. Awake put on thy strength ([arr PICKERING]; unascrib)
   A25:240 (inc)
2. My soul truly waiteth (*Pratt*)
   D19:126–32   D20v:124–8
3. For other adaptations from his music, *see* ALDRICH (3.6.)

**CARLTON, [Richard]** (*c.*1558–?1638)
Let God arise
   A2:279–80

**CARR, James** (?chor, Durham, 1612–17)
In thee O Lord
   C12:43–5

**CARTER, [Charles Thomas]** (*c.*1740–1804)
In C: Td, J
   A18:41–67

**CERVETTO** (MS 2nd half 18th cent.)
Violoncello Concerto in G
   M202

**CHARD, George William** (1765–1849)
1. In B♭: K, C
   A34:196–215   B3:1–4   B18:46–9   C20:37–41   C23:36–9
   C24:36–40   C25:37–40   D18v:109–14
2. Arr anthem by PAISIELLO

**CHAWNER, Claude F. Fox** (*c.*1840–67)
Devout men carried Stephen (*Ouseley 2*)
   B3v:29–32

**CHELLERI (KELLERY), Fortunato** (b. *c.*1686–90; d. 1757)
Sonata in A (Pr. M109(v))
   M69:72–5

**CHERUBINI, Luigi** (1760–1842)
Bow down thine ear (arr ASHTON)
   A10:199–206   B4:174–5   B15:106 (title only)   D19:79 (title only)

**CHESTERFIELD, Lord** (1694–1773)
Ah scribblers poor who write (Catch à 4) [*c.*1727]
   M70:54

CHILD, William (*c*.1606–97)

1. Blessed be the Lord God even the God
   B10:30  B17v:8  B29:6  C2:2  C11v:169  C14:12  C15:88–9
   C19:89–90  C27:76  C28:73  C34:65
2. Glory be to God on high ('in D sol re'; included as an anthem)
   C2:4  C11v:170  C14:16  C15:87–8  C27:157–8
3. Hear O my people
   A4:113–16  C2:125–6  C3:97–8  C7:65  C11v:20–1  C11v:52
   C14:81–2  C16:192–3  C19:232–3  C27:312
4. If the Lord himself (*Arnold 1*)
   B16:52–3  D20v:95–6
5. O clap your hands
   B10:53–4  B17v:9  B29:4  C2:3  C2:30  C11v:173a (imp)
   C14:4  C15:85  C19:90–1  C27:72  C28:72–3  C34:66
6. O God wherefore art thou absent
   A4:97–9  C11:151  C12:42–3  C15:114–15  C27:75–6
   C28:71  C34:60
7. O let my mouth be filled
   C2:1  C11v:167  C14:1
8. O Lord grant the king [I] (*Boyce 2*)
   A20:28–9  B6v:35–6  B9v:12  B10:21–2  B12:35–6  B17v:9
   B24:91  B26:22  B27:222–3  B29:8–9  C2:198  C11:148–50
   C12:39–40  C15:78–9  C17:104  C19:79–80  C27:73  C28:79
   C34:61
9. O Lord grant the king [II]
   B1:89–94  D23:117–18  D26/1–5:33–4  D26/6–9:34–6
   D30–5:49–50
10. O praise the Lord, laud ye
    A29:14–15  B6v:36–7  B9v:12–13  B10:28–30  B12:36
    B17v:6  B21v:10–12  B24:88  B29:5  C2:12–13  C11v:171–2
    C14:8–9  C15:89–90  C19:94–5  C27:69–70  C28:75–7
    C34:62–3
11. O pray for the peace (*Arnold 1*)
    B6v:39–40  B9v:15–16  B10:31–2  B17v:7  B27:223–5
    B29:6–7  C2:17–18  C11v:172–3 (imp)  C14:14–15  C15:86–7
    C19:91–3  C27:70–1  C28:77–8  C34:63–4  D20v:97–8
12. O sing unto the Lord a new song (*Boyce 2*)
    C2:2  C11v:168–9  C14:2
13. Praise the Lord O my soul and all (*Boyce 2*)
    A4:140–1  A20:41–2  B6v:37–8  B9v:14  B10:47–8  B12:31
    B17v:8  B21v:9 (inc)  B24:90  B26:21  B27:220–2  B29:7–8
    C7:131  C7:345  C14:169  C15:91  C27:74–5  C28:74–5
    C34:58–9

CHILD, WILLIAM (*cont.*)

14. Sing we merrily (*Boyce 2*)
    A4:144–8   A33:92–6   C7:132–3   C7:346–7   C14:170–1
    C15:92–3   C27:67–8   C28:80–2   C34:56–8   D18:32–9

15. The earth is the Lord's
    A4:159–61

16. Thou art my king, O God
    B1:95–6   C2:1   C11v:168   C14:1   D23:119   D26/1–5:35
    D26/6–9:36–7   D30–5:51

17. In A re, A re ♯, [ = a]: Td, J, S, K, C, M, N
    A4v: 152–70   C8:483–93   C12:81–8   C27:157 (S only)
    C33:199–209
    Td, J, K, C, M, N
    B28:121–3   C26:191–8   C31:194–201   C32:170–7
    Td, J, M, N
    B7:45–8   B8v:111–15
    Td, J
    A22:173–6   B5:45–9   B22:33–6   B23:97–9

18. Short Service, in C fa ut, C: Td, J, S, K, C, M, N
    Td, J, K, C, M, N
    A4v:133–51 (inc)   B28:108–20   C8:472–82 (+S)
    C12v:24–31 (+S; imp except S, K)   C26:199–206   C31:202–9
    C32:178–85   C33:208–16

19. In D sol re, D: Td, J, K, C, M, N
    A4v:18–34   C12v:78–86   C26:207–14   C31:210–17
    C32:186–93   C33:217–24

20. In D sol re ♯, D♯, [ = D]: Td, J, K, C, M, N (*Boyce 3*)
    B28:93–107   C12v:237–44 (N imp)   C26:215–22, 294–7, 327–31
    C30:63–73   C33:174–7, 225–32, 317–21   D18v:19–35
    M170:122–30
    Td, J, M, N
    A4v:115–31   A15:144–54   A22:103–15   B5:52–9   B7:51–9
    B8v:118–25   B19:156–68   B22:125–8, 131–3   B23:29–34
    B30:7–10 (−Td, J)   C31:218–25   C32:194–200
    D22:54–8 (−Td, J)

21. In E la mi flat, E♭: Td, J, S, K, C, M, N (*Arnold 1*)
    A33:220–31, 233–7   C12v:4–12 (imp except K)   C26:223–39 (−S)
    C31:226–32 (−S)   C32:201–7 (−S)   C33:240–6 (−S)   D20:27–41

22. In E la mi, E♯, E proper, [ = e]: Td, J, K, C, M, N (*Boyce 1*)
    A4v:35–54   A15:31–40   B3:188–98   B22:89–95   B28:68–77
    C12v:201–9   C26:230–6   C31:233–9   C32:208–14   C33:233–9
    M170:114–20

Td, J, M, N
A22:80–8   B5:59–64   B7:59–64   B8v:125–30   B19:10–15
B23:20–4   D20:17–20, 184–9
23.  In F fa ut, F: Td, J, K, C, Cd, Dm
A4v:1–17   B28:78–83, 88–92   B34v:28–38   C12v:87–96
C26:237–45   C31:240–8   C32:215–23   C33:247–55
Td, J, Cd, Dm
A15:202–10   A22:44–51   A34:180–95 (–Td, J)   B5:64–71
B7:64–70, 72   B8v:130–7   B18:1–9   B22:28–32   B23:99–104
B30:88–92 (–Cd, Dm)   C22:54–8 (–Td, J)   C30:132–8
24.  In Gamut, G: Td, Be, J, K, C, M, N
Be, J, K, C, M, N
A6:68–83   B28:132–46   C12v:128–38 (M, N imp)   C13:178–88
C26:181–90   C31:185–93   C32:161–9   C33:189–99
E11a:81–6, 283–5, 417–19
Td, J, M, N
A34:120–59   B15v:13–20   C20:126–36   C22:45–54
Td, J
B3:78–82   C25:130–5   D22:44–9
M, N
A15:227–30   A22:77–9   B5:49–51   B7:49–51   B8v:115–17
B18:9–12   B22:36–8   B23:104–5   B34v:38–41
25.  Unascrib single chant in F, numbered 3
C12v:273 (tenor)   C26v:3 (bass)   C28:507f (bass)

CHURCH, John (1675–1741)
1.  Blessed is he whose unrighteousness
C19:308–13
2.  I will alway give thanks
D30–5:53–4
3.  I will magnify thee O God
D30–5:52–3
4.  Praise the Lord O my soul and all
D30–5:54–5
5.  Righteous art thou
A28:222–4   B17v:24–5   B20:92–4   B21:151–3   B32:45–6
B36:8–10   C19A:135–7   C21:130a–2   C28:425–8   C29v:132–4
C35v:105–7
6.  Single chant in D sol re ♮ [= d]
A8:4

CLARI, Giovanni Carlo Maria (1677–1754)
1.  Be merciful (*Pratt*) (heading only)
D19:120   D20v:118

CLARI, GIOVANNI CARLO MARIA (*cont.*)
2. Out of the deep (*Pratt*)
   D19:117–19   D20v:116–18

CLARK, Thomas (1775–1859)
Praise the Lord ye servants (*Div Comp*)
   M174:6–7

CLARKE, Jeremiah (*c.*1674–1707)
T = *Thematic Catalog of the Works of Jeremiah Clarke*, T. F. Taylor (1977)
1. Awake my soul, awake mine eyes (Morning Hymn) (*Div Comp*;
   T160)
   M174:12–13
2. Bow down thine ear (*Page 2*; T101)
   B27:62–4   C27:371–3 (imp)
3. Hear my crying (*see* CROFT)
4. How long wilt thou forget me (*Boyce 2*; T102) (*see* 'I will sing of
   the Lord')
   A8:90–4   A29:68–73   B12:83   B17:30   B20:120–1   B26:36
   B32:65   B35v:4–5   B36:59   C19:476   C21:180   C29v:173–4
   C35v:175
5. I will love thee (*Boyce 3*; T105)
   A8:129–38   A8:198   A28:195–9   B6:37–9   B9:96–9   B24:76
   B26:64–6   B27:29–33   B29:163–6   B33:26–9   C19:320–1
   C27:353–8   C28:436–7
6. I will sing of the Lord (from 'How long wilt thou forget me') (*Div
   Harm 2, 1731,* arr ARMES)
   D23:115   D26/1–5:31   D26/6–9:32
7. My song shall be of mercy (*Div Comp*; T108) (arr ARMES)
   D23:223   D30–5:56
8. O be joyful in God (Annual Meeting, Sons of the Clergy) (T109)
   A8:174–9
9. O Lord God of my salvation (*Page 2*; T110)
   A20:62–5   A28:27–30   B6v:52–5   B9v:28–30   B10:265, 268–70
   B12:16–18   B20:83–5   B21:135–8   B24:31–3   B26:42–3
   B29:50–2   B31:86–8   B32:49–50   B34:28–30   B36:10–12
   C19:334–6   C19A:119–21   C21:107–10   C28:153–6
   C29v:108–11   C35v:88–91   D20v:168–72
10. O Lord how manifold (from 'Praise the Lord O my soul')
    D23:116   D26/1–5:32   D26/6–9:33
11. Praise God from whom all blessings (Chorus)
    M174:16–17
12. Praise the Lord O Jerusalem (*Boyce 2*; T113)
    A20:33–4   A25:154–6   B6v:60–1   B9v:37–9   B10:33–5

B12:25   B17v:10–11   B24:79   B26:66–7   B27:198–9
B29:203–4   B33:58–9   C19:324–6   C27:92–3   C28:456–8

13. Praise the Lord O my soul and all (*Div Comp*; T114) (D MSS arr ARMES)
   D23:223   D30–5:56   M174:10–11

14. Praise the Lord O my soul and all (T115)
   B27:65–8   C27:374–7

15. The earth is the Lord's (T116)
   C7:180   C15:219–20   C27:255–8 (imp)   C28:201–4
   C34:155–8

16. The Lord is full of compassion (T117) (*see* 'The merciful goodness of the Lord')
   A14:73–9   B6:164–7   B9:169–72   B12:49–51   B17:119–21
   B24:76   B26:140–3   B27:25–8   B32:91–4   B33:137–8a
   B36:116–18   C19:327   C27:346–9

17. The merciful goodness of the Lord (from 'The Lord is full of compassion') (*Div Harm 2, 1731*; arr ARMES)
   D23:114–15   D26/1–5:30–1   D26/6–9:31–2

18. [Ground] in C (Pr. M105)
   E32:53–5

CLARKE[-WHITFELD], John (formerly, CLARKE, John; 1770–1836)
   1. In Jewry is God known
      B15:178–9   D18:252–4   D19:197–9   D21:62–4
   2. O praise God in his holiness
      B4:86–9   B15:26–8   C22v:83–7   D20v:1–3   D22v:48–55
   3. The Lord's Prayer
      B18v:88–90   C20v:9–10   C23v:86–8   C24v:86–7
   4. In F: Td, J, M, N
      A21v:50–73   B18:15–23   C20:1–10   C23:1–11   C24:1–11
      C25:1–11   D18v:58–64 (−M, N)   D18v:92–8 (−M, N)

CLAUSSEN, J. (MSS late 17th cent.)
Sonata à 3 in G
   D5/1–3:2–3

CLUB ANTHEM (by HUMFREY, BLOW, and TURNER)
I will always give thanks
   A33:1   B10:105–7   C3:162   C7:138–40   C7:380   C14:181–2
   C15:157–9   C27:182–3 (inc)   C28:269–71   C34:203–5

COBBOLD, [William] (1560–1639)
In Bethlem town
   A2:281–3

COOKE, Benjamin (1734–93)

1. Wherewithal shall a young man
   B4:2   B18v:92   C20v:13   C23v:91   C24v:89
2. In G: Td, J, K, M, N
   Td, J, M, N
   A35:48–87 (+K)   B3:105–15   B15v:40–9   B30:27–35
   C22:68–80   D20:7–17

COOKE, Captain Henry (c.1615–72)

1. O Lord thou hast searched
   B1v:70–4
2. Put me not to rebuke
   B1v:64–9

COOKE, Robert (1768–1814)

In C: M, N
   A35:87–101   B18:41–5   C20:31–6   C23:26–30   C24:32–6
   C25:32–6

CORELLI, Arcangelo (1653–1713)

1. Op. 2
   [Sonata 1]
   M69:1 [Preludio, Largo]
   Sonata 3
   M69:24–5 (pt) M69:46–7 (Allemanda, [Presto])
2. Op. 3
   Sonata 2
   M70:10–17 (arr FINCH)
   Sonata 6
   M70:2–7 (arr FINCH)
3. [Op. 5]
   Sonata 8
   E32:77–82 (pt)
   Sonata 9
   E32:66–72   M70v:52–5
   Sonata 10
   E32:44
4. [Op. 5] (arr GEMINIANI)
   Sonata 6
   M157:74–7 (Allegro, Adagio, Allegro)
5. [Op. 6]
   Sonata 3
   M157:84–5

Sonata 9
M157:52 (Gavotta)
Sonata 11
M70:22–3 (Sicilian Air)    M157:62–3 (Giga)
6. [Posthumous Work, Sonata 2]
M175:43–9
7. Sinfonia à 4 in F (wrongly ascrib; by A. VERACINI)
8. Sonata à 4 in F
M199
9. Allemande in d
E11a:340–1

CORFE, [Joseph] (1741–1820)
★ = Church Music . . . by Joseph Corfe (c.1810)
1. ★Ponder my words
B11:104    B16:113    B18v:45    B34:143    C23v:26    C24v:23
D18:144–5
2. ★The king shall rejoice
A20:136–42    B8:98–101    B9:196–9    B11:38–41    B15:76–9
B16:44–7    B17:154–6    B26:157–62    B33:169–72    B34:90–2
B35v:144–7    C28:546

COSTE, [Thomas] (MS c.1630)
V, Td, Bs, M, N
C8:139–57, 323–8 (V inc)    C13:126–35 (– V)    E11a:142–8, 404–6 (– V)

COURTEVILLE, Raphael (before 1675–c.1735)
1. Ah! who can the joys discover (unascrib)
D9:10–11
2. Fly from Myrtillo
D9:6–8
3. Leave your ogling foolish lovers
D9:15

CRANFORD, William (fl. early 17th cent.)
1. Hear my prayer O Lord and consider (ascrib to CRANFORD in
C16, otherwise unascrib; possibly by BATH)
A3:19–22    C2:139–40    C3:111–12    C7:75–6    C11v:56–7
C14:96–7    C16:213–16    C19:251
2. I will love thee
A4:11–19    C2:121–2    C3:93–4    C7:64    C11v:19–20
C14:80–1    C16:200–3    C17:151–4    C19:228–31
3. O Lord make thy servant (King's Day)
A5:42–5    C1:130    C2:106–7    C3:79–80    C7:55–6
C11v:149–51    C14:64    C16:352–4    C19:396–7

CREIGHTON, Robert (*c*.1636–1734)

1.  I will arise (*Boyce 2*)
    A16:228–9
2.  Praise the Lord O my soul, O Lord my God
    D30–4:132–3
3.  In E♭: Td, J, M, N
    A22:188–92 (in D; − M, N; J inc)   A29v:55–63   B5:209–16
    B7:201–8   B17v:66–71   B19:225–35   B22:2–7   B23:112–16
    B28:365–71   B29v:27–33   B31v:5–11 (J imp)   B32v:14–19
    B33v:99–104   B35:63–9   B36v:69–75   C21v:150–9   C30:101–6
    C31:378–88

CROFT, William (1678–1727)

*Musica Sacra: or Select Anthems in Score . . . Compos'd by Dr. William Croft;*
★ = vol. 1 (1724); † = vol. 2 (1725)

1.  Behold now praise the Lord
    D13/1:38   D13/2:35   D13/3:32   D13/4:33   D14/1:38
    D14/2: 35–8   D14/3:33–6   D14/4:32–5
2.  Be merciful (*Arnold 2*)
    D31–4:129–31
3.  †Blessed are all they that fear him
    A7:35–41   A29:53–64   B24:67   B32:28   C19:318
    D13/1, 2:23–4   D13/3:20–1   D13/4:22–3   D14/1:23–4
    D14/2:22–3   D14/3, 4:21–2
4.  Blessed is the man
    D13/1, 2:12   D13/3:11   D13/4:12   D14/1, 2:12   D14/3, 4:11
5.  Blessed is the people (*Page 1*)
    A14:42–9   A28:75a–b, 76–82   B6:97–9   B9:10–12
    B10:336–44   B12:77–9 (inc)   B13:116–19   B16:27–31   B17:3–6
    B20:11–16   B21:49–50   B24:72   B27:6–9   B29:110–13
    B32:15   B33:15–17   C27:396–400   C28:435   C29v:9
6.  ★Burial Sentences (all but A29 and B27 include 'Thou knowest Lord'
    by H. PURCELL)
    A8:71–81   A13:39–42   A29:141–2   B10:85–90   B24:1–2
    B26:116–19   B27:217 (inc)   B29:196–9   C21:154–8
    C29v:154–8   C35v:132–6
7.  German (Hymn tune; to 'Ye children which do serve the Lord')
    B4:4–6   B18v:94–5   B27:165   C20v:15–16
8.  Give the king thy judgments (*Boyce 2*)
    B12:287–90   B20v:31–5   B21:63–7   B27:252–9   C19A:46
    C26v:25–31   C29v:43   C35v:27a
9.  God is gone up (*Boyce 2*)
    A13:48–51   B8:4–6   B9v:47–9   B10:291–4   B12:95–7

B13:29–31   B17:61–3   B26:70–1   B29:236–8   B31:28–30
B32:74–5   B33:84–6   B35v:41–3   C28:477–80

10. Hanover (Hymn tune; to 'My soul praise the Lord')
B4:18–19   B18v:93   C20v:14

11. Hear my crying (ascrib to CLARKE in B27)
B27:68–72   C27:362–6

12. †Hear my prayer O Lord and consider
A26:18–23   B12:68–73   B24:67–8   B29:169–72   B32:22
C19:471–3   C21:48–9   C29v:38–9   D13/1:24–6   D13/2:25–7
D13/3:22–4   D13/4:24–5   D14/1, 2: 24–6   D14/3, 4:23–5

13. ★Hear my prayer O Lord and let my crying
A14:118–21   A29:186–8   B8:51–2   B10:71–4   B12:211–12
B13:114–15   B17:98–9   B24:55   B26:89–90   B29:167–8
B31:73–4   B32:80–1   B33:130–2   B35v:87–8 (inc)

14. He loveth righteousness (see 'Rejoice in the Lord O ye righteous')

15. †I cried unto the Lord
A13:94–9   A26:142–7, 149   B12:220–2   B20:29–32
B21:29–33   B24:66–7   B26:97–9   B27:137–40   B29:186–9
B32:13   C19:404–5   C19A:25–6   C21:26–8   C35v:14–15
D13/1–4:5–6   D14/1–4:5–6   D30–5:90–1

16. I waited patiently
A13:80, 83–4   B6:158 (inc)   B8:33–4   B9:164–6   B12:99–100
B13:82–4   B17:84–6   B20:135–7   B24:44   B26:132–3
B29:264–5   B31:67–8   B32:76–7   B33:113–15   B35v:81–2
C28:484–6

17. †I will alway give thanks
A26:24–31   B12:298–305   B24:62   B26:91–6   B29:173–8
B32:23

18. I will give thanks unto thee
A14:180–91   A28:47–56   B6:92–6   B9:6–9   B10:170–8
B12:106–11   B17:104–7   B18v:4   B21:161–2   B24:75
B27:19–24   B29:106–10   B32:14   B33:10–14   B34:83–9
C19A:9–13   C19A:31–2   C21:137–9   C27:389–95   C29v:21–3
C29v:141–2   C35v:115–16

19. I will lift up mine eyes
A7:21–34   A28:91–8, 100–1   B21:45–9   D13/1–4:7–8
D14/1–4:7–8

20. ★I will sing unto the Lord
A14:28–32   A25:218–25   B12:273–5   B24:59   B26:83–5
B27:38–41   B29:157–9   B32:20–1   C19:319   C27:350–3
C34:316–19

21. Like as the hart (Div Comp; arr ARMES)
D23:225   D30–5:70

CROFT, WILLIAM (*cont.*)
22. *Lord what love have I
     A14:22–7   B10:120–2   B12:212–13   B24:3–5 (imp)
     B26:99–100   B29:137–8   B32:19–20   C19:469–71
     D30–5:79–80
23. My song shall be alway (*Div Comp*; D MSS arr ARMES)
     D23:225   D30–5:70   M174:3
24. My soul praise the Lord (to tune, 'Hanover')
25. O be joyful in God all ye lands
     B32:21   D13/1:40–1   D13/2:37–8   D13/3:34–5   D13/4:35–6
     D14/1, 2:40–1   D14/3:38–9   D14/4:37–8   D30–5:88
26. O be joyful in God all ye lands (*Div Comp*; D MSS arr ARMES)
     D23:226   D30–5:71   M174:4
27. O give thanks unto the Lord and call (*Div Comp*; arr ARMES)
     D23:224   D30–5:72
28. O give thanks unto the Lord and call
     A28:57–69   B6:99–105   B8:55–61   B9:12–18   B10:211–21
     B12:146–53   B20:44–56   B21:109–12   B29:122–9   B32:28–30
     B36:20–6   C19:424–37   C19A:88–96   C28:452–6   C29v:76–9
     C35v:68, 68a, 69–74   D13/1, 2:13–17   D13/3:12–16   D13/4:13–16
     D14/1:13–17   D14/2:13–16   D14/3:12–16   D14/4:12–15
29. †O give thanks unto the Lord for he is gracious
     A8:191, 193   A29:210–11, 213–15   B12:283–6, 223
     B17:99–100   B24:15–16   B31:76   B33:132–3   B35v:88–9
     D30–5:94–5
     The Lord taketh my part (last chorus; used separately)
     A29:214–15   B8:53–4   B12:223   B13:106–7   B32:87–8
30. O God of Hosts the mighty Lord (to tune, 'St Matthew')
31. O how amiable (*Div Comp*; D MSS arr ARMES)
     D23:224   D30–5:72   M174:14–15
32. *O Lord God of my salvation [I; in f]
     A8:164–70   B20v:7–9   B21:40   B24:95   B32:13   C26v:15–16
     C35v:15–17   D30–5:88–9
33. †O Lord God of my salvation [II; in e]
     A13:106–9   B10:81–4   B12:216–18   B20:3–5   B21:3 (inc)
     B24:21–2   B26:62–3   B27:189–91   B29:102–4   C19:457–9
     C19A:5–7   C21:3–5   C29:3–5   C29v:176–8   C34:93–5
     C35v:1–3
34. †O Lord grant the Queen/King
     A13:103–5   B10:74–7   B12:244–6   B20:6–8   B21:3–5
     B24:22–3   B27:192–4 (imp)   B29:104–6   C19:460–1
     C19A:7–9   C21:5–8   C27:94–6   C29:5–8   C29v:178–81
     C34:95 (frag)   C35v:3–5

35. †O Lord I will praise thee
    A26:49–59   A29:90–9   B12:261–8   B24:10–12 (imp)
    B26:119–25   B29:117–20   B36:64–6   C19:477–80   C21:185–8
    C29v:185, 185a–b, 186   C35v:178, 180–2   D13/1:26–8
    D13/2:28–30   D13/3:25–7   D13/4:26–8   D14/1–3:26–8
    D14/4:25–7
36. O Lord our Governor
    B21:113–21   C19A:97   C29v:80–8   C35v:75
37. †O Lord rebuke me not
    A13:109–12   B10:68–71   B12:214–15   B20:24–6   B21:22–3
    B24:54   B26:57–8   B27:237–9   B29:95–7   B36:61–2
    C19:113–15   C19A:20–4   C21:18–21   C29:8–10   C35v:7–9
    D30–5:73–5
38. *O Lord thou hast searched (*Page 2*)
    A14:98–111   B12:232–8   B13:128–32   B20v:15–20   B24:56–7
    B26:74–9   B27:151–6   B29:146–52   B32:12   C19:466–7
    C19A:37–8   C21:36–9   C29v:31–2   D13/1, 2:20–2
    D13/3:18–20   D13/4:19–21   D14/1:20–2   D14/2:19–21
    D14/3, 4:18–20   D30–5:84–5
39. †O praise the Lord ye that fear him
    A26:37–48   B12:311–17   B20v:1–5   B21:53 (frag)   B24:65–6
    B27:159   B29:182–6   C19:408   C19A:35   C21:31–4
    C26v:9–11, 13–14   C29v:32   D13/1–4:1–4   D14/1–4:1–4
    D30–5:89
    Save Lord and hear us (chorus; used separately)
    B13:107–8   B31:77–8   B32:88–9

    (l-c no. 3's copy of *Croft 2*, pp. 79–80, are ms replacement by
    Brass)
40. O render thanks and bless the Lord (Hymn)
    M174:5
41. O sing unto the Lord a new song
    A29:203–9   B6:110–14   B8:78–81   B9:25–9   B10:198–204
    B12:160–3   B13:84–8   B17:35   B17:108–11   B21:205   B24:82
    B26:128–31   B29:207–9   B31:3 (inc)   B32:82–4   B33:59–62
    B35v:8–11   B36:74–7   C21:195–6   C28:536–40   C29v:193
42. *Out of the deep
    B12:243–4   B21:52–3   B24:59   B27:143–7   B29:143–6
    B32:10   C15:135 (only 4 notes)   C19:464   C19A:26   C21:35
    C26v:4–8   C35v:26   D30–5:83
43. Praise God in his sanctuary
    A7:7–20   A14:143–61   A28:83–91   B6:87–92   B9:1–5
    B12:188–93   B13:119–24   B17:23–7   B21:34–5   B21:70–4
    B24:68–9   B27:180–1, 183, 185, 187–8   B29:130–5   B32:10–11

CROFT, WILLIAM (*cont.*)

> B33:43–8  C19:465  C21:49–55  C28:441–2  C29v:7–8
> D13/1, 2:9–10  D13/3:8–9  D13/4:9–10  D14/1, 2:9–10
> D14/3, 4:8–9

44. Praise the Lord O my soul, and all
> A13:12–19  B6:17–21  B9:112–15  B10:244–52  B12:170–5
> B13:16–20  B17:49–53  B27:9–13  B29:225–7  B31:18–21
> B33:75–7  B35v:31–4  C27:179–81 (inc)

45. ★Praise the Lord O my soul, O Lord my God (*Page 1*)
> A14:33–41  B12:229–32  B24:57–8  B26:85–9  B27:41–7
> B29:159–63  B32:15–16  C19:462–3  C27:366–71  C29v:11–12

46. Praise the Lord O my soul, O Lord my God (*Div Comp*; arr ARMES)
> D23:226  D30–5:71

47. Put me not to rebuke (*Boyce 2*)
> A14:173–7  B6:1–3  B8:48–50  B9:22–5  B10:229–32
> B12:38–9  B13:6–8  B17:40–2  B24:69–70  B26:125–8
> B29:210–12  B31:9–11  B32:84–6  B33:1–3  B35v:21–3
> B36:82–4  C28:540–4

48. ★Rejoice in the Lord O ye righteous
> B24:59–61
>
> 1st chorus
> A14:134–6  A29:189–91  B12:226–7  B13:104–5  B29:199–200
> B31:74–5  B32:86–7  C21:193–5  C29v:191–2
> He/The Lord loveth righteousness (last chorus; used separately)
> A14:137–9  A29:109–11  B12:227–9  B13:105–6  B20:126–7
> B29:120–1  B36:68–9  C19:481–2  C21:191–3  C29v:189–91

49. St Matthew (Hymn tune; to 'O God of Hosts, the mighty Lord')
> B4:98–9  B15:35–6  C22v:98–9  D20v:10–11  D22v:71–2

50. Save Lord and hear us (*see* 'O praise the Lord ye that fear him')

51. †Sing praises to the Lord (*Page 2*)
> A13:100–2  B10:78–81  B12:73–4  B24:16–18  B26:60–2
> B29:100–2  B32:7–8  B36:31–2  C19:453–5  C21:122–4
> C29v:123–5  C35v:112–15

52. ★Sing unto God O ye kingdoms
> A7v:3–6  A13:113–23  B10:112–19  B24:58–9  B29:136–7
> B32:18–19  D30–5:78–9

53. ★Sing unto the Lord, and praise
> A7:1–6  A14:55–64  B10:122–8  B12:293–7  B21:33–4
> B21:41–5  B24:57  B26:111–14  B29:139–42  B32:9
> C19:468–9  C19A:29–30  C21:55–7  C29v:13–14  C35v:24–5
> D30–5:81–2

54. †The earth is the Lord's
> A8:187  A25:225–32  B12:246–7  B24:62–3  B32:24

55. †The heavens declare
     A14:85–92   B12:306–10   B24:61   B29:178–81   B32:24–5
     C19:473   D13/1, 2:11   D13/3:10   D13/4:11   D14/1, 2:11
     D14/3, 4:10
56. The Lord is a sun and a shield (King's Coronation)
     B12:180–2   B17:16–18   B20:110–14   B21:193–7   B36:35–7
     C19A:164–8   C21:161–5   C29v:162–5   C35v:140–3
57. †The Lord is king, the earth (*Page 2*)
     A8:197   A25:203–12   C27:336–7   D13/1:36–7   D13/2:33–4
     D13/3:30–1   D13/4:31–2   D14/1:36–7   D14/2:33–4
     D14/3:31–2   D14/4:30–1
58. ★The Lord is my strength and my song, and he
     A8:195–6   B12:64–8   B13:110–14   B20:33–7   B21:35–40
     B24:24–5   B26:79–83   B27:14–18   B29:152–6   B32:16–17
     C19:331–2   C19A:27–8   C21:28–30   C27:407–11 (inc)
     C29v:10–11   D30–5:85–6
59. The Lord is my strength and my song, the joy (solo anthem)
     B17:10   B20v:95–6   B21:187   B32:54   C19A:157   C21:158–9
     C29v:158–9   C35v:136
60. The Lord is righteous
     D13/1:39   D13/2:36–7   D13/3:33   D13/4:34   D14/1, 2:39
     D14/3:37   D14/4:36
61. The Lord loveth righteousness (*see* 'Rejoice in the Lord O ye
     righteous')
62. The Lord of Hosts is with us (*see* 'This is the day')
63. The Lord taketh my part (*see* 'O give thanks unto the Lord for he is
     gracious')
64. The souls of the righteous (Funeral of Queen Anne)
     A7v:10–15   A26:115–19   A28:70–5   B6:106–10   B9:18–22
     B10:280–5   B12:130–3   B13:124–7   B17:27a–29   B21:171–2
     B24:109–10   B26:148–51   B27:47–51   B29:114–17   B32:17–18
     B33:18–21   C21:43–7   C27:401–6   C28:439–41   C29v:28–9
     C35v:22–3   D13/1, 2:17–19   D13/3:16–17   D13/4:17–19
     D14/1:17–19   D14/2:17–18   D14/3, 4:16–18
65. †This is the day
     A26:60–9   B12:141–4, 275–83   B24:63–5   B29:189–95
     B32:25–7   B36:70–4   C21:117–21   C29v:118–22
     1st chorus + Hallelujahs
     A13:25–9   B4:217–21   B6:31–2   B9v:42–3   B10:271–4
     B12:141–4   B13:21–2 (inc)   B17:53–5   B29:228–30   B31:22–4
     B33:78–80   B35v:34–6
     The Lord of Hosts is with us (used separately)
     A14:140–2   B13:108–10   B31:83–4   D30–D35:92–3

CROFT, WILLIAM (*cont.*)

66. Thou O God art praised
    B32:27–8   D13/1:42–3   D13/2:39–40   D13/3:36–7
    D13/4:37–8   D14/1, 2:42–3   D14/3:40–1   D14/4:39–40
    D30–5:99

67. ★We wait for thy loving-kindness
    A7v:28–35   A14:17–21   B12:224–5   B20v:13–14   B24:5–6
    B26:115–16   B27:156–7   B29:156–7   B32:11   C19A:36–7
    C21:40–1   C29v:30   D13/1:29–36   D13/2:31–2   D13/3:28–9
    D13/4:29–30   D14/1:29–35   D14/2:29–32   D14/3:29–30
    D14/4:28–9   D30–5:87

68. ★We will rejoice
    A14:50–4   B9v:64–7   B10:64–8   B12:218–20   B20:16–21
    B21:9–13   B24:52–3   B26:58–60   B27:232–6   B29:97–9
    B32:7 (inc)   C2:21–4, 28–9   C19:107–11   C19A:14–16
    C21:11–15   C27:113–15 (inc)   C29v:1–5

69. Ye children which do serve the Lord (to tune, 'German')

70. In A, A re: Td, J, S, K, C (*see* S. ELVEY for M, N)
    Td, J, K, C
    A13v:44–59   A34:226–64, 160–79   A35:1–48 (+S)
    B5:107–13, 216–19   B7:235–45   B8v:13–24
    B13v:37–40 (−Td; J inc)   B16v:138–51, 153–4   B17v:95–103
    B19:287–303   B23:3–7 (Td inc)   B28:332–40   B29v:52–61
    B31v:30–9   B32v:27–34   B35:88–97   C30:166–71 (−K, C)
    C31:388–95 (−K, C)

71. In b, B mi: Td, J, S, G (*Arnold 1*)
    B22:111–15, 168–70 (Td inc)   B23:80–4   B28:248–58, 221–2
    C19Av:1–6, 37–9   C21v:1–7, 27–9 (Td inc)   C29:13–19, 44–6
    D20:60–76
    Td, J
    A29v:36–47   B5:160–8   B7:146a–54   B19:277–87   B27v:1–9
    C19v:56–61   C26:331–40   C30:171–8   C31:359–66
    D18v:64–77
    S, G
    A7v:36–8   A13v:154–7   A14:128–30   A28:101–3   B6v:14–15
    B9v:53–5   B13v:130–2   B20v:91–2   B29v:21–2   B32v:12–13
    B35:51–2   B36v:20–2   C35:6–7

72. In E♭: Td, J, Cd, Dm (missing verse of J supplied by W. HAYES,
    so A18)
    A18:229–53, 253a–b, 256–88   B3:31–46   B18:76–92   B20:71–90
    C22:1–16   C24:70–78 (−Cd, Dm)   C25:70–85
    Cd, Dm
    B30:54–61   D21v:108–15   D22:1–7

CROTCH, William (1775–1847)

\* = *Ten Anthems . . . by Wm Crotch* [1804]

1. \*Be merciful unto me
   B4:64–6   D21:176–9
2. \*Blessed is he whose unrighteousness
   B4:69–70   D21:179–81
3. \*God is our hope and strength
   B4:48–53   D21:163–73
4. Holy holy holy Lord God Almighty
   D30–4:137   D35:135
5. \*How dear are thy counsels
   B4:59–60   D21: 175–6
6. \*My God my God look upon me
   B4:67–9   D21:181–4
7. O come hither and hearken
   B4:211–15   B15:133–6   D18:145–53   D19:147–51   D21:21–9
8. \*O Lord God of Hosts
   B4:53–5   D21:173–5
9. \*Rejoice in the Lord O ye righteous
   B4:60–4   D21:157–63
10. \*Sing we merrily
    B4:55–9   D21:145–50
11. \*The Lord even the most mighty
    B4:74–8   D21:150–7
12. \*Who is like unto thee
    B4:71–3   D21:184–6
13. Single chant in a
    B34:42

CURSCHMANN, [Carl] Fr[iedrich] (1805–41)

1. Der Schiffer fährt zu Land
   E38:6–8
2. Wach' auf du gold'nes Morgenroth (An Rose)
   E38:2–5

DAVIS, T. (*fl. c.*1720)

Single chant in B♭ (to start of V)
   C21v:48 (tenor)

DEANE, Thomas (*c.*1671–after 1731)

In B♭: Td, J, Cd, Dm
   C21v:39–48   C35:8–18

DERING (DEERINGE), Richard (*c.*1580–1630)

Almighty God which through thy only begotten Son (Monday in Easter Week)

DERING (DEERINGE), RICHARD (*cont.*)
  A5:158–63  C1:111–12  C2:53–4  C3:42–3  C7:31–2
  C11v:117–18  C14:34–5  C16:321–2  C19:367–8

DERRICK (early 17th cent.)
Short Service: Td, Bs, K, C (K ascrib to PATRICK in A1; *see* HUGHES
for M, N)
  A1:229–33 (−Td, Bs)  A3:211–21 (−K, C)  C8:89–97, 212–17
  C12v:1–3, 13–14, 244–8 (Td, Bs inc)  C13:83–90  C26:55–61
  C31:63–70  C32:132–5 (−K, C)  C33:155–62  E11a: 72–7, 269–72

[DEZEDE, Nicolas] (*c.*1745–92)
Lison dormoit dans un bocage
  E11a:446–7

D[IXON], F. (of Launceston; *fl. c.*1780)
  1. When all thy mercies (to Addison's Hymn)
    E11a:353
  2. Prelude in F, dated 1781
    E11a:348–9

DOUBIHON (*see* DU BUISSON)

[DRAKE, Thomas] (*c.*1693–1747; m-c, Durham, 1714–20; vicar of
Norham, 1720–47)
  1. Te Deum laeto celebramus hymno (Hymnus Ambrosianus)
    E1:1–88
  2. The night was dark and silent (Messiah, A Christ-Mass Song)
    D1:1–100

DU BUISSON (DOUBIHON) (2nd half 17th cent.)
Suite in e for viola da gamba
  A27:130–1

DUFAUT (du FAUT) (d. *c.*1682)
Suite in g for viola da gamba
  A27:108–10

DURANTE, Francesco (1684–1755)
O remember not the sins (*Latrobe 2*)
  B15:219–20a

DYKES, John Bacchus (1823–76; Durham; m-c, 1849–76; prec,
1849–62)
J. T. Fowler, *Life and Letters of John Bacchus Dykes* (1897); G. Roe &
A. Hutchings, *J. B. Dykes Priest & Musician* (1976)

1. Burial Sentences
   D29:1–7  D37/1–8:1–9  D37/9:1–7  D37/10–21:1–9
2. Come Holy Ghost (No. 2)
   D17:93–5
3. The Lord is my shepherd
   D30:116–18  D31:116–19  D32–4:116–21
4. In G: S1, K, Go, C, Sc, S2 (in C), G
   B30:135–40 (G inc)  D21v:116–20 (−Sc, S2, G)

EARLE, W[illiam] B[enson] (*fl. c.*1790)
In E♭: S, K
   A20:163–5  B8:102–3  B9:201–2  B11:49–50  B16:54–5
   B26:162–4  B34:95–6

EAST, Michael (*c.*1580–1648)
1. As they departed (St John Baptist)
   A5:197–203  C1:123–4  C2:85–6  C3:65–6  C7:43–4
   C11v:136–7  C14:51–2  C16:342–3  C19:385–7
2. O clap your hands (Ascension) [II]
   A2:294–300  A6:119–24  C1:114–16  C2:59, 60–1  C3:45–6
   C7:34–5  C11v:120–1  C14:38 (inc)  C16:323–5  C19:369–71
3. When Israel came out
   A5:74–9  C1:56–7  C4:85  C5:83–4  C6:93–4  C7:304
   C9:60  C10:76–7  C11v:160–60a  C16:176–7  C19:205–6

E[BDON], M[ary] (1766–1851; Durham; eldest daughter of Thomas EBDON)
1. Single chant in G (dated 2 Aug. 1797)
   A22:29
2. March in A
   D3:10
3. Rondo, Allegro, in A
   D3:20–1
4. Minuetto in A
   D3:21

EBDON, Thomas (1738–1811; Durham; chor, 1748–56; l-c, 1756–63; m of chor and org, 1763–1811) (*see* Index of Copyists)
★ = *Sacred Music, Composed for the Use of the Choir of Durham by Thomas Ebdon* (c.1790)
† = *A Second Volume of Sacred Music in Score . . . by Thomas Ebdon* (1811)
1. All kings of the earth
   A31:138–41  B16:137–9  B18v:71–3  B34:169–71  C23v:53–5
   C24v:52–4

EBDON, THOMAS (*cont.*)

2. †Behold God is my salvation (Feb. 1808)
   A30:91–3   A31:76–9   B11:112–13   B16:122–3   B18v:56–7
   B34:154–5   C23v:37–9   C24v:35–7

3. ★Behold how good and joyful
   A31:40–2

4. †Blessed is he that considereth (Sept. 1791)
   A30:45–9   A31:52–5   B8:107–9   B9:205–7   B11:57–9
   B16:56–9   B18v:23–5   B26:171–4   B34:98–100   C28:566–71

5. Blessed is he that hath the God of Jacob (Dec. 1804)
   A30:64   A31:100   B11:96   B16:105   B18v:37   B33:183–4
   B34:134–5   C23v:16–17   C23v:93   C24v:13   D18:130

6. Blessed is he whom thou chastness (Mar. 1810)
   A30:102   A31:110

7. ★Blessed is the man that feareth [1768 or 1769]
   A31:27–30   B6:179   B9v:62   B10:351–2   B12:155–6
   B13:140–1   B17:130–1   B24:90   B26:71–4   B29:274–6
   B31:96–7   B32:96–7   B33:142–4   B35v:103–5   C19:490
   C28:532–5

8. †Cry unto the Lord (Mar. 1804)
   A30:55–6   A31:84–5   B11:85 (frag; in pencil)   B11:88   B16:98
   B18v:30–1   B33:175–6   B34:126   C23v:3–4   C24v:3–4
   D18:120–1

9. †Deliver me from mine enemies (Dec. 1807)
   A30:121–2   A31:80–1   B11:99–100   B16:108–9   B18v:41
   B34:138–9   C23v:20–1   C24v:18–19   D18:138–9

10. Great is our Lord (Mar. 1810)
    A30:103–5   A31:111–13

11. Haste thee to help me (Jan. 1808)
    A30:124   A31:132   B11:101   B16:110   B18v:42   B34:140
    C23v:22–3   C24v:20   D18:140

12. Have mercy upon me O Lord (Mar. 1804)
    A30:58–9   A31:95   B11:89–90   B16:99–100   B18v:32
    B33:177–8   B34:128–9   C23v:6–7   C24v:6–7   D18:124

13. Hear me O Lord and that soon
    A31:142   B16:140   B18v:74   B34:172   C23v:56   C24v:55

14. †Hear me when I call (Jan. 1808)
    A30:125–6   A31:86–7   B11:102–3   B16:111–12   B18v:43–4
    B34:141–2   C23v:24–5   C24v:22   D18:142–3

15. Hear O Lord and have mercy (Aug. 1805)
    A30:69–70   A31:102–3   B11:98   B16:107   B18v:40   B33:186
    B34:137   C23v:19   C24v:16   D18:136

16. Help me now O Lord (June 1810)
    A30:120   A31:130   B16:134–5   B18v:69   B34:168   C23v:52
    C24v:51
17. Hide not thou thy face (May 1810)
    A30:110   A31:119   B16:129   B18v:63   B34:163   C23v:47
    C24v:45–6
18. How still and peaceful
    A30:50–1   A31:90–1   B11:93–4   B16:103   B18v:35–6
    B33:181   B34:131–2   C23v:13–14   C24v:10–11   D18:131–2
19. I called upon the Lord (1807)
    A30:72–3   A31:106–7   B11:98–9   B16:107–8   B18v:40
    B33:186–7   B34:137–8   C23v:20   C24v:17   D18:137–8
20. †I did call upon the Lord (Jan. 1804)
    A30:53   A31:83   B11:86–7   B16:96–7   B18v:29   B33:174
    B34:124–5   C23v:2   C24v:2   D18:118
21. I will give thanks unto thee
    A30:127   A31:129   B11:104   B16:112   B18v:45   B34:142–3
    C23v:26   C24v:23   D18:143–4
22. †I will give thanks unto the Lord
    A30:66–8   A30:99–101   A31:64–7   B11:95   B16:105   B18v:38
    B33:183   B34:134   C23v:16   C24v:14   D18:133
23. †I will magnify thee O God
    A30:75–8   A31:45–8   B11:106–8   B16:114–16   B18v:47–8
    B34:145–7   C23v:28–30   C24v:25–8
24. †I will remember thy name O Lord (Apr. 1809)
    A30:96–8   A31:73–5   B16:125–6   B18v:59–60   B34:157–8
    C23v:41–2   C24v:39–40
25. I will sing of the Lord (Jan. 1804)
    A30:54   A31:92   B11:87   B16:97   B18v:29–30   B33:175
    B34:125   C23v:2–3   C24v:2–3   D18:119
26. †Lord have mercy (Miserere, no. 2; in C)
    A30:74   A31:88   B11:92   B16:102   B18v:35   B33:179
    B34:131   C23v:11   C24v:10
27. †Lord have mercy (Miserere, no. 3; in g)
    A31:88   B11:100   B16:109   B18v:42   B34:139   C23v:22
    C24v:19
28. Lord how long wilt thou forget me
    A31:143–4   B16:140   B18v:74   B34:172–3   C23v:57   C24v:56–7
29. Lord I call upon thee (June 1811)
    A31:148
30. Lord thou knowest all my desire (May 1804)
    A31:97   B11:91   B16:101   B18v:33   B33:179   B34:129–30
    C23v:8   C24v:8   D18:126

EBDON, THOMAS (cont.)

31. Many one there be that say (Mar. 1804)
    A30:56–7  A31:93  B11:89  B16:99  B18v:31  B33:176–7
    B34:127  C23v:5  C24v:5  D18:121–2

32. My song shall be alway (Mar. 1810)
    A30:105–6  A31:114–15

33. O give thanks unto the Lord for he is gracious [I] (in g) (June 1804)
    A30:61  A31:98–9  B11:94–5  B16:103–4  B18v:36–7
    B33:182  B34:133  C23v:14–15  C24v:12  D18:128–9

34. †O give thanks unto the Lord for he is gracious [II] (in B♭)
    A30:89–91  A31:56–7  B11:111  B16:120–1  B18v:55
    B34:152–3  C23v:36–7  C24v:34–5

35. O Lord how manifold (chorus to MASON's anthem of same title)
    A26:112–13

36. †O Lord my God I cried unto thee (Mar. 1808)
    A30:94–5  A31:68–9  B11:114  B16:124  B18v:57–8  B34:156
    C23v:39–40  C24v:37–8

37. †O Lord my God I will exalt thee (Apr. 1809)
    A30:85–8  A31:60–3  B11:110  B16:118–20  B18v:52–3
    B34:150–2  C23v:34–5  C24v:32–3

38. *O Lord rebuke me not
    A31:31–4

39. O Lord the very heavens (July 1810)
    A30:113–15  A31:122–4  B16:136  B18v:70  B34:164–6
    C23v:48–50  C24v:47–9

40. O praise the Lord with me (May 1810)
    A30:111  A31:120  B16:134  B18v:68  B34:167  C23v:51
    C24v:50

41. O praise the Lord ye heathen
    A30:112  A31:121  B16:130  B18v:63–4  B34:161  C23v:45
    C24v:43–4

42. †O sing unto the Lord a new song (Feb. 1809)
    A30:81–2  A31:49–51  B11:109  B16:117  B18v:50
    B34:148–9  C23v:32  C24v:29–30

43. Ponder my words (Aug. 1805)
    A30:71–2  A31:104–5  B11:97–8  B16:106–7  B18v:39
    B33:185  B34:136–7  C23v:18–19  C24v:15–16  D18:134–6

44. †Praised be the Lord daily (Jan. 1804)
    A30:52  A31:82  B11:86  B16:96  B18v:28–9  B33:174
    B34:124  C23v:1  C24v:1  D18:117–18

45. Rejoice in the Lord O ye righteous (Feb. 1811)
    A30:128–9  A31:134–5  B16:142  B18v:77  B34:176  C23v:59
    C24v:59

46. Righteous art thou
     A31:144–5   B16:141   B18v:75   B34:174   C23v:58
     C24v:57–8
47. Shew me thy ways
     A31:136–7   B16:139   B18v:73   B34:176   C23v:60   C24v:60
48. Sing unto the Lord and praise (May 1804)
     A30:60   A31:96   B11:90   B16:100   B18v:33   B33:178
     B34:129   C23v:7–8   C24v:7   D18:125
49. *Teach me O Lord
     A31:35–8
50. The dead praise not thee
     A31:146–7   B16:143   B18v:77   B34:176   C23v:60   C24v:60
51. The eyes of the Lord (Mar. 1804)
     A30:58   A31:94   B11:89   B16:99   B18v:32   B33:177
     B34:128   C23v:6   C24v:6   D18:123
52. The king shall rejoice (June 1810)
     A30:116–19   A31:125–8   B16:131–3   B18v:65–7   B34:162
     C23v:46   C24v:44–5
53. The Lord helpeth them (June 1808)
     A30:79–80   A31:108–9   B11:108   B16:116–17   B18v:49
     B34:147–8   C23v:31   C24v:28–9
54. †The Lord is my shepherd (Dec. 1804)
     A30:62–3   A31:70–2   B11:95   B16:104   B18v:37   B33:183
     B34:134   C23v:16   C24v:13   D18:129–30
55. The Lord knoweth the days of the godly (Jan. 1808)
     A30:123   A31:131   B11:101–2   B16:110–11   B18v:43
     B34:140–1   C23v:23   C24v:20–1   D18:141–2
56. The Lord liveth (May 1810)
     A30:107–9   A31:116–18   B16:127–8   B18v:61–2   B34:159–60
     C23v:43–4   C24v:41–3
57. †The souls of the righteous (Mar. 1809)
     A30:83–4   A31:58–9   B11:109–10   B16:118   B18v:51
     B34:149–50   C23v:33   C24v:30–1
58. *To God O my soul be praises [1768–9] (words by Dean Cowper,
     so B10)
     A31:38–9   B6:178   B9v:58   B10:350–1   B13:138–9
     B17:128–9   B24:91   B29:273–4   B31:95   B32:94–5
     B33:146–7   B35v:106–7   C19:488–9   C28:530–2
59. To God the mighty Lord (Dec. 1804)
     A30:64–5   A31:101   B11:96–7   B16:105–6   B18v:38–9
     B33:184   B34:135   C23v:17–18   C24v:14–15   D18:133–4
60. Why art thou so vexed
     A31:133   B16:142   B18v:76   B34:175   C23v:59   C24v:58–9

EBDON, THOMAS (cont.)
61. *Preces and Responses
    A31:43
62. *In C: Td, J, K, C, S, G, M, N, Cd, Dm [1768]
    whole service:
    A31:1–26
    Td, J, M, N
    B5:280–9  B7:315–22  B8v:197–202  B13v:148–55  B17v:167–74
    B19:372–83  B23:64–7  B28:354–61  B29v:82–90  B31v:100–7
    B32v:74–80  B33v:81–92  B35:154–61  C30:87–97
63. *6 single chants, in C, c, A, a, C, g; double chant in b
    A31:44
64. †6 double chants, in G, C, A, g, C, B♭
    A31:89

*Glees for 3 voices:*
65. Fair Spring's approach (On Spring)
    D11:14–15
66. Hide not thou thy face
    D11:32 (inc)
67. Lord hear my prayer when I call
    D11:17
68. Lord in thee have I trusted
    D11:16
69. O praise the Lord with me
    D11:30–1
70. Peace decks the morn of Mira's life (Mira)
    D11:10–13
71. Play on happy youth
    D11:24–9
72. Sweet are the notes the lark begins (The Lark) (unascrib)
    D11:4–9
73. Sweet is the morning's golden beam
    D11:1–4
74. The king shall rejoice
    D11:18–19
75. The snows are desolving (Lapland Song)
    D11:20–3

*Instrumental:*
76. 13 harpsichord sonatas and concertos
    D6(i)–(xiii)
77. Incidental music, over 50 short items
    D3

EDWARDS, Richard (1524–66)

Deliver me O God (arr from 'In going to my lonely bed'; ascrib only in late Table to C20v)
  A11:91–4  B4:3–4  B18v:95–6  C20v:17  C23v:92  C24v:98–9

[ELLIS, William] (d. 1674)

My lady and her maid
  D9v:2

ELVEY, George Job (1816–93)
  1. Bow down thine ear
      B15:169–73  D18:239–43  D19:192–6  D21:50–4
  2. Wherewithal shall a young man
      B15:161–4  D17:183–8  D18:230–4  D19:183–7
  3. In F: Td, Bs, M, N
      B3:263–71

ELVEY, Stephen (1805–60)

In A (completing CROFT in A): M, N
  B15v:120–4  B30:130–4  D21v:1–6

FALLE, Philip (1656–1742; preb, Durham, 1700–42)
  1. It is a good thing
      B10:58  B21v:12  C19:326–7  C19A:33  C28:459
  2. Fantasie (hol)
      A27:320–1
  3. Passacaille (hol)
      A27:322–7
  4. Catalogue of his music (hol)
      Add. MS 154

FARINEL, [Michel] (1649–early 18th cent.)

Ground
  D2/1:70  D2/2: 72  D2/3:56  M70v:9

FARINELLI, Carlo Broschi (1705–82)

Regal Brittania (Ossequioso Ringraziamento; with extra copy of text, having translation interlined, on 'envelope' addressed to Edw. FINCH)
  M70v:178, 178a, 179–83

[FARNABY, Giles] (c.1563–1640)

Proper tune to Ps. 119 (melody)
  Pr.K.II.31

FARRANT

For Verses to the Organ: M, N
  A6:61–7   C18:31


FARRANT, John (?sen, *fl.* 1567–93; ?jun, 1575–1618)

Short Service, in D sol re: Td, J, K, C, M, N
  Td, J, M, N
    A3:387–97   C12v:166–72   C13:153–8 (+K)
    C13v:128–38 (+K, C)   C32:65–70   C33:56–60   E11a:90–4, 409–11


FARRANT, Richard (*c.*1525–80)

  1. Call to remembrance (*Boyce 2*)
    A20:68
  2. Lord for thy tender mercy's sake (*Page 1*; now attrib to HILTON)
  3. Short Service, in g: Td, Bs, 'J', K, C, M, N (*Boyce 1*)
    Td, Bs, K, C, M, N
    A5:121–37  A15:11–20  B3:142–57  B22:104–8 (−N; M inc)
    B23:7–13  B28:15–25  C8:19–27, 173–5, 253–7 (C inc)
    C12v:32–41 (Td, Bs imp)  C13:19–28  C26:62–72  C31:71–81
    C32:56–65  C33:47–56  D20:146–61  E11a:44–9, 258–60, 367–9
    Td, Bs, M, N
    A22:165–72  B5:17–25  B7:16–24  B8v:83–90  B13v:99–107
    B19:112–24  C30:112–19
    'J' (from Bs; arr PENSON)
    A34:7–13  B3:57–9  B18:104–5  B30:75–7  C20:102–4 (imp)
    C25:107–9  D22:21–3
    'J' (? composed by SHENTON)
    A18:9–12


du FAUT (*see* DUFAUT)


FELTON, William (1715–69)

  1. Burial chant, single, in c
    D37/1–8:3   D37/9:2   D37/10–21:3
  2. [Op. 1], Concerto 3, Andante Allegro
    M69:16–17   M108:2–3
  3. [Op. 2, Concerto 4], Andante
    M108:1


FERRABOSCO, Alphonso (1578–1628)

Have ye no regard
  A3:74–6

FERRABOSCO, John (1626–82)

1. By the waters of Babylon
   B1:86–86a, 87–8
2. I will sing a new song
   B1:81–5, 85a (imp)
3. Evening Service for Verses: M, N (unascrib)
   B1v:8

FERRETTI, Giovanni (*c.*1540–after 1609)

Plead thou my cause (arr PENSON)
   A11:75–82   B4:24   B18v:114–15   C20v:36–7   C23v:115–16
   D22v:5–6

FIDO, John (*c.*1570–*c.*1640)

Hear me O Lord and that soon
   A2:403–4   A5:80–5   C1:43–5   C4:76–7   C5:74–5   C6:79–80
   C7:292–4   C9:50–1   C10:65–7   C11v:30–1   C16:161–2
   C19:191–2

FINCH, Hon. Edward (1664–1738; preb, York, 1704–38)

Unascrib apart from the monogram 'EF' on some of the sonatas of (7.).
1. Bow down thine ear
   M179:27 (frag)
2. Grant we beseech thee merciful Lord
   M179:26 (frag)
3. Old 100th (arr in 5, 6, 7 pts)
   M200/1, 2:16
4. Single chant in G (6-pt and 7-pt versions)
   M70:i, 1
5. When Gammar Gurton first I knew
   M208:5
6. 2 sonatas for German flutes (dated 1716 and 1717)
   M70v:1–8
7. 11 sonatas (dated 1717–20)
   M70v:12–51, 56–9
   Nos. 1, 2, 4, altered by BOCCHI (1720)
   M70v:66–75
8. Division on FARINEL's Ground (*c.*1685–9)
   M70v:9–11
9. Arr CORELLI, Op. 3, Sonatas 2 and 6
   M70:10–17, 2–7 [*sic*]
10. For other items possibly by FINCH, *see* ANON (38.47.63.102–9.)

FINGER (FINGHER), Gottfried (c.1660–1730)

1. Op. 1
   M195/3 (Sonatas 10–12)   M195/5 (Sonatas 8–12; 8, 12 inc)
   M196 (Sonatas 8, 9, 7)
2. Pastorelle in G, Sonata in F, for 3 flutes
   M197
3. Prelude in e for viola da gamba
   A27:123

FIOCCO, [Pietro Antonio] (c.1650–1714)

Give thanks unto the Lord (arr NALSON)
   A26:90–6   B6:189–90   B9:182–4   B12:338–9   B17:145–45a
   B18v:20–3   B24:99   B27:133–6   B31:117–19   B33:162–4
   B34:80–3   B35v:129–31   C10:114–15   C19:333   C21:21–4
   C27:63–6

FIORE, Angelo Maria (c.1660–1723)

Op. 1
   A27:168–9, 231–3 (2 items)

FORCER, [Francis] (c.1650–1705; chor, Durham, 1661–5; org to Bishop
of Durham until 1669, when ran away; at death, partner in Sadlers Wells)

O give thanks
   C7:381–3   C14:209–11   C15:207–9   C28:218–20   C34:182–3

FORD, Thomas (c.1580–1648)

1. Look shepherds look (unascrib; possibly by FORD)
   B1:16–20
2. Haste thee O Lord (Canon à 3)
   M174:1 (imp)

FOSTER, John (c.1620–77; Durham; chor, c.1632–8; m of chor and org,
1661–77) (see Index of Copyists)

With the exception of no. 12, the entries in MSS A3 and A5 are
holograph.

1. Almighty and everlasting God who art always more ready
   A5:292–3   C11:147–8   C12:38–9   C17:73–4   C19:23–4
2. Almighty God who seest (22 Aug. 1671)
   A3:421–2   C11:150–1   C12:49–50   C17:105   C19:80–1
3. Glory be to God on high (included as an anthem, not as part of
   Second Service)
   A3:10b, 11–14   C1:85–6   C7:341–2   C9:73 (inc)
   C10:99–100 (inc)   C11:101–3   C15:60–1   C17:74–6   C19:37–8

Sc, S
A3:10–11   B28:182 (–S)   C1:86, 88   C4:92 (imp)   C5:92
C7:314   C10:86   C33:186 (–S)
G
*see* 'Glory be to God on high'

FRIEND, [John] (l–c, Durham, 1782–1819) (*see* Index of Copyists)
  1. Again the day returns (Morning Hymn)
     A16:190   B11:84   B16:95   B18v:27–8   B26:174   B34:123
  2. Hear O Lord consider
     A16:142–7   B11:84   B16:95   B18v:27   B26:110   B34:122

FROST (MS *c*.1630)
For Verses: M, N
  C18:32–3

FUSSEL (*fl*. 1774–d. 1802)
In A: Cd, Dm
  A11:1–31   A22:194–8 (–Dm)   B3:5–11   B18:50–6   C20:41–8
  C23:40–7   C24:41–8   C25:41–8

GALE, Thomas (MSS *c*.1635)
O how amiable
  C2:128–30   C3:99–100   C7:66–7   C11v:11   C14:84   C16:185–7
  C19:235–7

GALLIARD, John Ernest (*c*.1680–1749)
  1. Completion of TALLIS's Litany
     A8:53–6
  2. Merlin, or the Devil of Stonehenge (Opera; hol)
     E30(i)
  3. [Apollo and Daphne] and ?[The Triumphs of Love] (Operas; hol)
     E30(ii)

GALUPPI, Baldassare (1760–85)
Minuet in F
  M69:92

GARTH, John (1722–1810; org to Bishop of Durham, 1793)
  1. Dust thou art
     A26:184–9   B6:200–2   B8:89, 91–3   B12:354   B13:165–6
     B24:106, 111, 114   B31:129   B35v:136
  2. Out of the deep
     A20:22–5   B6:198–9   B8:90–1   B9v:76–7   B12:352–3
     B13:164–5   B24:112–13   B26:136–7   B31:130–1   B33v:118–19
     B34:15–17   C22v:8–9   C22v:78–80   C28:554–7   D21:97–9

3. Unto thee O God
   A16:199–201  B11:91–2  B16:101–2  B18v:34  B33:180
   B34:130–1  C23v:12–13  C24v:8–9  D18:126–8
4. [Op. 2, Sonata 1] (unascrib)
   M69:52–5

GASPARINI, Francesco . . . Lucchesi (c.1665–1737)

*L'Armonico Practico al Cimbalo*, Chapter 9 (1745 edition)
   E24(i)—in English   E24(iv)—in Italian

GEERES, John (l-c, King's College, Cambridge, 1623–8; l-c Durham, 1628–d. 1642) (*see* Index of Copyists)

1. Merciful Lord, we beseech thee (St John the Evangelist)
   A1:324–5  C1:92–3  C2:14  C3:12  C7:8  C11v:91  C14:10
   C16:299  C19:345–6
2. O praise the Lord of heaven (hol in A1, C4–7, C10)
   A1:48–9  C4:30–1  C5:22–3  C6:28–9  C7:238–9  C9:10–11
   C10:20–1  C11:67–8  C15:63–4  C17:32–3  C19:9–11
3. The eyes of all (hol in C4–10)
   A5:46–7  C1:6  C2*:21  C4:47  C5:39  C7:252  C9:26
   C10:33  C11:66–7  C15:46–7  C16:43  C17:64–5  C27:32
   C28:34  C34:17

GEMINIANI, Francesco (1687–1762)
Only in MSS M157 and M185 are composer and exact title given. Otherwise, Geminiani is named only before the first concerto in MS E13; two concertos are numbered in MS E25, and the Table to MS E13 gives some concerto numbers.

1. Op. 2
   Concerto 1
   E13:69–76
   Concerto 2
   E13:1–11
   Concerto 3
   E13:127–35  M157:36 [Presto]
   [Concerto 4]
   E13:76–87
   Concerto 5
   E13:42–54
   [Concerto 6]
   E13:97–109
2. Op. 3
   Concerto 1
   E13:110–26  M157:31–3 (inc)

GEMINIANI, FRANCESCO (*cont.*)
     Concerto 2
     E13:55–66
     Concerto 3
     E13:19–33    M70v:156–78    M157:64–5 (Allegro 2)
     Concerto 4
     E13:34–41
     Concerto 5
     E13:88–96    M157:60–1 (Allegro)
     Concerto 6
     E13:11–18
  3. [Op. 4] (as Concertos; arr from Sonatas 1, 11, 2, 5, 7, and 9 respectively)
     Concerto 1
     E25(viii) (inc)
     Concertos 2–6
     E25(ix)–(xiii)
  4. [*Pièces de Clavecin* (1st Collection)]
     E25(xiv):1–31 [lacks Minuets]    E25(xv) [part of 1st Suite]
  5. [*A Treatise of Good Taste*]
     E24(vii) [Ex. 1]    E25 (xiv):32–4 [Exs. 1–2]
  6. Minuet in F + variations
     M185:7–8
  7. [Variations on Sarabande theme of CORELLI, Op. 5, Sonata 7]
     E25(xvi)
  8. Affettuoso in d
     E11a:346–7

GIBBONS, Christopher (1615–76)
   1. Have pity upon me
      C2:176    C3:143    C7:103    C14:129    C19:285–7
   2. How long wilt thou forget me
      B1:108–11
   3. O praise the Lord all ye heathen
      B1:112–13
   4. Teach me O Lord
      A4:117–20    C11v:211

GIBBONS, [Edward], of Exeter (1568–1650)
What strikes the clock (textless)
     Hunter 33: ff. 6v–7

GIBBONS, Orlando (1583–1625)
*A Collection of the Sacred Compositions of Orlando Gibbons*, ed. F. A. G.
Ouseley (1873)

1. Almighty and everlasting God mercifully look (*Boyce 2*)
   A1:61–2   A14:16   B6v:20   B9v:36–7   B10:62–3   B12:133
   B13:98–9   B24:78–9   B27:246   C2★:37   C4:27   C5:19
   C6:25   C7:235   C9:5   C10:17   C11:36   C15:30   C16:60
   C17:30   C19:6   C28:544–5
2. Almighty God who by thy Son (St Peter)
   A4:92–7   C1:126–7   C2:89–90   C3:69   C7:45   C11v:138
   C14:53   C16:344   C19:389–90
3. Awake up my glory (*see* Preces & Ps., Easter Evensong)
4. Behold I bring you glad tidings (Christmas)
   A2:316–19   C1:89–90   C2:7–8   C3:7   C7:5   C11v:88   C14:5
   C16:295–6   C17:190–1   C19:341–2   D30–5:47–8
5. Behold the hour cometh (now attrib to T. TOMKINS)
6. Behold thou hast made my days
   A1:54–8   C1:50   C4:80   C5:78   C6:86   C7:298 (inc)   C9:55
   C10:70   C11v:21–2   C16:177–8   C17:140   C19:197
   C27:118   C28:141–2   C34:120
7. Blessed are all they
   A4:26–31   C1:45–7   C4:77   C5:75–6   C6:81–2   C7:294–5
   C9:52   C10:67–8   C11v:4–5   C16:137–9   C19:193–4
8. Blessed be the Lord God of Israel (2nd pt of 'Deliver us O Lord')
   D17:156–7
9. Deliver us O Lord (*see above*)
   D17:153–5
10. Glorious and powerful God (Whitsunday)
    A2:197–200   B1v:10   C1:33–4   C2:68–9   C3:53–4   C4:69
    C5:67–8   C6:70   C7:37–8   C7:281–3   C10:57–8   C11v:126–7
    C14:43–4   C16:331–3   C17:129–30   C19:176–8   C27:121–4
11. Grant Holy Trinity (King's Day)
    A2:352–5   A4:64–9   C1:20   C2:103   C3:76–7   C4:59   C5:57
    C6:56   C7:52–3   C7:265   C9:38   C10:45   C11v:148   C14:61
    C16:356–7   C19:159–60
12. Have mercy upon me O God (now attrib to BYRD)
13. Hosanna to the Son of David (*Boyce 2*)
    A1:86–8   A9v:4, 5, 8–9   A14:12–13   A29:16–17   B6v:18–19
    B9v:2–3   B10:17–19   B12:32–4   B17v:16–17   B24:51
    B27:204–5   B29:3–4   C2★:18–19   C4:28   C5:20   C6:26
    C7:236   C9:7   C10:18   C11:27–8   C15:31–2   C16:21–2
    C17:27–8   C19:7–8   C27:18   C28:37–8   C34:42–3
14. If ye be risen again (Easter)
    A1:92–5   C1:109–10   C2:51–2   C3:40–1   C7:30   C11v:116
    C14:32–3   C16:320–1   C19:365–6   D30–5:46–7

GIBBONS, ORLANDO (*cont.*)

15. Lift up your heads
    A6:357–9   A14:14–15   A29:18–19   B6v:17–18   B9v:3–4
    B10:19–21   B12:10–12   B17v:17   B21:183–4   B24:45
    B27:202–4   B29:2–3   C1:244–5   C2:181–2   C3:146 (inc)
    C7:120–1   C11:10–12   C14:134–5   C15:77–9   C16:30–2
    C17:81–2   C19:47–8   C27:19–20   C28:35–6   C34:8–9
    D18:30–2

16. O clap your hands (*Boyce 2*)
    D18:40–50

17. O God the king of glory (Ascension) (D MSS arr ARMES)
    C1:113–14   C2:63–5   C3:49–50   C7:33   C11v:124–5
    C14:37–8   C16:325–6   C19:376–7   D23:120–1   D26/1:36–8
    D26/2–5: 36–7   D26/6–9:37–8   D30–5:104–5

18. O Lord I lift my heart
    D17:158

19. O Lord increase my faith (now attrib to LOOSEMORE)

20. Sing unto the Lord O ye saints
    A2:252–5   A5:140–4   B4:130–1   B15:59–64   C1:19   C4:58
    C5:56   C6:54–5   C7:264–5   C9:37   C10:44   C11v:46
    C16:140–1   C17:118–20   C19:157–9   C22v:136–42   C27:120–1
    C34:117–19   D20v:33–9   D22v:109–15

21. The eyes of all (*see* Preces & Ps., Whitsunday Evensong)

22. The secret sins (probably by W. MUNDY; in C7 the text has been
    altered to 'The Lord is only my support')
    C1:20–1   C4:59   C5:57   C6:56   C7:265–6   C9:38   C10:45
    C19:160

23. This is the record of John (4th Sunday in Advent)
    A5:145–8   C1:51–2   C2:5   C3:5   C4:81–2   C5:79–80   C6:88
    C7:3   C7:299–300 (inc)   C9:56–7   C10:71–2   C11v:87   C14:3
    C16:294   C17:141   C19:199   C27:119   C34:116–17

24. We praise thee O Father (Easter)
    A2:244–7   C1:27–9   C2:49–50   C3:39–40   C4:64   C5:62
    C6:64–5   C7:28–9   C7:274–5   C9:44 (inc)   C10:51–2
    C11v:114–15   C14:30–2   C16:318–19   C17:125–6   C19:167–8

25. Why art thou so heavy (now attrib to LOOSEMORE)

26. Preces & Ps., Easter Evensong (although MSS imply Ps., 'Awake up
    my glory', is by GIBBONS, it is probably by W. SMITH)
    Preces only
    C1:294   C13v:12   E4–11:17   E11a:11–12

27. Preces & Ps., Whitsunday Evensong (The eyes of all) (D MSS arr
    ARMES)
    A2:10–12   C1:211–13   C13v:22–3   C18:3–4   D23:90–2

D26/1–3:6–9    D26/4–9:6–8    E4:33–5    E5:33–6    E6:33–4
E7:33–6    E8–11:33–5    E11a:22–5

28. Short Service, in F (in G in some later MSS): Td, Bs, 'J', K, C, M, N
(*Boyce 1*)
Td, Bs, K, C, M, N
A1:170–84    A15:21–30    A22:64–76    B3:173–88    B5:35–45
B7:34–45    B8v:101–11    B13v:118–28    B16v:7–16    B19:124–40
B23:140–6    B28:57–67    C8:98–102, 218–22, 303–7 (– Bs)
C12v:227–37 (all imp)    C13:94–103    C19Av:67–9 (just M, N)
C26:83–92    C30:16–25    C31:93–102    C32:78–85    C33:38–47
D18v:11–18 (– Td, Bs)    D20:170–83    E11a:77–81, 272–4, 393–5
'J' (from Bs; arr PENSON)
A34:14–20    B3:59–61    B18:106–7    B30:77–9    C20:105–6
C25:109–11    D22:23–5
'J' (from Bs; arr SHENTON)
A18:5–8
29. For Verses, Second Service: M, N
A2:13–19    C1:180–3    C12v:256–60    C13v:69–72    C18:29–30
E11a:510–12

GIBBS, John (*fl.* 1605–15)

To the Organ: Td, J, M, N
C18:18–21

GIBBS, Richard (*fl.* 1620–40)

See sinful soul (Good Friday)
A5:259–64    C2:40–42    C3:30–1    C7:22    C11v:105–6    C14:24–5
C16:312–13    C19:358–9

GILES, Nathaniel (*c.*1558–1634)

1. Everlasting God which hast ordained (St Michael and All Angels)
A4:69–73, 73a, 74    C1:63–4    C2:93–4    C3:71    C4:89    C5:88
C7:47    C7:309–10    C9:64–5    C10:82–3    C14:55    C16:345
C19:390–1
2. God which as at that time (Whitsunday)
C1:117–19    C2:69–71    C3:54–5    C7:38–9    C11v:128–9
C14:44–5    C16:333–4    C19:377–9
3. Have mercy upon me O God
A3:228–33    C1:248–50    C1:266–8    C2:162–3    C3:132–3
C7:92–3    C11v:59–60    C14:116–17    C16:226–8    C19:273–4
4. He that hath my commandments (men's voices)
A1:292–3    A3:161–2    A5:288–9    C4:65    C5:63    C6:66
C7:276    C10:53    C11:118–19    C17:97–8    C19:72–3

GILES, NATHANIEL (*cont.*)

5. I will magnify thee O Lord
A1:42–6  C1:60–1  C2:124–5  C3:96–7  C4:87–8  C5:86–7
C6:96 (inc)  C7:306–7  C9:62–3  C10:80–1  C11v:6–7
C14:73  C16:144–5  C17:144–5  C19:206–7

6. O give thanks unto the Lord for he is gracious
A6:87–9  C2★:25–6  C4:5  C5:①(imp)  C6:5  C7:215
C10:1 (imp)  C11:21–2  C12:1–2  C15:5–7  C16:1–2  C17:5

7. O hear my prayer Lord
A3:7–10  C1:263–5  C2:138–9  C3:110–11  C7:74–5
C11v:68  C14:95–6  C16:211  C17:159  C19:249–50

8. O how happy a thing it is (I)
C1:8–9  C4:52  C5:50  C6:45–6  C7:256  C9:30  C10:38
C11v:38  C16:169  C19:146

9. O how happy a thing it is (II)
A5:112–15

10. O Lord my God in all distress
C1:13–15  C4:54–5  C5:52–3  C6:49–50  C7:259–60  C9:33
C10:40–1  C11v:32–3  C16:166  C19:149–50

11. O Lord turn not away thy face
A5:10–15  C1:70–1  C9:75 (imp)  C10:101–2  C11v:84–5
C16:239  C17:147–8  C19:221–2

12. Out of the deep
A4:32–8  C1:269–70  C2:159  C3:129  C7:89  C11v:70
C14:113  C16:222–3  C17:164–5  C19:267–9

13. Thou O God that guidest (now attrib to BYRD)

14. First Service: Td, J, K, C, M, N
A1:105–28  A2:56–68, 70–5 (−K)  C1:154–64  C13v:37–46
C18:13–17 (−K)  E4:93–8, 125–8, 153–6
E5:95–101, 125–8, 153–6  E6:91–5, 119–21, 147–9
E7:95–100, 127–30, 155–8  E8:99–104, 127–9, 155–8
E9:87–91, 117–19, 149–52  E10:93–8, 121–3, 145–8
E11:103–7, 129–31, 155–7  E11a:211–15, 328–30, 486–9

15. Second Service, Last Service: Td, J, K, C, M, N
A2:78–101  C1:168–79  C13v:59–68  C18:23–8 (M, N both imp)
E11a:216–21, 331–3, 489–92

GODFREY, William (MS early 18th cent.)

When first Dorinda charming eyes (text only)
D9:36–8

GOLDWIN, John (*c*.1667–1719)

1. Hear me O God
A28:228–30  B9v:25–7  B12:89–90  B20v:77–8 (inc)

B21:101–2  B32:44  C19:419–21  C19A:81–2  C21:91–2
C28:143–5  C29v:72–3  C35v:61–2
2. I have set God always (*Boyce 2*)
   A20:5–7  B6v:51–2  B9v:27–8  B10:40–2  B12:22–3  B17:2–3
   B20:39–40  B24:29–30  B26:46–7  B27:195–7  B29:58–9
   B32:48–9  B33:21–2  C2:35 (frag)  C8:515–16 (inc)
   C14:131–2 (imp)  C19:461–2  C27:97–100  C28:423–4
   C29v:23–4  C34:91–2
3. I will sing unto the Lord (*Page 1*)
   A16:196–8  D19:42–4
4. O Lord God of Hosts
   A20:36–8  A28:225–8  B6v:49–51  B9v:24–5  B12:3–6
   B20v:74 (inc)  B21:99–100  B24:52  B26:101–2  B29:59–60
   B32:43–4  B34:23–4  B36:5–6  C19:416–18  C19A:79–80
   C21:89–90  C28:126–8  C29v:70–1  C35v:59–60
5. O Lord how glorious
   A8:147–51  A13:51–4  B13:134
6. O praise God in his holiness (*Page 2*)
   A14:162–8  B21:75  B27:170, 173–4  C19:126  C19A:60
   C21:68  C26v:40–2  C29v:54  C35v:35
7. In F: Td, J, S, K, C, M, N (*Arnold 1*)
   D18v:40–54 (−S)  D20:89–107  M170:148–54 (−S, K, C)

GOODSON, [Richard] (1655–1718)

In C: Td, J
   A22:177–87  B5:203–8  B7:221–7  B19:208–17  B21:31–5
   B21v:36–42  B22:74–80  B23:73–4 (−J; Td inc)  B28:227–34
   B33v:121–6 (Td inc)  B36v:16–20  C19v:13–20  C19Av:54–8
   C21v:49–55  C29:61–6  C30:178–83  C31:344–51  C35:36–40
   M170:155–7 (−J; Td inc)

GOSS, John (1800–80)

1. If we believe that Jesus died
   B4:216–17
2. Praise the Lord O my soul while I live
   D17:67–73
3. In E: M, N
   D17v:115–19

GRAUN, Carl Heinrich (1703–4 to 1759)

1. Behold the Lamb of God (*Latrobe 1*)
   B15:214–15  D21:214–15

GRAUN, CARL HEINRICH (*cont.*)
2. Great is the Lord
   A11:55–74   B4:16–18   B18v:107–9   C20v:28–30   C23v:107–9
   D22v:2–4
3. O Zion mark what pity (*Latrobe 5*)
   D21:203–5
4. Sing to Jehovah (*Latrobe 2*)
   B15:190–2   D18:266–9   D19:219–21   D21:77–9

GREATHEED, Samuel Stephenson (1813–87)
Blessed is the man that feareth (St Matthew) (*Ouseley 2*)
   B3v:54–7

GREATOREX, Edward (*c.*1823–1900; Durham; m-c, 1849–99; prec, 1862–72)
Have mercy Lord on me
   D30–3:143–5   D34:143–5, 147a–b   D35:141–3

GREATOREX, [Thomas] (1758–1831)
?arr PERGOLESI (2.)

GREEN, James (*c.*1700–after 1751)
Td
   E11a:233

GREENE, Maurice (1696–1755)
*Forty Select Anthems in Score . . . by Dr. Maurice Greene* (1743); ★ = vol. 1;
† = vol. 2.
1. ★Acquaint thyself with God
   A12:149–59   A29:40–4   B20v:65–73   B21:98   B24:84
   C19A:78   C29v:69   C35v:58   D17:80   D21:194–5
2. ★Arise shine O Zion
   A29:172–8   D17:95–9
3. As pants the hart (Canon à 3; unascrib)
   M174:11
4. †Behold I bring you glad tidings (Christmas Day, 1728)
   A7:74–94   A29:25–30   B20v:55–7   B21:88–90   C19:142–4
   C19A:67–9   C21:78–80   C29v:60–2   C35v:47–9
5. Blessed is the man that hath not walked
   B20:73–7   B21:128–32   C19A:111   C21:99   C28:428–9
   C29v:105–6   C35v:80
6. Blessed is the man whose strength (*see* HOWARD)
7. Bow down thine ear (*Page 3*)
   A7:52–62   A29:47–50   B6v:47–9   B9v:22–4   B20v:49–51

B21:82–4   B27:175–6, 179   B32:51–2   B36:54–5   C19:135–8
C19A:61–3   C21:72–4   C28:468–70   C29v:55–7   C35v:41–3
D19:14–16

8. †God is our hope and strength
A16:84–95   A29:112–17   B8:105–7   B9:202–5   B11:54–6
B16:59–68   B26:165–71   D30–3:124–6   D35:122–4

9. Hast not thou forsaken us (*see* AVISON)

10. †Have mercy upon me
A29:34–8   B20:57–68   B21:122–3   C19:422–3   C19:438–9
C19A:109–10   C21:93–4   C29v:89–90   C35v:76–7

11. Hear my crying (*Page 2*)
B20:71–2   B21:126–7   C19:440–5   C19A:100–1   C21:97–8
C28:446–7   C29v:99–103

12. †Hear O Lord and consider
A29:158–61   B20:69–70   B21:124–5   C19:446–7   C19A:98–9
C21:95–6   C28:447–9   C29v:94–8   C35v:78–9

13. *I will give thanks unto thee O Lord
A29:162–71   D17:160–71

14. I will magnify thee O God (*Arnold 2*)
B12:112–15   B20v:37–40   B21:67–8   B27:259–62   C19A:53–4
C21:62–3   C26v:21–5   C29v:44–5   C35v:32–4

15. †I will seek unto God
B21:157–9   C19A:141   C21:135–6   C29v:137–9
C35v:110–11

16. *I will sing of thy power
A28:8–11   B12:241–2   B17v:23–4   B20:89–92   B21:142–4
B24:83–4   B26:11–12   B32:47–8   B36:7–8   C19:338–40
C19A:126–9   C21:114–17   C28:150–2   C29v:115–17
C35v:95–8   D17:76–9   D21:191–4

17. Kyrie eleison [à 4: in C; also in B♭]
M70:64, 90–1

18. *Let God arise
A29:178–85   D17:99–106

19. †Let my complaint
A17:83–92   A29:127–9   B12:242–3   B24:85

20. Like as the hart (*Arnold 2*)
A14:122–7   A28:157–62   B9v:55–6   B12:103–4   B20v:79–80
B21:103–4   B24:95–6, 99   B31:131–2   B34:77–8   C19:451–2
C19A:83–4   C28:442–4   C29v:74–5   C35v:63–4   D19:6–8

21. *Lord how long wilt thou be angry
A7:43–51   A28:16–19   B12:238–9   B20v:40–2   B21:68–70
B24:94   B27:262–3   B32:50–1   B36:50–1   C19:123–5
C19A:51–2   C21:63–5   C26v:32–3   C28:466–8   C29v:45–6

37. ★Praise the Lord O my soul while I live (*Arnold 2*)
    A29:130–5   D19:8–9   D30:128   D31–4:128–9
38. ★Praise the Lord ye servants
    A29:135–40
39. ★Sing unto the Lord ye that go down
    B20v:82–4   B21:163–5   C19A:143–4   C21:139–45
    C29v:143–4   C35v:120–5
40. †The Lord even the most mighty
    A26:178–83
41. †The Lord is my shepherd
    A17:158–66   A29:192–9   B20v:84–90   B21:165–71
    C19A:145–7   C21:145–7   C29v:145–7   C35v:117–18
42. †Thou O God art praised
    A17:144–51   A29:142–6   B24:68   D17:87–8   D21:196–7
43. In C: Td, J, M, N (*Arnold 2*)
    B19:16–26   B20v:96–105   B21v:58–67   B22:143–50
    B28:259–65   B36v:1–7   C19A:87–96   C21v:62–9   C29:73–9
    C31:167–73   C35:56–65   D19v:57–76

*Secular item*:
44. Air + variations in A [from *A Collection of Lessons for the Harpsichord* (1750)]
    M69:86–9

GREGGS, William (?1652/?62–1710; songman, York, 1670–7; m of chor, York, 1677–81; m of chor and org, Durham, 1682–1710) (*see* Index of Copyists)

   1. Hear my prayer O Lord and let my crying
      A25:26–7   C7:200–1   C14:130   C15:136 (inc)   C19:97
      C27:59   C28:61   C34:90
   2. If the Lord himself
      A25:33–7
   3. I will sing a new song (Thanksgiving for a General Peace 1697)
      A25:126–30   C14:85–8   C27:323–7   C28:418–21
   4. My heart is inditing
      A4:153–8   C27:126   C27:333–6   C28:215   C34:180
   5. O Lord our Governor
      A25:56–8 (imp)   C27:133   C28:213   C34:179
   6. The Lord hear thee
      A4:173–5 (inc)   C7:336–9   C11v:233   C14:167   C15:110
      C27:134–6   C28:239–42   C34:251–3

GREGORY, Edward (Durham; m-c, 1731–d. 1753)
Christian name only in MS B35

GREGORY, EDWARD (*cont.*)
  1. In Eb: M, N
     A13v:32–43   B7:227–35   B17v:88–95   B19:265–76   B22:38–47
     B28:381–8, 389–90   B29v:33–41   B31v:22–9   B35:80–7
     C33:100–9   M207:1–51
  2. Arr MARCELLO (2.)

[GREVILLE, Robert] (service acquired 1791)
In C: M, N (unascrib)
   A15:175–81   B13v:191–4   B23:181, 184–5   B35:188–92

HACQUART, Carolus (*c.*1640–?1701)
Op. 3
   A27:35–7, 39, 62–3, 75–7, 82, 144–7, 174–6, 225–9, 245–8, 274–8
   (16 items)

HALL, Henry (*c.*1656–1707)
  1. By the waters of Babylon
     A33:63–9   C7:188–90   C7:385   C14:220   C15:204   C27:261–4
     C28:256–9   C34:269–72
  2. Comfort ye my people
     B4:131–42   B15:64–8   C22v:142–5   D20v:39–42   D22v:115–17
  3. In thee O Lord
     A13:5–11   B6:14–17   B10:240–4   B12:157–9   B13:13–15
     B17:46–8   B29:222–4   B31:16–18   B33:72–4   B35v:28–31
     B36:89–91
  4. Praise the Lord O ye servants
     A34v:74–82   B4:45–7   B15:18–19   C20v:79–81   C22v:50–2
     D22v:32–4
  5. The souls of the righteous
     A13:1–5   B6:11–14   B10:236–40   B12:122–4   B13:10–12
     B17:44–6   B29:220–2   B31:14–15   B33:70–2   B35v:26–8
     B36:87–9
  6. In Eb: Td (*see* HALL *and* HINE)
*Secular item*:
  7. Oil and vinegar are two pretty things (Catch for 3 voc; unascrib)
     M193/1:39

HALL, Henry *and* HINE, William
In Eb: Td (by HALL), J (by HINE) (*Arnold 3*)
   A15:220–6   B5:190–5   B7:175–80   B16v:92–8   B19:26–31
   B20v:105–10   B21v:67–71   B23:57–9 (inc)   B28:265–9
   B34v:23–7   B36v:7–10   C19v:29–33   C19Av:96–101   C21v:70–4
   C29:80–4   C30:151–4   C31:367–70   C35:65–70   D19v:45–53

HANDEL, George Frederick (1685–1759)

1. As pants the hart (Chandos anthem 6, various forms)
   6A, with symphony
   B36:46–8   C35v:158–65
   6B, without symphony
   A7v:17–28   A26:73–83   B8:61–4   B9:105–8   B10:204–8
   B12:248–55   B20v:21–5   B21:54–9   B24:81–2   B27:161–5
   B29:200–3   B35v:11–14   B36:104–7   C19A:39–43   C29v:33–7
   C35v:18–21   E26(v) (inc)
   6D, with variant (19th cent. MSS)
   D19:21–9   D20v:162–7

2. Be ye sure that the Lord (Utrecht Jubilate)
   E15:6–9

3. Dettingen Te Deum
   A32:47–154 (full score)   D7 (25 single pts)   D19v:128–45

4. Gloria Patri
   A31v:23–5   B3:29–31   B18:73–5   C20:68–71   C23:66–8
   C24:67–9   C25:67–9

5. Hallelujah Chorus (Messiah)
   A14:65 (frag)   B26:137–40

6. Hast not thou forsaken us (see AVISON)

7. Have mercy with me O God (Chandos anthem)
   B36:42–5   C35v:144–52

8. He gave them hailstones (Israel in Egypt)
   A21:35–8   B4:96–7   B15:34–5   B15:150–1   B21v:1–2
   C22v:96–7   D19:169–70   D20v:9–10   D22v:69–71

9. He that dwelleth in heaven (Messiah)
   B8:29–33   B9:161–4   B17:82–4   B29:262–4   B33:111–13

10. How beautiful are the feet (Messiah; for two altos)
    A11:44–52   B6:191–2   B9:185–91   B13:160–2   B17:145a–46
    B31:120–2   B33:165–6   B35v:132–3   C22v:75–6   D22v:40–2
    D30–5:96–8   M173:42–4 (for 2 oboes)

11. How long wilt thou forget me [I]
    A13:90   B8:46–8   B9v:52–3   B12:127   B13:97–8   B17:96–7
    B24:98   B26:10–11   B32:79–80   B33:125–7   B34:41–2
    B36:113–14   C28:525–6

12. How long wilt thou forget me [II] (arr from 'Amadigi')
    E15:1–5

13. In the days of Herod (Pratt)
    D19:107–9   D20v:109–11

14. Israel in Egypt (see 'He gave them hailstones', 'The Lord is a man of war', 'I will sing unto the Lord'; see also Oratorios)
    E3:iv, 1–331 (full score; unascrib)

HANDEL, GEORGE FREDERICK (*cont.*)
    B29:205–6  B32:54–6  B35v:122–4  B36:15–16  C19A:147–9
    C21:148–50  C23v:8–11  C29v:148–50  C35v:126–7  E25(xix)
    E35(iii)/3

*Oratorios and secular choral works:*
45. Abel (wrongly ascrib; by ARNE)
46. [Aci, Galatea e Polifemo (2)] (only 1 pt ascrib)
    E26(ii)
47. Acis and Galatea (unascrib, apart from 1 pt in E26(iii))
    Full score
    E17:1–246 (inc; some pp. blank)
    Overture and 1st Chorus
    M184–6:14–15  M187:13–14  M188–9:14–15
    Selections
    E26(iii)
48. Alexander's Feast (unascrib, apart from M172 and 1 pt of E20(iii))
    All
    E20(i)—19 single pts  M172—10 single pts
    Selection
    E20(ii)
    Concerto No. 2 ( = Concertante)
    E20(iii)—15 single pts
    Softly sweet in Lydian measures
    M88:1–5
49. Angelico splendor (insert in 'Israel in Egypt')
50. Athalia (unascrib)
    Blooming virgins
    M88:29–32
    Gentle airs
    M88:32–4
51. [Carco sempre di Gloria] (Cantata II, in praise of St Cecilia; unascrib)
    E20(iv)/6—1 instr pt
52. [Cecilia volgi un sguardo] (Cantata I, in praise of St Cecilia; only 1 pt ascrib)
    E20(iv)—6 instr pts
53. Deborah (unascrib)
    E12:1–200 (full score)
54. Esther (unascrib, apart from a few pts in D15)
    D15—31 single pts  E35(iii)—12 single pts
55. From harmony, from heavenly harmony (Ode for St Cecilia's Day)
    Full score + 8 single pts
    E23

What passion cannot music raise (unascrib)
M88:38–47
56. Israel in Egypt (*see also* no. 14)
Angelico splendor (insert)
E26(x)—full score (inc)
The sons of Israel do mourn (arr from 'The ways of Zion')
E35(i)—2 single pts
57. Jephtha
Farewell ye limpid springs
M173:38–42 (for 2 oboes)
The smiling dawn of happy days
M173:44–6 (for 2 oboes)
Ye sacred priests
M173:38 (for 2 oboes)
58. Joshua
A24:1–322 (full score)    D8—30 single pts
59. Judas Maccabaeus
Pt of full score (unascrib)
E35(ii)
O lovely peace
M173:12–13 (for 2 oboes)
60. L'Allegro (unascrib)
But O sad virgins
M88:13–24
[Far from all resort]
E33/3:8    E33/4:6    E33/5:6–7
61. Messiah (*see* no. 20)
62. Occasional Oratorio (unascrib)
O Liberty
M88:35–7
63. Saul
Overture (unascrib)
M184:20    M185–8:18–19    M189:18–20
Sin not O king
M173:37 (for 2 oboes)
64. Semele (unascrib)
Author of peace
M88:24–7
O Sleep
M88:27–9
65. Theodora
Angels ever bright and fair
M173:36–7 (for 2 oboes)

HANDEL, GEORGE FREDERICK (*cont.*)

*Operas and operatic stage works*:

Of nos. 65–86, only no. 66 (2nd item) is ascrib

66. Alcina
Overture
M157:52–3
Verdi prati selve amene
E26(vi)—full score
67. Amadigi
Overture
E25(xviii)—frag
S'estinto e l'idol mio
M70:18–21
68. Ariadne, Overture
M157:40–1
69. Ariodante (all no text)
[Al sen ti stringo e parto]
E33/3–5:3
Cieca notte
E33/1–2:3    E33/3:4    E33/4:3    E33/5:4
[Il tuo sangue]
E33/1v:3–4    E33/2v:3    E33/3v:4–5    E33/4v:3–5    E33/5v:4–5
[Voli colla sua tromba]
E33/1v, 2v:4    E33/3v:7    E33/4v:5    E33/5v:5–6
70. Atlanta
Sol prova
E33/3:1–2    E33/4, 5:1
71. Berenice, Overture
M157:90–1 (Allegro)
72. Faramond, Overture
M157:91 (Allegro)
73. Flavius, Overture
M184–6:10    M187:9    M188–9:10
74. Floridant, Overture
M185–6:9    M187:8    M188–9:9
75. Hercules
How blest the maid
M88:5–13
76. Hymen, Overture
M157:92
77. Il Pastor Fido (I), Overture
M157:37–9

78. Il Pastor Fido (II), Overture
M157:46–8
79. Muzio Scaevola
Overture to Act III
M184–6:13   M187:12   M188–9:13
[Lungo pensar e dubitar]
M70:50–2
80. Ottone
Full score
D16:1–203
Overture (= Op. 3, Concerto 6, 1st movement)
E34(ii)   M185:10–11   M186:11   M187:10   M188–9:11
81. Pernasso, Overture
M157:93
82. Ptolemy, Overture
M185–6:21–2   M189:23–4
83. Radamistus, Overture
D16:204–6   M184–6:12   M187:11   M188–9:12
84. Richard the First, Overture
M183:24   M185–6:20   M189:21
85. Rinaldo
Overture
E32:11–17   M185–6:6   M189:6
[Bel piacere]
E32:73–4
86. [Rodelinda, Overture]
E32:88 (Adagio)
87. Sosarmes, Overture
E33/1, 2:10–11   E33/3:11–12   E33/4:9–10   E33/5:12–13
*Instrumental*:
88. [Op. 3]
[Concerto 4] (as 1st edn., 1734)
E33/1–5:1–3
Concerto 6, 1st movement
*see* 'Ottone', Overture
2nd movement
E32:25–7
89. [Op. 4]
Concerto 1
E26(i)—9 single pts
90. [Op. 6] (ascrib and numbered only in M157)
Concertos 1–4 (all inc)
E25(i)–(iii)

HANDEL, GEORGE FREDERICK (*cont.*)
    Concerto 5
    M157:98–100
    Concerto 6
    M157:95–7   E24(ix)   E25(iv)   E34(i)
    Concerto 7
    E25(v) (inc)   M157:110–11
    Concerto 8
    M157:104–5
    Concerto 10
    M157:100–1 (Allegro Moderato)
    Concerto 11
    E25(vi) (inc)   M157:106–10
    Concerto 12
    E25(vii)
91. Concerto Grosso in C major ( = Concertante)
    E20(iii)—15 single pts
92. [Fugue in F] (unascrib)
    E24(xi):45 (inc)
93. [Suite de Pièces: 'Harmonious Blacksmith'] (*see* STANLEY)
94. Minuet in G
    E32:43

HARTE
Thou O God art praised (although attrib to HARTE in Table to MS C34, the version in MS A4, copied in 1679, excludes Philip HARTE (1674–1749). Possibly by John HAWKINS)

HASSE, Johann Adolph (1699–1783)
  1. O praise the Lord of heaven
    A10:1–12   B4:78–80   B15:20–1   C20v:82–3   C22v:53–61
    D22v:35–6
  2. Artaxerxes, Overture
    E18—full score + 11 single pts
  3. [Op. 3], Concerto 2
    M157:102–3
  4. [Op. 4], Concerto 1
    E26(iv)—7 single pts

HAVERGAL, William Henry (1793–1870)
  1. Give thanks unto the Lord
    B15:182–6   D18:257–62   D19:208–13   D21:70–4
  2. In E♭: Cd, Dm
    B3:116–28   B15v:50–9   B30:79–88   C22:80–91   D20:121–30

HAYDN, FRANZ JOSEPH (*cont.*)

3. *Great is the Lord
   A16:61–6   D20v:160–1
4. I have set God always
   D30–5:34
5. Lo from the hills (Hymn)
   A16:130–1   B9:210–11
6. *Lord how long wilt thou be angry
   A16:80–4   D30–5:39–41
7. *Lord thou hast been our refuge
   A16:23–9
8. *O be joyful in God
   A16:70–9   A19:548–60
9. *O worship the Lord
   A16:13–23   D20v:145–51
10. *Praise the Lord O Jerusalem
    A16:39–45   D20v:138–42
11. *Save Lord and hear us
    A16:6–12   A19:536–47   D20v:142–5   D30–5:25–8
12. *The Lord even the most mighty
    A16:46–60   D20v:151–9   D30–5:28–31
13. The Lord is good
    D30–5:24
14. *The Lord preserveth
    A16:1–5   D20v:137–8
15. *In D: Td (see P. HAYES for Bs)
    A21v:1–9
16. *In E♭: Cd, Dm (completion of Service by HALL and HINE)
    A13v:60–7   B5:220–5   B5:262   B7:245–51   B8v:24–30
    B13v:40–5   B16v:122–7   B17v:104–8   B19:303–11
    B23:52–4 (Dm inc)   B28:349–53   B29v:61–6   B31v:39–44
    B32v:35–8   B35:97–102   C30:1–6   C31:432–9
17. In E♭: O go your way (verse omitted from CROFT's Jubilate)
    A18:253a–b

HEARDSON, Thomas (MSS 1660s)
Keep we beseech thee
    A3:407–8   C11:145–6   C12:35–6   C17:72–3   C19:22

HENLEY, Phocion (1728–64)
1. As pensive by the streams we sat (Hymn; *Div Harm 1798*)
   M174:19–21
2. The Lord is my shepherd
   A16:216–23   A20:166–73   B8:103   B9:199–200   B11:50–4
   B16:55–6   B26:164   B34:96

HENLEY, PHOCION (*cont.*)
  3. To God whom I trust (Hymn; *Div Harm 1798*)
    M174:18

HENRY VIII (1491–1547)
O Lord the maker of all things (*see* W. MUNDY)

HENSHAW, William (*c.*1791–1877; m of chor and org, Durham, 1814–62) (*see* Index of Copyists)
Single chant in D
  B27:191

HESLETINE, James (*c.*1692–1763; m of chor and org, Durham, 1710–63) (*see* Index of Copyists)
  1. I will give thanks unto thee
    B21:15  B27:81–5  C19:321–2 (imp)  C27:100–5
  2. O let my mouth be filled
    A17:198 (inc; only first 4 bars)  B12:272  B24:94  M206:1–19
  3. Praise the Lord ye servants
    A17:189–98  B6:184–8  B9:178–82  B10:99–104  B12:268–71
    B15:70–5  B24:71  B27:57–62  B31:113–16  B33:32–4a, 35
    C7:213–14  C10:112–13  C27:378–82 (imp)  C29v:25–6
  4. This is the day
    B27:78–80  C27:175–9
  5. 2 single chants, in D, f
    C12v:275 (tenor)

HEUDELINNE (HEUDELINE), Louis (*fl.* 1700–10)
  1. Liv. I
    A27:46–9, 66, 67 (6 items)
  2. *Trois Suites* (nos. 29–41)
    A27:133–40

HIGGINS, Edward (*fl.* 1760–70)
  1. In D: Td, J
    A18:179–204
  2. Double chant in F♮ [= F]
    A18:228

HILTON, John (d. 1608)
  1. Call to remembrance
    A1:219–21  B10:7–8  B17:33–4  C1:3a–b  C4:43–4  C5:35–6
    C6:41  C7:250–1  C9:22–3  C10:30–1  C11:59–60  C12:23–4
    C15:45 (inc)  C15:124–5  C16:70–1  C17:48–9  C19:17–19
    C27:55–6  C28:20–2  C28:56–7  C34:18–19

2. Hear my cry O God
   C1:271–2   C2:153–4   C3:123–4   C7:87–8   C11iv:203–4
   C14:108–9   C16:219–21   C17:163–4   C19:264–7
3. Lord for thy tender mercy's sake (ascrib to R. FARRANT in MSS
   and in *Page 1*)
   A16:204–5   D19:44–5   D24/1–6:1
4. Save me God
   A4:75–81   C2:142   C3:114   C7:77–8   C14:98–9   C19:253–4
5. Td, J, K, M, N
   A6:303–17   C1:282–6 (– M, N)   C13:136–42
   Td, J, M, N
   C12v:149–54 (N inc)   C26:297–304   C32:86–91   C33:120–6
   E11a:94–8, 415–17

HIMMEL, Friedrich Heinrich (1765–1814)
Incline thine ear (arr NOVELLO; text by PATTEN)
   B15:168–9   D18:243–5   D19:201–2   D21:54–6

HINDE, Richard (*fl. c.*1630;a Richard Hynd was chor, Durham, 1592–8)
O sing unto the Lord a new song
   A5:204–9   B1:132–8   C1:31–2   C2:123–4   C3:95–6   C4:68
   C5:66–7   C6:69   C7:60–1   C7:280–1   C10:56–7   C11iv:9–11
   C12:63–5   C14:76–7   C16:159–60   C17:127–8   C19:174–5

HINE, William (1687–1730)
1. Save me God
   A8:161–3   B9:116   B10:279   B12:155   B17:57–8   B26:102
   B29:231   B31:25   B33:81   B35v:37–8
2. In E♮: J (*see* HALL and HINE)

HITCHECOCKE, Walter (*fl. c.*1670; l-c, Westminster Abbey, 1689–90)
Bow down thine ear (hol; dated '69')
   B1:124 (frag)   B1:126–31

HODGE, [Robert] (l-c, Durham, 1691–3)
1. I will give thanks
   C34:263–5
2. O clap your hands
   C34:261–3

HOLDEN, George (MSS *c.*1850)
Arr HAYDN (2.14.), and MOZART (2.)

HOLMES, George (chor, Durham, 1688–94; org to Bishop of Durham;
org, Lincoln, 1704–d. 1721)

HOLMES, GEORGE (*cont.*)
1. Arise and shine (*Page 3*)
   C7:1–2   C19:313–17
2. I will sing of thy power
   A25:146–50

HOLMES, [John] (d. 1629)
1. O God that art the well-spring (ascrib to T. HOLMES)
2. M, N
   C13v:139–43

HOLMES, Thomas (?1580–1638)
O God that art the well-spring (possibly by J. HOLMES)
   B1:42–7

HOOPER, Edmund (*c.*1553–1621)
1. Almighty God which hast given us (Christmas)
   A3:112–14   C1:3b–4   C4:44–5   C5:37–8   C6:42 (inc)
   C7:251–2   C9:24–5   C10:31–2   C11:82–3   C15:45–6
   C16:75–6   C17:46–7   C19:19–20
2. Almighty God which hast made thy blessed Son (Circumcision of
   Christ)
   C1:93–4   C2:15   C3:13   C7:9   C11v:93–4   C14:11   C16:301
   C19:346–7
3. Behold it is Christ
   A1:81–2   B10:12–14   B27:217–18   C2*:1–2   C4:3   C6:3
   C11:30–1   C12:④–⑤ (imp)   C15:3–4   C16:23–4   C17:3
   C27:2–3 (imp)   C28:3–4   C34:32–3
4. I will magnify thee O God
   A3:86–8   C1:245–6   C2:180–1   C3:145–6   C7:119–20
   C11:1–2 (imp)   C14:133–4   C15:75–6   C16:29–30   C17:109–10
   C34:123–4 (text only)
5. O God of Gods (King's Day)
   A2:192–6   C1:22–3   C2:101–2   C3:75–6   C4:61–2
   C5:59–60   C6:59–60   C7:51–2   C7:269–70   C9:40–1
   C10:47–9   C11v:146–7   C14:59–60   C16:354–6   C17:120–2
   C19:162–3
6. O Lord in thee is all my trust
   A5:16–20   C1:68–70   C4:92   C5:91   C7:313–14   C9:68
   C10:85   C11v:43–4   C16:173–4   C19:209–10
7. O Lord turn not away thy face
   C1:25–6   C4:63–4   C5:61   C6:63–4   C7:273   C9:43–4
   C10:50–1   C11v:39   C16:170   C19:166

8. O thou God Almighty (ascrib to MUNDY)
   A3:91–2  C2*:17  C4:19  C5:13  C6:19  C7:229  C9:1
   C10:11  C11:37  C12:17  C16:45  C17:22
9. Teach me thy way (ascrib to W. MUNDY)
   A6:352–3  C1:77–8  C7:318–19  C9:72 (inc)  C10:90–1
   C11:69–70  C11:91–2  C15:52–3  C16:53–4  C17:34
   C27:47–8  C28:54–5  C34:15–16
10. The blessed Lamb (Good Friday)
    A2:329–33  A6:279–84  C1:104–6  C2:43–4  C3:32–3
    C7:23–4  C11v:107–9  C14:25–6  C16:313–15  C19:359–61
11. Of 5 parts, to PARSONS of Wells's Flat Service: M, N
    A2:25–32  C8:268–75  C13:56–9  C18:55–6  E11a:374–9
12. For Verses: M, N
    A2:37–47  A5:149–57  C1:188–92  C13v:101–3  C18:77–9
    E11a:513–17

HOPKINS, Edward John (1818–1901)

1. Out of the deep
   B15:195–9  D18:276–80  D19:225–9  D21:86–90
2. In F: Td, Bs, S, K, M, N
   D17v:85–100

HORSELEY, [?John] (a John Horsley was l-c, Durham, 1576–after 1619)

O Lord of whom I do depend
A5:27–32

HOSIER, Richard (?at King's College, Cambridge, 1637; ?at Bristol, 1660)

All hol; unique to this MS

1. Now that the Lord hath readvanced (The Consecration Anthem)
   B1:21–4
2. O give thanks unto the Lord for he is gracious
   B1:64–71
3. O love the Lord all ye
   B1v:6–7
4. Praise the Lord ye servants
   B1:72–6
5. Thou O God art praised
   B1:56–9
6. Unto thee do I cry
   B1:114–18

HOWARD, Samuel (1710–82)

Blessed is the man whose strength (ascrib to GREENE in B12, C19A, and C36, and in the Tables to several other MSS; 'HOWARD or GREENE' is found in the Table to C19A, and the former is named in pencil in A28)

    A28:200–7   B12:176–9   B17:13–15   B20:105–9   B21:188–92
    B36:26–9   C19A:160–3   C21:159–60   C29v:161–2   C35v:138–40

HUCHESON (HUTCHESONNE), Richard (Durham; bapt ?1590; chor, 1600–7; m of chor and org, 1613–d. 1646)

  1. Lord I am not high minded
     A1:212–13   C1:29–30   C4:66   C5:64   C6:67   C7:278   C10:54
     C11v:25–6   C16:165   C17:180   C19:170–1

  2. O God my heart prepared is
     A1:206–11   A2:238–43   C1:54–6   C4:84   C5:82   C6:92–3
     C7:303   C9:59   C10:74–5   C11v:36–7   C16:153–5   C17:142–4
     C19:202–4

  3. Ye that fear the Lord
     A5:98–101   C1:232–4   C2:202–4   C3:175–6 (inc)   C7:112–14
     C11:142–4   C14:156–8   C15:73–5   C16:91–4   C17:60–3
     C19:44–6

HUDSON, Robert (1732–1815)

In A: S, K, C (to C. KING in A, [I])
    D19v:40–5

HUGHES (HEWES) (a Thomas Hughes was l-c, Durham, 1627)

To DERRICK's Short Service: M, N
    C8:294–302   C13:90–4   E11a:388–92

HUMFREY, Pelham (1647–74)

  1. Haste thee O God (*Boyce 3*)
     A25:150–4   A28:171–4   B1:148–56   B6:81–3   B9:80–3
     B10:136–9   B12:138–9   B13:90–3   B24:91–2   B29:34–5
     B33:68–9   C27:340–2   C28:449–50

  2. Have mercy upon me O God (*Boyce 2*)
     A28:179–83   A33:111–16   B1v:42–8   B6:76–8   B9:88–90
     B12:84–6   B17:1–2   B21:173–5   B24:89   B29:40–2   C19A:35
     C27:192–4   C28:281–4   C34:199–202

  3. Hear O heavens (*Boyce 3*)
     A33:18–19   B6:72–3   B9:79–80   B10:129–31   C7:146–8
     C7:354   C14:179   C15:162–4   C27:186–8   C28:275–7
     C34:196–9

  4. I will always give thanks (*see* CLUB ANTHEM)

HUMPHRIES, [John S.] (*c.*1707; d. before 1740)
[Op. 2] Concerto 1
  M157:113–14
Concerto 6
  M157:101 (Allegro)

HUTCHINSON, John (*fl.* 1628–45; it was James not John Hutchinson, who was bapt at Durham, 2 July 1615)
  1.  Behold how good and joyful
     C11:138–9  C12:34–5  C15:80–1  C17:71–2  C19:39–40
     C27:40–1  C28:59–60  C34:89
  2.  Grant we beseech thee merciful Lord
     A3:272–3  C7:239  C11:112  C12:47  C15:69  C16:94
     C17:49–50  C19:26
  3.  O God the proud
     C11v:227  C12:79  C14:161–2  C15:113–14  C27:139–40
     C28:138–41  C34:113–15
  4.  O Lord let it be thy pleasure
     A3:273a–4  C7:326  C11:113–14  C12:48  C15:70  C16:95
     C17:50  C19:25  C27:45  C28:27  C34:30
  5.  Out of the deep
     A4:1–6

HUTCHINSON, Richard (*see* HUCHESON, Richard)

IONS, Thomas (1817–67)
By the waters of Babylon
  B15:173–8  D18:246–51  D19:202–8  D21:56–62

ISAAC, Elias (1734–93)
O Lord grant the king
  A31v:17–22  B9v:105–8  B18v:78–81  B18: loose  B34:177–8
  C23v:61–2  C24v:61–2

[?ISAAK, Benjamin] (d. 1703)
O how amiable
  B1:170–2

ISHAM (ISUM), John (*c.*1680–1726)
  1.  Bow down thine ear
     C2:155–8
  2.  O clap your hands
     A25:187–94

JACKSON, John (*c*.1630–d. 1688)
Halleluiah, the Lord said
  A4:166–9

JACKSON, William (1815–66)
Awake put on thy strength (The Deliverance of Israel)
  B4:190–5  B15:119–23  D18:63–8  D19:94–9  D21:126–31

[JEFFREYS, George] (*c*.1610–85)
With notes that are both loud and sweet
  B1:1–8

JEFFRIES, Matthew (*fl. c.*1590)
  1. Praise the Lord ye servants
     C2:186–8  C14:139–41  C17:84–6  C19:50–2
  2. Rejoice in the Lord O ye righteous
     A1:275–7  C2:183–4  C2*:33–5  C4:21–2  C5:15  C6:21
     C7:122–3  C7:231  C9:3  C10:13  C11:3–4  C14:136–7
     C15:24–6  C16:10–11  C17:24–5  C19:1–2
  3. Sing we merrily
     C2:185–6  C7:124–5  C14:138–9 (imp)  C15:78 (heading only)
     C17:83–4  C19:48–50
  4. For Meanes (dated 1639 in A2): V, Td, Bs, K, C, M, N
     A2:162–88  C18:84, 87–90 (− V, K, C; Td, Bs inc)

JENKINS, John (1592–1678)
RC = 'Janet Richards's Thematic Index' (*Chelys* for 1971)
*For viols and bass continuo:*
  1. 2 fantasias, in a, g (unascrib)
     D2/1:20–5  D2/2:22–7  D2/3:20–3
  2. 13 ayres, sarabandes, courantes, fantasias, and allemandes (RC 24–34,
     36, 35; unascrib; apart from last two are in same order as in Brit.
     Lib. Add. MS 29369)
     D2/1:47–64  D2/2:49–66  D2/3:43–53
  3. [Fancy à 2] in a (RC 19; unascrib)
     D2/1:68–9  D2/2:70–1
  4. 3 fantasias in d (RC [63], 37, 38; the 1st ascrib to YOUNG)
     D4/1, 2:2–8  D4/3:2–3
  5. Fantasia in a (RC 14; ascrib to P. POUL)
     D4/1, 2:8–10  D4/3:3
  6. 2 fantasias, in d, g (RC 40, 39; the 1st ascrib in D4 to YOUNG)
     D4/1, 2:1–2, 12–14  D4/3:1, 4–5  D5/1, 2:20–1, 22–3
     D5/3:18–19, 20–1

JENKINS, JOHN (*cont.*)
7. 2 sonatas, in d, A
   D5/1–3:10–13
8. Sonata in e (RC 15)
   D5/1, 2:18–19   D5/3:18
9. Sonata in a (8 movements; unascrib; RC 53, 54, 51, 56, 52, 59, 57, 58)
   D10:1–11
10. Sonata in a (6 movements; the 1st, ascrib to NICOLAI, is RC 55; rest unascrib)
    D10:20–8
11. 36 sonatas, forming 'Set B' in MSS (only nos. 1–19 are complete; ascrib in 3 places)
    M179:62–124 (Lyra, in tablature)   M179:167–88 (Treble)
    M180:19–51, 107–11, 114–47 (Bass)
12. 15 sonatas, forming 'Set D' in MSS (all imp; unascrib, though no. 6 is entitled 'The pleasing slumber')
    M179:30–59 (Lyra, in tablature)   M180:151–66? [*sic*] (Treble)

JOMMELLI, Nicolo (1714–74)
  1. Oratorio della Passione (unascrib)
     M176:1–120 (Pt. 1; inc)   M177:1–20 (Pt. 2; inc)
  2. In E♭: S, K (from Chacone in Overture)
     C20:137   C25:138

JONES (MS mid 18th cent.)
Suite in C
  M69:70–2

JONES, William (1726–1800)
Arise O Lord into thy resting place
  A20:78–81   B34:93–4   C28:550–4

JUXON, [George] (d. 1599)
Christ rising again (Easter)
  A5:36–8   C1:107–8   C2:45–6   C3:35–6   C7:24–6   C11V:110–11
  C14:27–8   C16:73–4   C17:107–8   C19:361–3

[KEISER, Reinhard] (1674–1739)
Croesus, Overture
  M186:2   M189:2

KELLER, Charles (1784–1855)
Zu meinen Aügen leuchten sie nicht (Der Blinde)
  E38:12, 15–17

KELLER, Gottfried (d. 1704)
1. Sonata in d for 3 flutes
   M201(ii)—3rd flute pt
2. 12 sonatas for 3 flutes (all imp; only 1st is ascrib), forming 'Set A' in MSS
   M179:3–25 (Treble)   M180:2–? [sic] (1st flute)
   M180:169–85 (Treble)
3. Sonata à 5 in C
   M193/2–4, 6, 7:23

KELLERY (see CHELLERI, Fortunato)

KELWAY, Thomas (c.1695–1749)
1. Verse Service in A: M, N
   A34:21–37  B3:61–4  B18:107–10  B30:1–4  C20:107–11
   C22:26–9  C25:111–15  D22:25–9
2. Full Service in a: M, N
   A34:107–20  B3:74–7  B15v:10–12  C20:123–6  C22:41–5
   C25:126–30  D22:40–4
3. In B mi, b: M, N
   A13v:113–17  B7:280–3  B8v:59–62  B13v:74–7  B17v:135–7
   B19:359–64  B22:1 (−N; inc)  B23:158–60  B28:330–2
   B31v:71–4  B32v:60–2  B33v:56–8  B35:131–3  C30:74–6
   C31:407–11

KENT, James (1700–76)
★ = Twelve Anthems composed by James Kent (1773)
† = A Morning & Evening Service with Eight Anthems . . . by the late James Kent . . . Vol. 2d, ed. J. Corfe (c.1777)
1. ★All thy works praise thee
   B9v:81–2  B11:14–15  B12:341–5  B24:100  B34:70–4
   B36:157–9
2. ★Blessed be thou Lord God of Israel
   A20:53–7  B9v:95–8  B11:28–31  B16:1–3  B26:151–4
   B31:133–5  B34:32–4  C28:572–7  D22v:117–21
3. ★Hear my prayer O God and hide not
   B9v:81  B11:14  B16:15  B34:40  C28:578–81  D22v:128
   M173:23–7 (for 2 oboes)
4. ★In the beginning was the Word
   A20:92–102  B9v:98–103  B11:31–6  B16:4–11  B34:62–9
5. ★Lord how are they increased
   A20:81–4  B9v:103–5  B11:36–7  B16:12–13  B26:154–7
   B34:35–6  C28:581–5  D22v:121–3

KENT, JAMES (*cont.*)

6. *Lord what love have I
   B9v:82–3　B11:15–16　B16:14　B31:138　B34:76–7
   D22v:126–7　M173:18–22 (for 2 oboes)

7. *My song shall be of mercy
   B9v:86　B11:19　B16:32　B34:76　C28:589　D22v:126

8. †O Lord our governor (*Page 1*)
   A13:74–80　B6:158　B8:29　B9:157–60　B12:125–6　B13:82
   B17:82　B20:139　B31:66　B33:110　B35v:80　B36:104
   C28:488–9

9. *Sing O heavens
   A26:97–106　B9v:78–80　B11:11–13　B12:340–1　B24:99–100
   B34:37–40　B36:159–60　C28:600–5　D17:135–40

10. Teach me O Lord
    A13:68–73　B6:157–8　B8:28–9　B9:153–6　B12:126
    B13:81–2　B17:81–2　B20:137–8　B31:65–6　B33:109–10
    B35v:79　B36:103–4　C28:486–8

11. *The Lord hath prepared
    B9v:83–4　B11:16–17　B16:32–6　B34:50–4

12. *When the Son of Man
    B9v:87–9　B11:20–2　B16:36–9　B34:54–61

13. *Who is this
    A20:143–52　B9v:90–5　B11:23–8　B16:39–43　B34:46–50
    C28:590–9　D22v:130–1

14. *Why do the heathen
    A20:74–7　B9v:84–6　B11:17–19　B16:15–17　B34:74–5
    C28:585–8　D22v:123–5

15. †In C: Td, J, Cd, Dm
    Td, J
    A15:113–20　A21v:18–49 (+Cd, Dm)　B5:296–301
    B7:329–34　B13v:162–7　B16v:1–7　B17v:180–5　B19:395–400
    B23:59–62　B31v:119–24　B33v:105–10　B35:168–72
    B36v:131–5 (Td inc)

KING, Charles (1687–1748)

1. Hear O Lord and have mercy (*Arnold 1*)
   D20v:92–3

2. O pray for the peace (*Arnold 2*)
   D19:18–20

3. Rejoice in the Lord O ye righteous (*Arnold 1*)
   D20v:93–5

4. Unto thee O Lord (*Page 1*)
   A16:206–8

5. In A [I]: Td, J, M, N (*Arnold 2; see* HUDSON for S, K, C)
   B30:50–4 (– Td, J)   D18v:115–25 (–M, N)   D19v:76–96
   D22:66–71 (–Td, J)
6. In A [II]: Td, J (*Arnold 3*)
   D18v:125–35   D19v:29–39
7. In B♭: Td, J, S, K, C, Cd, Dm (*Arnold 1*)
   Td, J, K, C, M, N
   B5:168–80   B7:154–6   B16v:98–113   B17v:52–62, 141
   B19:45–58   B23:85–9 (–K, C)   B28:284–95   B35:1–9
   B36v:31–40   C8:533–47   C19v:47–55   C21v:90–101
   C29:99–111   C30:119–25 (–K, C)   C31:174–81   C35:84–95
   D20:42–60 (+ S)
8. In C: Td, J, K, C, M, N (*Arnold 3*)
   A15:155–64   B3:281–91   B7:341–9   B8v:212–20
   B13v:180–3, 186–90   B16v:60–8   B22:60–3 (– C, M, N)
   B23:174–80, 182–3   B30:163–72   B34v:19–22 (just M, N)
   B35:180–8   C30:212–22   D22:86–96, 66–71
9. In D: Td, J, K, C, M, N
   A18:124–60, 160a, 161–78   B3:12–28   B18:56–73
   C20:49–58a, 59–68   C23:48–65   C24:49–66   C25:49–66
10. In F: Td, J, K, C, M, N (*Arnold 2*)
    A13v:79–93   B5:234–40, 243–4 (C, M inc)   B7:259–69
    B8v:37–47   B13v:53–63   B16v:79–89   B17v:115–24
    B19:324–39   B23:68–73   B28:340–8   B29v:73a, 73b–81
    B30:172–81   B31v:51–61   B32v:44–51   B33v:34–43
    B35:110–19   C30:25–34   C31:395–407

KING, Robert (1676–1728)
1. I will always give thanks (*Div Comp*) (D MSS arr ARMES)
   D23:222–3   D30–5:59   M174:8–9
2. The fire of love in youthful blood (unascrib)
   D9:12–13

KING, [William] (1624–80)
1. I will always give thanks
   C11v:187–8   C12:60   C19:301–2   C27:130–1   C34:102–3
2. Lord how are they increased
   C2:9
3. Praise ye the Lord
   A4:100–4   C2*:24   C9:25   C11v:175

KYNASTON, E. C. (MSS late 19th cent.)
1. Rend your heart
   D30–5:76–7

KYNASTON, E. C. (*cont.*)
  2. In F: M, N
     D30v:43–6    D31v:41–4    D32v:41–2 (−N; M frag)
     D33v–5v:41–4

LAMB, Benjamin (1674–1733)
  1. In e: Cd, Dm
     A13v:125–37   B17v:142–6   B21v:43–50   B22:150, 153 (both inc)
     B36v:98–103   C19Av:58–67   C21v:56–61   C29:67–72
     C31:351–8   C35v:41–9
  2. Single chant in G
     E32:76

LAMPE, John Friedrich (1703–51)
Cuckoo Concerto
  M184:57   M189:87–8

LANZETTI, Salvatore (*c.*1710–*c.*1780)
  1. [Op. 1, Sonata 5, Minuet] (unascrib)
     M69:78–9   M108:6–7
  2. Op. 2, Sonata 3
     M201(i)

LAWES, Henry (1596–1662)
  1. I know that my redeemer (Funeral Anthem; unascrib; = Bod. Lib.
     MS Don. c. 57)
     B1:60–3
  2. My song shall be alway
     C7:137 (frag)   C7:330   C11v:228–30   C14:164   C15:154–6
     C17:146   C19:216   C27:117   C34:99

LAWES, William (1602–45)
  1. O God my God wherefore dost thou forsake me
     B1:97–107
  2. The Lord is my light (*Boyce 2*)
     B1:32–7   B10:92–4   C12:61–3 (imp)   C15:214
     C27:116–17 (inc)   C34:97–9

LEO, Leonardo (1694–1744)
  1. Bow down thine ear (*Pratt*)
     D19:132   D20v:128–9
  2. God shall send forth (*Pratt*)
     D19:120–3   D20v:119–21

LINGARD, Frederick (1811–47; temporary l-c, Durham, 1835; l-c, Durham, 1837–47)

Arr BEETHOVEN (1.), HAYDN (9.), MOZART (3.4.), WINTER

LOCKE, Matthew (c.1621–77)

H = R. E. M. Harding, *A Thematic Catalogue of the Works of Matthew Locke* (1971)

1. And a voice came out of the throne (The Marriage of the Lamb; H1; unascrib)
   B1:38–41
2. I know that my redeemer (unascrib; differs from H18 after a few notes; not by LOCKE, but by [H. LAWES])
3. Lord let me know mine end (*Boyce 2*; H9; ascrib to Silas TAYLOR in B1)
   A26:32–6  A29:8–11  B1v:49–54, 54b–56  B6:83–5  B9:99–101
   B12:135–6  B13:99–100  B17:113–14  B20:1–3  B27:94–6 (inc)
   B29:80–1  B33:38–9  C19A:2–4  C21:3 (inc)  C27:172–4
   C28:438–9  C29:1–3  C29v:26–7
4. Not unto us O Lord (H14)
   A33:70–4  C7:176  C15:209–12  C28:265–8  C34:254–6
5. O give thanks unto the Lord for he is gracious (H4)
   B29:78–9  B36:14–15

*Secular item*:
6. Hark I hear my passing bell (from 'The Passing Bell'; H19; unascrib)
   D9:3

LOEILLET (LUILEY), Jean (1680–1730)

Non nobis Domine (arr of BYRD's Canon)
   M70:46–9

LOGG, Cath (MS early 18th cent.)

Textless song in C
   D9:23

LOGGINS, J. (MS c.1670)

Be thou my judge O Lord
   B1:167–70

LOOSEMORE, Henry (c.1600–70)

1. Fear not shepherd (Christmas)
   A2:341–3  C11v:157–8  C17:178–9  C19:293
2. Give the king thy judgments (King's Day)
   A2:333–7, 337a  C2:113–14  C3:84–5  C11v:156–56a
   C14:69–70  C16:359–60  C19:289–90

LOOSEMORE, HENRY (cont.)
  3. Glory be to God on high [II] (Anthem Collect for Communion)
       A2:338–41   C17:177–8   C19:291–2
  4. I will give thanks unto thee
       C5:40   C11v:184–7   C12:65–9   C17:182–3   C19:329–30
  5. O Lord increase my faith (ascrib to O. GIBBONS)
       D17:152–3
  6. Praise the Lord O my soul while I live
       A3:351–3   C11:109–10   C12:36–8   C15:83–4   C16:98–9
       C17:50–1   C19:20–1   C27:46–7   C28:17–18   C34:31–2
  7. Why art thou so heavy (ascrib to O. GIBBONS)
       D17:155–6
  8. First Service: Td, J, L, K, Go, C, M, N
     Td, J, K, C, M, N
       A3:331–51 (+L, Go)   C8:508–10 (just Td, J; J inc)
       C12v:105–16 (+Go; Td imp)   C13v:144–57 (+Go)
       C26:93–102   C31:103–12   C32:92–100   C33:75–9, 117–19

LOTTI, Antonio (c.1667–1740)
Turn thy face from my sins ('for Litany Mornings'; ascrib only in D22;
English text to 'Miserere', *Latrobe 5*)
    A21:71–2   B4:106   B15:43   C22v:108–9   D20v:18   D22v:81–2

LUILEY (*see* LOEILLET)

LUTHER, Martin (1483–1546)
Great God what do I see (Hymn)
    A11:85–90   B4:84–5   B18v:117   C20v:88–9   C22v:80
    D22:52–3

V. M. (MS 18th cent.)
Concerto no. 14 in d
    M203 (inc)

MACE, Thomas (c.1612–?1706)
For viola da gamba, in d (*Musick's Monument*)
    A27:80–1

MACFARREN, George Alexander (1813–87)
Wherewithal shall a young man (*Ouseley 2*)
    B3v:11–14

[MANCINI, Francesco] (1672–1737)
Hydaspe
  Overture
    E32:17–22   M185–6:4   M189:3

Largo
E32:65
Lusinga del mio core
E32:57–9
[Bianca man tu sei di neue] (no text)
E32:38–41
All' Ombra alle catene (no text)
E32:8–10

MARAIS, Marin (1656–1728)
  1. Liv. 1
  A27:2–7, 10–17, 19–21, 42–5, 77, 86–7, 97–9, 161–7, 192–8, 203–7, 286–9 (28 items)
  2. Liv. 2
  A27:1, 8–9, 18, 22, 40–1, 45, 78, 85, 93, 199 (11 items)
  3. Ex MSS, Sarabande in F
  A27:121

MARCELLO, Benedetto (1686–1739)
  1. Give ear unto me (with add by NOVELLO)
  B15:186–7   D18:262–4   D19:213–15   D21:67–9
  2. O Lord give ear (arr GREGORY)
  A13:60–7   B6:156   B8:6   B9v:49   B12:318–21   B13:63–8
  B20:128–35   B35v:78–9   B36:91–2   C21:197–8   C29v:39
  C35v:17
  3. O Lord our governor (*Page 2*)
  A26:190–3   B26:143–8

MARENZIO, Luca (*c.*1553–99)
  1. Dolorosi martir, fieri tormenti
  E15:12–16
  2. Giunto a la tomba
  E15:17–20
  3. Save Lord, hear us (*Page 3*)
  D19:12–13

MARSH, John (1752–1828)
In D: Td, J, S, K, C
  B3:47–53   B18:93–9   B30:63–72   C20:90–8   C22:17–25
  C25:86–94   D21v:97–107   D22:8–16   D36:1–20

MARSON, George (*c.*1573–1632)
Td, J, M, N
  A6:290–302   C1:275–82   C13:294–302   E11a:106–11, 412–14

M[ARTIN], R[obert] (org, Launceston, late 18th cent.)

Alas the blooming pride of May (1786)
    E11a:350–1


MARVELL, Andrew (1621–78)

Think'st thou that this Love can stand
    D9:44 (text only)


MASON, William (1725–97)
    1. All flesh is grass
        A21:61–70  B4:102–3  B15:39–40  C22v:103–4  D20v:14–15
        D22v:76–7
    2. Help us O God of our salvation
        A17:199–201   B24:108
    3. I will go forth in the strength
        A17:203–5
    4. Let us devote this consecrated day (Hymn; see PLEYEL)
    5. Lord of all power and might (*Page 1*)
        A20:173–4  B6:188  B9:184  B17:145  B24:95  B26:96
        B29:286  B31:117  B33:162  B34:24  B35v:129  C21:201
        M173:14–15 (for 2 oboes)
    6. O Lord how manifold
        A26:107–13 (with add by T. EBDON)  B6:170  B9:177
        B12:339  B13:159  B17v:173  B24:100–1  B26:133–4
        B29:209  B31:120  B33:164  B34:79–80  B35v:131  B36:124
        C21:201
    7. In C: K
        B7:350  B8v:221  B11:80  B16:91  B18:12  B19:401  B20v:6
        B28:398  B30:62  B34:118–19  C19v:1  C30:223


[?MATTEIS, Nicola] (d. ?1707)

Sonata à 3 in D (ascrib 'M1t23s')
    D2/1, 2:4–5   D2/3:6–7


MELANI, Alessandro (1639–1703)

Piu' non puole il mio core
    E29(i):1–23


MENDELSSOHN-Bartholdy, Felix (1809–47)
    1. As the hart pants
        B15:207–14  D18:284–94  D21:107–20
    2. Cast thy burden upon the Lord (Elijah)
        B4:215  B15:221  C22v:151  D18:283–4  D21:90–1

3. Christus
   D23:169–71   D30:158–60   D31, D32:156–8   D33:157–62
   D34:158–60   D35:156–8
4. Daughters of Zion
   D30–4:148–50   D35:146–8
5. Grant us thy peace
   B15:192–3   D18:269–71   D19:221–2   D21:79–81
6. Holy holy holy is God the Lord (Elijah)
   D17:11–12   D21:216–17
7. How lovely are the messengers (St Paul)
   B4:175–7   B15:107–9   D19:79–81   D21:211–13
8. See what love hath the Father (St Paul)
   B15:193–4   D18:272–3   D19:222–3   D21:82–3
9. In A: Td, J
   B15v:71–5, 98–100   B30:103–7, 112–14   D18v:82–6, 152–5
   D19v:166–70, 185–7   D21v:67–75
10. In B♭: M, N
    B15v:100–7   B30:114–20   D18v:155–63   D19v:188–96
    D21v:75–83

MITZER, a mis-reading of 'M1t23s', which may be a representation of
MATTEIS; it has also been suggested that SCHMELZER is intended.

MONK, Edwin George (1819–1900)
Blessed are all they that fear (*Ouseley 2*)
   B3v:14–18

MOREIRA, Antonio Leal (1758–1819)
  1. O pray for the peace (arr PATTEN)
     B15:226–7   D21:138–9
  2. Praise ye the Lord (text by PENSON, 1817)
     A11:35–44   B4:14–15   B18v:105–7   C20v:26–8   C23v:106–7
     D22v:1–2

MORGAN, John [?1688–?1734; Welsh cleric, scholar, author]
Blessed be the Lord God of Israel (dated, Christmas Day 1731)
   A8:171–3

MORLEY, Thomas (*c.*1557–1602)
  1. De profundis (= Out of the deep [I])
     E15:21–30
  2. How long wilt thou forget me
     A2:220–2   A5:48–50   C1:52–3   C4:82–3   C5:80–1   C6:89–90
     C7:300–1   C9:57–8   C10:72–3   C11v:29–30   C16:163
     C19:200–1

MORLEY, THOMAS (*cont.*)

3. Out of the deep [I] (full anthem; *see* 'De profundis')
   A1:188–90   B10:9–10   C2★:4–5   C4:7   C5:1   C6:7   C7:217
   C11:39–40   C12:4–6   C15:8–9   C16:78–9   C17:7   C27:5–6
   C28:40–1   C34:22–3

4. Out of the deep [II] (verse anthem)
   A5:8–9   C1:7   C4:51   C5:49   C6:44–5   C7:255   C9:29
   C10:37   C11v:34–5   C16:167   C19:145

5. First Service, for Verses, Best Service: Td, Bs, K, C, M, N
   A2:102–22   A6:29–47   C1:141–50 (Td inc)
   C12v:260–3 (just M, N)   C13v:47–58   C18:5–10
   E4:99–105, 129–32, 157–61   E5:101–8, 128–31, 157–61
   E6:97–101, 123–6, 151–4   E7:101–7, 130–3, 159–64
   E8:104–9, 130–3, 158–62   E9:93–8, 121–4, 153–6
   E10:99–104, 124–7, 149–53   E11:108–13, 132–5, 158–61
   E11a:205–10, 325–7, 481–5

6. Second Service, 3 Minhams: M, N
   A2:123–8   A6:48–53   C1:150–3   C13:280–3   C18:11–12
   E11a:442–6


MORNINGTON, Earl of (1735–81)

Double chant in E♭
  A18:24


MOZART, Wolfgang Amadeus (1756–91)

1. Blessed is he that cometh (from 'Requiem')
   A16:236–41   A16:242–61   B4:7–14   B11:105–6   B16:113–14
   B18v:46   B18v:98–105   B34:144–5   C20v:18–25   C23v:27–8
   C23v:94–105   C23v:116   C24v:24–5   C24v:100–7

2. Grant O Lord we beseech thee (arr HOLDEN)
   B15:159–61   D17:140–2   D18:228–9   D19:181–3   D21:206–7

3. I will arise (arr LINGARD)
   B4:210–11   B15:132–3   D18:1–2   D19:145–7   D21:16–18

4. I will cry unto God (from 12th Mass; arr LINGARD)
   A10:207–41   B4:177–88   B15:109–17   D18:68–79   D19:82–92

5. I will magnify the Lord
   A34v:5–8   B4:31–2   B18v:115–16   C20v:45–6   C22v:17–18
   D22v:13–15

6. O God to whom the night shines (= 'O God when thou appearest'
   = Motet no. 1, 'Splendente te Deus')
   B15:136–9   D18:193–6   D19:151–5   D21:4–7

7. Plead thou my cause (from 12th Mass; *Pratt*)
   D19:136–42   D20v:131–6

8. Praise the Lord O my soul and forget (from 1st Mass; *Pratt*)
   D19:114–17    D20v:114–16
9. Thou wilt keep him in perfect peace
   D23:173–8

MUDD, Thomas (possibly in Durham in 1648 and 1653; d. Durham, 1667, after numerous brief post-Restoration appointments. Much is simply ascribed 'MUDD', and could be by an earlier Thomas MUDD, *c.*1560–after 1619)

1. God which hast prepared
   A3:294–5    C1:234–5    C2:195    C7:111    C11:111    C14:155
   C15:68 (imp)    C16:97    C17:65–6    C19:60
2. I will always give thanks
   A4:87–92    C11v:180–2    C12:58–9    C15:149 (inc)    C19:298–300
   C27:128–9    C28:129–31    C34:104–5
3. Let thy merciful ears
   A3:16    C1:76–7    C7:318    C9:72    C10:90    C11:72    C11:90
   C15:52    C16:44    C17:35    C19:11
4. Lift up your heads
   A4:127–30    C11v:224    C12:77–8    C14:161    C27:124–5
   C28:132–4    C34:107–8
5. O God thou art my God
   A4:123–6    C11v:223    C12:78    C14:162    C27:127    C28:131–2
   C34:106

MUNDY

The lack of precise ascription at Durham and elsewhere means that either John or William could be the composer. Personal inclination, based on the possible history of a set of Durham books used in the 1660s, but no longer extant, favours William.

1. He that hath my commandments (men's voices)
   A3:152–3    C11:119–21    C17:98–9    C19:73–4
2. Let us now laud (men's voices)
   A3:156–8    C11:116–17    C17:96–7    C19:70–1
3. O thou God Almighty (now attrib to HOOPER)
4. Rejoice in the Lord alway (men's voices)
   A3:126–8    C11:114–15    C17:94–5    C19:68–70
5. For 2 basses: V, Td, Bs, K, C, M, N
   A3:192–206, 209–10, 115–26
6. Three parts for men: Td, Bs, K, C, M, N
   A3:165–78, 128–39
7. Four parts for men: Td, Bs, K, C, M, N
   A3:179–91, 140–52

Mundy (*cont.*)

8. In C fa ut: M, N
   A3:234–42  C8:328–9, 400–5, 407

MUNDY, John (*c.*1555–1630)

1. Blessed art thou that fearest God
   A5:102–6  C1:11–13  C4:53–4  C5:51  C6:47–8  C7:258–9
   C9:32  C10:39–40  C11v:2–3  C16:136–7  C19:148–9

2. Give laud unto the Lord
   A1:322–3  C2*:41–2  C4:35  C5:27–8  C6:33  C7:243–4
   C9:14  C10:23  C11:12–13  C15:37–8  C16:2–3  C17:38–9
   C27:17

3. O give thanks unto the Lord for he is gracious
   A1:285–7  C2*:29–31  C4:15–16  C5:9–10  C6:15–16
   C7:225–6 (imp)  C11:23–5  C12:20–2  C15:20 (inc)  C16:5–7
   C17:16–17

4. O God my strength and fortitude
   C1:9–11  C4:52–3  C5:50–1  C6:46–7  C7:257  C9:31
   C10:38–9  C11v:35–6  C16:168  C19:146–7

5. O Lord our Governor (Ascension) (in C1, C13v, E4–E11, and E11a,
   it is implied that it is by Edw. SMYTHE)
   A2:304–8 (inc)  A5:253–7  C1:298–9 (inc)  C2:61–3  C3:47–8
   C7:36 (inc)  C11v:122–3  C13v:14–16  C14:39 (inc)
   C16:327–30  C19:371–5  E4–11:21–3  E11a:15–16

6. Send aid
   A5:107–11  C1:65–6  C4:90  C5:89  C7:311–12  C9:66
   C10:83–4  C11v:44–5  C16:174–5  C19:213–14

MUNDY, William (*c.*1529–*c.*1591)

1. Ah helpless wretch
   C4:50  C5:48  C6:43–4 (inc)  C7:254  C9:28  C10:36

2. O Lord I bow the knees
   A1:89–92  B10:42–5  C2*:14–15  C4:17–18  C5:11–12
   C6:17–18  C7:227–8  C10:9  C11:44–6  C12:14–16  C15:21–2
   C16:67–9  C17:19–20  C27:10–11 (imp)  C34:46–7

3. O Lord the maker of all things (ascrib to MUNDY in C19;
   HENRY VIII in A20, B26, C19A, C21; SHEPPARD in B10,
   C7–C17)
   A3:301–3  A20:16–17  A33:255–6 (inc)  B10:60–2  B20:114–15
   B26:7–8  C7:106–7  C11:78–9  C14:150–1  C15:64–6
   C16:47–8  C17:68–9  C19:62–4  C19A:169  C21:171–2

4. O Lord the world's Saviour (ascrib to WOOD)
   A3:303–6  C7:107–9  C11:80–1  C14:151–3  C15:66–8 (imp)
   C16:48–50  C17:69–71  C19:64–6

5. Teach me thy way (now attrib to HOOPER)
6. The secret sins (ascrib to O. GIBBONS but probably not by him;
   in C7 the text has been altered to 'The Lord is only my support')
   C1:20–1  C4:59  C5:57  C6:56  C7:265–6  C9:38  C10:45
   C19:160
7. This is my commandment (men's voices; authorship not established:
   TALLIS in A1, A3; MUNDY in Table to MS C17; unascrib in
   C11, C19; D MSS 19th cent.)
   A1:294–5  A3:159–61  C11:123–5  C17:101–2  C19:76–7
   D23:122  D26/1:38–9  D26/2–5:38  D26/6–9:39
8. 1st Service, 1st in D sol re, 'of fower parts': V, Td, Bs, K, C, M, N
   A3:49–70 (–V)  C13:230–43 (–V)  C18:57–65 (–V)
   E4:71–80, 117–20, 143–6  E5:69–80, 117–21, 141–4
   E6:69–77, 111–14, 137–40  E7:69–80, 118–21, 143–7
   E8:70–9, 118–21, 143–7  E9:67–74, 109–10, 137–40
   E10:68–75, 78, 113–16, 137–40  E11:70–9, 122–5, 145–8
   E11a:163–70, 296–9, 428–31 (–V)
9. Second Service, in F fa ut: V, Td, Bs, M, N
   A3:248–72  C8:316–22 (–V, Td, Bs)  C13:115–25 (–V)
   E11a:135–41, 400–3 (–V)
10. Short Service: Td, J, K, C (see READ for M, N)
   A1:191–201  C8:41–8, 182–7  C12v:42–4 (–K, C; J inc)
   C13:38–45  C26:141–5 (–K, C)  C32:136–40 (–K, C)
   C33:167–73  E11a:55–9, 263–5
11. Of 5 parts, to R. PARSONS [I]'s 5-pt Service: M, N
   A3:284–93  C13:270–4  C18:39–40  E11a:424–8

MURPHY, [Samuel] (*fl. c.*1759–d. 1780)
Oh! praise the Lord ye that fear him (23 October)
   A19:611–50

NALSON, Valentine (1682–1722)
  1. In G: Td
     M170:104–6
  2. Arr FIOCCO

NARES, James (1715–83)
★ = *Twenty Anthems in Score . . . by Dr. Nares* (1778)
  1. ★Behold how good and joyful
     A26:172–7
  2. Blessed be the Lord God of Israel (*Page 2*)
     D19:20–1  D20v:168
  3. ★By the waters of Babylon
     B33:194  D19:53–4

Nares, James (*cont.*)

4. ★Call to remembrance
   A29:45–6   B6v:58–9   B9v:34–5   B12:15–16   B17:22–3
   B21:202–4   B24:9–10 (imp)   B26:45–6   B29:56–7   B32:58–9
   B33:190–2   B36:49–50   C19:456–7   C19A:170   C21:172–3
   C28:523–5   C29v:166–7   C35v:165–6   D19:50–3

5. ★God is our hope and strength
   D19:61–2

6. ★It is a good thing
   D19:58–9

7. ★Not unto us O Lord
   B33:193

8. ★O come let us sing
   A29:100–3   B17v:28   B20:125   B21:204   B35v:6–8   B36:67–8
   C21:189–91   C29v:187–9   D19:56–7

9. ★O Lord my God I will exalt thee
   D19:54–5

10. Rejoice in the Lord O ye righteous
    A20:85–91   D19:60   M173:29–35 (for 2 oboes)

11. Save me O God
    B12:83   B17:30   B20:120   B24:9   B26:36   B32:62   B34:17
    B35v:1   B36:56   C21:174   C28:64   C29v:168   C35v:167

12. ★The Lord is righteous
    D19:59

13. ★The souls of the righteous
    B33:194–5   D19:55–6

14. Wherewithal shall a young man
    A29:88–90   B12:83   B17:30   B20:119   B32:66   B35v:6
    B36:62   C19:475   C21:180   C29v:174   C35v:172

15. In C (No. 1): Td, J
    A29v:48–54   B5:197–203   B7:196–201   B16v:128–33
    B17v:62–6   B19:218–25   B23:62–4   B28:362–5   B29v:23–7
    B31v:1–5   B35:52, 59–63   B36:65–9   C19v:72–6
    C21v:144–50   C30:97–101   C31:371–7

16. In C (No. 2): Td, J
    A18:68–85   A21v:90–101   B18:32–6   B30:36–41   C20:20–5
    C23:21–6   C24:21–6   C25:21–6

17. In C: M, N
    B15v:68–71   B30:100–3   D18v:78–81   D19v:165–6 (−M; N inc)

18. In F: Td, J, K, C, M, N (*Arnold 3*)
    A18:87–98 (M, N only)   B3:272–81   B30:11–21   D19v:1–14
    D22:76–86, 59–62

19. Double chant in D♯ [ = D]
  A18:98

NAVARRA, Francesco (?b. Rome, c.1660; 'Maes. di Cap^la di S.A.S. di
Mant . . . 1697')
  1. Sinfonia à 5 in a (1697)
    M175:11–16   M193/2–4, 6, 7:18–19
  2. Sinfonia à 5 in C
    M175:3–7   M193/2–4, 6, 7:16–17

NICHOLLS, John (Durham; l-c 1661–77; m of chor, 1677–d. 1681) (see
Index of Copyists)
  1. I will give thanks unto thee O Lord
    C2:129   C10:106   C11v:166   C17:162   C19:294–5   C27:131–3
    C34:100–1
  2. O pray for the peace
    A3:109–11   C1:78–9   C4:47 (frag)   C7:320–1   C10:92–3
    C11:93–4   C15:53–4   C16:85–6   C17:56–7   C19:31–2
    C27:43–4   C28:52–4   C34:28–9
  3. In G: Td, J, M, N
    C12v:194–201   C26:103–9   C31:113–19   C32:101–6   C33:65–9

NICHOLSON (MSS late 19th cent.)
The sacrifices of God
  D30, D31:151–2   D32:159a–b   D33:151–2   D34:155–6
  D35:149–50

NICOLAI, Johann Michael (1629–85)
  1. Sonata in g for 2 violins and viola (ascrib to 'N3C4L13')
    D2/1–3:16–17
Sonatas for 2 and 3 viole da gamba
  2. In a (probably by JENKINS)
    D10:20–8
  3. In C
    D10:11–19
  4. In D
    D10:29–33

NORCOMBE (NORCUM), Daniel (fl. 1602–55)
  1. Sonata in d for 2 viols and bass continuo
    D2/1:70   D2/2:72   D2/3:56
  2. Divisions in a for viola da gamba
    D10:106–7

NORRIS, Thomas (1741–90)

Hear my prayer O Lord and let my crying
  B4:160–2   B15:92–6   D18:5–10   D19:1–6

NORRIS, William (c.1669–1702)
  1. Blessed are those that are undefiled
      A25:50–5   C7:398–9   C15:116–17   C27:285–6   C28:212–13
      C34:178–9
  2. In Jewry is God known
      A25:45–9   C14:234   C15:118   C15:205   C27:156   C28:214
      C34:181

NOVELLO, Vincent (1781–1861)
  1. Rejoice in the Lord O ye righteous (arr PATTEN)
      B15:221–4   D21:132–5
  2. Therefore with angels
      B15:194–5   D18:274–6   D19:224–5   D21:84–6   D21:213–14
      D24/1–6:2–3
  3. Arr HIMMEL, MARCELLO (1.)

NUSSEN (fl. c.1750)
  [Six Solos for a Violin, Sonata 2]
    M69:46 [Gratiosa]

OGLE, Miss (MSS c.1800; ?Susannah, d. 1825; daughter of Newton
Ogle, preb Durham, 1768–1804)
  In E♭: K
    B7:352   B8v:196   B16v:152   B18:13   B21:208   B27:182, 184
    B28:399   B30:61–2   B34v:41   C22:60   C30:255

OTTLEY, Edward J. (fl. 2nd half 19th cent.)
  Rejoice in the Lord O ye righteous (Ouseley 2)
    B3v:18–25

OUSELEY, Frederick Arthur Gore (1825–89)
  ★ = Special Anthems for Certain Seasons, ed. F. A. G. Ouseley, vol. 2 (1886)
  1. ★And there was a pure river
      B3v:6–11
  2. Blessed is he
      D30–4:141   D35:139
  3. In Jewry is God known
      D30–5:100–3
  4. ★I saw the souls of them
      B3v:38–41

5. Jerusalem on high
D31–5:60
6. My song shall be alway
B3v:45–6
7. The Lord preserve thy going out
D31–5:61
8. The salvation of the righteous
D30–4:134  D35:132
9. ★They that wait upon the Lord
B3v:36–8
10. Trust ye in the Lord
D31–5:61
11. ★Who shall ascend
B3v:41–5
12. In C, for double choir (dedicated to J. B. Dykes: 1866): Td, Bs, K,
C, Sc, S, G, M, N
Td,Bs, K, C, S, G, M, N
D23:51–84  D25/1, 2:1–28  D25/3:1–32 (+Sc)  D25/4, 5:1–28
E2:1–74 (+Sc)

PACIERI, [Giuseppe] (d. after 1700)

In Palaggio Regal da tetto d'oro (L'ucello in Gabbia)
E29(ii):17–48 (inc)

PAISIELLO, Giovanni (1740–1816)

Have mercy Lord on me (arr CHARD)
B15:190  D18:265–6  D21:76  D23:193–4

PALMER, Henry (l-c, Durham, 1627–d. 1640) (see Index of Copyists).
Entries hol in MSS A1, A5, A6

1. Almighty and everlasting God we humbly beseech (Purification of
Mary the Virgin)
C2:83  C3:62–3  C7:42 (inc)  C11v:135  C14:48–9  C16:341
C19:384
2. Almighty and everlasting God which hatest nothing (Ash Wednes-
day)
A5:70–3  C1:100  C2:27  C3:20–1  C7:15  C11v:100–1
C14:18 (inc)  C16:307–8  C19:353–4
3. Almighty and everlasting God who of thy tender love (Sunday next
before Easter)
A6:285–9  C1:102  C2:33–4  C3:25–6  C7:19  C11v:103
C14:21  C16:310  C19:355–6

PALMER, HENRY (*cont.*)
  4. Almighty God whose praise this day (Innocents' Day)
      A1:326–7   C1:95   C2:16–17   C3:14   C7:10   C11iv:92
      C14:12   C16:300   C19:347–8
  5. Hear my prayer O Lord and with thine ears
      A5:33–5   C16:58–9
  6. Lord what is man
      A1:69–72
  7. O God whose nature and property
      A5:138–9   C2*:38   C4:33   C5:25   C6:31   C7:241   C9:12
      C11:47–8   C12:28–9   C15:35–6   C16:41–2   C17:36–7
      C19:13–14
  8. The end of all things
      A5:280–1
  9. This is the day (*see* Preces & Ps., Easter Evensong)
 10. Thou O God art praised (*see* HARTE, Jn HAWKINS)
 11. Preces & Ps., Easter Evensong (This is the day)
      C13v:27–9   E11a:28–30
 12. K, C
      A3:221–7   C8:194–7   C13v:85–6   E11a:337–8

PARSLEY, Osbert (1511–85)

Flat Service: Td, Bs (to TYE's Evening Service, which is ascrib to
PARSLEY in A6)
      A6:334–45   C8:72–80   C13:66–70   E11a:63–7

PARSONS, Robert [I] (*c.*1530–70)
  1. Deliver me from mine enemies (ascrib to BYRD)
      A1:214–15   C2*:7–8   C2*:22–3   C4:11   C5:5   C6:11
      C7:221   C10:5   C11:42–3   C15:14–15   C16:39–40   C17:11–12
      C27:13–14 (imp)   C28:10–11   C34:38–9
  2. Holy holy holy Lord God Almighty
      A1:83–5   C2*:11–12   C4:14   C5:8   C6:14   C7:224
      C10:8 (imp)   C11:28–30   C12:13–14   C15:18–19   C16:20–1
      C17:15–16   C27:6–7   C28:32–3   C34:36–7
  3. First Service, for Meanes: V, Td, Bs, K, C, M, N
      C13:203–15 (−V)   E4:50–60, 108–11, 135–8
      E5:50–9, 111–13, 133–6   E6:50–60, 103–6, 129–32
      E7:50–9   111–14, 135–9   E8:50–60, 111–14, 135–9
      E9:48–58, 100–3, 127–31   E10:49–58, 107–9, 129–32
      E11:49–59, 115–18, 137–40
  4. For Countertenors, of 5 parts: Td, Bs, K, C (*see* W. MUNDY for
      M, N)
      C13:260–70   C18:34–8   E11a:156–62, 293–6

PARSONS, Robert [II], of Exeter (1596–1676)
1. Above the stars
   C1:272–3  C2:151–2  C3:122–3  C7:86  C11v:49–50
   C14:107–8  C16:218  C19:263–4
2. Ever blessed Lord ('A Collect for the Quire')
   A3:296–8  C1:229–30  C11:73–4  C12:40–2  C15:71–2
   C16:79–81  C17:106–7  C27:39–40 (imp)  C28:30–1  C34:34–5
3. How many hired servants
   C1:37–8  C4:72  C5:70  C6:74  C7:288–9  C9:46–7  C10:61
   C16:178–80  C19:184–6
4. Td, Bs, K, C, M, N
   A3:358–81  C1:217–28  C8:494–507  C12v:155–60 (inc)
   C13:167–78  C26:110–22  C31:128–39  C32:106–16
   C33:137–48

PARSONS, [?William], of Wells (fl. 1545–63)
Flatt Service: Td, Bs (see BLANCKS and HOOPER for M, N)
   C8:49–63  C13:48–55  C18:66–70  E11a:118–26

PATRICK, Nathaniel (d. 1595)
Short Service, in g (in a in later MSS): Td, Bs, 'J', K, C, M, N (Arnold 1;
ascrib there and in B30 to Richard PATRICK)
   Td, Bs, K, C, M, N
   A15:191–202  A22:33–43  B5:25–35  B7:24–34  B8v:91–101
   B13v:107–17  B19:140–55  B22:7–9, 14–17 (−K)  B23:116–22
   B28:35–44  B30:181–90 (N inc)  C26:122–9, 170–3  C30:76–86
   C31:120–7, 151–3  C33:18–22, 180–6  D20:107–21
   Td, Bs, M, N
   A1:222–4, 227–9, 234–7 (Td, Bs inc)  C8:64–71, 278–82
   C12v:219–26 (M, N imp)  C13:60–5  C32:117–22
   E11a:59–63, 380–2
   K, C
   A15:230–3  C19v:12 (headings only)  C19A:34–6  C29:41–3
   D18v:36–9
   'J' (from Bs; arr PENSON)
   B3:54–5  B18:100–1  B30:72–4  C20:98–100  C25:103–4
   D22:17–18

PATTEN, William (1803–63)
Arr HAYDN (12.), HIMMEL, MOREIRA (1.), NOVELLO (1.)

PEERSON, Martin (c.1572–1651)
1. Blow up the trumpet
   A6:116–18  C1:240–2  C2:188–90  C7:125–6  C11:7–8

PEERSON, MARTIN (*cont.*)

C14:143–4   C15:107–9   C16:12–13   C17:86–8   C19:53–5
C27:48–50 (imp)   C28:48–50   C34:9–11

2. I will magnify thee O Lord
A2:364–8   C1:16–17   C4:56–7   C5:54   C6:52   C7:261–2
C9:35   C10:42   C17:114–16   C19:154–6

PENSON, Peter (*c.*1788–1870; m–c, Durham, 1815–48; prec, Durham, 1815–44)

1. Responses and Litany [ = A]; conclusion to TALLIS's Litany [ = B]; Amens in Communion Service [ = C]
A34:216–25 [B]   B3:83–96 [ABC]   B15v:21–32 [ABC]
C20v:56–72 [ABC]   C22v:29–45 [AB]   C25:136–7 [BC]
D22:50–1 [BC]

2. Arr FERRETTI, HANDEL (25.), MOREIRA (2.); in R. FARRANT (3.), O. GIBBONS (28.), PATRICK, TALLIS (14.) has arr J from composer's Bs

PEPUSCH, Johann Christoph (1667–1752)

O praise the Lord laud ye
A8:141–6   A13:54, 57–9 (inc)   B13:101–4

PERGOLESI, Giovanni Battista (1710–36)

1. Glory in the highest (no. 1; 4 pts)
A21:39–52   B4:99–100   B15:36–8   C22v:99–101   D20v:11–13
D22v:72–4

2. Glory in the highest (no. 2; 5 pts; arr [T.] GREATOREX)
A21:73–86   B4:114–15   B15:50–1   D20v:25–6

3. O Lord haste thee (unascrib, copied *c.*1765. The much later *Novello Octavo Anthems No. 926* states that 'O Lord have mercy upon me'—a movement here—was adapted from PERGOLESI by Vincent Novello)
A17:130–5   B17:123

PEZ, Johann Christoph (1664–1716)

[*Duplex genius*], Sonatas 1, 2, 3, 7, 5, 8
M200

PICKERING, Theophilus (preb, Durham, 1692–d. 1711)

1. Every day will I give thanks
A20:184   B15:181–2   B18v:77   C2*:43   C15:181   C24v:108
C27:60   C28:460   D18:256–7   D21:66–7

2. Arr CARISSIMI (1.)

PIERSON, Henry Hugo (1815–73)
  1. Lo he comes with clouds descending (no. 39—not 41—of 'Jerusalem')
     D23:195–6
  2. Of the Rock that begot thee
     D23:197–8
  3. What are these
     D23:199–200

PILBROW, of Exeter (MSS early 19th cent.)
In B♭: K
   A10v:22–3   B3:96–7   B9:160   B15v:33   B30:1   C20:144
   C22:59   D22:52

PLEYEL, Ignace Joseph (1757–1831)
Let us devote this consecrated day (Hymn; unascrib except PLEYEL in
B8, B13; MASON in Table to B16)
   A16:139   B7:350–1   B8v:222   B9:209   B11:81–2   B13v:184–5
   B16:92–3   B34:119–20   C30:224

POOLE, Anthony (*fl. c.*1670)
Divisions to a Ground in d, for the viola da gamba
   A27:253–6

PORTER, Samuel (1733–1810)
O Lord our Governor
   A20:1–3   B6:193   B9v:70   B12:346–7   B17:152–3   B24:102
   B26:134–5   B31:122–3   B33:167–8   B34:14–15

PORTMAN, Richard (d. *c.*1655)
  1. Behold how good and joyful
     C1:34–5   C4:70   C5:68–9   C6:71–2   C7:284–5   C10:58–9
     C11v:1–2   C16:134–6   C17:130–1   C19:179–81
  2. I will always give thanks
     C2:120–1   C3:92–3   C7:61–2   C11v:17–18   C14:78–9
     C16:184–5   C19:226–8
  3. Rejoice in the Lord O ye righteous
     A4:82–7   B1:14–16
  4. Save me O God
     C1:18   C4:57   C5:55   C6:53–4   C7:262–3   C9:36   C10:43
     C17:117–18   C19:156–7

POUL, P. (MSS late 17th cent.)
Sonatas for 2 viols and bass continuo
  1. In a (probably by JENKINS)
     D4/1, 2:8–10   D4/3:3

POUL, P. (*cont.*)
2. In e
   D4/1:20–2   D4/2:21–3   D4/3:8
3. In g
   D4/1, 2:14–17   D4/3:5

POWLEY (MSS late 19th cent.)
1. Grant we beseech thee merciful Lord
   D30–5:111
2. Have mercy upon me O God
   D30–5:106–10
3. In F: Td, J
   D30v:5–9   D31v–5v:1a–5

PRESTON, Thomas (jun, so A33; 1662–1730; not Durham, in spite of Brit. Lib. K.7.e.2; probably org, Ripon, 1690–1730)
When Israel came out
   A33:86–91   C7:369–70   C14:196   C15:194   C27:252–4
   C28:165–7   C34:133–5

PRIEST, [Nathaniel] (*fl. c.*1750)
In F: Td, J, M, N (acquired in 1748)
   A13v:13–31   B6v:1–13   B7:209–21   B8v:1–13   B17v:78–88
   B19:247–65   B23:89–90 (−Td, J)   B28:371–80   B29v:41–51
   B31v:11–22   B32v:19–27   B35:69–79   C30:184–94   C31:416–24

PRYCE, Sir John (1698–1761; 5th Baronet, of Newton Hall, Montgomery)
5 single chants, in A re ♯ [ = A], Gamut ♯ [ = G], E la mi ♮ [ = e], D sol re ♯ [ = D] (dated 20 July 1736), and B♭ (dated 14 July 1738)
   A8:3–5

[PURCELL]
Z = *Henry Purcell—An analytical catalogue of his music*—F. B. Zimmerman (1963)
At Durham all the late 17th cent. chants lack ascription. Elsewhere several are ascribed to different members of the Purcell family, but the information is conflicting. Doubts persist over:
1. 5 single chants, in a, g, g, d, A, numbered 5–9 (no. 7 = Z D33, but is possibly by T. PURCELL)
   C12v:273 (tenor)   C26v:3 (bass)   C28:507f (bass)
2. 2 single chants, in d, G, numbered 10 and 11 (no. 10 = Z123; no. 11 = Z121)
   C12v:273–4 (tenor)   C28:507g (bass)

3. Single chant in d, numbered 21
   C28:507h (bass)

PURCELL, Henry (1659–95)

Z = *Henry Purcell—An analytical catalogue of his music*, F. B. Zimmerman (1963)

1. Behold I bring you glad tidings (*Boyce 3*; Z2)
   A25:138–41   A28:148–52   B6:57–8 (inc)   B9:53–5   B10:186–90
   B12:119–20   B27:72–6   B33:50–2   C27:328–32   C28:402–5

2. Be merciful unto me (*Boyce 2*; Z4)
   A26:194–200   A28:126–30   A33:34–8   B6:21–5   B8:68–71
   B9:57–60   B10:150–5   B12:80–2   B24:87–8   B27:105–9
   B29:19–22   C7:161–6   C14:222–7   C15:218–19   C27:218–22
   C28:292–6   C34:232–7

3. Blessed is he that considereth (*Page 2*; Z7)
   B21:105–8   C19A:84–7   C35v:65–7

4. Blessed is the man that feareth (Z9)
   B4:107–11   B6:6–8   B9:68–70   B10:222–5   B12:167–70
   B13:1–3   B15:44–7   B17:36–8   B29:215–17   B31:4–6
   B33:5–7   B35v:16–19   B36:77–9   C22v:109–14   D20v:19–22
   D22v:83–7

5. Christ is risen (ZS2; now attrib to E. WHITE)

6a. Hear my prayer O God and hide not (Z14)
   A25:66–7   C27:207–9   C27:312–15   C28:297–9   C34:237–9

6b. Hear my prayer O Lord and let my crying (Z15)
   D23:227

7. Help us O God (Z25/3; from 'Lord how long wilt thou be angry')
   D23:182–3

8. I was glad (*Page 2*; Z19)
   A8:183–4   A8:188–90   A9:3–6   A16:112–19   A28:130–3
   A33:54–8   B6:28–30   B9:55–7   B12:57–9   B18v:1–4
   B24:72–3   B26:29–31   B27:117–20   B29:17–18   C7:166–70
   C7:383–4   C14:211–12   C15:121   C27:204–6   C28:303–5
   C34:243–5

9. I will sing unto the Lord (Z22)
   A20:39–40   A28:139–40   A33:24–5   B6v:24–5   B9:66–7
   B10:50–1   B12:30–1   B17v:3   B18v:18–19   B24:39–40
   B26:27–8   B27:213–14   B29:13–14   B32:33   C7:368–9
   C11v:216–17   C12:76   C15:192–3   C27:89 (inc)   C28:90–1
   C34:68–9

10. Jehova quam multi sunt (Z135; *see* 'Lord how are they increased')

11. Let God arise (Z23)
    C27:210   C28:216   C34:188

PURCELL, HENRY (*cont.*)

12. Lord how are they increased (from 'Jehova quam multi sunt hostes'; arr ARMES)
    D30:166–7   D31, D32:164–5   D33:170–1   D34:166–7
    D35:164–5
13. Lord how long wilt thou be angry (Z25; *see* 'Help us O God')
14. My song shall be alway (Z31)
    A8:109–18   A12:159–68 (inc)   A17:109–17   A25:19–23
    A28:145–8   B27:248   B29:25–30   C27:211–17   C28:168–75
    C34:136–42
15. My heart is inditing (*see* 'Praise the Lord O Jerusalem')
16. O all ye people clap your hands (Z138)
    A21:131–46 (inc)   B4:111–13   B15:48–9   C22v:114–16
    D20v:23–4   D22v:88–90
17. O give thanks unto the Lord for he is gracious (*Boyce 3*; Z33)
    A8:181–2   A8:185–6   A9:25–33   A25:14–18
    A28:141–3b, 144–5   B9:61–3   B10:179–86   B12:59–63
    B24:19–20   B26:31–3   B27:52–6   B29:22–5   B33:40–2
    C7:192–5 (frag)   C7:407–13   C14:111–12 (frag)
    C15:137–40   C19A:102–6   C27:277–80   C28:327–8, 400–1
    C34:301–4
18. O God they that love thy name (Z D4) (D MSS arr ARMES)
    A33:98–9   C28:109   C34:86–7   D23:109   D26/1–5:25
    D26/6–9:26
19. O God thou art my God (*Boyce 2*; Z35)
    A20:10–12   A28:136–8   A33:101–3   B6v:22–4   B9:65–6
    B10:24–6   B12:23–4   B17v:2–3   B21:5–7   B24:34–5
    B27:208–10   B29:14–15   B32:30–1   C7:172–3   C15:130–1
    C27:85–6   C28:92–3   C34:76–7   C35v:5–7   D18:56–8
20. O God thou hast cast us out (*Boyce 2*; Z36)
    A20:14–16   A28:133–6   A33:100 (inc)   B6v:21–2   B9:63–4
    B10:22–4   B12:53–5   B17v:1–2   B24:30–1   B26:28–9
    B27:210–12   B29:15–16   B32:31–2   C7:170–1   C15:132–3
    C27:87–8   C28:94–5   C34:78–9   D18:59–61
21. O Lord God of Hosts (*Boyce 2*; Z37)
    D18:107–13
22. O Lord how manifold (Z48/6; from 'Praise the Lord O my soul')
    A10:53–4   B4:113   B15:49   C22v:117   D20v:24   D22v:90
23. O Lord rebuke me not (Z40)
    A25:23–5   C27:209   C28:220   C34:187
24. O praise the Lord all ye heathen (Z43)
    A4:121–2   C11v:225–7   C12:80   C14:163   C15:120   C27:222
    C28:210   C34:176   D23:185–7

25. O sing unto the Lord a new song (Z44)
A10:55–69, 100–4, 104a–18   B4:125–9   B15:54–8   C22v:128–33
D20v:29–33   D22v:101–6

26. Praise the Lord O Jerusalem (Z30/7a from 'My heart is inditing')
D23:189–90

27. Rejoice in the Lord alway (Z49)
A21:112–30   B4:103–6   B15:40–2   C22v:104–7   D20v:15–17
D22v:78–81

28. Remember not Lord (Z50)
D23:191–2

29. The earth trembled ('A Hymn on our Saviour's Passion') (Z197)
A8:120–1

30. The Lord is king, the earth (Z54)
A25:195–202   C7:181–2   C27:236–41   C28:182–8   C34:143–8

31. They that go down (*Boyce 3*; Z57)
A29:199–202   B9:70   B10:190–3   B17:35–6   B21:206
B29:210   B36:77   C21:197   C29v:194

32. Thou knowest Lord (Z58C)
By itself:
A20:181   B12:118   B27:245   B32:32   C5:44   C10:116
C19:455   C19A:24   C26:348   D22v:129
D37/1–7, 10–16, 18–21:10
With CROFT's Burial Sentences:
A8:78–9   A13:40–1   B10:88–9   B24:2   B26:118–19   B29:198
C21:156–7   C29v:157   C35v:134–5

33. Thy righteousness O God (Z59) (D MSS arr ARMES)
A33:96–7   C28:108   C34:85–6   D23:108   D26/1–5:24
D26/6–9:25

34. Thy way O God (*Boyce 2*; Z60)
A14:80–4   A25:233–9   A28:153–6   B9:67   B10:194–8
B12:26–7   B24:75   B29:30–2   B33:62–5   B35v:14–16
C19A:34   C27:344–5 (inc)

35. Thy word is a lantern (*Boyce 3*; Z61)
A25:28–30   C7:386–9   C15:134–5   C27:287–9   C28:300–2
C34:240–2   D18:155–9

36. In B♭: Td, Bs, K, C, M, N, Be, J, Cd, Dm (*Boyce 3*; Z230)
Td, Bs, K, C, M, N (known as 1st Service)
A33:153–63, 166–72   B28:235–48   C26:305–15   C26:317–27
C31:302–11   C32:275–84   C33:297–306   D21v:28–43
Td, Bs, M, N
A9v:29–31 (Td only; frag)   A22:135–44   B5:139–46   B7:126–33
B8v:146–52   B19:1–9 (Td imp)   B21v:50–7   B22:137–42
B23:39–44   C19Av:70–6   C35:49–55   M170:135–6 (Bs only)

PURCELL, HENRY (*cont.*)

Be, J, Cd, Dm (known as 2nd Service)

A29v:13–25   B5:147–56   B7:134–43   B17v:37–45   B19:86–102
B20v:123–37   B23:44–9   B29v:6–15   B31v:88–97   B32v:1–7
B35:21–9   B36v:51–9   C19v:64–72   C21v:125–37   C29:127–39
D21v:43–58   M170:144–7 (Cd, Dm)

Cd, Dm, M, N

D18v:99–108

37. Grand, in D: Td, J (Z232)

A12:129–47   A26:121–41   B5:156–60   B7:143–6
B17v:72, 77–8 (inc)   B19:235–47   B22:47–53   B23:79–80
B27v:10–17   B28:391–7   B30:155–60   B36v:75–80
C19Av:10–15   C21v:14–18   C29:20–4   C30:194–201
C33:321–8   C35:1–5

38. In g: M, N (Z231)

M170:133–4

39. Unascrib single chant in a, numbered 12 (Z120)

C12v:274 (tenor)   C28:507g (bass)

See [PURCELL] for possible further chants.

*Secular vocal:*

Only nos. 41, 43, 44, and 49 are ascrib

40. Ah Belinda I am pressed [Dido and Aeneas] (Z626/3a)
D9:18–19

41. A quire of beauties (Z D130)
D9:20–1

42. Bring the Bole and cool Nants (Z243)
D9v:3–4

43. Corinna I excuse thy face [The Wives' Excuse] (Z612/3):
D9:14

44. Hail bright Cecilia (St Cecilia's Song) (Z328)
M102:1–68, 77–88 (inc)

45. Now the maids and the men (Fairy Queen) (Z629/22b)
E11a:448–55

46. Next winter comes slowly (Fairy Queen) (Z629/36b)
M193/1:40

47. On the brow of Richmond hill (Z405)
D9:4–5

48. The danger is over (The Fatal Marriage) (Z595)
D9:32–5

49. This poet sings the Trojan wars [Anacreon's Defeat] (Z423)
D9:24–31

50. Thus happy and free [Fairy Queen] (Z629/44)
D9:22

*Instrumental*:

51. Overture in D (unascrib) (Z T691)
    E32:60–2
52. Trumpet tune in C (unascrib) (Z630/4a)
    E32:7

[PURCELL, Thomas] (d. 1682)
Unascrib single chant in a, numbered 20
   C12v:274 (tenor)   C28:507h (bass)
*See* [PURCELL] for possible further chants.

QUARLES (QUARLESI), Charles (Carlo) (*fl.* 1688–d. 1727; org, York, 1722–7)
Cantabile
   M70v:76–83

RAMEAU, Jean-Philippe (1683–1764)
  1. [Op. 3: Rondeau: La Soyeuse]
     M69:15   M108:4
  2. [Op. 3: Menuet en Rondeau]
     M69:15   M108:4
  3. Minuet in B♭
     M69:13

RANDALL, Greenwood (*fl.* 1610; d. between 1645 and 1660)
M, N
A2:226–33   C18:41–3

RAVENSCROFT, Thomas (*c.*1582–*c.*1635)
  1. Come Holy Ghost (unascrib)
     A3:14–15
  2. O let me hear thy loving kindness
     A6:154–8   C1:253–5   C2:143–4   C3:115–16   C7:81–2
     C11v:74–5   C14:102–3   C16:233–4   C17:161–2   C19:254–5
  3. O Lord in thee is all my trust
     A6:165–70

RAYLTON, [William] (*fl.* 1736–d. 1757)
In E♭: S, K, C, M, N
   A13v:68–78   B5:226–33   B7:251–9   B8v:30–7 (−S)
   B13v:46–53   B17v:108–15   B19:311–23   B28:50–6   B29v:66–73
   B31v:44–51   B32v:39–44 (−S)   B35:102–9
M, N
   A34:38–60   B33v:31–3 (M inc)   C20:138–44
   C31:439–42 (−M; N inc)

READ, [?Richard] (*fl.*1570–1616)
1. God standeth
   A1:205   B10:56–7   C2*:42–3   C4:36   C5:28–9   C6:34
   C7:244–5   C9:15   C10:24   C11:56–7   C15:39   C16:50–1
   C17:39–40   C27:28   C28:16–17   C34:19–20
2. To [W.] MUNDY's Short Service: M, N
   A1:201–4   C8:263–7   C12v:66–8   C13:45–7   C26:130–2
   C31:140–1   C32:148–9   C33:153–4   E11a:372–4

REDFORD, John (*fl.* 1534–d. 1547)
Rejoice in the Lord alway (now attrib to ANON)

REYNOLDS, John (d.? 1778)
My God my God look upon me (*Page 1*)
   A16:202–4   D18:153–4   D19:47–8

RICHARDSON, Vaughan (*c.*1670–1729)
O how amiable (*Page 1*)
   D19:45–6

ROGERS, Benjamin (1614–98)
1. Behold now praise the Lord (*Boyce 2*)
   A20:4
2. I beheld and lo (I beheld in a Revelation) (unascrib)
   B1:9–13
3. Lord who shall dwell (*Page 3*)
   D19:10–11
4. Teach me O Lord (*Boyce 2*)
   A20:35   A29:5–6   B6v:63–4   B9v:41   B10:59–60   B12:35
   B17v:13–14   B26:24–5   B27:219–20   B29:11   C7:357–8
   C14:180–1   C15:166–7   C27:84–5   C28:83–4   C34:54–5
5. In a: M, N
   A34:94–106   B3:72–4   B15v:7–9   C20:120–2   C22:38–41
   C25:123–6   D22:37–40
6. In D, De sol re, D♯: Td, J, K, C, S, M, N (*Boyce 1*)
   Td, J, K, C, M, N
   A15:41–50   B3:198–211   B5:80–7 (−M, N; +S)   B7:81a–90
   B16v:36–45   B23:146–52   B27v:20–4 (−M, N; C inc)
   B28:159–66   C19v:21–9   C19Av:16–24   C21v:19–27
   C26:146–57   C29:25–33   C30:54–63   C31:322–31   C35:18–26
   M170:76 (just N)
7. In F: Td, J, M, N
   A34:60–94   B3:65–71   B15v:1–7   C20:111–19   C22:30–8
   C25:115–22   D22:29–36

8. In Gamut: Td, J, M, N
   A10v:24–64    A35:115–44    B1:139–45 (−Td, J)    B3:253–63
   B15v:59–67    B30:92–100    D19v:146–56    D23:86–90 (−Td, J)
   D26/1–9:2–5 (−Td, J)

ROLLE, Johann Heinrich (1716–85)
In thee O Lord (*Latrobe 1*)
   A10:130–7    B4:149–50    B15:82–3    C22v:149–50    D20v:104–5
   D21:95–6

ROSEINGRAVE, Ralph (*c*.1695–1747)
1. In C: Td, J, K, C, Cd, Dm
   A18:289–334
2. In F: Td, J, K, C, Cd, Dm
   A18:335–73
3. Single chant in A♮ [= a]
   A18:359
4. Double chant in D♯ [= D]
   A18:374

RUSSELL, [William] (1777–1813)
In A: Td, J, M, N
   D30v:23–32    D31v–3v:21–30    D34v:21–3, 24–30    D35v:21–30

RUTTER, George (1561–1623; a George Rutter was chor, Durham, 1600–*c*.1607)
Blessed is he that feareth
   A3:101–3    C1:1 (inc)    C4:39–40    C5:31–2    C6:37–8    C7:247
   C9:18–19    C10:27    C11:32–3    C12:25–6    C15:41–2    C16:24–5
   C17:42–3    C27:29–30    C28:28–9    C34:39–40

SABADINI (SABATTINI), [Bernardo] (d. 1718)
God be merciful (*Latrobe 2*)
   B15:217–19

STE COLOMBE, le fils (*fl. c*.1713)
*For the viola da gamba*:
1. Fantaisie en Rondeau in g
   A27:110–11
2. 2 gavottes, in g, f
   A27:112, 319
3. Sarabande in f
   A27:318
4. 5 suites, in g, a, F, e, b
   A27:104–6, 113–15, 117–20, 124–9, 291–4

STE COLOMBE, LE FILS (*cont.*)
  5. Tombeau in f, 'pour Mr Ste Colombe le père'
    A27:314–18

SALISBURY, Edward (*fl.* 1727–41; org, York, 1727–35)
  1. O praise the Lord all ye heathen (arr and adapt)
    M70:68–9   M70:84–5
  2. Arr STEFFANI (1.)

SALVATORE (*fl.* 17th cent.)
O hide not thy face ('for Litany mornings'; unascrib apart from in pencil
in A10; English text to 'Recessit pastor', *Latrobe 3*)
  A10:51–2  B4:107  B15:43  C22v:108  D20v:18  D22v:82

SARTI, Giuseppe (1729–1802)
O my God wash thou me (arr from 'Amplius lava me', *Latrobe 2*)
  A34v:8–16  B4:32–6  B15:1–4  C20v:47–51  C22v:19–23
  D22v:15–19

SCARLATTI, Domenico (1685–1757)
Concertos (ed. AVISON, 1744)
No. 1
  M157:70–3 (Allegros 1, 2)
No. 3
  M157:34 (Allegro 2)
No. 5
  M157:35 (Allegro 2)
No. 8
  M157:63 (Vivace)
No. 9
  M157:82–4 (Allegro 2, Con spirito)
No. 10
  M157:49 (Giga)

SCHENCK, Giovanni (*c.*1660–*c.*1712)
  1. Op. 2
    A27:26, 29, 31, 38, 51–4, 58–61, 65, 73, 94–7, 151–61, 221–5, 236–44,
    264–73, 300–10 (24 items)
  2. Op. 6
    A27:24, 28, 30–1, 70–3, 147–51, 176–90, 209–21, 260–3, 283–6,
    297–300 (15 items)

SCHICKHARDT (SCHICKHARD), Johann Christian (b. *c.*1682;
d. before 1762)
[Op. 19], Concerto 1
  M157:103 [Allegro]

SCHMELZER (SMELTZER), Johann Heinrich (1623–80)
Sonatas à 3 viols
1. In F
D2/1, 2:8  D2/3:10
2. In G
D2/1:32–3  D2/2:34–5  D2/3:28–9 (dated [16]72)
3. In D (ascrib 'M1t23s', who may be ?MATTEIS, ?SCHMELZER)
D2/1, 2:4–5  D2/3:6–7

SCHNITTELBACH, Nathanael (1633–67)
Sonata in D for 2 viols + bass continuo
D2/1, 2:12–13  D2/3:14–15

SCHUBERT, Franz (1797–1828)
1. Am Bach viel kleine Blumen stehn (Des Müllers Blumen)
E38:1
2. Laue Lüfte Blumendüfte (Lob der Thränen) (unascrib)
E38:22–3

SCHUTZ, G[abriel] (1633–1710)
Sonata in a for 2 viols + bass continuo
D4/1:17–19  D4/2:18–20  D4/3:5–7

SHARP, John III (1723–92; Vicar of Hartburn, 1749, and Bamburg
1772; Archdeacon of Northumberland, 1762; preb, Durham, 1768–92)
Catalogues and lists of his music
M174(ii)—loose sheet (hol)  M194 (hol; inc)

SHARP, Thomas II (1725–72; Vicar of Bamburgh, 1757–72)
*Hymn tunes*:
1. Bamburgh
Behold the morning sun begins
M90:50–1
My soul repeat his praise
M89:12–14  M215 (no text)
2. Beadnell
Say heavenly muse and teach my song
M89:5–11  M215 (no text)
3. Hartburn
With one consent let all the earth
M89:1–4
4. Leyden
The spacious firmament on high
M89:15–22  M90:53–4

SHARP, THOMAS II (*cont.*)
5. Out of the deep of sad distress (arr from 'Dr. Boyce's Sonata')
M89:23–8
6. Rothbury (unascrib)
In all my vast concerns with thee
M90:23   M215 (no text)

SHAW, Alexander (chor, Durham, 1660–4; ?org, Ripon, 1677; org, Durham, 1677–81; d. 1706) (*see* Index of Copyists)
1. I will sing unto the Lord
A4:54–8
2. The Lord is my shepherd
A4:6–11
3. In E lo mi: Td, J, M, N
A4v:77–92
4. In G: Td, J, K, C, M, N
A4v:55–68, 73–6 (C, M inc)   C12v:184–94
C13v:29–30 (Td only, frag)

SHENTON, Robert (*c.*1730–98)
1. O give thanks unto the Lord and call (dated 1777)
A19:482–502  B6:194–8  B8:84–9  B9v:71–5  B11:1–5
B12:348–52  B17:147–51  B24:104–5  B31:125–8  B34:1–5
2. In E♭ (dated 1777): Td, J, K, C, Sc, S, G, M, N, Cd, Dm
A19:375–420, 423–81
Td, J, M, N
B15v:75–90
Td, J
A15:121–30  B5:302–8 (J inc)  B7:335–41  B8v:203–11
B17v:186–92  B22:54–60  B23:166–72 (+ text of K, C (inc))
B33v:111–16  B34v:1–8  B35:173–80
M, N
B30:107–11  D18v:146–51  D19v:178–84
3. In BEVIN, BYRD (30.), ? R. FARRANT (3.), O. GIBBONS (28.), TALLIS (14.) has arr J from composer's Bs

SHEPPARD (SHEPHERD), John (*c.*1515–*c.*1560)
1. O Lord the maker of all things (now attrib to W. MUNDY)
2. Submit yourselves
A3:163–5  C11:128–9  C17:93–4  C19:66–8
3. Second Service, in F fa ut: V, Td, Bs, 'K', C, M, N
V, Td, Bs, C, M, N
A5:225–39, 246–52 (−V, C)   C13:216–22, 224–9 (−V)

E4:63–9, 113–15, 140–1b (— V, heading only, p. 61)
E5:60–8, 115–17, 137–40  E6:63–8, 108–10, 133–6 (— V, as E4)
E7:60–8, 115–17, 139–42  E8:61–9, 116–18, 139–43
E9:61–6, 106–7, 132–5 (— V, as E4, but p. 59)
E10:59–67, 111–13, 133–6  E11:60–9, 119–21, 141–4
E11a:149–56, 290–2, 420–3 (— V)
Td, Bs, 'K', M, N (19th cent. MSS; 'K' arr ARMES from Bs)
D23:201–15  D27/1–10:1–13  D28/11:10–22

SIMPSON, Christopher (c.1605–69)
 1. *The Division Viol*
    A27:68–9, 106–7, 120, 132, 190–1, 278–82, 295–6 (9 items)
 2. *Practical Compendium Appendix*
    A27:107–8 (3 items)

SIMPSON, H[enry] Purver (1766–1842; of Finedon, Northants)
In the midst of life
    B6:203–5  B11:76–80  B16:90  B34:118

SKELTON, [George] (1773–1859)
In D: Td, J, S, K, Go, M, N
    D17v:100–10

SMART, George Thomas (1776–1867)
In G: Td, J, K, Go, C, Sc, S, G, M, N
    D30v:10–18, 20–2 (— Sc, S, G)  D31v, D32v:6–20
    D33v:6–17 (— M, N)  D34v, D35v:6–20

SMELTZER (*see* SCHMELZER)

SMEWEN, [Thomas] (m of chor, York, 1684)
In Gamut: Td
    M170:77–9 (inc)

SMITH, Edward (*see* SMYTHE, Edward)

SMITH, Elias (*see* SMYTH, Elias)

SMITH, John Stafford (1750–1836)
In E♭: K
    B3:83  B15v:20  C20:136–7  C22:59  C25:135  D22:49

SMITH, William (1603–45; Durham; chor, 1614–c.1617; m-c, 1627–45)
(*see* Index of Copyists) MS A1:1–41 is hol
 1. Almighty and everlasting God we humbly beseech (Candlemas:
    Purification of Mary the Virgin)
    A1:30–1  C1:122  C2:82  C3:62  C7:42  C11v:134  C14:48
    C16:340  C19:383

18. Preces & Ps., Whitsunday Matins (God be merciful)
    A1:25–7  C1:302–4  C13v:20–1  E4–11:29–31  E11a:20–2
19. First Service: K, Go, C
    A1:1–5  C8:188–91 (−Go)  C13v:87–8 (−Go)
    E11a:334–6 (−Go)
20. Second Service: K, Go, C
    A1:5–8  C8:192–3 (−Go; both inc)  C13v:89–90 (−Go)
    E11a:336 (−Go)
21. K ('10 several ways')
    A6:243–6  E11a:287–90
22. Fantasia [I] in d (unascrib, but in his hand)
    A1:328–30
23. Fantasia [II] in d (unascrib, but in his hand)
    A1:331–3 (imp)

SMYTH, Elias (Durham; m-c from 1628; prec, 1661–d. 1676) (*see* Index of Copyists)

How is the gold become dim (King Charles the Martyr)
    A3:403–7  C2:79–80  C3:85–6  C7:67–8  C11v:162–3
    C14:71–2  C19:400–3

SMYTHE, Edward (Durham; chor, 1597–1601; m of chor and org, 1608–d. 1612. It is possible that a slightly later Edw. SMYTHE (d. 1647) may have been responsible for some of the items)

1. Blessed are those that are undefiled (*see* Preces & Pss., All Saints)
2. If the Lord himself (5 November)
    A5:64–9  C1:38–9  C2:109–10  C3:81  C4:73  C5:71
    C6:75–6  C7:57  C7:289–90  C9:47–8  C10:62  C11v:154–5
    C14:65–6  C16:403–4  C17:134–5  C19:186–7
3. Let my complaint (*see* Preces & Pss., All Saints)
4. O Lord consider my distress
    A5:85–9  C1:67–8  C4:91  C5:90  C7:312–3  C9:67  C10:84
    C11v:41–2  C16:172–3  C19:208–9
5. O Lord my God to thee I do complain
    A2:272–4  A5:116–20
6. O Lord our Governor (by J. MUNDY; *see* SMYTHE's Preces & Ps., Ascension Matins)
7. O praise God in his holiness
    A2:359–62  A5:90–4  C1:42–3  C4:75  C5:73  C6:77–8
    C7:291–2  C9:49–50  C10:64–5  C11v:183–4  C16:151–3
    C17:136–7  C19:189–90
8. Preces & Ps., Ascension Matins (Preces are SMYTHE's; and although it is implied Ps. 'O Lord our Governor' is his too, it is by

SMYTHE, EDWARD (*cont.*)
J. MUNDY to whom it is ascrib in those other MSS where it appears as an anthem)
Preces only
C1:297   C13v:14   E4–11:21   E11a:14
9. Preces & Pss., All Saints (Blessed are those that are undefiled; Let my complaint)
A1:99–104   A2:1–5   C1:208–10   C13v:24–6
C18:3 (2nd Ps. only, inc)   E4–5:37–40   E6:37–9   E7–8:37–40
E9:37–9   E10–11:37–40   E11a:25–7

SNEP, Jean (*fl. c.*1700–10)
Op. 1
A27:27, 32–5, 56–7, 88–93, 141–3, 171–4, 233–5, 257–9 (16 items)

SPOHR, [Louis] (1784–1859)
1. As pants the hart (Crucifixion; arr STIMPSON)
B15:188–9   D18:264–5   D19:215–6 (inc)   D21:74–5
2. Blest are the departed (Last Judgment)
A10:119–29   B4:142–4   B15:68–70   C22v:134–6   D20v:43–4
D22v:107–9

STAINER, John (1840–1901)
1. Drop down ye heavens (*Ouseley 2*)
B3v:32–6
2. I saw the Lord (Trinity Sunday) (*Ouseley 2*)
B3v:46–53
3. They were lovely and pleasant (*Ouseley 2*)
B3v:57–61

STANLEY, John (1712–86)
Variations on [HANDEL's 'Harmonious Blacksmith']
M69:90–1

STEFFANI, Agostini (1654–1728)
*Anthems, motets, and madrigals:*
1. By the waters of Babylon (≠ Super flumina; arr SALISBURY from duet 'Soavissime catene' in 'La lotta d'Hercole con Achelo')
M70v:116–20
2. Cingite floribus
M192:18–46
3. Gettano i rè dal Soglio
E15:48–54
4. I will give thanks unto thee (= Qui diligit Mariam)
M70:70–83

5. Sonitus armorum
   M192:80–104
6. Videte gentes
   M192:47–79

*Cantatas for two voices, possibly by* STEFFANI (unascrib in E22):

7. Ad supernam coeli mensam
   E22:73–92
8. Benedicam Dominum in omni tempore
   E22:21–40
9. Cantate Domino canticum novum
   E22:41–54
10. [Che m'importa]
    E22:115–19 (inc)
11. Omnes gentes ad Iesum venite
    E22:92–113
12. Quemadmodum desiderat cervus
    E22:54–73
13. Super flumina babilonis ( ≠ By the waters)
    E22:2–20

STEFFKIN, Frederick (?son of below)
Suite in G, for viola da gamba
   A27:251–2

STEFFKIN (STOEFFKEN), Theodore (Ditrich) (early 17th cent.–
1673)
Divisions in a, for viola da gamba
   D10:101–5

STEPHENS, [John] (*c.*1720–80)
1. In E♭: Cd, Dm
   B13v:168–70   B19:391–4 (inc)   B22:170 ( − Dm; Cd inc)
   B28:45–9   C33:96–100
2. Single chant in E♭
   A18:22

STEVENSON, [Robert] (*fl.* 1570–1600)
1. When the Lord turned again
   A3:46–8   C1:237–8   C2:177–9   C3:159–60   C7:128–30
   C11:76–7   C14:146–8   C16:71–3   C17:90–1   C19:57–8
2. V, Td, Bs, K, C, M, N
   A3:23–46   C8:107–20, 223–8, 308–14 (V, Bs inc)
   C13:103–15 ( − V)   E11a:127–35, 275–7, 396–9

STIMPSON, James (1820–86; chor, Durham, 1827–33; org, Carlisle, 1841–2)
Arr SPOHR (1.)

STONARD (STONNARD), William (c.1550–75 to 1630)
1. Hear O my people
   A6:366–9
2. My God my God look upon me
   A6:360–5   C11v:159–59a
3. When the sorrows of hell
   A6:370–2 (inc)

STRADELLA, Alessandro (1644–82)
1. Clori son fido amanti
   E15:55–62
2. Piangete occhi dolente tanto
   E15:31–47

STROGERS, Nicholas (fl. 1560–75)
1. O God be merciful unto us
   A3:356–8   C2:197–8   C7:109–10   C11:136–7   C14:153–4
   C16:99–100   C17:66–7   C19:61–2
2. Short Service: V, Td, Bs, K, C, M, N
   A6:15–28 (−V)   C8:28–40, 176–81, 258–62   C13:29–38 (−V)
   E11a: 50–4, 260–2, 369–72 (−V)

STROUD, Charles (c.1705–26)
Hear my prayer O Lord and hide not (Page 1)
   A20:58–61   A28:23–6   B6v:40–3   B9v:16–19   B12:7–9
   B20v:26–9   B21:59–63   B24:46–8   B26:53–5   B27:249–52
   B29:76–8   B32:37–8   B34:25–7   C19:118–22   C19A:47–50
   C21:57–61   C26v:17–21   C28:116–19   C29v:40–3
   C35v:28–31 (imp)   D19:37–41

SÜSSMAYR (SÜSSMAYER), [Franz Xavier] (1766–1803)
He is blessed (Requiem)
   D23:179–80

TALLIS, Thomas (c.1505–85)
1. All people that on earth do dwell (see ALDRICH)
2. Arise O Lord and hear my voice
   A3:299–300   C1:235–6   C2:196   C3:161   C7:105   C11:75
   C14:149   C16:46   C17:91–2   C19:59
3. Blessed are those that be undefiled
   D23:218–19   D30:45   D31–2:45–6   D33–5:45

TALLIS, THOMAS (*cont.*)

    Td, Bs, R, L, K, Go, C, S, G, M, N
    B23:133–9 (– Go, S, G)    B28:400, 3–14 [*sic*]    C33:1–13 (– R, G)
    D20:21–7, 161–70 (– R, L)
    L, S, K, R
    B30:149–55
    S
    B17:33    B20v:137    C21v:137    C29:139    C35v:177
    'J' (from Bs; arr PENSON)
    A34:1–6    B3:56–7    B18:102–3    B30:74–5    C20:100–2
    C25:105–6    D22:19–20
    'J' (from Bs; arr SHENTON)
    A18:1–4
    *See* Litany, and Preces and Responses
  15.  Single chant in F fa ut ♮ [ = F]
    A8:3

TARTINI, Giuseppe (1692–1770)

T = *Le sonate per violino di Giuseppe Tartini—catalogo tematico*, P. Brainard (1975)

  1.  [Op. 1, no. 11] (T E5; in D here)
    E11a: 342–5
  2.  7 sonatas, in B♭, G, B♭, g, B♭, C, E♭, for 'Solo Violino con basso obligato' (nos. 5–7 are ascrib to TARTINI, but in nos. 6 and 7 this has been crossed out. No. 5 = T B15, which describes the attribution as 'uncertain')
    M159:1–39

TAYLOR (MS 1770s)

Single chant in E♭
  A18:23

TAYLOR, Daniel (d. 1643)

Sing we merrily
  A2:377–8a    C4:25–7    C5:18–19    C6:24–5    C7:234–5    C9:5 (inc)
  C10:16–17    C11:14–15    C15:28–9    C16:7–9    C17:28–9
  C19:4–5

TAYLOR, Silas (1624–78)

Lord let me know mine end ( = anthem by LOCKE)

TESSARINI (TESSARINA), Carlo (1690–1766)

[Op. 1]
Concerto 2
  M157:42–5 (Allegro 2)

Concerto 8
  M157:54–9 (Allegro 1)
Concerto 9
  M157:78–81 (Allegro 2)
Concerto 12
  M157:66–9 (Allegro 1)

THALBERG, Sigismond (1812–71)
  1. Hier an dem grünen Walde (Des Jägers Haus)
     E38:9–11
  2. Weit, weit, über das Thal
     E38:24–5

THORNE, John (c.1519–73)
Td
  C13:302–4

TOMKINS, John (1586–1638)
Turn thou us O good Lord (Good Friday)
  A5:39–41   C1:103–4   C2:39–40   C3:29—30   C7:21   C11v:104
  C14:23–4   C16:311–12   C19:356–8

TOMKINS, Thomas (1572–1656)
  1. Above the stars
     A2:248–50   C1:257   C2:131–2   C3:105   C7:69   C11v:48
     C14:89   C16:195–6   C19:242–3
  2. Almighty and everlasting God we humbly beseech (Purification of
     Mary the Virgin)
     A4:39–42   C1:121–2   C2:81   C3:61   C7:41   C11v:133
     C14:47   C16:339   C19:382
  3. Almighty God the fountain
     A1:63–67   C2*:32–3   C4:19–21   C5:13–14   C6:19–20
     C7:229–30 (imp)   C9:1–2   C10:11–12   C11:34–5   C11:133–5
     C12:18–20   C15:23–4 (inc)   C16:56–8   C17:22–4
  4. Almighty God which hast knit together (All Saints)
     A1:73–7   C1:62–3   C2:97–8   C3:73   C4:88   C5:87   C7:49
     C7:308–9   C9:63–4   C10:81–2   C11v:142–3   C14:57   C16:349
     C19:391–2
  5. Behold the hour cometh (Whitsunday; ascrib to O. GIBBONS)
     C1:119–20   C2:72   C3:56   C7:40   C11v:130   C14:46
     C16:335   C19:379–80
  6. Blessed be the Lord God of Israel
     A2:373–4   A3:81–2   C1:51   C4:81   C5:79   C6:87   C9:56
     C10:71   C11v:5–6   C16:139   C19:198

TOZAR, Salomon (MSS 1630s)

O Lord let me know mine end
A5:1–4   C1:250   C2:164   C3:133–4   C7:93–4   C11iv:73
C14:117–19   C16:228–9   C17:167–8   C19:275–6

TRAVERS, John (c.1703–58)

1. Ascribe unto the Lord (*Arnold 3*)
D22v:60–5
2. The earth is the Lord's
A19:561–76
3. In D: Td (*Arnold 3*)
D19v:15–23
4. In F: Td, J, S, K, C, M, N (*Arnold 2*)
A15:81–92   B19:32–45   B28:270–83   B36v:22–30
C8:517–33   C21iv:75, 78–9   C29:85–98   C35:71–83
D19v:111–127
Td, J, K, C, M, N
B5:103–7 (– Td, J, K; Cd inc)   B7:288–97   B16v:69–78
B17v:29–36   B22:1 (just N)   B23:122–8   B35:36–45
C19v:33–46   C30:125–31 (–K, C)   C31:154–66
5. Single chant in D
A19:421

TUCKER, William (d. 1679)

1. Comfort ye my people (St John Baptist)
A4:162–5   B1v:74–9   C11iv:199   C15:146   C17:186–7
C27:145–6   C28:226–8   C34:215–17
2. I was glad
A4:136–9   B1v:80–3   C7:134–5   C7:349–50   C14:172
C27:143–4   C28:231–2   C34:211–13
3. I will magnify thee O God
A33:44–8   C7:177–9   C11iv:208–10   C14:205–8 (imp)
C14:212–13   C15:215   C27:141–3   C28:233–5   C34:209–11
4. Lord how long wilt thou be angry
A4:109–12   C11iv:193–5   C12:70b (imp)   C15:150–2   C27:150
C28:217   C34:189
5. My heart is fixed
A4:149–52   C11iv:197   C12:55–6   C15:145   C17:185
C27:149–50   C28:224–5   C34:213–15
6. O give thanks unto the Lord and call (*Page 1*)
A4:142–3   A20:73–4   B6v:62–3   B9:40   B10:48–9   B12:34
B17v:14–15   B24:98   B26:23–4   B27:225–6   B29:10
C7:136–7   C7:348–9   C11iv:196   C12:54–5   C14:168   C15:94

TURNER, William (1651–1740)

1. Deliver us O Lord
   A33:249–50
2. I will always give thanks (*see* CLUB ANTHEM)
3. Lift up your heads (*Div Comp*; arr ARMES)
   D23:221   D30–5:57
4. Lord thou hast been my refuge (*Boyce 3*)
   A25:184–6   B27:124–7   B33:56–8   C27:106–8
5. Lord what is man
   A25:161–2   C7:116–18
6. O Lord God of Hosts
   A20:65–7   A28:186–8   A33:10–12   B6v:27–8   B9v:4–6
   B10:26–8   B12:37   B17v:5–6   B24:43–4   B26:25–7
   B29:12–13   B33v:117–18   B35v:94–5   C7:362–3   C14:187–9
   C15:174–6 (imp)   C27:79–80   C28:87–9   C34:70–1
7. O praise the Lord (*Div Comp*; arr ARMES)
   D23:221–2   D30–5:58–9
8. The Lord is king
   C19A:44–6   C21:41–3   C29v:37–8   C35v:21–2
9. In D: Td, J, K, C, M, N
   A33:238–49, 251–4
10. In G: S, G
    A4v:171 (G inc)   C7:343–4   C10:107–8   C15:95–6
    C27:159–60 (imp)   C28:507a–c
11. 6 single chants, in A, A, D, A, b, g, numbered 13–18 (unascrib
    except in A8)
    Nos. 13–18
    C12v:274 (tenor)   C28:507g (bass)
    [No. 14]
    B1v:1 (bass; set to V)
    [No. 15]
    A8:4 (4 pts)

*Secular item*:

12. How happy! how happy's the soul [chorus of 'Thus mortals
    submit to fate'] (unascrib)
    D9:2–3

TYE, Christopher (*c.*1505–72)

1. From the depth (*Page 3*)
   D23:228   D30–5:43
2. I lift my heart to thee
   A1:299–301   C2★:27–9   C4:10–11   C5:4–5   C6:10–11

Tye, Christopher (*cont.*)

C7:220–1   C10:4   C11:64–5   C12:9–11   C15:12–14   C16:65–7
C17:10–11

3. I will exalt thee (*Boyce 2*)
   D18:21–5
4. O Lord thy word
   A34v:71–4   B4:47–8   B15:19–20   C20v:81   C22v:52–3
   D22v:34–5
5. The proud have digged pits
   A11:83–5   B18v:90   C20v:11   C23v:89   C24v:88–9
6. Evening Service: M, N (to PARSLEY's Morning Service; ascrib to
   PARSLEY in A6)
   A6:346–51   C8:283–8   C13:70–3   E11a:382–5

VALENTINI, Giuseppe (*c.*1680–after 1759)

[Op. 7]
Concerto 3
   M157:114–16 (Allegros 1, 2)   M192:2–3 (Adagio)
Concerto 4
   M157:112–13 (Allegro 2)
Concerto 6
   M157:94 (Allegro 1)
Concerto 8
   M157:86–9 (Vivace, Allegro)
Concerto 11
   M157:105 (Allegro e Piano)

[VERACINI, Antonio] (1659–1733)

[Op. 1, Sonata 6] (ascrib to CORELLI)
   M175:51–6

VERACINI, Francesco Maria (1690–1768)

Partenio, Overture
   M183:21–3   M184:18   M185–9:16–17

VINCENT, [Thomas] (jun; *c.*1720–83)

6 Minuets, in D, A, F, G, D, C, drawn from [Op. 1: *Six solos* . . .]
   M69:34, 37–9

[VITRY, Philippe de] (1291–1361)

*Polyphonic motets*:
   1. [O canendo vulgo per compita]
      C.I.20, f. 337ᵛ
   2. Vos quid admiramini
      C.I.20, ff. 336★ᵛ–7

WALKLEY (WAKELEY), Anthony (1672–1717)

In F, in F fa ut: Td, J, K, C, M, N
  A29v:1–13  B7:181–90  B19:70–86  B20v:110–23
  B22:71–4 (−Td, J, K)  B23:160–5  B28:299–310  B35:12–20
  B36v:43–5, 45a–b, 46–51  C21v:112–25  C29:115–26

WALMISLEY, Thomas Attwood (1814–56)

★ = *Cathedral Music . . . A Collection of Services & Anthems composed by the late Thomas Attwood Walmisley, ed. T. F. Walmisley (1875)*

1. ★Behold O God our defender
   D17:12–15
2. ★Blessed is he that considereth
   D17:38 (inc)
3. ★Father of heaven
   D17:25–7
4. ★Hear O thou shepherd of Israel
   D17:19–23
5. ★Not unto us O Lord
   D17:27–8
6. ★O give thanks unto the Lord, the righteous
   D17:15–19
7. ★O God the king of glory
   D17:23–4
8. ★Ponder my words
   D17:28–37
9. ★Remember O Lord (Dublin Prize Anthem)
   B15:139–41  D18:196–201  D19:155–8  D21:139–45
10. ★The Lord shall comfort Zion
    D17:132–5
11. ★In B♭: M, N
    B15v:107–19  B30:120–30  D17v:47–54  D18v:164–79
    D19v:196–202  D21v:83–97  D30v–3v:63–6  D35v:63–6
12. ★In C: Td, J, S, M, N
    D17v:4–14
13. ★In D: Td, Bs, S, K, C, M, N
    D17v:14–30
14. ★In d: M, N
    D17v:1–4
15. ★In F: Td, J, S, K, C, Cd, Dm
    D17v:30–40  D32v–3v:53–61, 67–9 (−S, K, C)
    Td, J
    D30v:55–60  D31v, D34v–5v:53–8

WALSH, [George] (*fl.* 1747–d. 1765)

1. In D: Td, J
   A18:99–123   A21v:74–89   B18:24–31   B30:41–9   C20:11–19
   C23:12–20   C24:12–21   C25:12–20
2. 2 double chants, in A♯ [ = A], G♯ [ = G]
   A18:123

WANLESS, [Thomas] (*c.*1640–1712)

1. Litany
   A7:129–30   A29:66   B17v:26   B28:296–7   B35:10   B36v:41
   C8:548–9   C21v:101–2   C29:112–13   C29v:8   C35:96–7
2. O clap your hands
   C34:299–300
3. Save me O God
   A29:64–5

WARD, John (1571–1638)

Let God arise
   A1:270–4   A2:394–9   C1:15–16   C4:55–6   C5:53   C6:50–1
   C7:260–1   C9:34   C10:41–2   C11v:23–5   C16:156–8
   C17:111–13   C19:150–3

WARWICK (WARROCK), Thomas (*fl.* 1580–1620)

O God of my salvation
   A6:354–5   C2*:19–20   C4:29, 32   C5:24   C6:30   C7:240   C9:9
   C10:22   C11:46–7   C15:34–5   C16:51–2   C17:35–6   C19:12–13
   C27:27 (imp)   C28:38–9   C34:21–2

WEBB, William (*c.*1600–after 1656)

Let me sleep this night away (Canon in Unison)
   M174:7

WEBBE, Samuel (The Elder) (1740–1816)

★ = *Eight Anthems in Score . . . by Samuel Webbe* (1797/8)

1. ★Let everything that hath breath (chorus of 'Thou Lord in the
   beginning')
2. ★The Lord is the portion
   A16:224–7
3. ★Thou Lord in the beginning
   A16:132–8   B15:24–5   C20v:87–8   C22v:81–2   D22v:42–3
4. ★When the fullness of time
   A16:191–5

WEBSTER, Maurice (Maarit) (*fl.* 1621–36)
Divisions in a, for the viola da gamba
  D10:98–100

WEELKES, Thomas (1576–1623)
  1. Alleluia, I heard a voice (All Saints)
    A1:96–8   C1:5   C1:128–9   C2:99–100   C3:74   C7:50
    C11v:188–9   C14:58   C16:350–1   C17:189–90   C19:393–4
  2. Give the king thy judgments (King's Day)
    A2:201–3   A2:390–3   A5:60–3   C1:40–1   C2:104–5   C3:77–8
    C4:74   C5:72   C6:76–7   C7:53–4   C7:290–1   C9:48–9
    C10:63   C14:62   C16:357–8   C19:188
  3. In thee O Lord
    A3:397–403   C2:149–51   C3:121–2   C7:84–5   C11v:62–3
    C11v:179–80   C14:106–7   C16:216–17   C19:261–3
  4. O how amiable
    A2:380–1   C2*:10–11   C4:13   C5:7   C6:13   C7:223 (inc)
    C10:7 (imp)   C11:50–1   C12:11–12   C15:17–18   C16:26–7
    C17:14   C27:14–15   C28:19–20   C34:41–2
  5. O Lord how joyful is the king (5 November)
    A5:21–6   C2:110–13   C3:82–4   C7:58   C14:66–8
    C16:405–7   C19:397–400
  6. For Trebles: M, N
    A2:344–52   A6:54–60   C1:183–8   C13v:104–6   C18:75–6
    E11a:517–19
  7. Short Service: Td, J, M, N
    Td, J
    A6:318–24   C13:143–8 (+M, N)   C26:133–6   C31:142–5
    C32:141–3   C33:163–6   E11a:98–101
  8. Of 7 parts: M, N
    C1:304–10 (imp)   C18:80–3

WELDON, John (1676–1736)
  1. Blessed art thou O Lord (*Div Harm 1, 1731*; arr ARMES)
    D23:111   D26/1–5:27   D26/6–9:28
  2. Blessed be the Lord my strength
    A17:104–8
  3. Hear my crying (*Boyce 2*)
    A20:46–9   A28:219–22   B6v:45–7   B9v:20–2   B12:97–9
    B20v:46–8   B21:79–81   B24:35–6   B26:3–7   B27:166–7, 169
    B29:63–5   B32:40–1   B36:1–2   C19:131–4   C19A:57–9
    C21:69–71   C26v:37–40   C28:123–6   C29v:51–3
    C35v:38–40

WELDON, JOHN (*cont.*)

4. In thee O Lord (*Boyce 2*)
    A20:50–2    A28:216–18    B6v:43–5    B9v:19–20    B12:104–6
    B20v:43–5    B21:76–8    B24:49–50    B26:48–9    B27:265–7
    B29:61–3    B32:38–40    C19:127–31    C19A:55–6    C21:66–7
    C26v:34–7    C28:120–3    C29v:48–50    C35v:36–7

5. I will lift up mine eyes (*Page 1*)
    A29:104–8    B12:137    B17:31–2    B20:121–2    B24:88–9
    B32:65–6    B35v:5–6    B36:60–1    C19:474–5    C21:181–2
    C28:529–30    C29v:174–5    C35v:173–4

6. O God thou hast cast us out (*Arnold 1*)
    D20v:98–100

7. O how pleasant
    A8:155–60

8. O Lord rebuke me not
    A8:152–4    A14:131–3    A17:92–5    B9:150–2    B21:198–201

9. O praise God in his holiness
    A21:53–7    B4:100–1    B15:38    B15:238–9    C22v:101–2
    D20v:13    D22v:74–5

10. O praise the Lord of heaven
    A8:103–8    A21:58–60    B4:101–2    B15:39    C22v:102–3
    D20v:14    D22v:76

11. The Lord shall preserve me (from 'I will lift up mine eyes'; *Div Harm 1, 1731*; arr ARMES)
    D23:112    D26/1–5:28    D26/6–9:29

12. Thou art my portion
    A8:83–9    A17:96–103    A20:153–62    B8:104    B9:200    B11:57
    B16:56    B26:165    B34:97

13. Turn thy face from my sins (*Div Harm 1, 1731*; arr ARMES)
    D23:113–14    D26/1–5:29–30    D26/6–9:30–1

WESLEY, Samuel (1766–1837)

I said I will take heed (*Page 2*)
    D20v:172–7

WESLEY, Samuel Sebastian (1810–76)

★ = *Anthems by Samuel Sebastian Wesley*, vol. 1 (1853)

1. ★Ascribe unto the Lord
    D17:116–22

2. ★Blessed be the God and Father
    D17:122–5

3. ★Man that is born
    D17:128–9

4. *O Lord my God hear thou the prayer
   D17:115–16
5. Praise the Lord O my soul and all
   B3v:1–5
6. *The wilderness
   D17:107–15
7. *Thou Judge of quick and dead (from 'Let us lift up our heart')
   D17:125–8
8. *Wash me throughly
   D17:130–2
9. In E major: Td, J, K1, K2, S, C, M, N
   B3:291–300 (– Td, M, N)   D21v:6–27
10. Chant Service in F: Td, J, M, N
    B30:161–3 (M, N)   D17v:110–15 (Td, J)

[WHITE, E.] (*fl.* *c.*1700; MS 1770s)
Christ is risen (attrib to H. PURCELL)
   A19:577–610


WHITE, Robert (*c.*1538–74)
1. O how glorious art thou
   A1:58–60   C2*:2–3   C4:4   C6:4   C11:20–1   C12:⑤–⑥
   C15:4–5   C16:15–16   C17:4   C28:58–9   C34:88
2. The Lord bless us
   A1:283–4   A5:298–9   C4:1   C7:331   C11:61–2
   C12:①–② (imp)   C15:1–2   C16:34–5   C17:1

WHITE, William ('Will: White of Durham'—so MS A1:280; chor,
1578–*c.*1587; at Durham School, 1588–90; d. after 1622)
1. Behold now praise the Lord
   A1:278–80   C1:2–3   C4:41–2   C5:34–5   C6:39–40   C7:249–50
   C9:21–2   C10:29–30   C11:25–6   C15:44 (inc)   C16:18–19
   C17:45–6   C19:15–17
2. O praise God in his holiness
   A1:185–7   C4:23–4   C5:16   C6:22   C7:232   C9:4   C10:14
   C11:18–19   C15:26–7   C16:16–17   C17:26–7   C19:2–3

WILKINSON, [?Thomas, as MS A2:388; ?William, as MS C2:118]
(*fl.* 1579–96; a Thomas, 'musitioner', married in Durham, 22 Feb.
1603/4)
1. Behold O Lord
   A6:140–3   C2:145–6   C3:117–18   C7:79–80   C11v:13–14
   C14:100–1   C16:187–9   C19:257–8

C11:85–9   C12:50–4   C15:48–51   C16:81–4a   C17:52–5
C19:27–30   C27:23–6   C28:22–6   C34:125–8 (text only)

WINTER, [Peter von] (1754–1825)
Have mercy upon me O Lord (arr LINGARD)
  A10:242–7   B4:188–9   B15:118   D18:61–2   D19:93

WISE, Michael (c.1647–87)
1. Awake put on thy strength (*Boyce 2*)
  A9:10–15   A28:189–92   A33:14–17   B8:64–6   B9:71–3
  B10:143–7   B12:42–4   B17:114–16   B26:38–9   B29:44–6
  B35v:92–4   B36:32–4   C7:148–53   C7:360–1   C14:190–1
  C15:169–73   C27:195–8   C28:248–51   C34:220–4
2. Awake up my glory (*Boyce 3*)
  A4:170–2   A20:178–80   A28:231 (inc)   B1:146–8   B9:74
  B10:147–9   B12:44–5   B24:77   B26:37   B29:42–3
  B35v:121–2   C7:153–5   C7:372–4   C14:203–4 (text only)
  C15:199   C19A:43   C27:199–200   C28:252–3   C34:225–6
3. Blessed is he that considereth (*Boyce 3*)
  A13:30–2   B6:69   B9:116–17   B10:275–7   B12:144–5
  B17:55–6   B29:230   B31:24   B33:80   B35v:36–7
4. By the waters of Babylon
  A4:45–8   C11v:192   C12:70   C19:305–7   C27:315–18
  C34:246–8
5. Have pity on me
  A4:43–5   B1:119–23   C11v:190   C12:69   C19:303   D23:107
  D26/1–3:22–3   D26/4, 5:23   D26/6–9:23–4
6. How are the mighty fallen (*see* 'Thy beauty O Israel')
  A4:131–5   C11v:213–15   C12:71–3   C15:217   C27:281–2
  C28:254–5   C34:249–50
7. I charge you daughters (unascrib)
  B1:164–6
8. Prepare ye the way (*Boyce 2*)
  A28:193–4   B9:73–4   B10:90–2   B12:40–1   B17:100–1
  B24:50–1   B27:127–9   B29:46–7   B33:22–3   C14:110
  C27:108–10   C28:433–4
9. The Lord is my shepherd
  C2:152   C11v:177   C14:77   C15:109   C17:110   C27:225
  C28:223   C34:185
10. The ways of Sion (*Boyce 3*)
  A7v:1–2   A16:120–9   A16:230–5   A28:212–15   B6:69   B9:74
  B12:79   B20:21–3 (imp)   B24:56   B26:40–2   B27:4–5
  B29:48–50   B33:24–6   C19:323   C27:383–6 (imp)   C28:434

WISE, MICHAEL (*cont.*)
11. Thy beauty O Israel (*Boyce 3*) (revision by ALDRICH—to whom
    ascrib in B27, B36, and C27—of 'How are the mighty fallen')
    A13:20–5   B12:297   B27:1–3 (imp)   B33:128–30   B36:108–10
    C27:386–8b
12. In d: Td, J
    A29v:26–31 (in e)   B7:191–3   B17v:46–9   B19:103–8
    B22:161–3   B28:83–5   B29v:1–3   B32:8–10   B35:45–8
    B36v:59–62   C21v:138–41   C29:140–4
13. In E♭: M, N
    A29:32–5   A35:102–14   B5:195–7   B7:193–5   B16v:89–92
    B17v:49–51   B19:109–12   B28:86–7   B29v:4–6   B31v:97–9
    B32v:10–12   B35:48–50   B36v:62–4   C19v:62–3   C21v:141–3
    C29:144–7   M170:131–2
14. In E♯ [ = e]: K, C
    A18:25–33
15. In f: K, C
    A18:33–40

WOLF, Ernst Wilhelm (1735–92)
Saints and angels (*Latrobe 1*)
    B15:215–17

WOOD
O Lord the world's Saviour (now attrib to W. MUNDY)

WOODSON, Leonard (*c.*1565–1641)
Arise O Lord God
    A2:312–15

WOODWARD, Richard (?1743–77)
4 double chants in G♯ [ = G], C♮ (= C) (dated 1776), G♯ (dated 1777), and
D♯ [ = D]
    A18:25,86,86 [*sic*], and A19:421

[WORREL] (*fl.* early 18th cent.)
Not unto us O Lord (Canon à 4)
    M70v:121

YARROW, Thomas (*fl. c.*1630)
Almighty and everlasting God which dost govern
    A6:356–7   C1:80   C7:321–2   C10:93–4   C11:71   C15:55–6
    C16:54, 56   C17:63–4

YOUNG, John (1822–97; chor, Durham, 1833–8; articled to Henshaw the Durham organist, 1838–43, and assistant org, 1843–4; org, Lincoln, 1850–95)

In D: Td, J, K, S
  A11:95–167 (−S)  B15v:90–7  D18v:136–46  D19v:171–8
  D21v:58–67 (−K, S)

YOUNG (JOUNGH, JUNG), William (d. 1662)

*Sonatas à 3 viols*:

1. In d
  D2/1:30  D2/2:32  D2/3:26  D10:223–5
2. In C
  D2/1:34  D2/2:36  D2/3:30
3. In D
  D2/1:44–6  D2/2:46–8  D2/3:40–1  D10:226–30
4. In d (ascrib to JENKINS in D5; probably by him)
  D4/1, 2:1–2  D4/3:1  D5/1, 2:20–1  D5/3:18–19
5. In d (probably by JENKINS)
  D4/1, 2:2–4  D4/3:2
6. [?Fancy] à 2 in d
  D2/1:66–7  D2/2:68–9

*For the viola da gamba*:

7. Divisions in g (possibly by BUTLER)
  D10:139–42
8. Divisions in g
  D10:152–5
9. 3 suites, in g, d, D
  D10:162–5, 166–70, 170–5
10. In d
  D10:175

ZAMPONI, [Gioseffo] (b. 1610–20; d. 1662)

Sonata à 3 in g (authorship uncertain—ascrib to BUTLER in D2, ZAMPONI in D5, unascrib in D10)
  D2/1:42–3  D2/2:44–5  D2/3:38–9  D5/1–3:4–5  D10:219–22

ZIANI, [Pietro Andrea] (c.1616–84)

6 sonatas, in B♭, g, e, f, A, F. (The first three sonatas = Op. 1, nos. 1–12; even so, are probably by ALBINONI)
  M193/1:1–36 (full score)  M193/2–4:1–13  M193/5:1–4, 7, 8 (inc)
  M193/6, 7:1–13

# INDEX OF DATES OF
# MANUSCRIPTS

*Monastic fragments*:

| | |
|---|---|
| 10th cent. | B.IV.9, A.II.17 |
| mid 11th cent. | A.IV.19, B.III.32 |
| 11th cent. | B.II.11, B.III.11 |
| *c.*1200 | A.IV.6, Inc. 3, Inc. 4 |
| early 13th cent. | C.III.12 |
| early 14th cent. | C.I.8, C.III.29 |
| 14th cent. | B.III.12, C.I.20, End Paper 23 |
| late 14th cent. | Communar's Cartulary |
| *c.*1400 | A.III.11, Inc. 15A |
| 15th cent. | A.III.32; Hunter 99, 103, 104; End Papers 24, 25 |
| *c.*1500 | A.IV.23 |

*Later MSS* (indicating only when begun):

| | |
|---|---|
| early 17th cent. | A1–3, A5–6, C2, C3–11, C13–14, C16, C18, E4–11, E11a; Hunter 33, 125 |
| late 17th cent. | A4, A25, A33, B1, C1, C2★, C12, C15, C17, C19, C26–8, C31–4, D2, D4–5, D10, ?E22, ?E29, Pr. K.II.31, Misc. Chs. 7116–17, M170, M179–80 |
| early 18th cent. | A7–9, A27, B10, B17, B19–21, B27–8, B32, B36, C19A, C21, C29, C35, D1, D9, D13–16, E1, E15, ?E22, ?E29, E30–2, Add. 154, M70, M102, M175, M192–3, M195–7, M199–201, M203, M208 |
| mid 18th cent. | A12–13, A28–9, B5–9, B13, B29, B31, B33, B35, E3, E12–14, E16–21, E23–8, E33–5, M108, M157, M159, M172, M176–7, M183–9, M201, M204, M206–7, M215–16 |
| late 18th cent. | A14–20, A22–4, A26, A32, B11–12, B16, B22–6, B34, C30, D3, D6–8, D11, M69, M88–90, M173–4, M194, M202, M205 |
| early 19th cent. | A10–11, A21, A30–1, A34–5, B3–4, B15, B18, B30, C20, C22–5, D18–20, D22, D36, E37, M71 |
| late 19th cent. | D12/1–8, D17, D21, D23–35, D37, E2, E38 |
| early 20th cent. | D12/9–10, E36 |

# SIGNATURES RELATING TO
# PAYMENTS FOR COPYING

In the manuscripts are signatures certifying that the work had been paid for 'thus far'. From the 1680s to the 1810s they are usually those of the current Precentor (see Chapter Minute, 20 Nov. 1702), and only if the person held a different position is comment made below. As the signature is not always supported by a date (and vice versa), it has been deemed advisable to give the full terms of office of the Precentors from 1682 to 1815.

| | |
|---|---|
| 1638 | Antho: Maxton (Treasurer) |
| 1671 | Alexander Shaw (copyist) |
| 1679 | Thomas Smith (Treasurer) |
| 1682–8 | E[dward] K[irkby] |
| 1689–1705 | John Milner |
| 1705–11 | P[exall] F[orster] |
| 1711–16 | A[braham] Y[app] |
| 1716–21 | R[obert] L[eeke] |
| 1721–32 | J[ohn] W[aring] |
| 1728–9 | [?Bryan] Turner (copyist) |
| 1732–8 | Bryan Turner (now prec) |
| 1738–65 | William Forster |
| 1765–73 | A[braham] G[regory] |
| 1773–83 | J[ohn] W[heele]r |
| 1783–1815 | Thomas Hayes |
| 1814–62 | William Henshaw (org, acting in place of the prec) |
| 1862–1907 | P[hilip] A[rmes] (org; dates not of payment but of editing) |
| 1862–72 | Matthew Brown (copyist) |
| 1886 | Joseph Walker (l-c, sub-prec) |
| 1892 | C[harles] H. N[utton] (copyist) |
| 1892–7 | G. W. Shaw (copyist) |
| 1909–13 | Joseph S. Lisle (copyist) |

# COPYISTS OF DURHAM'S LITURGICAL MANUSCRIPTS

BEGINNING with John Todd in 1600 references to named copyists occur in the Treasurer's Account Books and in the Act Books of the Dean and Chapter of Durham. From 1678–9 onwards they are located in the Audit Books. These books itemized every expense connected with the cathedral, those for transcribing music usually occurring in the section headed, 'In Billis', though that headed 'E Decretis' is always worth examining for other musical matters. As the former heading indicates the payment was made following the submission of a suitable bill. For the period from 1681 to 1700 some fifteen of these bills survive; and there are others for 1709, 1729, 1730, the 1760s, 1780s, 1790s, 1805, and the 1830s. In many cases they state how many pages had been copied into the different manuscripts; and, of course, they themselves provide much lengthier examples of the copyist's handwriting than the quarterly signatures in the Treasurer's Account Books. Ensuring that the bills made no false claims was the responsibility of the Precentor—it became mandatory in 1702—and he both certified the bill and dated and initialled the manuscripts at the latest points covered by it.

The task of correlating the evidence of the Audit Books and the copyists' bills with the dated signatures in the manuscripts is fraught with difficulties. For instance, over thirty manuscripts date from before the start of the system of payments, and there are a number of extra manuscripts produced at private expense. Again, there are dates in the manuscripts for which the Audit Books state the amount expended but fail to name who submitted the account. Conversely, the names of some of the copyists are known but their handiwork has not been identified. Finally, it becomes apparent from a multiplicity of styles of writing that particularly from c.1765 onwards the presenter of the account was not himself responsible for all the work done.

Ranging over the periods, the identification of the work done by Todd, William Smith, Henry Palmer, and John Geeres in the

1620s and 1630s is almost certainly correct. Doubts, however, persist whether Toby Brookinge was assisted by his wife. James Greene's contribution in 1637 has not been identified, even though his hand is well known from Hunter MSS 11 and 33. With Greene, as with various later copyists, it is quite possible that he worked on manuscripts which are no longer extant.

For the 1660s and 1670s what has been identified as by John Foster, Elias Smyth, Alexander Shaw, and John White, seems secure. What is in doubt is what their hands were like before and after their 'prime', and whether some of them had less formal styles too. The survival of bills by Shaw, White, William Greggs, and Mathew Owen provides decisive information for the 1680s and 1690s.

During the last few years of the seventeenth century and the first three decades of the eighteenth many hands worked at the manuscripts. The contributions of Robert Softley (also active in London), Robert Leeke, and Thomas Laye, all named in the records, have been identified; that of Nicholas Harrison of Gateshead in 1709 has not, even though his bill has survived. Among unnamed contributors the handiwork of John Thoresby (c.1697) and William Parkinson (1709) has been recognized through the recurrence of interesting details found in their signatures.

After [?Bryan] Turner, named for 1729, there follows a period of stability, for from late 1729 to 1761 Cuthbert Brass was copyist. A single item copied by Thomas Ebdon in 1761 is easily detected. So too is the work of John Mathews who brought with him manuscripts he had copied at Salisbury, and later sent over two manuscripts from Dublin. But it is with Mathews that the position changes, and the statements in the Audit Books and even the bills begin to prove unhelpful. There can be no doubt that Mathews was the main copyist from 1764 to 1776, and yet for all that period Ebdon the organist is named as the recipient of the payments for copying music. Apart from the period from 1796 to 1803 when George Chrishop, the deputy organist, submitted his own bills, Ebdon continued to be the recipient until his death in 1811. He himself acted as copyist from 1804 onwards, but those from 1777 to 1795 pose many problems. One of them no doubt was John Friend, known from his catalogue of John Sharp III's books at

Durham. His hand at its best is certainly present in the manuscripts, but uncertainties arise when one contemplates what his ordinary hand might have been like. The reverse is true of James Radcliffe, whose shaky hand dates from 1811 to 1813.

From 1813 to 1862 William Henshaw, the organist, is named as the recipient of the payments. But whereas Ebdon had done some of the copying, it has not been established whether Henshaw did any. From 1819 these doubts intensify, for from that date the certifying signature is not the Precentor's but Henshaw's. Moreover, after Henshaw's retirement, the recipient is named as Matthew Brown, and his complaint in 1866 about the loss of income resulting from Chapter's decision to change from manuscript to printed copies confirms his activity. From the 1830s the copyist could have been Brown, but as he had been a chorister under Henshaw their hands could well have similarities.

Finally, Philip Armes's contribution is readily recognizable, for much of it is both dated and initialled by him. These details, however, no longer relate to payments.

In the notes below, selected biographical details are followed by those of copying activity.

★ Indicates inclusion in the Index of Composers.

★ARMES, Philip: b. 1836; org and m of chor, 1863–1907, previously at Oxford and Chichester; d. 1908. His transcriptions, made mainly in the 1870s and 1880s, include his own editings of earlier music.

BRASS, Cuthbert: chor 1717–27; l-c 1727–81, acting as m of chor for five months in 1748 when Hesletine at Finedon; d. 1782. Copyist 1729–61, with limited activity until 1772. The bills for 1729–30 and 1730 are extant.

BROOKINGE, Toby: counter-tenor l-c c.1623–42, previously at Bristol where in trouble on account of drink; injured by Hucheson in pub brawl in 1628; d. 1642. Copyist in late 1620s and 1630s. Earned £14. 6s. 8d. in 1632 to 1634; not known whether a further £6. 6s. 8d. collected by his wife Magdalen was on her own behalf. In 1635 agreed to act as copyist for Abraham Coates (Hunter MS 27); hand evident in Peterhouse MSS.

BROWN, Matthew: chor 1810–18; l-c 1832–77; d. 1886. In 1847 given £20 and a fortnight's leave of absence to go to London to

London to procure a set of false teeth. Named as copyist 1862–72, but possibly active from 1830s—*see* HENSHAW. Recompensed to tune of £25 p.a. from 1866 onwards to compensate for lack of earnings following decision to purchase printed folio and octavo music.

CHRISHOP, George: deputy org 1796–1803; previously org at Staindrop (*Ebdon 1*). Described in MS C15 as 'Organist of the Cathedral Church of Durham'; but not featured in Treasurer's Account Books. The Act Book has Minutes granting him (i) permission to furnish the Song School with a bed, table, and chairs, and (ii) three weeks' leave of absence in 1801. The bill submitted in connection with (i) describes him as 'deputy organist'. He appears as a minder of music in 1795; and from 1796 to 1803 the Audit Books record an allowance 'E Decretis', and pay him for copying music. His music bills for 1797 and 1798 survive, confirming he did the actual copying.

★EBDON, Thomas: b. 1738; chor 1748–56; l-c 1756–64; dep on organ for six months during Hesletine's final illness; org and m of chor 1763–1811, though Chrishop seems to have taken over duties, 1796–1803; d. 1811. Appointed org, only Dean approving. Displaced Brass as copyist but then gave way to Mathews. With Ebdon procedure for payment altered—he is named as recipient when, e.g., Mathews clearly did the copying.

★FOSTER, John: chor *c*.1632–*c*.1638; ?matriculated, Magdalene College, Cambridge, Dec. 1638; org and m of chor 1661–77; d. 1677. Only his copying activity in the organ books has been identified.

★FRIEND, John: l-c 1782–1819. Copyist *c*.1790, though nowhere named as such. Hand known from his catalogue of John Sharp III's Durham books (Gloucester Record Office, D3549, Box 52).

★GEERES, John: l-c 1629–41/2, but on scene by Oct. 1628; previously l-c and graduate at King's College, Cambridge; d. 1641/2. Copied one service dated 1639 in MS A2, and two hol anthems in e.g. MS C4; hand is evident at Peterhouse.

GREENE, James: m-c 1631–67; d. 1667. Paid for copying *c*.200 pp. in 1637, but hand not identified in part-books. The last hand of Hunter MS 33 is his, as is Hunter MS 11 gathering 98. Responsible as Sacrist for compilation of Misc. Ch. 7116–17. In Peterhouse MSS.

*GREGGS, William: org and m of chor, 1682–1710, having previously held office at York. In 1686 given three months leave of absence to go to London to improve skill in music. Copied end of MS A4 and most of MSS A25 and A33 (organ books); also active in part-books. His bills for 1687, 1691, 1694, 1694–5, 1699–1700, and 1708–9 survive.

HARRISON, Nicholas: named in Audit Book for 1709. His bill, dated 18 Nov., bases him at Gateshead. The services he copied have not been identified.

*HESLETINE, James: b. c.1692; chor Chapel Royal under Blow, leaving in 1707; org and m of chor, Durham, 1711–63; d. 1763. Few of his compositions survive at Durham—is said to have destroyed them supposing he had been slighted by the Dean and Chapter. Never named as copyist, but MS A9 is in his hand (also Brit. Lib. Add. MS 30860).

*HENSHAW, William: org and m of chor 1814–62 (retired); d. 1877. Inactive as a composer, only one chant discovered. Named as copyist 1816–62, but probable similarity between his hand and Matthew Brown's (chor under him) makes his contribution uncertain.

HUSBANDS, [?Charles, Gentleman of Chapel Royal, d. 1678]. Paid in 1674 'for pricking 20 Tunes for ye Psalms', presumably those now found in slightly later MSS C12, C26, and C28.

LAYE, Thomas: l–c 1710–29; ?m of chor for three months in 1711 during inter-regnum; d. 1729. Copyist in at least 1717–18 and 1727–8. An untidy hand. Bill for 1728 survives.

LEEKE, Robert: m–c 1694–1721; prec 1716–21; d. 1726. Copyist in 1706–7, 1707–8, and c.1711. Hand known from Parochial Register, vol. 1.

LISLE, Joseph S.: chor 1894–9; l–c 1910–39. Copied MS D12/10 in 1913.

MATHEWS, John: l–c 1764–76, previously at Winchester and Salisbury, later at Dublin where d. 1799. A fine hand. Named as copyist only in 1764–5, but clearly active throughout time at Durham. Brought with him from Salisbury MSS A24, A32, D7,

D8, and part of A17. Sent (on commission) MSS A18, A19 from Dublin.

*NICHOLLS, John: l-c 1661–77; m of chor (but not org) 1677–81, resigning Mastership of Langley Song School which he had held from 1667; d. 1681. Hand not identified, but named for 1678–9.

N[UTTON], C[harles] H.: chor 1886–92; articled to Armes 1892 onwards. Copyist in 1892—the only person to fit initials found in MS D30.

OWEN, Matthew: l-c 1687–9; m-c 1689–95; d. 1699. Copyist 1687–8 to 1693–4, succeeding White. The first copyist since 1630s to use round notation in part-books. His bills for 1688, 1688–9, 1689–91, and 1693–4 survive.

*PALMER, Henry: l-c 1627–40; acted as m of chor in 1628 when Hucheson suspended and still drawing coal allowance in 1633; d. 1640. Copyist in 1631 and c.1637–9. Copied Organ Books MSS A1, A5, and A6, but nothing else obvious at Durham except one line on MS C8:181. Peterhouse script supports this, but number of anthems in e.g. MS C2 with no title against his name is disturbing.

PARKINSON, William: b. 1692; chor 1702–11; l-c 1711–14; d. 1714. Not named as copyist, but anon bill of 1709 and a few pp. in MS C27 have 'P' very much as in his signature.

RADCLIFFE, James: l-c 1795–1818, previously at Dublin. Taught choir for two months in 1802; given permanent leave of absence in 1816; copyist 1811–14.

*SHAW, Alexander: chor 1661–4; sackbutter 1664–72; org (but not m of chor) 1677 to Christmas 1681 when said to have been sacked for contumacy; possibly org at Ripon earlier in 1677; married Foster's widow; d. 1706 being described as 'musician'. Copied MS C19 and Brit. Lib. Add. MS 30479 by 1671, and may have made additions to MS C11 and C13 c.1664 (cf. 'A' in C11v:161 and his signature in the Treasurer's Book for 1663–4). During absence copied parts of Brit. Lib. K.7.e.2; on return copied MS A4, etc. His bill for ?1681 survives.

SHAW, G[eorge] W.: chor 1887–92; articled to Armes 1892 onwards. Copied much of MSS D30–5 between 1892 and 1897.

*SMITH, William: b. 1603; chor. 1614–c.1617 (not earlier as some have supposed); [Christ's College, Cambridge]; m-c 1627–45, prec at various times. Acted as org for a month in 1627 when Hucheson in jail; d. 1645. Never named as copyist, but hand is evident in MSS A1–3, A1:1–41 being hol collection of his own works. Contributed to Peterhouse MSS.

*SMYTH, Elias: m–c 1628–76; prec 1661–76; formerly at Gloucester. Librarian 1633–76; Headmaster, Durham School 1639–62; d. 1676. Extent of work not known, the only record being in 1672 when paid £4. 4s. 0d. (= at least 250 pp.). Copied anthem by Child in MSS C12 and C15; also a few pp. for Peterhouse in the 1630s. Hand well known from MSS A.IV.32, B.IV.47, and Hunter MSS 11 and 125.

SOFTLEY, Robert: chor 1689–97; l–c 1697–1704. Copyist 1701–4, some whilst in London where he had gone in 1701–2 to improve singing and handwriting. Because of date must be last hand of MS C7.

THORESBY, John: m–c 1695–8. Not named as copyist. Responsible for a few pp. in MSS C7, C14, C15, C26, and C27. Identified from his signature, particularly the 'r'.

TODD, John: m–c c.1598 to d. Jan. 1630/1; prec in 1620s. Copied some of MS A2, many being 'loose' pieces, and much of early 17th cent. MSS. Named as copyist in 1600, 1627, and 1630, signing an indication of the extent of his activity in the Act Book. A few items went to Peterhouse.

TURNER, [?Bryan: m–c 1719–38, prec from 1733; d. 1738]. Paid £2. 12s. 6d. in 1728–9. Hand not identified.

WALKER, Joseph: l–c 1858–1901; given £12. 12s. 0d. in 1860 to assist him to purchase a set of false teeth. Copyist 1882 onwards.

WHITE, John: chor 1664–c.1669; l–c c.1671–87; took over from Nicholls at Langley Song School in 1677; d. 1687. Copyist 1674–87. MS C17 is in his hand. The bills for 1683, 1684, 1687, and 1687 [sic] survive, the last being presented by his widow.

# INDEX OF MUSICAL GENRE

*(Other than Anthems and Services)*

# INDEX OF FIRST LINES

| | |
|---|---|
| Cantate Dominum canticum novum | [?Steffani] |
| Carco sempre di Gloria | Handel |
| Cast thy burden | Mendelssohn |
| Cecilia volgi un sguardo | Handel |
| [Che m'importa] | [?Steffani] |
| Christ being raised | Blow |
| Christ is risen | H. Purcell, [E. White] |
| Christ rising again | Byrd, Juxon |
| Christus | Mendelssohn |
| Cieca notte (Ariodante) | Handel |
| Cingite floribus | Steffani |
| . . . Clemens creator eloy te tremunt omnes angeli | Anon |
| Clori son fido amanti | Stradella |
| Come here's a good health | Blow |
| Come Holy Ghost | Dykes, [Ravenscroft], Tallis |
| Comfort ye my people | Aldrich, Hall, Tucker |
| Corinna I excuse thy face | H. Purcell |
| Crown me with roses | Anon |
| Cry unto the Lord | Ebdon |
| Daughters of Zion | Mendelssohn |
| Deborah | Handel |
| Dei preco fit baptista | Anon |
| Delirai mia bella | Astorga |
| Deliver me from mine enemies | Byrd, Ebdon, R. Parsons [I] |
| Deliver me O God | Bull, Edwards |
| Deliver me O Lord | Hall, Wilkinson |
| Deliver us O Lord | Batten, Battishill, O. Gibbons, Turner |
| Deo gratias | Anon |
| De profundis | Morley |
| Der Blinde | C. Keller |
| Der Jägers Haus | Thalberg |
| Der Mondenschein | Anon |
| Der Schiffer fährt zu Land | Curschmann |
| Des Müllers Blumen | Schubert |
| Dettingen Te Deum | Handel |
| Devout men carried Stephen | Chawner |
| Dialogue in Amphitrion | Boyce |
| Dolorosi martir fieri tormenti | Marenzio |

Drop down ye heavens      *Stainer*
Dust thou art      *Garth*

Esther      *Handel*
Eternal God, Almighty Power      *Beethoven*
Ever blessed Lord      *R. Parsons [II]*
Everlasting God who hast ordained      *Giles*
Every day will I give thanks      *Pickering*

Fair spring's approach      *Ebdon*
Farewell ye limpid springs (Jephtha)      *Handel*
[Far from all resort] (L'Allegro)      *Handel*
Father of heaven      *Walmisley*
Father we adore thee      *Haydn*
Fear not shepherd      *Loosemore*
Fly from Myrtillo      *Courteville*
For Sion's sake      *Aldrich*
For thou only art holy      *Arnott*
From harmony, from heavenly harmony      *Handel*
From the depth      *Tye*
Fusa cum silentio      *Anon*

Gentle airs (Athalia)      *Handel*
German (Hymn tune)      *Croft*
Gettano i rè dal soglio      *Steffani*
Give ear unto me      *Marcello, Novello*
Give laud unto the Lord      *J. Mundy*
Give peace in our time      *Callcott*
Give sentence with me      *T. Tomkins*
Give thanks unto the Lord      *Fiocco, Havergal*
Give the king thy judgments      *Aldrich, Boyce, Croft, Loosemore, Weelkes*

Gloria in excelsis      *Anon*
Gloria Patri      *Handel*
Glorious and powerful God      *O. Gibbons*
Glory be to God on high      *Beethoven, Child, Foster, Haydn, Loosemore*

Glory in the highest      *Pergolesi*
God be merciful      *Sabadini, W. Smith*
God is gone up      *Croft*
God is our hope and strength      *Aldrich, Blow, Crotch, Greene, Nares*

God shall send forth      *Leo*

| | |
|---|---|
| O give thanks unto the Lord, let them give thanks | Greene |
| O give thanks unto the Lord, the righteous | Walmisley |
| O God be merciful unto us | Strogers |
| O God my God wherefore dost thou forsake me | W. Lawes |
| O God my heart prepared is | R. Hucheson |
| O God my strength and fortitude | J. Mundy |
| O God of Gods | J. Bennet, Hooper |
| O God of Hosts the mighty Lord (t. St Matthew) | t. by Croft |
| O God of my righteousness | Greene |
| O God of my salvation | Warwick |
| O God the king of glory | O. Gibbons, Walmisley |
| O God the proud | Byrd, J. Hutchinson |
| O God they that love thy name | H. Purcell |
| O God thou art my God | Greene, Mudd, H. Purcell |
| O God thou art the well spring | T. Holmes |
| O God thou hast cast us out | H. Purcell, Weldon |
| O God to whom the night shines | Mozart |
| O God wherefore art thou absent | Anon, Blow, Child |
| O God whose nature and property | Palmer |
| O God which hast taught | W. Smith |
| O hear my prayer Lord | Giles |
| O hide not thy face | Salvatore |
| O how amiable | Anon, Croft, Gale, Greene, [?Isaak], Richardson, Weelkes |
| O how glorious art thou | R. White |
| O how happy a thing it is | Giles |
| O how pleasant | Weldon |
| Oh praise the Lord ye that fear him | Murphy |
| Oil and vinegar are two pretty things | [Hall] |
| Old 100th (Hymn tune) | Anon, arr Finch |
| O let me hear thy loving kindness | Ravenscroft |
| O let my mouth be filled | Child, Hesletine |
| O Liberty (Occasional Oratorio) | Handel |
| O Lord call to remembrance | Haydn |
| O Lord consider my distress | Edw. Smythe, Wilkinson |
| O Lord give ear | Byrd, Greene, Marcello |
| O Lord God of Hosts | Crotch, Goldwin, Greene, H. Purcell, Turner |
| O Lord God of my salvation | Clarke, Croft |